PRISONS AND THE PRISONER

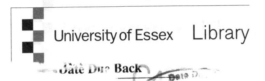

PRISONS AND THE PRISONER

An introduction to the work of Her Majesty's Prison Service

Edited by Shane Bryans and Rachel Jones

London: The Stationery Office

Contents © Crown Copyright 2001

Published for Prison Service Training Services under licence from the Controller of Her Majesty's Stationery Office

The typographical copyright in this work is held by The Stationery Office Limited. Applications for permissions to reproduce this copyright work should be made in writing to: The Copyright Unit, Her Majesty's Stationery Office, St Clement's House, 2–16 Colegate, Norwich NR3 1BQ.

First published 2001
ISBN 0 11 341228 2

Published by The Stationery Office and available from:

The Stationery Office
(mail, telephone and fax orders only)
PO Box 29, Norwich, NR3 1GN
Telephone orders/General enquires 0870 600 5522
Fax orders 0870 600 5533

www.thestationeryoffice.com

The Stationery Office Bookshops
123 Kingsway, London WC2B 6PQ
020 7242 6393 Fax 020 7242 6394
68–69 Bull Street, Birmingham B4 6AD
0121 236 9696 Fax 0121 236 9699
33 Wine Street, Bristol BS1 2BQ
0117 926 4306 Fax 0117 929 4515
9–21 Princess Street, Manchester M60 8AS
0161 834 7201 Fax 0161 833 0634
16 Arthur Street, Belfast BT1 4GD
028 9023 8451 Fax 028 9023 5401
The Stationery Office Oriel Bookshop
18–19, High Street, Cardiff CF1 2BZ
029 2039 5548 Fax 029 2038 4347
71 Lothian Road, Edinburgh EH3 9AZ
0870 606 5566 Fax 0870 606 5588

The Stationery Office's Accredited Agents
(see Yellow Pages)

and through good booksellers

This book is dedicated to

Elizabeth, Jamie, Hannah and Jemma Bryans

and

J.A.F. Jones

CONTENTS

NOTE:

1. Lists of all text references are found at the ends of chapters; a further reading list is found at the end of this book. All publishers' locations are London, unless stated otherwise.

2. All photographs have been supplied by the Prison Service and are Crown copyright.

FIGURES AND TABLES

Figures

Tables

NOTES ON CONTRIBUTORS

Editors

Shane Bryans is Governor of HM Young Offender Institution (HMYOI) Aylesbury. He joined the Prison Service in 1986, having gained a law degree and a Master's degree in Criminology from the University of Cambridge. He has served in three prisons as a governor grade, completed two postings to Prison Service Headquarters and worked as Head of Management and Specialist training at the Prison Service College. While working in the Prison Service he obtained an MBA degree from the Open University and an M.Ed. from the University of Sheffield. In 1998 he was seconded to Cambridge University to take up a Cropwood Fellowship, and in 1999 was elected a Fellow of the Royal Society of Arts. He has published numerous articles on the Prison Service and in 1998 published a book, *The Prison Governor: Theory and Practice* (with David Wilson), which is now in its second edition. He advises the Mongolian government on prison conditions and has undertaken Human Rights inspections in Mongolia and Romania.

Rachel Jones is Head of Security and Estates at HMYOI Aylesbury. She joined the Prison Service on the accelerated promotion scheme in 1996, having previously worked as a civil servant in the Immigration and Nationality department of the Home Office. She has a degree in modern history from the University of Liverpool. She has worked in Wormwood Scrubs and Coldingley Prisons, and was recently seconded to the International Centre for Prison Studies, King's College, London, where she completed work on international aspects of life imprisonment for HM Chief Inspector of Prisons, and on TB in prisons in the former Soviet Union. She has contributed to articles published in the *Prison Service Journal*.

Contributors

Bill Abbott was Governor of HM Prison (HMP) Liverpool until he retired in 1999. He joined the Prison Service in 1966, and has also served as governor of HMYOI Glen Parva and HMP Pentonville. He was Head of Security for the Prison Service following prisoner escapes from Parkhurst and Whitemoor. He has been involved with Tavistock Services in leading and developing training experiences for governors, on the role of the governor.

Zoë Ashmore is Principal Psychologist at Prison Service Headquarters and was previously Head of Regimes at HMYOI Aylesbury. After gaining a psychology degree she joined the Prison Service in 1978. She has worked in psychology units at Usk Detention Centre and Borstal (later to become Usk YOI), Birmingham Prison, Swinfen Hall YOI and Holloway Prison. In 1988 she obtained an M.Sc. degree in psychology from Birmingham University and in 1998 began reading for a Master's degree in criminology and management (prison studies) at the University of Cambridge. Zoë moved to HMYOI Aylesbury in 1996.

Neil Beales is staff officer to the Governor at HMYOI Aylesbury. He joined the Prison Service in 1991, having previously trained as an actor and been drafted into the South African Navy. He has worked at Risley and Camphill Prisons. Neil was involved in the project to set up the correctional training facility at Colchester Military Prison, and was recently selected for the Prison Service developing managers programme.

Gina Beaton is in the second year of the Prison Service's accelerated promotion scheme, her first year having been completed at Holloway Prison. She joined the Prison Service in 1997 after obtaining a law degree at Dundee University and a Master's degree in human rights at Durham University.

Richard Booty is Governor of HMP Gloucester. He joined the Prison Service in 1985, having previously worked in local government. He has worked in Chelmsford, Oxford, Campsfield House, Bullingdon and Reading Prisons, and has completed a short secondment to the Oxfordshire and Buckinghamshire probation service. Until recently he was Head of Management Development Training at the Prison Service College.

Andrew Coyle is Director of the International Centre for Prison Studies, King's College, London. He was previously Governor of Brixton Prison and, prior to 1991, held senior posts in several Scottish prisons. He has a PhD degree in criminology from the University of Edinburgh. He is the author of *The Prisons We Deserve* (1994) and *Inside: Rethinking Scotland's Prisons* (1991), as well as numerous articles on imprisonment. He is currently managing editor of *Punishment and Society – The International Journal of Penology*.

Colin Edwards is project co-ordinator for the Dangerously Severe Personality Disorder Project in the Home Office. He joined the Home Office in 1995 from the NHS, as a nurse advisor and later a healthcare advisor. He has a number of clinical nursing qualifications and a diploma in criminology from Cambridge University. He is currently studying for his Master's degree.

David Godfrey was Governor of HMP and YOI Guys Marsh until he retired in 1999. He joined the Prison Service in 1969 after obtaining a psychology degree from St Andrews University. He has previously worked at Morton Hall and Deerbolt Borstals; as a tutor at the Prison Service College; and at Wormwood Scrubs, Camp Hill, Albany, Northeye and Ford Prisons. He has also had two postings at Prison Service Headquarters and a secondment to the Home Office. In his spare time he obtained an M.Phil. degree from Leeds University on the effectiveness of the borstal system, an Open University diploma in applied social sciences, and an advanced diploma in criminology for research on the use of penal custody for male juvenile offenders. In 1996 he took unpaid leave to study criminology at Cambridge University, researching 'short, sharp shock' custodial regimes and gaining a further M.Phil. degree. He has contributed numerous articles to the *British Journal of Criminology*, the *Howard Journal of Criminal Justice* and the *Prison Service Journal*.

Jim Gomersall is Governor of HMP Winchester and was previously Deputy Governor of Grendon and Springhill Prisons. He joined the Prison Service at Grendon Prison as an officer in 1974 and has worked at Wellingborough, Bullingdon and Oxford Prisons and at Prison Service Headquarters. He is currently studying part-time for a Master's degree at the University of Cambridge.

Roger Haley is currently working on the Quantum Business Change Programme for the Prison Service. He joined the Prison Service in 1981 as an assistant governor and served at Dorchester, Portland Borstal/YCC, Maze, Frankland and Wandsworth Prisons. He has worked at Prison Service Headquarters in a variety of departments including area office and as Head of the Population Management Unit. Roger graduated from Lancaster University with a degree in European studies, has a diploma in criminology, and is currently researching the determinants of prison population fluctuations for his Master's degree at Cambridge University.

Sue James is the lifer governor at HMP Leyhill. She joined the Prison Service on the direct entry scheme in 1998. Sue was previously employed in the probation service, and undertook a full range of probation duties while working as a probation officer, including specialisation in young prisoners in custody. Following a promotion to senior probation officer in 1989 she completed a four-and-a-half-year secondment to HMP Bristol. In 1999 Sue obtained an MBA degree from the University of the West of England, her dissertation being concerned with improving the joint performance of the Prison and probation services.

WD2310 Jennings was working as an architectural technician for a district council before entering the prison system. Upon release he took up a place, offered while in prison, to study architecture, although he left the course after two years. He is currently in his final year of an interior design degree at the same university and intends to pursue an MA degree immediately afterwards. From there he hopes to enter the teaching profession at university or further education level.

Kevin Leggett is Deputy Governor of HMYOI Aylesbury, where he chairs the race relations management team (RRMT). He joined the Prison Service in 1988 and, after five years as a prison officer, was selected for the accelerated promotion scheme and subsequently worked at Bullingdon and The Mount Prisons. He has also worked in the Security Group at Prison Service Headquarters, and was staff officer to the Head of Training and Development. In 1999 he was awarded a certificate in management by the Open University and is now working on his diploma.

Peter Leonard is at present on secondment to the Prison Service of Northern Ireland and was previously Head of the Prison Service Standards Audit Unit. He joined the Prison Service in 1968 as a prison officer. He successfully completed the 27th assistant governors' course and was posted to HMP Wormwood Scrubs, and then to the Officers' Training School in Wakefield. He spent almost five years as Deputy Governor of Wellingborough Prison before being given his first command, Morton Hall, which he re-opened in 1985. After three years in the Director General's office he became Governor of Lindholme Prison and then, after being promoted to governor grade 1, was technical advisor to the Learmont Inquiry. In 1995 he was appointed Governor of Frankland Prison, and in 1998 was posted to the Secretariat at Prison Service Headquarters to work on the *Prisons–Probation Review* and the implementation of the *Prison Service Review*. Peter has published a number of studies in the *Prison Service Journal* and has been technical advisor to the Albanian Prison Service.

Dr Steve Lowden joined the Prison Service in 1996 as Head of Training Policy, he is at present on secondment to the Civil Service College. He previously worked at the Police Staff College, Bramshill, and in educational establishments as diverse as an approved school and an independent school. Steve's previous publications include management material for the Open University and commentaries on the 'logic' of education policy.

Martin Narey is Director General of the Prison Service. He started his career in the NHS and moved to the Prison Service in 1982, where he worked as an assistant governor for seven years. In 1989 he moved to a policy post at Prison Service Headquarters and from there, in 1990, to the Home Office, to work as Private Secretary to the minister at the time, Lord Ferrers. Martin then went on to various policy posts within the Home Office, including leading work on what have become known as the Narey reforms, which aimed to tackle delay within the criminal justice system. He then moved back to Prison Service Headquarters as

Head of Security Policy and Director of Regimes. He assumed his current role in April 1999.

Nicola Padfield is a criminal barrister by training. She is currently President of Fitzwilliam College, Cambridge, and Director of Studies of a Master of Studies part-time degree course for senior prison managers at the University of Cambridge Institute of Criminology. Her research interests cover legal topics in a wide range of criminal justice areas. Her books include *The Criminal Justice Process* (1995), *Sentencing Theory, Law and Practice* (1996), *Criminal Law* (1998) and *A Guide to the Crime and Disorder Act* (1998). She is editor of the criminal law practitioners' monthly magazine, *Archbold News*.

John Powls has been Head of the Correctional Policy Unit since its formation in August 1998. Prior to that he spent three years at Prison Service Headquarters managing a number of major development projects in planning and IT. After leaving university John spent three years as a court liaison officer for Teesside Social Services department, joining the Prison Service as an assistant governor in 1978. He served at HMP Manchester, Frankland and Wakefield as well as the Prison Service College. His last job of 'honest work' was as Governor of HMP Dartmoor. At Wakefield and Dartmoor Prisons, he was closely involved in developing the offending behaviour programmes, particularly for sex offenders. He has published a number of articles in management and other professional journals, and contributed to a number of books. John is also a published poet.

Stephen Pryor is Governor of HMP Highpoint. His career has spanned various establishments, officer training and Prison Service Headquarters. He has published papers on numerous themes associated with human rights in prison. His chapter draws on a presentation made to staff joining HMP Highdown, which he opened in the early 1990s.

Charlotte Rendle is a principal officer at HMP Grendon, working in the Regimes and Services department. She joined the Prison Service on the accelerated promotion scheme in 1997 and subsequently worked at HMP Bullingdon. Before joining the Prison Service she undertook post-graduate research in ethics at Oxford University, being particularly concerned with the historical justification for imprisonment and with penal reform. Charlotte has a degree in theology from the University of Durham.

Gareth Sands is a principal officer at HMYOI Huntercombe. He joined the Prison Service on the accelerated promotion scheme in 1997 and has worked at Grendon and Springhill Prisons. Prior to joining the Prison Service he worked for the Shaftsbury Society as a support worker for adults with challenging behaviour.

Gareth obtained a degree in sociology and social policy from the University of Durham, and has contributed to the *Prison Service Journal*.

Stephen Shaw is HM Prisons Ombudsman for England and Wales. His chapter was written when he was Director of the Prison Reform Trust, a post held from 1981 to 1999. Previously he worked as a research officer in the Home Office and for the National Association for the Care and Resettlement of Offenders (NACRO). In the past twenty years Stephen has visited most of the prisons in the United Kingdom. He is a frequent contributor to the media – radio, television and the newspapers – and is the author of many articles, reports and pamphlets on the penal system.

Sally Swift is currently Deputy Governor at HMP Bristol. Previously she was a civil servant with the Export Credit Guarantee department and the Environment Research Council. She joined the Prison Service in 1979 as an assistant governor and served at HMP Holloway and HM Borstal Bulwood Hall, then the only closed borstal for young women in England and Wales. She has served in a number of male establishments, at Prison Service Headquarters and, in 1993, she was appointed Governor of HM Remand Centre Puklechurch. Sally obtained a B.Sc. degree in sociology from the University of London. Her particular interest is female crime and the treatment of women in custody and she is currently working on a Master's degree dissertation on the causes of female crime.

Ed Tullett is currently working at Brixton Prison. His previous employment includes casework, construction, a government inner-city project and working at HMYOI Dover. He was Head of the Prison Service Security Group policy unit and is responsible for the Service's current *Security Manual*.

Chris Watts worked for the Prison Service Training Services for two years. He has a degree in English literature from the University of London and a Master's degree in English at Warwick University. He is editor of *Warwick Work in Progress: A Journal of Comparative Literary Studies*. He is at present Head of Research and Development for the London Ambulance NHS Trust.

Yvonne Wilmott works in the Women's Policy Group in the Prison Service Directorate of Regimes. She joined the Prison Service as Assistant Head of Nursing Services in May 1993. She qualified as a nurse in 1968, a midwife in 1969, a district nurse and health visitor in 1977, and a nurse teacher in 1986. Yvonne also has a diploma in criminology. Until her move to the Women's Policy Group she was nurse advisor to the Directorate of Healthcare.

Robert Young currently works in the Regimes Directorate at Prison Service Headquarters as project manager for the Purposeful Activity Expansion Scheme (PAES). He joined the Scottish Prison Service from a career as an electronics engineer. While in the Scottish Service he worked at a YOI and Headquarters, later transferring to the Home Office as a marketing manager. He recently obtained a diploma in Criminology from the University of Cambridge.

FOREWORD

Crime is not an abstract social problem. Everyday crime diminishes the lives of innocent people, restricts their civil liberties and causes fear, anger and loss. The government is taking tough action to deal with crime, and to tackle its causes.

The Prison Service has a key part to play in our strategy by protecting the public and by reducing re-offending. It has achieved much in recent years by coping with an increase in the prison population and at the same time dramatically reducing escapes from prisons. This record on escapes must be maintained but we must focus our attention on reducing re-offending. The government is investing an additional £226 million in our prisons over a three-year period to provide constructive regimes which will help prisoners avoid returning to crime on release. We have prioritised three areas in particular: offending behaviour programmes, tackling poor literacy and numeracy, and driving down drug misuse.

We have developed offending behaviour programmes, using what we know about characteristics of effective intervention, which are accredited by an independent panel of experts as likely to reduce re-offending. These programmes have been shown to work. Re-offending after release by those who had undertaken such programmes is almost half that of a control group of prisoners.

We know that many prisoners lack basic literacy and numeracy skills, and rule themselves out of over 90% of jobs when released. By improving literacy and numeracy we will give prisoners a fresh chance on release.

Finally, £76 million is dedicated to reducing the supply of drugs coming into prisons, and providing effective rehabilitation programmes for prisoners with addictions. All establishments now offer CARAT (counselling, assessment, referral, advice and throughcare) services to all prisoners with a drug problem. One of its innovative features is that it provides continuity between treatment in prison and that it is available on release for up to eight weeks.

The continuity that has been achieved between delivering drug treatment programmes in prison and in the community must be replicated in other areas of our work. Although joint working between the Prison Service and the probation service is not a new idea – in England and Wales the two services have successfully worked together to develop the Prison/Probation joint accreditation panel and to review and revise sentence planning – it is only by willing and effective collaboration that prisoners will be equipped to get jobs, find homes and, ultimately, commit fewer crimes. Formal links have now been established between prison healthcare and the NHS and I am determined that this partnership arrangement will dramatically improve the substandard healthcare I have seen in a number of establishments. By raising standards to match those in the NHS we will ensure that important health gains which occur in prison are maintained on release.

I welcome the publication of this book as it provides a comprehensive account of the work of Her Majesty's Prison Service. It usefully sets the work of the Prison Service within the wider context of the criminal justice system, as well as outlining what happens in our prisons. The book is not an official publication but is written in most part by Prison Service staff. It therefore provides a real insight into how and why our prisons function; an understanding of the people who run, live and work in them; and the issues they face on a daily basis.

I am sure that *Prisons and the Prisoner* will give readers a realistic insight into what happens in our penal institutions and how the Prison Service is uniquely placed to have major impact on reducing re-offending.

Paul Boateng
Minister of State
Home Office

ACKNOWLEDGEMENTS

This book would not have been possible without the hard work of many people. The editors are particularly grateful to the authors of the various chapters for their patience and enthusiasm during the long gestation period of the book.

We also extend our thanks to the following people who have contributed to the book in various ways: Carole Allen, Nicky Baldock, Norma Beddell, Jim Boniface, Simon Charnock, Dominic Clayton, Tony Corcoran, Peter Dawson, Vicky Foot, Roger Hemmings, Wayne Hickey, Stuart Hoskins, Phil Kielman, Havilah Lobban, Michael Loughlin, Gavin Marney, Tim Morris, James Neville, William Payne, Tony Pearson, Peter Quinn, Steve Sale, Aston Tew, Roger Thasan, John Walford and Phil Wheatley.

In addition, our gratitude goes to Catherine Fell and Rebecca Mann of the Prison Service Library for tracking down many references for the authors, and to Julia Carlton for typing the final drafts.

ABBREVIATIONS

ACAS   Advisory Conciliation and Arbitration Service
ACOP   Association of Chief Officers of Probation
ACPO   Association of Chief Police Officers
ADP   average daily population
AFC   accommodation fabric check
AG   assistant governor
APS   accelerated promotion scheme
BOV   Board of Visitors
C & R   control and restraint
CARAT   counselling, assessment, referral, advice and throughcare
CCF   core competence framework
CJA   Criminal Justice Act
CJPO   Criminal Justice and Public Order Act
CNA   certified normal accommodation
CSR   comprehensive spending review
CYPA   Children and Young Persons Act
DCMF   designed, constructed, managed and financed [prisons]
DHC   Directorate of Healthcare
DLP   discretionary lifer panel
DTO   Detention and Training Order
DYOI   detention in a Young Offender Institution
ECHR   European Convention on Human Rights
HM CIC   Her Majesty's Chief Inspector of Constabularies
HM CIP   Her Majesty's Chief Inspector of Prisons
HMP   Her Majesty's Prison
HMYOI   Her Majesty's Young Offender Institution
IR   industrial relations
IT   information technology
JSAC   Job Simulation Assessment Centre
KPI   Key Performance Indicator
KPT   Key Performance Target
LGA   Local Government Association
LMU   Lifer Management Unit
LRU   Lifer Review Unit
NACBV   National Advisory Council for the Boards of Visitors of England
            and Wales
NACRO   National Association for the Care and Resettlement of Offenders
NAPO   National Association of Probation Officers
NGO   non-governmental organisation
NHS   National Health Service

NPV	net present value
NTO	national training organisation
NVQ	national vocational qualification
OBPU	Offending Behaviour Programme Unit
OPCS	Office of Population Censuses and Surveys
OPG	Operational Policy Group
OSG	operational support grade
PAES	Purposeful Activity Expansion Scheme
PAR	parole assessment report
PCU	Prisoner Casework Unit
PE	physical education
PFI	Private Finance Initiative
PGA	Prison Governors' Association
PMS	prison medical service
POA	Prison Officers' Association
POINT	prison officer initial training
PRT	Prison Reform Trust
PSA	public service agreement
PSO	Prison Service Order
PSTS	Prison Service Training Services
RAPT	Rehabilitation of Addicted Prisoners Trust
ROTL	release on temporary licence
RRLO	race relations liaison officer
RRMT	race relations management team
SCP	sentencing and correctional policy
SCWS	staff care and welfare service
SMART	specific, measurable, achievable, realistic and time-bounded [objectives]
SOTP	sex offender treatment programme
STC	secure training centre
STO	Secure Training Order
TC	therapeutic community
UDHR	Universal Declaration of Human Rights
UKCC	United Kingdon Central Council for Nursing, Midwifery and Health-visiting
VP	vulnerable prisoner
VPU	Vulnerable Prisoner Unit
WRVS	Women's Royal Voluntary Service
YJB	Youth Justice Board
YO	young offender
YOI	Young Offender Institution
YTC	youth training centre

INTRODUCTION

Shane Bryans and Rachel Jones

The Prison Service has not, since an official publication in 1977, been the subject of such an in-depth study as this book provides. This multi-authored work is about the people who live and work in the prisons that make up Her Majesty's Prison Service for England and Wales (referred to as the Prison Service throughout this book). It contains contributions from Prison Service staff, an ex-prisoner, academics and a pressure group. The book reflects the individual authors' personal views rather than the Prison Service official position. By doing so, it provides a unique insight into the work and problems faced by the Prison Service in providing a vital public service.

The book begins with Part One looking at the operating context of the Prison Service. Chapter 1 considers the historical debate about the purposes of imprisonment. It highlights how the theory of prisons has moved away from an emphasis on punitive institutions to prisons as places of rehabilitation. It offers a perspective on the human rights surrounding the issue of imprisonment as well as an overview of the major themes of prison work in the last 200 years. Chapter 2 offers a history of the Prison Service: showing how prisons have progressed and tracing the key reforms that have changed imprisonment and the criminal justice system in England and Wales. It looks at major developments and crises within the Service, and examines the work of prison reformers such as John Howard. Chapter 3 considers Home Office correctional policy and the increase in joint working between the Prison Service and other agencies, particularly the probation service. It provides a policy context and a strategic overview for the full range of planning documents and all aspects of work with offenders undertaken by the services, both separately and together. Chapter 4 deals with the current structure and organisation of the Prison Service. It examines how and why the Prison Service was accorded agency status and looks at relationships between the government and those that run the Service. The structure at Headquarters and establishment level is explored, and the chapter goes on to outline how performance targets are set and managed. Chapter 5 examines the role played by the private sector within the Prison Service. It outlines the key issues and debates concerning privatisation, and illustrates how the seven private prisons are contracted and run. It examines the issue of accountability in private establishments as well as cost comparisons, and asks whether the Service can expect continued growth in contracting-out. Chapter 6 considers the Prison Service's commitment to, and policies on, race relations in the context of an overview of ethnic groups in prison. It highlights the important issues surrounding racial equality in the Service and looks at the Service's RESPOND initiative, launched in 1999 to help ensure racial equality for staff and prisoners.

Part Two considers the prison population as a whole and looks at distinct groups of prisoners, their specific needs and management. Chapter 7 examines trends in the prison population, tracing the causes of population fluctuations and the dramatic increase in population between 1989 and 1999. It looks at the links between the law, crime rates, the amount of court business and the size of the prison population. It then examines the prison population to answer the question, 'Who are the prisoners?' and studies how the Prison Service copes with the problems caused by a rising prison population. Chapter 8 focuses on the historical context for, and the current treatment of, high-security prisoners – from the abolition of the death penalty to the inception of the high-security prison estate and the dispersal system. It examines how high-profile incidents and Inquiries, such as the Mountbatten Report and those concerned with the Whitemoor and Parkhurst escapes, have influenced developments in the estate It provides an overview of the problems and issues facing the Service in holding high-security prisoners effectively in custody. Chapter 9 considers the treatment of life-sentence prisoners in the Prison Service. It examines the historical context of life imprisonment and details how life-sentenced prisoners are treated in custody. It takes a detailed look at sentencing trends, sentence progression, release and recall of prisoners serving Britain's most severe penal sanction. Chapter 10 looks at the issues surrounding the imprisonment of women. It examines trends in the female prison population and considers the impact on families when women are imprisoned. It looks at the key, and sometimes overlooked, differences in holding women in prison and outlines their needs and issues. Chapter 11 focuses on what happens to young people held in custody by the Prison Service. It begins with an examination of the young offender population: their offences, backgrounds and particular needs; and moves on to look at effective regimes and key relationships, such as those with family on the outside and staff acting as role models inside prison.

Part Three looks at the people who work in prison. Chapter 12 provides an account of the staff who work in prison establishments and at Prison Service Headquarters. It discusses the largest group of prison staff, prison officer grades, and outlines the work of other staff including administrative and industrial grades. It explores the Prison Service human resource management strategy, including the core competence framework (CCF), leadership charter, staff culture and industrial relations. Chapter 13 discusses the role of prison governors within the Service. It examines the complex managerial and operational context in which governors operate and considers how governors run their prisons effectively given the myriad demands placed upon them. It demonstrates the essential role that governors play in how their prison functions and explores the leadership themes this raises. Chapter 14 explores how the Prison Service is facing the challenge of developing a learning organisation against a background of increased efficiencies and performance delivery. It details the training and development new recruits receive at the start and during their service to enhance their skills and professionalism. It charts developments in training and best practice, and highlights the importance of well-trained, supported and committed staff. Chapter 15 offers a personal insight into the role and work of the prison officer, by prison officers themselves. It shows the conflicts of interest in the job, as well as the preconceptions about prisons, prisoners and prison staff, both from inside and outside the Service. It explores how decisions are interpreted on 'the ground floor' and how the Service can achieve a greater degree of co-operation and cohesion between prison staff and prison management. Chapter 16 sees the world of the Prison Service from the perspective of a senior prison governor. It considers major developments and changes in the Service, reflects on the difficulties of balancing demands and resources while governing, and looks to the future of efficiency in the Service.

Part Four looks in detail at what happens in prison. Chapter 17 examines prison regimes and the development of constructive and purposeful activity for prisoners. It explores the foundation of constructive regimes and how they are designed to attempt to reduce re-offending. It looks at the work and activity available to prisoners and at the Purposeful Activity Expansion Scheme (PAES), the Prison Service initiative to increase the value of regime activity within prisons. Chapter 18 discusses how the Prison Service delivers the second part of its Statement of Purpose ('… our duty is to look after them with humanity and help them lead law-abiding and useful lives in custody and after release.') by helping prisoners to address their offending behaviour and substance-misuse problems. It looks at the development of offending behaviour programmes and the growth of 'what works' analysis, which seeks to measure the effectiveness of such programmes. Chapter 19 considers the development, role and function of therapeutic communities (TCs) within prisons. It covers the efficacy of such treatment and programmes plus their unique place within prisons and within the wider context of TC theory. Chapter 20 examines security, custody and order and how these elements interact to provide safe and secure prisons. It considers the relationship between physical, procedural and 'dynamic' security, and goes on to review how order and control can be maintained, offering evidence of how disturbances can be prevented. Further, the chapter covers the administration of the reward and punishment system and the appropriate use of force. Chapter 21 looks at healthcare services in prisons and prisoners' health. It presents an overview of prison healthcare staff, their duties and terms and conditions. It also examines the relationship between prison health services and the NHS, and considers proposals for further integration of services/joint working, and the impact of this on prisoner care. Chapter 22 examines how prisoners cope with imprisonment and the essential part played by relationships in ensuring a safe and fair prison. It provides an insight into some of the conflicts inherent in imprisonment and the importance of the judgement and personal standards of staff as the foundation of their work. Chapter 23 looks at how the Prison Service works with other agencies to prepare prisoners for release into the community. It examines the place of risk assessment, the management of risk in the release process, and highlights the importance of the sentence management and throughcare system. It looks at the mechanisms for reintegration, including release on temporary licence (ROTL) and parole, and the need for offending behaviour work and community liaison. Chapter 24 offers an ex-prisoner's perspective of imprisonment through a sentence served in a number of Prison Service establishments. It offers an insight into some of the frustrations and problems of serving prisoners, as well as what makes a positive difference to life after a custodial sentence.

In Part Five, Chapter 25 asks, 'Who guards the guardians?' It examines the role of the Inspectorates, the Prisons Ombudsman and Boards of Visitors; those whose role it is to safeguard the fair treatment of prisoners and staff. It looks at the powers of these bodies, their accountability and the standards they work to, and asks if their roles and powers are clear, well defined and appropriate for the work they do. Chapter 26 offers a view of the Prison Service from a pressure group. It examines the conflicts within the Service and its relationship with those outside. It highlights the difficulties facing prisoners, prisons and prison staff. It examines the misrepresentation of all three, and suggests solutions such as better communications for changing the situation for the better.

Part Six looks to the future and provides a vision of what prisons should be like in the early part of the 21st century. Chapter 27 presents the Director General's view of the Prison Service. He examines the challenges faced by the Service and the strategies needed for the future. He goes on to highlight, through an examination of key themes such as the imprisonment of under-18s, the importance of a robus, long-term strategy to secure the future of the Prison Service.

The final part of the book contains two annexes that are referred to throughout the text. Annex A lists the Prison Service's Aims, Objectives and Principles; Annex B, its Key Performance Indicators (KPIs) for 1999–2000. A list of further reading may be found before the index; all other references are at the ends of individual chapters.

This book should give the reader an idea of the complexity of the world of prisons and prisoners. It was written for members of the public, students and new practitioners in the criminal justice field. We started the book out of a desire to shed some light on the 'world behind the wall'. We hope that it does so.

PART ONE:
THE OPERATING CONTEXT

THE PURPOSES OF IMPRISONMENT

Andrew Coyle

Introduction

There are a number of large institutions that are common to most modern societies. They include schools, hospitals, the armed services, the police – and prisons. Most of them have very clear objectives. There may be debates about the finer details of their purpose in society, but in broad terms there is a consensus about their role (Cayley 1982). For example, the school exists to educate young people. The hospital exists to restore sick people to health. The purpose of the armed services is to protect society from real or potential enemies. The main objective of the police is to prevent crime from happening and, where it does, to detect those responsible. As regards the purpose of the prison, however, there is a degree of ambivalence.

Over the years there has been a lively debate, which continues today, about the purpose of imprisonment. The classical interpretation suggests four major purposes (see, for example, Walker 1965). Some commentators argue that its main purpose is **to punish** people for the crimes they have committed. Others insist that its main purpose is **to deter** individuals who are in prison from committing further crimes after they are released, as well as to deter others who might be inclined to commit crime. A further suggestion is that people are sent to prison **to be reformed or rehabilitated**. That is to say, during the time they are in prison they will come to realise that committing crime is wrong and they will learn skills that will help them to lead a law-abiding life when they are released. Sometimes it is argued that such personal rehabilitation is more likely to come about if the prisoner experiences hard labour. In some instances, people may be sent to prison because the crimes they have committed shows that they present **a grave threat to public safety**. Before examining each of these claims in more detail, it is worth considering the development of the modern prison as an institution.

The growth of imprisonment

Until a few hundred years ago prisons were generally places in which men and women were held while waiting for something to happen: that something might be trial; or the payment of a ransom, a debt or a fine; exile; or execution. Occasionally, individuals who posed a particular threat to the local ruler or state might be deprived of their liberty for a long period. Such men or women would be held in prisons that belonged to the local ruler, frequently attached to his castle or palace (Morris and Rothman 1998). The prison building used for ordinary criminals was often an annexe of the court and the jailer was an officer of the court. The prison as an institution was regarded as an adjunct of the court, the final element in the criminal justice process.

Modern prisons have their genesis in North America and western Europe. As originally conceived, these prisons were little more than warehouses where offenders were punished by being deprived of their liberty (Howard, J. 1791). Their existence was an extension of the earlier notion that wrongdoers should be punished by being exiled from the community. Now, instead of being sent to another part of the country or being transported to the colonies, prisoners were punished for their crimes by being exiled behind the high walls of the prison. The punishment of the court consisted of deprivation of liberty, and the authorities had little concern for what went on inside the prison. Physical conditions in most prisons were often appalling. Prisoners were frequently dependent on their families or friends for food and clothing. Jailers made their living by charging prisoners for access to the essentials of life (HM Chief Inspector of Prisons for Scotland 1839).

At the end of the 18th and beginning of the 19th centuries a number of influential individuals turned their attention to the poor state of the prisons. Penal reformers in the United Kingdom advanced the notion that prisons should not be places of depravity and inhumanity but that they should be decent and austere. John Howard spread this principle to other countries in Europe (Howard, J. 1791). The genesis of the Silent System of imprisonment at Auburn Prison in the state of New York, in which prisoners were allowed to mix with each other at work but were forbidden to communicate in any way, and of the Separate System at the Eastern Penitentiary in the state of Pennsylvania, in which prisoners were not allowed to come into any contact with each other, have been well documented (McConville 1981). At the same time or before, similar developments were taking place in United Kingdom prisons such as Gloucester and Glasgow Bridewell.

After these reforms there was an unforeseen consequence – a change in the type of person who worked in prison. Senior staff, particularly, became more reputable. Gradually, the men and women involved developed a rationalisation for their task of locking up other human beings. This went beyond simple deprivation of liberty. It was suggested that criminals might be reformed by the very experience of imprisonment. This notion owed much to the religious beliefs of the first prison reformers. Prisoners were locked up in small cells, rather like early Christian hermits, and were left to contemplate the error of their ways with only the Bible for company. The chaplain became second only to the governor in the prison hierarchy (McConville 1981).

Simultaneously, the new academic discipline of criminology was beginning to expand. Academics were turning their attention to the phenomenon of crime: how it is to be defined, who commits it, why and how might they be prevented from doing so (Ignatieff 1978). In the following generation criminologists had a new set of half-brothers who were known as penologists. They studied the philosophy and practice of punishment, particularly in respect of imprisonment.

Out of all of this grew the belief that crime was an aberration from the norm and that, rather like a young tree which is growing in a crooked manner, people, particularly young people, who committed crime could be trained to live law-abiding lives. The human expression of this training became known as rehabilitation (Garland 1985). The new breed of experts who began to work in prisons – assistant governors, social workers, probation officers, teachers, psychologists and psychiatrists – took on the task of rehabilitating men and women who had originally been sent to prison as punishment for the crime they had committed.

The notion that people could be trained out of criminality in the prison setting, like plants forced on in a greenhouse, was an attractive one on several counts. It raised the possibility that crime might eventually be eliminated. This vision was articulated by Sir Alexander Paterson, one of the foremost prison administrators in the early part of this century. Giving evidence to the Persistent Offenders' Committee in 1931, Paterson noted: 'The problem of Recidivism is small, diminishing, and not incapable of solution' (Ruck 1951).

Once the positive potential of imprisonment was recognised it was logical to move on to the next step. If one could identify soon enough in life people who were likely to become serious offenders in the future it would be proper to send them to prison at an early stage in their criminal career in order to rehabilitate them. This would be particularly appropriate if they were sent to prisons for young people, where the emphasis would be on reform and training. Thus was born the concept of prisons for juveniles and, in due course, of borstal institutions.

So, to the original view of prison as a place where people were sent as punishment for crimes which they had committed was added the notion that prison could also be used as a tool for the control and prevention of crime by diverting those who were in prison from a life of future crime.

The next logical step was the principle that the length of time that men and women were to spend in prison should be determined not merely by the gravity of the offence for which they were sent to prison in the first place but also as a result of an assessment of the likelihood that they would commit further crime in the future. This consideration was expressed in two forms. It could be based on the number of similar crimes that the person had already committed. This was the justification for preventive detention as it existed in the United Kingdom in the first half of the 20th century. It could also be based on an assessment of the likelihood of future offending. This assessment was to be undertaken while the man or woman was in prison. As a consequence, the length of time that a man or woman could spend in prison would be determined not by the sentencing court but by some form of administrative or quasi-judicial process according to how the prisoner responded while the sentence was being served. This led to the introduction of the indeterminate sentence in its many forms and to the concept of release on parole. The implications of these developments for the system of criminal justice did not go unnoticed:

> There can be no doubt that the increase in the control of the Executive over the offender after he has been sentenced has been one of the major features of twentieth century penal history in this country (Cross 1971).

In recent years there has been increasing emphasis on the part that imprisonment has to play in preventing crime. This has been based on the concept that most offences are committed by an identifiable group of people. To the extent that they can be identified and taken out of society, the rest of us, as law-abiding citizens, can get on with our lives in peace. This was the basis of the recently popular aphorism, 'Prison Works' (Howard, M. 1993).

The purposes of imprisonment today

This very brief look at the development in the use of imprisonment in this country has shown how its objectives have usually been articulated after the event rather than as a set of principles agreed in advance in order to justify its subsequent use. So, what conclusions can now be drawn from the stated objectives of punishment, deterrence, reform and public protection? An important starting-point for this discussion is the recognition that one cannot consider prisons in a vacuum. The manner in which imprisonment is used will be determined by what society expects of its criminal justice process. In most western countries the criminal justice system is considered to have two main aims. One is to punish those who have committed crime; the other is to prevent future crime. We must, therefore, consider how the expressed purposes of imprisonment contribute to the realisation of these aims.

Punishment

Prison plays an important part in the punishment of criminals. In the United Kingdom it is the most severe sentence that a court can apply and its symbolic effect is very important. The picture of the judge ordering the convicted person to be 'taken down' carries great resonance. For this reason, as well as in the interest of justice, it should not be over-used. In determining the length of sentence the court should take account of the gravity of the offence that has been committed and the circumstances in which it was committed. Traditionally, the judge in each case has made a determination based on the evidence in that case. This has been an important element in the principle of an independent judiciary, a principle of which we were justifiably proud. An exception to this was the obligation placed on the judge to pass a life sentence after a conviction for murder. Even this exception came under extensive criticism, not least from the House of Lords. In a number of cases the law laid down maximum sentences that could not be exceeded. For example, the maximum sentence for burglary in a dwelling is fourteen years. In recent years, following precedents used extensively in other countries such as the United States, legislation has been enacted imposing mandatory minimum sentences that the judge is obliged to impose (Crime (Sentences) Act 1997).

There is less unanimity now than in previous years about how the punishment element of imprisonment is to be achieved. Until recently in the United Kingdom there was little challenge to Alexander Paterson's aphorism: 'Men come to prison as a punishment, not *for* punishment' (Ruck 1951).

According to this principle, the punishment of imprisonment consisted solely of the deprivation of liberty. In reality, the coercive nature of the prison environment meant that the punitive element of imprisonment extended far beyond the mere deprivation of liberty into many features of daily life in prison. Nevertheless, Paterson's point was that it was no responsibility of the prison system to impose punitive regimes on prisoners. There has been an increasing sentiment in some quarters in recent years that there should also be a punitive element within prison – that the experience of imprisonment should be an unpleasant one in itself (*Sunday Express*, 29 August 1993). In any event, Paterson's dictum never applied in many other prison systems, where it was a function of the administration to impose punishment on prisoners.

Imprisonment is a blunt instrument of punishment. For some prisoners the pains of deprivation of liberty and separation from family are almost unbearable. For others, prison may be some sort of place of safety from the pressure and severity of normal life. These opposing views should be in the mind of the judge who passes a sentence of imprisonment.

Deterrence

If it is true that human beings value freedom above all else, then it is reasonable to conclude that we will ensure that we never do anything which will put that freedom at risk. On that basis, one might assume that the threat of imprisonment is likely to act as a strong deterrent against crime. The truth is that the use of prison as a means of crime control, let alone crime prevention, is much more problematic. In terms of deterrence the statistics speak for themselves: out of every hundred offences committed, only two result in a criminal conviction. In the unlikely event that a potential criminal will apply actuarial considerations, these are pretty good odds. In terms of preventing future offending the statistics do not give much more cause for optimism: 56% of males and 40% of females released from prison are re-convicted within two years. Two-thirds of offenders under the age of 21 are re-convicted within two years (Home Office 1995).

It is true that these statistics tell us little about the number of people who might have committed a crime had they not been aware of the possibility that they might go to prison as a consequence, but by definition it is difficult to produce evidence to support such an argument. Such evidence as there is tends to support the assertion that potential offenders are more likely to be deterred by the certainty of detection than by the prospect of punishment.

Reform

The notion that prison can be a place where individuals are taught to change their behaviour is an attractive one on a number of counts. It provides a positive justification for what would otherwise be a merely negative punishment of the criminal. Prison as a place of reform is also attractive to those public-spirited men and women who work within the prison system and who wish to do more professionally than merely deprive prisoners of their liberty. For society, which regards crime as something that is committed by a relatively small, identifiable group of men and women, it holds out an expectation that there will be less crime in the future if these individuals can be encouraged to lead law-abiding lives. All of these considerations encourage belief in the principle of rehabilitation through imprisonment, that people who have broken the law can be encouraged to obey the law as a consequence of spending a time in prison.

The principle that human beings can be encouraged to change their patterns of behaviour is a sound one. The application of the principle in a prison setting is very problematic, however. Change of this nature comes about primarily as a result of a personal decision by the individual concerned; it cannot be imposed by external agents. In the coercive world of the prison it is very difficult for an individual to make a truly personal decision. Much activity is predetermined and allows for little variation. Even when there is an element of choice, the consequence of any decisions has to be weighed carefully as it may have a bearing on decisions made by others about the prison in which the sentence is to be served, or even the date of release.

No matter how open a prison may strive to be the reality is that it is essentially a world set apart from normality. The prisoner's links with social structures, which the rest of us take for granted, are tenuous. If a prisoner is to prepare for a law-abiding life after release he or she has to overcome the rules and regulations, formal and informal, of the abnormal world of the prison. It would be wrong to create the impression that someone who has had problems at home, at school, in the workplace, in social relationships – as many prisoners have had throughout their lives – could be altered by a few months in prison and then sent back to the world, from which he or she came, as a changed person. That is not to devalue the sterling work that goes on in many prisons, where prisoners are provided with opportunities to change themselves and their behaviour. Some people are changed for the better by the experience of imprisonment. But it can be argued that this happens despite the prison environment rather than because of it.

Public protection

There are a small number of people whose behaviour is such that it presents a serious threat to the safety of society. Some of them may already have committed serious crimes and give every indication that, if they are released, they will continue to do so. The starting-point for any discussion about how these people are to be dealt with should be a recognition that they are very few in number. Most of them have a high public profile because of the offences they have committed. It is quite proper that these people should be in prison for as long as they present a threat to

Prison Service perimeter security fencing. The wire and protective cladding are designed to make climbing as difficiult as possible.

the public, however long that may be. What is important is that decisions about their detention or release should be made by a properly constituted judicial body and that the prisoner should have a recognised avenue of appeal against any such decisions. It is not appropriate that decisions about these individuals should be made behind closed doors by executive or political agencies.

The detention of prisoners who have not been sentenced

Our discussion so far has been about prisoners who have been sentenced to a period of imprisonment. Special considerations apply to prisoners who are detained without conviction. These prisoners can fall into a number of categories. They may be awaiting trial; facing a civil charge; or awaiting some administrative decision, for example about an immigration matter. The situation faced by these people is quite distinct from those who have been convicted of an offence. They have yet to be found guilty of any offence and should, therefore, be regarded as innocent in the eyes of the law. The reality is that they are often held in the most restricted conditions, conditions which in some cases can be considered to be an affront to human dignity. In a number of countries the majority of people who are in prison are awaiting trial; the proportion sometimes exceed 60%. In England and Wales the proportion is 20% (Home Office 1998).

The future use of imprisonment

What is to be concluded from all of this about the future use of imprisonment? What should society expect of it and what can imprisonment be expected to achieve? One way of dealing with these questions is to differentiate between the **act** of imprisonment and the **experience** of imprisonment.

The **act** of imprisonment is carried out by the judge or magistrate who sends a person to prison. It is he or she who decides that the person appearing in court should be deprived of liberty. That decision should be made on the basis of the principles described above. The duty of punishment is clearly laid down in criminal justice legislation and is to be determined by the seriousness of the crime. The arguments for deterrence are not strong but the judge may also feel a need to take account of public sentiment about the type of crime that has been committed. However, how is this public sentiment measured? To what extent is it justified and how is it expressed? Given the arguments presented above, a judge should never send someone to prison in order to be reformed. That may be a desired outcome of the prison sentence but it should not be a justification for imposing it. Finally, the issue of public protection is a very narrow one. When it is necessary to impose a prison sentence for this reason the judge should make clear that this is what is being done. When a sentence is imposed on grounds of public safety this fact may well have a bearing on how the sentenced person is subsequently treated in prison. Once the sentence has been passed the task of the judge has been completed.

So much for the act of imprisonment. Once the prisoner passes through the gates of the prison, the experience of imprisonment commences. This is the point at which the work of the Prison Service begins. It is the responsibility of those who work within the prison system to encourage and help the prisoner to put the experience of imprisonment to best advantage. This is not an easy objective to meet. One of the most frequently quoted aphorisms about the reality of imprisonment is from the 1990 White Paper:

> For most offenders, prison has to be justified in terms of public protection, denunciation and retribution. Otherwise it can be an expensive way of making bad people worse (Home Office 1991).

The task of the Prison Service is to try to ensure that *no one*, never mind only those who are 'bad' (whatever that means), is made worse by the experience of imprisonment.

The Prison Service of England and Wales has set itself a higher target than merely making sure that people are not damaged or 'made worse' by the experience of imprisonment. It has set a series of outcomes that spread across a wide spectrum. These range from basic education, through work and training skills, the ability to survive in our demanding society, and on to the very complex issues surrounding personal behaviour. These outcomes are more likely to be achieved if prisons do not operate as isolated entities but instead have clear links with the 'real' world existing outside them, a world from which the prisoner has come and to which, with all its complexities, he or she will return.

A prison system is also more likely to realise these outcomes if it is asked to work only with the relatively small number of men and women for whom there is no alternative but that they be deprived of their liberty – those who have committed the most serious crimes or from whom society needs to be protected. It should not be asked to be an asylum, a place of safety, for all those for whom society has no other solution: the mentally disturbed, the homeless, the drug and alcohol abuser. The prison has a very specific and narrow role to play in a democratic society. It should not be used to solve the many ills of society.

Prisons in context

Prisons do not exist in a vacuum. They exist because society has decided that they should be used as a method of responding to serious crime. The manner in which they are organised is subject to the general rule of law. The prison system is also subject to a whole range of international covenants, treaties and standards to which the government of the United Kingdom is a signatory. Some of these standards, such as those set by the United Nations, are universal in application. Others, such as those of the Council of Europe, are regional.

It is important to stress that these are not standards which have been imposed on us by foreign powers. The United Kingdom has been one of the driving forces behind many of the international human rights covenants, particularly the original ones drawn up in the aftermath of the Second World War. The United Kingdom was one of the prime drafters of the Universal Declaration of Human Rights (UDHR), which was adopted by the General Assembly of the United Nations in December 1948. The UDHR is not a legally binding instrument but its provisions are held to constitute general principles of law or to represent elementary considerations of humanity. The International Covenant on Civil and Political Rights (1966) was adopted by the UN General Assembly on 19 December 1966 and came into force on 23 March 1976. It has the legal force of a treaty for the states that have signed it. The United Kingdom has done so. Article 10 of this covenant requires that: 'All persons deprived of their liberty shall be treated with humanity and with respect for the inherent dignity of the human person.'

Other UN conventions that are relevant to the treatment of people deprived of their liberty include the Convention against Torture and Other Cruel, Inhuman or Degrading Treatment or Punishment (1984), the Convention on the Elimination of All Forms of Racial Discrimination (1966) and the Convention on the Elimination of All Forms of Discrimination against Women (1979). These conventions are not theoretical or academic treatises: they compose a body of international law which must be respected by the community of nations. Their relevance to the United Kingdom has been exemplified by the debate over recent years about what should be done with young people who break the law. A recent judicial review and HM Chief Inspector of Prisons have drawn attention to the fact that increasing numbers of young people under the age of 18 are being held in prisons. The UN Convention on the Rights of the Child (1989) defines a child as 'every human being below the age of 18 years' (Article 1). The United Kingdom has ratified, and is therefore bound by, this convention. That is not to say that the actions of children cannot be bound by law, but it does mean that when dealing with these actions the law and the legal system have to take account of the fact that they are children.

The European Convention on Human Rights makes specific reference to punishment and to those deprived of their liberty. The decision by the present government to incorporate this convention into domestic law (the Human Rights Act 1998) has attracted a great deal of public comment. Some of the criticisms of this proposal give the impression that incorporation will involve imposing the will of a foreign power on a sovereign state. This is ironic, given that the United Kingdom played a leading role in drafting this convention, which was signed in 1950 and came into force in 1953. Its provisions include many of the principles which our parents fought so strenuously to defend in two world wars.

The general principles contained in the covenants and conventions mentioned above are covered in more detail in a number of international instruments that refer specifically to prisoners. These include the Standard Minimum Rules for the Treatment of Prisoners (1957). These covenants and conventions are crucial to any understanding of the principles that apply to the practice of imprisonment at the beginning of the 21st century. They should be known to everyone who works within a prison environment.

Conclusion

It is proper to remind ourselves that the United Kingdom carries a heavy responsibility for the development of the prison and for its export to many countries. It is equally important to recognise that many countries today look to the Prison Service of England and Wales as a model service that strives to carry out its duty within a context of humanity, decency and fairness. The conditions in a number of our prisons still fall far short of what should be expected in a civilised society. The increase in the prison population and a reduction in resources in past years have led to a reversal of some of the significant improvements which followed in the wake of the Woolf Report (Woolf and Tumim 1991) and the subsequent White Paper (Home Office 1991). What is important is that no one denies the need for improvement to meet our own, as well as international, standards. The criticisms of campaigning bodies and pressure groups are taken into account by government ministers and officials. The independence of HM Chief Inspector of Prisons, of the Prisons Ombudsman, and of Boards of Visitors are held up as models for other countries. On the international front, the United Kingdom has played a key role in developing standards and in taking account of constructive criticism when offered.

Imprisonment as a punishment of the court is a fairly recent invention. In the course of a few hundred years its use has extended to almost every country in the world. In the United Kingdom it is the most extreme punishment that can be imposed on a citizen. It has been suggested that the extent to which prisons operate in a decent, humane and just fashion is a measure of the civilisation of a society (Mandela 1994). If that is the case, we have to be ready to question ourselves continually about the extent to which we in the United Kingdom, at the start of the 21st century can consider ourselves to be a civilised society.

References

Cayley, D. (1982) *Ivan Illich in Conversation*, House of Anasi Press

Crime (Sentences) Act 1997, c. 43

Cross, R. (1971) *Punishment, Prison and the Public*, Stevens & Sons

Garland, D. (1985) *Punishment and Welfare*, Aldershot: Gower

HM Chief Inspector of Prisons for Scotland (1839) *Annual Report of the Inspector of Prisons for Scotland*, HMSO

Home Office (1991) *Custody, Care and Justice: The Way Ahead for the Prison Service in England and Wales*, Cm 1647, HMSO

— (1995) *Digest: Information on the Criminal Justice System in England and Wales*, Home Office Research and Statistics Department

— (1998) *Prison Statistics England and Wales 1997*, Cm 4017, The Stationery Office

Howard, J. (1791) *An Account of the Principal Lazarettos in Europe*, (2nd edition), Johnson, Dilly & Cadell

Howard, M. (1993) speech to the Conservative Party Conference, Conservative Party Central Office

Human Rights Act 1998, Royal Assent 9 November 1998, c. 42

Ignatieff, M. (1978) *A Just Measure of Pain: The Penitentiary in the Industrial Revolution 1750–1850*, New York: Columbia University Press

Mandela, N. (1994) *Long Walk to Freedom*, Little Brown

McConville, S. (1981) *A History of English Prison Administration, Vol. I, 1750–1877*, Routledge & Kegan Paul

Morris, N. and Rothman, D.J. (1998) *The Oxford History of the Prison*, Oxford University Press

Ruck, S.K. (ed.) (1951) *Paterson on Prisons: Being the Collected Papers of Sir Alexander Paterson*, Frederick Muller

Walker, N. (1965) *Crime and Punishment in Britain*, Edinburgh University Press

Woolf, Lord Justice and Tumim, Judge S. (1991) *Prison Disturbances April 1990: Report of an Inquiry by the Rt Hon. Lord Justice Woolf and His Hon. Judge Stephen Tumim* (The Woolf Report), Cm 1456, HMSO

Newspaper article
Sunday Express (29 August 1993) 'Soft touch jails are an insult to victims'

NOTE: All publishers' locations throughout this book are London, unless noted otherwise.

THE HISTORY OF THE PRISON SYSTEM

Chris Watts

The modern Prison Service in England and Wales is the result of a complex history of development and reform that can be traced back to before the Norman Conquest. This chapter notes the seminal events in the emergence of the Prison Service, though it does not to provide a guide to every convolution of the last thousand years that has contributed to our current comprehension of imprisonment.

Early prisons

> Art thou poor and in prison? Then thou art buried before thou art dead
> (Salgado 1977, p. 169)

The notion of the prison as a place of punishment, let alone of reform, is a recent innovation. Pre-18th-century punishment consisted of flogging, torture, mutilation and execution. Prisoners in early prisons were subject to appalling conditions. There was no segregation: men, women and children were held together whether tried or not, and regardless of their crimes, age and state of health. Little consideration was given to sanitary arrangements, and disease, such as gaol fever (typhus), was unchecked and uncontainable. The moat surrounding the Fleet Prison in London was ten feet wide and deep enough to take 'a boat laden with a tun of wine, filled with effluent from various latrines and sewers while butchers used it to deposit cattle entrails, the whole becoming so clogged that it was possible to walk across it' (Harding et al. 1985, p. 42).

Conditions of confinement at this time were subject to status: the affluent could buy relative comfort, even the freedom to go 'wandering', that is, being allowed outside the prison to practise religion and sometimes even swordsmanship. The majority of those imprisoned were debtors, confined until they had repaid their debts. For the wealthy, terms of imprisonment could be reasonably short, with many debtors being able to work off their debt in the relative freedom money afforded them. For the poor, there was little hope of being able to repay debts while confined. Their situation was made worse by the fact that the jailers themselves were unpaid and made their living by charging inmates for food and drink. Corrupt jailers would demand fees for hammering irons on or off. Prisoners could even be charged to be released.

Around the turn of the 18th century a number of new laws were enacted that began to change this grim prison regime. In 1699 an Act was passed that allowed county justices to build and repair jails. In 1702 Newgate and Marshalsea Prisons were inspected by the Society for the Promotion of Christian Knowledge, which advocated the keeping of prisoners in separate cells. Marshalsea was inspected again in 1728, along with the Fleet, this time by a parliamentary committee. In the same year, an Act allowing for the relief of debtors in prison required jailers to post an inventory of (regulated) fees.

Bridewells, transportation and prison ships

An early effort at reformation of the prison system was the Bridewell, or House of Confinement. First established in London in 1556, the first Bridewell was an attempt to deal with increasing levels of vagrancy. Inmates were put to work, with the difficulty of their labour being graded by the nature of their crime. They were encouraged into industriousness by this labour, but the work itself is unlikely to have been financially profitable. Bridewells were originally intended to be self-funded, though in reality most came to depend upon the income of a compulsory levy on the local community. Corruption was considerably reduced by the presence of salaried staff, no longer reliant on extorted fees for their livelihood.

The Bridewells were initially a success, with an Act being passed in 1609 making their construction compulsory in every county. However, the lack of a clear purpose increasingly led to them being used by justices as an alternative to imprisonment. As a result the distinction between Bridewells and ordinary prisons became blurred. Instead of fulfilling their original purposes of providing labour, discipline and reducing the cost of poor relief, Bridewells developed the same inherent problems that were plaguing the prisons.

The search for alternative forms of punishment that resulted in the popularity of the Bridewells is indicative of a shift in penal practice away from the public spectacle of execution and towards punishment as a retributive and reformatory concept. This way of thinking also led to the advent of transportation (the shipping of prisoners to the colonies) as a form of punishment. It was thought that time spent in the 'New World' under conditions of hard labour was a suitable alternative to the death penalty for those found guilty of capital offences. The first transportations took place in 1615, and the punishment grew in popularity so much so that between 1715 and 1775 30,000 convicts were transported to the Americas. In spite of the popularity of its usage, transportation was to come under attack as lacking in deterrence: there were stories of those sent out for punishment but having prospered.

With an increase in convicted crimes and the sudden cessation of transportation the government turned to prison ships, or 'hulks', as temporary vessels in which to imprison convicts. A strict punitive regime was imposed on the hulks, with prisoners carrying out hard physical labour on meagre diets. Disease was rife on the overcrowded ships, and a third of prisoners were to die as a result of being confined in them. Despite the dreadful conditions, the last English hulk did not go out of service until 1857. In the same year transportation was abolished as a judicial sentence.

The beginnings of reform

In 1777 John Howard published *The State of the Prisons in England and Wales*. Howard was appalled by the conditions he discovered when visiting a prison under his jurisdiction as sheriff in Bedfordshire. He protested to the magistrates, who asked for evidence that jails in other counties were any different. As a result Howard visited every prison in England, recording observations in his book. Its publication caused an outcry, and the resulting public awareness initiated a process of reform that was to change the prison system radically.

Howard's greatest achievement was to realise the potential of a reformed prison system and in so doing to marginalise other forms of punishment. He shifted the focus of imprisonment on to administrative reform and sought to abolish profit as a motivating factor. He had faith in prison as an institution, one that could genuinely bring about social reform, and he was critical of a failure to administer that institution properly. Howard's targets were simple – the jailers' fees, poor health amongst inmates, lack of categorisation – but they struck at the very foundations upon which the prison system was based. The immediate result of Howard's work was three reformative Acts: the Discharged Prisoners Act 1774, the Health of Prisoners Act 1774, and the Penitentiary Act 1779.

The opening of London's Millbank Penitentiary in 1816 marked official recognition of the need to reform the prison system. Millbank's reformative regime combined solitary confinement with religion and work, and was known as the

Separate System. For the first time inmates were categorised according to their sentence. The Prison Act 1835 established a prison inspectorate, the first time an inspectorate body had come under central government authority. The inspectorate included William Crawford and Reverend Whitworth Russell, the chaplain at Millbank, both strong advocates of the Separate System. This regime was to fail at Millbank by 1842, when its severity was criticised for causing the inmates to go insane. The completion of Pentonville Penitentiary in 1842 marked the high point for constructing a disciplinary system within a prison. Inmates were kept completely separate, even at exercise and chapel. In spite of its success (Pentonville had been used as a model for 50 prisons by 1850) it was still criticised for causing insanity and failing to prevent recidivism. The deaths of Crawford and Russell in 1847 marked the end of reformation and the advent of an increasingly severe prison system for the next twenty years.

Nationalisation and the Gladstone Committee

The Prisons Act 1877 brought about the nationalisation of the prison system, which transferred charge of the prisons to the Home Secretary. Nationalisation brought prisons under central control and with that control came a unification of philosophy and responsibility. A Prison Commission was established to administer the new system, with the Head of the Prison Commission supported by an inspectorate body.

Sir Edward Du Cane was the first Head of the Prison Commission. A military man, Du Cane advocated a regime of austerity and deterrence. Prisoners were fed a minimal diet and made to undergo hard labour, much of it of an arbitrary nature, such as the crank or the treadmill. It was Du Cane's paramilitary staff structure, with a pyramidal hierarchy of authority and the introduction of uniforms, that originated a single career structure for prison officers. The introduction of a Prison **Service** was to prove important to staff, providing them a place within a body working towards a national policy.

The prison regime under Du Cane was criticised for failing to prevent recidivism and for an over-emphasis on solitary confinement. As a result the government set up a parliamentary committee on prisons, chaired by Herbert Gladstone. The report of the Gladstone Committee in 1895 marked a move away from the oppressive punitive regime put into place by Du Cane and led to the implementation of measures of deterrence and reform. The report ushered in the abandonment of useless labour, less emphasis on solitary confinement and more on association, and the introduction of better living conditions for prisoners. The Committee emphasised that prisons should be training institutions, capable of releasing physically and morally improved prisoners. Du Cane resigned after the Gladstone Committee's report and was replaced by Sir Evelyn Ruggles-Brise, a more liberal Head of the Prison Commission. Ruggles-Brise implemented many of the recommendations of the Gladstone Committee, including the introduction of prison industries and the discontinuance of separate confinement.

Borstals and open prisons

The first half of the 20th century was marked by a sense of optimism in the Prison Service, brought about by the implementation of a number of the reformatory initiatives outlined by the Gladstone Committee. In 1922 Sir Alexander Paterson was appointed Head of the Prison Commission. Paterson built upon the reformatory objectives Ruggles-Brise had inaugurated, most significantly developing borstals and open prisons.

The Gladstone Committee had proposed the idea of a penal reformatory that was to house young offenders, and in 1901 the first such institution was set up in Borstal, Kent. In time, the name 'borstal' came to be applied to all establishments for young offenders. Under Paterson the borstals enjoyed initial success. He introduced an operating system based on that of the English public school, with separate house blocks being overseen by individual housemasters. A more relaxed regime favoured sport, education and recreation, and the inmates, or 'lads' as they were referred to by the officers, were encouraged into a sense of individualism.

But the success of the borstal was to be short-lived. Although the Criminal Justice Act 1948 promoted wider use of borstals, it led to an increase in the number of offenders less suited to the more easy-going routines. Rising crime rates in the 1950s caused public opinion to turn against the paternalistic methods of Paterson's borstals, and their success rate began to decline. Detention centres, with their emphasis on 'firm and brisk' disciplinary measures, caused an increased emphasis on a punitive regime for young offenders. After enjoying a short-lived increase in popularity during the 1970s, borstal training was formally replaced in 1982 by youth custody.

Post-Gladstone methodology had introduced a growing sense of the prisoner as an individual, and penal policy became more centred on a liberal humanitarianism. Criticism of the effects of the institutionalisation of prisoners led to the development of open prisons. These establishments waived the strict security of ordinary prisons, allowing prisoners greater physical and mental freedom. Since the success of the first open prison at New Hall in 1936, the Prison Service now runs a number of its establishments as open prisons.

Security, staff and management

In 1963 the Prison Commission was abolished and replaced by the Prison Department of the Home Office. At the time, a growing prison population was causing unrest among staff and prisoners: with overcrowding, security and staff safety were being jeopardised. The publication of the Mountbatten Report in December 1966 addressed the growing public concern over prison security.

Mountbatten observed that many of the prisons were outdated, some having been designed for a penal system over a hundred years old. He considered that 'the modern policy of humane liberal treatment aimed at rehabilitating prisoners rather than merely exacting punishment is right' (Mountbatten 1966, p. 4), and put forward security changes that would maintain, rather than disrupt, that methodology. He proposed higher perimeter security to prevent escapes, and a four-class system of categorisation (A to D) to differentiate between prisoners. He also suggested that a new maximum security prison be built on the Isle of Wight, to house prisoners 'whose escape would be highly dangerous to the public or the police or to the security of the state' (Mountbatten 1966, p. 5). This proposal was never realised, instead it was replaced by a number of high-security establishments called 'dispersals', amongst which high-risk prisoners would be 'dispersed'. Mountbatten also addressed staffing problems and indicated that morale was much in need of boosting. He recommended that there should be more staff with a broader range of abilities, the new rank of senior prison officer be introduced (staff previously had to wait sixteen years for promotion), a greater emphasis on specialised security training, and the appointment of a professional head of the Prison Service.

In spite of the changes brought about by the Mountbatten report, staff unrest was to continue throughout the 1970s. Increasing industrial action culminated in the publication of the report *Committee of Inquiry into the United Kingdom Prison Services*, the Committee being chaired by Sir John May. The May Committee suggested that:

> reasons for the current unrest include loss of confidence in treatment objectives, the distancing of staff and inmates as a result of the changing nature of the prison population, increased emphasis on security and growing numbers of specialists in prisons . . . poor working environments . . . apparent changes in the general industrial relations climate and the effects of this on the comparatively isolated position of prison officers . . . the failure of management to take the initiative in responding to industrial unrest, and to support governors faced with disputes (May 1979, p. 287).

The May Committee proposed that a new policy of 'positive custody' should replace the previous objective of 'treatment and training' laid down by the Prison Department in 1964. The thinking behind 'positive custody' was to recognise work, education and other activities in prison as playing a role in maintaining the physical and mental vitality of prisoners, rather than the prison system simply acting as an authority over prisoners' demeanour. The Committee also recommended a reformed Prison Inspectorate, to be headed by someone independent of the Prison Service. It drew the attention of the Boards of Visitors to the welfare of prison staff as well as that of prisoners. Finally, a single-attendance system for staff was introduced, thereby reducing the high levels of overtime that diminished the effectiveness of staff deployment.

In 1987, the Fresh Start initiative introduced a new rank structure and set of working hours for prison officers:

> The purpose of Fresh Start was to produce a more flexible approach to the organisation of work, a more rational management structure, a more rewarding job, and improved conditions of service to staff (HM Prison Service 1987, p. 1).

In order to achieve this purpose, Fresh Start had three key principles:

> Managerial accountability; more effective use of staff time; and a clearer shared sense of purpose for all staff within the Service (HM Prison Service 1987, pp. 2–3).

The Prison Service in the 1990s

On 1 April 1990 a prolonged and turbulent riot broke out in Manchester (Strangeways) Prison. Over the next 25 days, with high-profile media attention, rioting spread to another twenty establishments, causing millions of pounds worth of damage to the prison estate. The consequence of these riots was the publication, in February 1991, of the most exhaustive and progressive report into the state of the Prison Service since the Gladstone Committee in 1895. Conducted by Lord Justice Woolf and Sir Stephen Tumim, *Prison Disturbances April 1990: Report of an Inquiry* addressed the long-term problems of poor conditions and inadequate management that had culminated in the serious rioting of the previous year. The Report called for a fundamental reassessment of the objectives of imprisonment:

The Prison Service must set security, control and justice in prisons at the right level and it must provide the right balance between them . . . Security here refers to the need to prevent prisoners escaping. Control refers to the obligation, ultimately, to prevent prisoners causing a disturbance. Justice encapsulates the obligation on the Prison Service to treat prisoners with humanity and fairness and to act in concert with its responsibilities as part of the Criminal Justice System . . . Lapses in control affect both security and justice. Prisoners did not escape during the April disturbances. But they might easily have done so (Woolf and Tumim 1991, p. 17).

The Woolf Report [sic]was condensed into twelve key recommendations: There should be a general increase in responsibility at a higher level, starting with 'visible leadership' from the Director General. Governors of establishments should be given increased responsibility, and the role of the prison officer enhanced. Each prisoner should be given a 'compact' or 'contract' that outlines expectations and responsibilities in their own establishment. They should be located as near to their families or home community as possible. Overcrowding should cease, except in exceptional circumstances, and establishments divided into 'small and more manageable and secure units' (Woolf and Tumim 1991, p. 20). All prisoners should have access to sanitation. Prisoners should be given reasons for decisions affecting them and a grievance procedure should be established, with access to an independent complaints adjudicator. Finally, Woolf recommended closer co-operation within the divisions of the criminal justice system, and the creation of a national system of accredited standards to which all prisons must conform (Woolf and Tumim 1991, pp. 19–20).

In response to the Woolf Report, the government published a White Paper, *Custody, Care and Justice: The Way Ahead for the Prison Service in England and Wales* (Home Office 1991). This document charted a course for the Prison Service for the rest of the 20th century and beyond. Its proposals sought to improve the Prison Service's performance in the three keys areas of custody, care and justice. The aim was to provide a better prison system, with more effective measures for security and control; a better and more constructive relationship between prisoners and staff; and more active, challenging and useful programmes for prisoners (Home Office 1991, p. 1).

Although there was to be no statutory prescriptions on prison overcrowding, *Custody, Care and Justice* stated that Woolf's other recommendations were to be realised, albeit without the allocation of further resources and over a designated period of 25 years.

In December 1991 Admiral Raymond Lygo published his report, *Management of the Prison Service*, which recommended that the Prison Service should take on agency status. This was the type of structural modification that Woolf had encouraged, providing the Prison Service with a greater sense of autonomy and unification. As a 'Next Steps' agency the Prison Service would be headed by a Chief Executive/Director General, to be appointed by open competition, who would be responsible for meeting performance requirements. Matters of Prison Service policy were to remain in the government's charge.

Also that year, the Criminal Justice Act (CJA) 1991 made important changes to the sentencing of offenders. An increased emphasis on community sentences for minor crimes, coupled with more severe sentences for violent and sexual offenders, led to a decline in the prison population. A new system of remission and parole was set up, with remission being replaced by an 'at risk' period after release, to run until the end of the sentence itself. Three identifiable groups of sentences were established:

- up to (not including) twelve months, with release at the halfway point;
- twelve months up to (not including) four years, with release under supervision at the halfway point; and
- four years and above, with parole possible between the halfway and three-quarters point of the sentence.

Lifers, sex offenders, fine defaulters and deportees were exceptions to this structure.

Perhaps the most important aspect of the CJA 1991 was the introduction of private sector involvement at three levels of the criminal justice system: court security officers, prisoner escorts and contracted-out prisons. The first contracted-out prison, The Wolds in Humberside, opened on 6 April 1992. By 1998 six contracted-out prisons were operational, and all court security officers and prisoner escorts had been contracted out.

On 1 April 1993 HM Prison Service for England and Wales became an executive agency of the Home Office, presided over by Derek Lewis, the first Director General to be appointed from the private sector. *The Framework Document* that accompanied the implementation of agency status outlined the Prison Service's Statement of Purpose:

Her Majesty's Prison Service serves the public by keeping in custody those committed by the courts. Our duty is to look after them with humanity and

help them lead law-abiding and useful lives in custody and after release
(HM Prison Service 1993, p. 4).

The Conservative Party Conference of October 1993 marked a new emphasis by
the government, and in particular by the Home Secretary Michael Howard, on a
belief in imprisonment as a method of reducing crime and requiting the victims
of crime. Howard's 'Prison Works' approach marked the beginning of a new
crisis of prison overcrowding and a move away from reform towards the conviction that austerity is the better form of correction.

The situation was exacerbated by the advent of a new security crisis. On
9 September 1994 six Category A prisoners, one of them armed, escaped from
Whitemoor Dispersal Prison by climbing over the outer wall using a rope ladder
made from self-manufactured equipment. A search of their belongings discovered Semtex, fuses and detonators. In spite of their almost immediate recapture,
the Prison Service found itself the subject of severe criticism in the report
resulting from the Inquiry into the incident, headed by Sir John Woodcock at the
end of December 1994. The Woodcock Report castigated a nebulous management system and neglect of basic security procedures, and recommended an
extensive tightening of security.

Less than four months later three life-sentence prisoners, two of whom were
Category A, escaped from Parkhurst Prison on the Isle of Wight. The subsequent Inquiry, carried out by General Sir John Learmont (1995), incorporated a
comprehensive review of all Prison Service high-security establishments. The
Inquiry proposed a return to custody as the primary objective of imprisonment
(as opposed to Woolf's balance between security, control and justice), and highlighted critical problems in the Service's management structure. In response to
the ensuing furore about who was ultimately answerable for prison organisation,
Michael Howard sacked the Director General, Derek Lewis. (Lewis was later to
sue the Secretary of State for wrongful dismissal and won an out-of-court settle-
ment.)

In spring 1997 the new Director General, Richard Tilt, established the Prison
Service Review to take a strategic look at the management and organisation of the
Prison Service, which would provide a framework for the delivery of prison
services into the next century (HM Prison Service 1997, p. 1).

The Review suggested that organisational change should be a continual process,
with strategic management rather than 'one off' structural shake-ups in response
to crises. The Prison Service, the report proposed, required organisational capacity
for change management of this nature. The need to refocus on the rehabilitative

aspect of imprisonment led to a consideration of the probation service's interests and 'closer and more integrated work between the Prison Service and the probation services of England and Wales' (HM Prison Service 1997, p. 3), an outline that was realised by the publication of the Prisons–Probation consultative document in 1998 (Home Office 1998).

The newly elected Labour government made clear its commitment to 'joined up government in action' (Home Office et al. 1999, p. 2) and the publication of a criminal justice system strategic and business plan in 1999 brought the Prison Service firmly within an integrated system aimed at 'working together to reduce crime and secure justice' (Home Office et al. 1999).

References

Criminal Justice Act 1991, Royal Assent July 1991, entered into force October 1992

Harding, C., Hines, B., Ireland, R. and Rawlings, P. (1985) *Imprisonment in England and Wales: A Concise History*, Croom Helm

HM Prison Service (1987) *A Fresh Start: The Revised Offer*, Home Office

— (1993) *National Framework for the Throughcare of Offenders in Custody to the Completion of Supervision in the Community*, Home Office

— (1997) *Prison Service Review*, Home Office

Home Office (1991) *Custody, Care and Justice: The Way Ahead for the Prison Service in England and Wales*, Cm 1647, HMSO

— (1998) *Joining Forces to Protect the Public: Prisons–Probation*, A consultative document, The Stationery Office

Home Office, Lord Chancellor's Department and Attorney General's Office (1999) *Criminal Justice System Strategic Plan 1999–2000 and Business Plan 1999–2000*, Home Office et al.

May, J. (1979) *Committee of Inquiry into United Kingdom Prison Services*, HMSO

Mountbatten, Earl (1966) *Report of the Inquiry into Prison Escapes and Security* (The Mountbatten Report), HMSO

Salgado, G. (1977) *Elizabethan Underworld*, Dent

Woolf, Lord Justice and Tumim, Judge S. (1991) *Prison Disturbances April 1990: Report of an Inquiry by the Rt Hon. Lord Justice Woolf and His Hon. Judge Stephen Tumim* (The Woolf Report), Cm 1456, HMSO

3

THE CORRECTIONAL POLICY FRAMEWORK: PROVIDING A CONTEXT FOR MORE EFFECTIVE JOINT WORKING

John Powls

The Prison Service and the probation services of England and Wales have recently found themselves the subjects of a range of planning documents emerging from Government sources: the *Criminal Justice System Strategic Plan 1999–2002 and Business Plan 1999–2000* (Home Office et al. 1999); the *Prison Service Corporate Plan 1999–2000 to 2001–2002 and Business Plan 1999–2000* (HM Prison Service 1999); and *Probation Circular 3/2000* (Home Office 2000). Supplementing these national plans are local prison planning documents and local probation area plans. The Government's demand for more effective joint working between the two services has also led to a detailed agenda of action and initiatives, which is continually developing. Both services can therefore be in no doubt about the action, priorities and targets required of them by the Government. They can be assured that change is now regarded as the norm.

However, while the 'what' requirements have been clarified, until recently there was a vacuum surrounding the 'why'. Why have particular priorities emerged? Why has the Government set this direction? why does joint working need to be more effective than in the past? *The Correctional Policy Framework* (Home Office 1999), published in September 1999, seeks to fill that vacuum by providing, for the first time, the policy context and a strategic overview for the full range of planning documents and all aspects of work with offenders undertaken by the services, both separately and together.

Before considering the *Framework*, its genesis through the Prisons–Probation Review and the subsequent public consultation in 1998, a little background may provide some useful insight.

Joint working between the services – a brief history

Probation service links with the Prison Service date back to the 1950s when boys sent to a detention centre were offered voluntary after-care from a probation officer in the community after their release. A variety of voluntary agencies offered support to others released from custody.

Following recommendations in a report published by the Advisory Council on the Treatment of Offenders in 1963, the probation service was given statutory authority for all work with prisoners after release. The report also examined whether probation officers should assume the tasks of welfare officers within prisons, undertaken then by a voluntary organisation on behalf of the Prison Service. Some considered that such a move might weaken the efforts of prison staff to prepare prisoners for release. The report, therefore, proposed that the Home Secretary appoint social workers to multidisiplinary teams within each prison. The Home Secretary of the day, Roy Jenkins, held the opposite view. By 1966 probation officers, on secondment from their own probation service areas, were placed in prison establishments. The rational for this was to improve communication between prison and probation staff so that after-care for prisoners might be more effective.

Stimulated by legislative developments (that is, the Criminal Justice Act (CJA) 1991), the importance of the relationship was re-emphasised in 1993 when the Home Office published the *National Framework for Throughcare of Offenders in Custody to the Completion of Supervision in the Community* (HM Prison Service 1993). For the first time, a government document provided guidance on both services. Responsibilities for prisoners and a joint process for planning and managing prisoners' sentences was introduced. The Framework particularly sought to note best practice, and validated the view that a prison sentence is a process which begins at a prisoner's reception into prison and continues until supervision ends in the community. This view formed the foundation of the relationship that exists today.

The Prison–Probation Review and outcome of consultation

The Prisons–Probation Review was set up in July 1997 and commissioned to identify ways in which:

- the two services can work better together on programmes which are effective in reducing the likelihood that offenders will re-offend;
- the services can co-ordinate efforts to prepare prisoners for release and resettlement in the community

- resources, information, knowledge and skills – about how to reduce offending and protect the public – may be shared; and
- changes in organisation and structure will help to deliver these improvements and provide best value.

The Review identified many factors limiting joint effectiveness. Focusing on these problems in turn, it was established that there was a need for:

- a new, rigorous and substantial national 'corrections' policy framework which would ensure standards, consistency of service delivery, and high levels of effectiveness and efficiency across the country without inhibiting the beneficial elements of the existing system (for example, local discretion, community involvement, and responsiveness to local needs and circumstances);
- a plan of common policies, standards, and performance targets;
- agreement on respective resource contributions in some areas (for example, joint training or probation officers working in prisons to a wider remit, or prison officers working with probation staff in resettlement units);
- performance accountability of the senior management of both services (ultimately leading to some means of sanction for non-performance);
- cultural change, by engineering new attitudes to core tasks and encouraging staff to see themselves working across a spectrum of sanctions determined by the courts; and
- a detailed examination of the scope for more effective management of the prison population.

The last point has a direct bearing on the effectiveness of resettlement work. The more prison overcrowding forces prisoners to be moved around the country, the harder it is to plan resettlement effectively and therefore minimise re-offending risks.

The Review led directly, in August 1998, to the publication of the consultation document *Joining Forces to Protect the Public* (Home Office 1998), which set out ministers' preferred options for a wide-ranging programme to modernise joint working practices between the two services.

Consultation issues include:

- a proposal to rename the new probation service and the term 'throughcare' to 'resettlement';
- the organisation of operational service delivery in London;
- the need for mechanisms to secure responsiveness to local requirements and circumstances including:

- work with local authorities
- community-based initiatives on crime reduction and
- the possible roles, membership and appointment of local reference groups and/or advisory boards;
- restructuring Prison Service areas into regions, matching the Government's Offices for the Regions; and
- the possible future role of HM Inspectorate of Probation.

Central to the proposals set out in the consultation document was reorganising the probation services nation-wide into a unified service for England and Wales. The reorganisation, with 42 operational commands (versus the current 54), would be co-terminus with police areas and focused on effective local partnerships.

It was concluded that the day-to-day running and management of the probation service should remain the responsibility of the chief officers. Chief officers will become statutory officers appointed by, and accountable to, the Home Secretary. Further, it was to be led by a national director with a range of operational responsibilities, and funded entirely by central government, with full ministerial accountability to Parliament for it. The local focus would be provided by a governing board for each of the 42 services.

Joint strategic planning forum

Joining Forces to Protect the Public indicated Ministers' intention to form a joint strategic planning forum to plan the delivery of the package of improvements known as the Zero Plus Agenda. This included a national correctional policy framework plus monitoring the progress of any joint work undertaken by the Prison Service and probation services of England and Wales. The terms of reference described in *Joining Forces* are that the forum will:

- meet, identify and agree the elements of the services they need to plan together;
- develop plans, performance targets and standards;
- agree what respective resource contributions are necessary;
- resolve timing issues encountered during the planning cycle; and
- agree the means of performance management (that is, monitoring delivery and responding effectively to non-performance, should it become evident).

The forum, chaired by Sue Street, Director of Sentencing and Correction Policy, is comprised of members from the Central Probation Council, the Association of

Chief Officers of Probation, the Prison Service, Her Majesty's Inspectorate of Probation and Home Office Correctional Policy Unit.

Prison Service Strategy Board

The Home Secretary sets the strategic direction of the Prison Service, specifies the outputs and targets which it is required to achieve, and allocates resources accordingly. He or she determines the strategic direction given the wider ministerial planning for the criminal justice system as a whole and, within the Home Office, in the context of overall policy for correctional matters and greater collaborative working between the Prison Service and the probation services. Accordingly, the Home Secretary's designated Minister on prison matters chairs the Prison Service Strategy Board. Membership includes: Martin Narey, the Director General and other executive directors of the Prison Service; Sue Street, Director of Sentencing and Correctional Policy (SCP); and non-executive directors appointed by the Home Secretary. The Board advises Ministers on matters relating to correctional policy as a whole, for other parts of the criminal justice system and the work of the Prison Service. The Home Office has four strategic aims. Co-ordination of programmes that contribute to these and 'aim owner' is Sue Street. The Director General of the Prison Service is responsible, with the probation services, for delivering Aim 4, the 'effective execution of the sentences of the courts so as to reduce re-offending and protect the public' (Home Office 1999, p. 4).

The Board provides a forum for discussing the strategic direction of the Prison Service and its performance. Each year, the Director General submits a draft Corporate Plan to the Prison Service Strategy Board and the Home Secretary for final approval. The Plan is for three years, the first year of the planning period being covered in more detail. The Plan includes:

- Prison Service objectives, in support of Home Office aims, together with KPIs and targets;
- strategies to achieve the objectives;
- operating assumptions about the prison population and planned capacity;
- information about any sensitivity to variations in those assumptions;
- how the resources and assets will be deployed, consistent with totals and outputs agreed; and
- proposals for securing agreed efficiency improvements, including public–private partnerships.

The Correctional Policy Unit and its *Framework*

To help manage action points arising from the Prisons–Probation Review, the Correctional Policy Unit was formed in August 1998. The Unit, headed by John Powls, is charged with taking forward the Structural Change programme for probation services and is primarily engaged in co-ordinating, reviewing, analysing and contributing to initiatives for closer integration and improved joint working of the Prison Service and the probation services.

One of the Unit's key documents, *The Correctional Policy Framework*, is sharply focused on the essential requirement of delivering Home Office Aim 4: 'The effective execution of the sentences of the courts so as to reduce re-offending and protect the public.' Although delivery of that aim requires a range of key stakeholders, inside and outside the criminal justice system, to work in close collaboration, the *Framework* focuses on the measures provided by the Prison Service and probation services themselves. Joint working between the two services has been placed at the heart of the Government's correctional policy, with a stronger focus on resettlement work than has existed in the recent past. The *Framework* includes the range of initiatives the Government set out in its consultation document, *Joining Forces to Protect the Public* (Home Office 1998), plus a wider agenda, with vital links to the Crime Reduction Programme, the work of the Social Exclusion Unit, the 'Rough Sleepers' initiative, and the Welfare to Work programme. Therefore, strategic links between various government initiatives, including those aimed at combating crime, is a key theme of the *Framework*.

Measures adopted to reduce re-offending also provide the services and their partners with the opportunity to make direct contributions to the achievement of Home Office Aim 1 – crime reduction – through the better achievement of Aim 4. For example, offending behaviour programmes, based on the 'what works' principles both services have embraced, enable them to tackle volume crime (multiple and frequent offences that are committed by single offenders, such as burglary and car theft) and serious, violent and sex crimes in a more systematic way. The object is to increase methodically the number of offenders attending these programmes. Among mixed offender populations, well-run programmes can expect to achieve a reduction in recidivism of 10–15% versus an untreated comparison group. Improvements of up to 25% have been demonstrated where programmes are targeted at high-risk offenders (Home Office 1999, p. 4). Since offenders under supervision in the community and in prison tend to be repeat offenders, reductions in their offending will have a more pronounced effect on the overall crime rate.

Five main categories of offence account for three-quarters of recorded crime. These are burglary, theft of and from vehicles, criminal damage, wounding and shoplifting. In addition, research suggests that 20% of male offenders account for 60% of known offences (Home Office 1999, p. 8). The Government's strategy for correctional policy is, therefore, to impact directly on these key areas of volume crime and target those offenders generating high volumes of repeat offences.

Unlike the planning documents for which it provides a context, the *Framework* has no obvious life span. It is a living document that describes a strategy capable of absorbing new initiatives and innovative ideas in the future, which may involve a more strategic integration of correctional and sentencing policy. The long-term objective is to integrate the policies more closely so that the range and combination of measures available to sentencers is complemented by seamless operational practice undertaken by those charged with the effective execution of the courts' sentences.

Effective sentencing, like correctional policy, is essential to the delivery of Home Office Aims 1 and 4. We can expect to see the Government pursuing sentencing strategies that punish in ways that deter re-offending, and this will include severe punishments for serious repeat offenders. The key outcome of Aim 4, to reduce re-offending, will therefore be served; it will also impact on the Aim 1 requirement to reduce crime and the fear of crime. (Ministers are at pains to emphasise the connections between the Aims, not the distinctions.)

Like the action plans for which it provides a policy context, the *Framework* represents a strategy based unequivocally on outcomes: a reduction in re-offending and improved public protection. The key measure to be used for the delivery of these outcomes will be national re-conviction rates. The intention is to drive rates down, with policy and operations working in concert. This strategy will be achieved by improving effectiveness.

As well as requiring key stakeholders to work closely with each other, the *Framework* also requires a wider range of co-operation and partnerships with other organisations, within and outside the criminal justice system. The important contribution of other organisations – such as the police, the Youth Justice Board, Social Services, the NHS, employment services, housing associations and other accommodation specialists, and partner agencies in the public and private sectors – is also recognised.

The Government has chosen to highlight with the *Framework* some of the most important aspects of their wider policy. As well as resettlement, these include:

- young offenders;
- women offenders;
- short-term prisoners;
- drug-related crime; and, significantly,
- the fight against racism.

The *Framework* recognises that short-term prisoners are an important omission in the current sentencing and correctional legislative framework. The Government intend to provide a remedy by making this group a key area of development for correctional policy.

In addition, the report of the Inquiry into the murder of Stephen Lawrence has influenced the development of the *Framework* in several ways. The policy document is not only committed to confronting and changing the behaviour of racially motivated criminals, it also requires both services to recognise the challenge of eradicating institutional racism from their organisations and from the criminal justice system generally. It places responsibility for changing the present situation firmly on the shoulders of every individual member of staff.

The *Framework*'s development is also closely linked to the public service agreement (PSA) which the Home Office has concluded with HM Treasury. The Aim 4 contribution to the Home Office PSA is:

- to conduct research and develop targets for introduction by 2001–02 including:
  - ensuring that the two-year re-conviction rate for those receiving custodial and community sentences remains below the rate predicted for those offenders
  - reducing the re-convictions rate for persistent young offenders. Work is under way to collect the baseline data and establish a target;
- to improve supervision programmes run by the probation service and prison regimes that require offenders to face up to their behaviour, and introduce a system of independent accreditation covering probation as well as prison programmes;
- to increase the number of completions of accredited offender behaviour programmes run by the Prison Service from 3,000 to 6,000 a year by 2001–02, including an increase in those completing sex offender programmes from 110 to 680;
- to reduce by 15% the proportion of prisoners discharged from their sentence who are at level 1 (equivalent to GCSE) or below for literacy and numeracy skills, by April 2002;

- to reduce the rate of positive results from random drug tests from a 20% target in 1998–99 to 16% in 2001–02, and to provide access to voluntary drug-testing for all prisoners by April 2001;
- to pilot the Drug Treatment and Testing Orders that allow the courts to place offenders on treatment programmes quickly and to review their progress;
- to provide treatment for problem drug-users in prison, which is then followed through under post-release supervision;
- to ensure that more offenders enter treatment programmes as a result of arrest referral schemes and post-release supervision;
- to maintain the existing target of no escapes of high-risk (Category A) prisoners;
- to ensure the overall rate of escapes from prisons is no higher than 0.17% of the average prison population; and
- to ensure that the number of escapes from contracted-out escorts is no more than 1 per 20,000 prisoners handled (HM Prison Service 1999, Annex A).

In addition, there are closely related targets in the PSAs for the criminal justice system, Sure Start and Action against Illegal Drugs programmes.

The *Correctional Policy Framework* provides a focus on the common concerns shared by all those engaged in the punishment and treatment of offenders, presents a policy context for the difficult and demanding operational practices in which they are already engaged, and forms the basis for 'seamless sentences' designed to protect the public and reduce re-offending.

References

HM Prison Service (1993) *National Framework for the Throughcare of Offenders in Custody to the Completion of Supervision in the Community*, Home Office

— (1999) *Corporate Plan 1999–2000 to 2001–2002 and Business Plan 1999–2000*, Home Office

Home Office (1998) *Joining Forces to Protect the Public: Prisons–Probation*, A consultative document, The Stationery Office

— (1999) *Protecting the Public: The Correctional Policy Framework*, Home Office

— (2000) *Probation Service Objectives and the Home Secretary's Priorities and Action Plans for the Service 2000–01*, Probation Circular 3/2000, Home Office

Home Office, Lord Chancellor's Department and Attorney General's Office (1999) *Criminal Justice System Strategic Plan 1999–2000 and Business Plan 1999–2000*, Home Office et al.

The author extends thanks to Susan James, who contributed to the writing of this chapter.

4

THE STRUCTURE AND ORGANISATION OF THE PRISON SERVICE

Richard Booty, Gina Beaton and Rachel Jones

Introduction

This chapter looks at how the Prison Service is structured in the light of its current status, remit and powers. It begins by examining agency status and the issue of accountability to ministers, then draws a picture of how the Service is organised at a national and local level, and how management structures have developed and continue to evolve to accommodate the diverse needs of the Service. The role of the Statement of Purpose, Aim, Objectives and Principles is described. How targets are set from these and the management tools that exist to ensure performance meets these targets are then considered. Developments in the management of standards and performance are looked at, together with the decision-making process within the Service.

Agency status

Kenneth Clarke, the then Home Secretary, specified 1 April 1993 as the date when the Prison Service would acquire agency status. This had first been suggested by the 1991 Lygo Report, which suggested that the Prison Service should be established as a 'modified agency'. The Prison Service was awarded agency status because 'it was considered that the greater managerial, financial and personal authority such status is intended to provide would lead to more effective performance with improved quality of service, (Home Office 1999b, p. 4). The Prison Service remains the largest and, indeed, most notable of government agencies. Overall, agency status was intended to provide the Prison Service with a clearer set of objectives and targets, and increased autonomy which would lead to more cohesion in a service traditionally regarded as divided. The theory behind executive agencies as a whole was that they would clarify the respective jobs of ministers and civil servants and thus provide a more efficient public service. Chief executives are normally appointed on fixed contracts that are linked to targets set for them by ministers. Within this new structure, common to many areas of government work, ministers look after policy while chief executives look after the day-to-day business of the agency.

It is clear that the Prison Service has not been and is not a typical agency. Those agencies that do not attract much political interest meet the standard agency model better. The Prison Service has been described as a 'large, complex and politically sensitive ... organisation ... notable for the fact that there is no residual Prison Department within the Home Office dealing with policy on the basis that prisons policy and operations are so inextricably linked that the responsibility for both must be in the same organisation' (HM Prison Service 1997, p. 31). Clearly there have been difficulties in separating policy and operational functions between the minister and chief executive within the Prison Service: 'Like marriage, it will probably work if both partners are prepared to compromise, but otherwise it is likely to be a miserable existence' (Dunbar and Langdon 1998, p. 27).

The difficulties the relationship could generate became publicly apparent during Derek Lewis's period as the first Director General of the new agency. The then Home Secretary, Michael Howard, sacked Derek Lewis in 1995 following the escapes from HMP Parkhurst and HMP Whitemoor. In his autobiography Lewis wrote: 'It was a battle for reputation, and I had a great deal to lose. Integrity and honesty had always meant a great deal to me, and I was determined to fight' (Lewis 1997, p. 204). This situation illustrated the tension between operational and political responsibilities for the Prison Service.

The change to agency status did not lead to an unambiguous relationship between ministers and civil servants, perhaps because of the highly politicised nature of the Prison Service. Indeed, the structure may ultimately be less important then the individuals that operate within it. The Prison Service Review was set up by the Director General in 1997, partly to take a strategic look at the organisation of the Prison Service. The Review team concluded that the agency's framework document was 'on the whole a clear and concise description of the division of responsibilities between the Home Secretary, the Permanent Secretary and the Director General' (HM Prison Service 1997, p. 31). However, the *Review* also noted a recent Home Affairs Committee report on the relationship between the Home Secretary and the Director General which had concluded that it was not possible to exercise a rigid divide between roles of ministers and of the Director General.

As a result of the *Quinquennial Review* of the role of the Prison Service (Home Office 1999b), the Home Secretary announced in February 1999 that agency status had been retained. This *Review* concluded that despite some difficulties in inception and definition, agency status for the Prison Service had been a success. Shortly after that, the *Framework Document* that defines the role of the Service and those who work in and support it, was reissued (HM Prison Service 1999b). This redefined relationships between ministers, the Prison Service and the rest of the Home Office. The new document:

- reflects the government's commitment to ensuing proper ministerial responsibility for the Prison Service;
- integrates the aims, objectives and principles of the Prison Service into the new planning arrangements for the wider criminal justice system; and
- focuses on management responsibility and accountability issues with greater clarity for the roles of the principle players.

The *Quinquennial Review* acknowledged problems that had occurred during the period after agency status was introduced and identified a number of key improvements made in the Prison Service since 1993 (Home Office 1999b, p. 5). These include:

- coping with a 40% increase in the prison population without a serious loss of control;
- reduced costs of keeping prisoners in custody by 7%;
- a reduction of escapes (of 78%) and assaults (down 7.8%);
- ending the use of police cells for overcrowding and slopping out (from 1996); and
- increases in time out of cell for prisoners, and purposeful activity (by 32%).

In reviewing agency status, the *Review* attempted to correlate these improvements in delivery with agency status, concluding that it had contributed through:

- delegated freedom for the Director General;
- focus on outputs and targets; and
- a cohesive organisation with a visible Director General (p. 5).

The role of ministers

The Home Secretary is responsible for the Prison Service in England and Wales, and as such is accountable to Parliament. The Home Secretary sets the strategic direction of the Prison Service, specifies outputs required, and allocates resources accordingly. A detailed account of outputs and resources is set out each year in the Prison Service Corporate and Business Plan (HM Prison Service 1999a). This is agreed annually with the Director General. To report on Prison Service matters, the Home Secretary commissions and presents to both Houses of Parliament the Prison Service *Annual Report*.

The Home Secretary designates a minister to be responsible to him/her on Prison Service matters. This person is known as the designated minister, and in the current structure also holds ministerial responsibility for the probation service.

The Director General and Deputy Director General

The Director General is appointed by the Home Secretary, with the approval of the Prime Minister, and has designated authority for the day-to-day management of the Prison Service. He or she is responsible for the performance within the Service, as set out in corporate plans and targets and agreed with the Home Secretary. In addition, the Director General is responsible for ensuring that the public funds allocated to the Prison Service are well and properly managed. The Director General is the principal advisor to the Home Secretary on matters relating to Prison Service activities, and has delegated authority on financial and personnel matters. Prison Service staff are civil servants and are therefore accountable to the Home Secretary, via the Director General.

While the Director General is directly responsible for the operational performance of the Prison Service, the full-time role of the Deputy Director General has been expanded to cover operational and performance management. The Deputy Director General has direct managerial responsibility for all area managers (who were formerly managed by two operational directors) and three directors; the Director of High-security Prisons, the Director of Security and the Director of the Female Estate.

Headquarters' structure: key features

Strategy Board

The former Prisons Board has been replaced by the Prison Service Strategy Board. This is chaired by the minister for prisons and probation, and includes the Director General, the Director of Sentencing and Correctional Policy in the Home Office, and other executive and non-executive directors. The Board meets eight times a year to discuss long-term strategy (four meetings) and high-level monitoring of the performance of the Service (also four meetings). Policy matters are discussed with a focus on how the Prison Service can contribute to

Aim 4 of the Home Office policy on crime and criminal justice, which reads: 'Effective execution of the sentences of the courts so as to reduce re-offending and protect the public' (Home Office 1999a).

Management Board

The agency *Framework Document* allows the Director General to appoint a Management Board, which replaces the old Executive Committee. This deals with more immediate issues, meeting in full monthly, but more frequently on an informal basis. Its day-to-day business includes:

- monitoring prisons;
- deciding on priorities and expenditure;
- authorising projects and initiatives;
- approving important internal communications; and
- deciding what the Strategy Board might discuss.

The Management Board comprises all the executive directors and *ex officio* members appointed by the Director General. At the present time these include the Board Secretary, the Home Office legal advisor, the Head of Media Relations, the Head of Internal Communications and the Prison Service Racial Equality Officer. The role of the non-executive directors is to:

- challenge existing practices and assumptions;
- contribute a source of new ideas and wider experience;
- provide independent oversight of propriety;
- act as a sounding board for the development of policies; and
- supply independent scrutiny of establishments requiring special managerial attention.

Non-executive directors have the right of direct access to the Home Secretary and the Permanent Secretary on matters affecting the Prison Service.

The sub-committees

The Strategy and Management Boards are formally supported by two sub-committees, the Operational Policy Group and Audit Committee.

The Operational Policy Group (OPG)

The OPG does not exercise **decision-making** powers, but has delegated responsibility vested by the Deputy Director General to co-ordinate the business of the Management Board. It ensures the adequacy of the mandatory assessment of operational impact on any recommended change of operational policy. Its purpose, therefore is to consider proposed policy changes affecting establishments before substantive work begins, and to check the adequacy of operational impact assessments, which are required of originating groups prior to a paper being accepted for the Management Board agenda. In this way the OPG ensures that all proposals developed by directorates and submitted to the Management Board are properly assessed.

The Audit Committee

The other committee supporting the Management Board is the Audit Committee. Its role is to advise the Director General on all aspects of internal financial control systems and the co-ordination of internal and external audits. It advises on performance in response to audit reports, education about audit requirements, and the workings of the internal audit. The Audit Committee is chaired by a non-executive director, who is an independent appointee of the Director General.

Directorate structure

Each executive director has functional responsibility for particular aspects of the activities of the Prison Service (high-security prisons, security, personnel, corporate affairs, finance, and regimes). This structure and the areas of responsibility are shown in Figure 4.1.

The Prison Service national structure illustrates that its 'business' is constantly moving so its own management structure has to constantly evolve to meet the challenges that arise. For example, the Prison Service has responded to a call for distinct management of the female estate by setting up a model for functional management of this estate. The *Prison Service Review* recommended that, 'There should be a Director of Regimes with clear responsibility for regime policy and for prisoner administration for all prisoner types … there should be separate … posts with responsibility for prisoner administration; regime development for young offenders; regime development for women; regime development for adult males, and parole and lifers' (HM Prison Service 1997, p. 68). That recommendation was accepted and the new post integrated into the current structure.

Figure 4.1: Responsibilities of executive directors

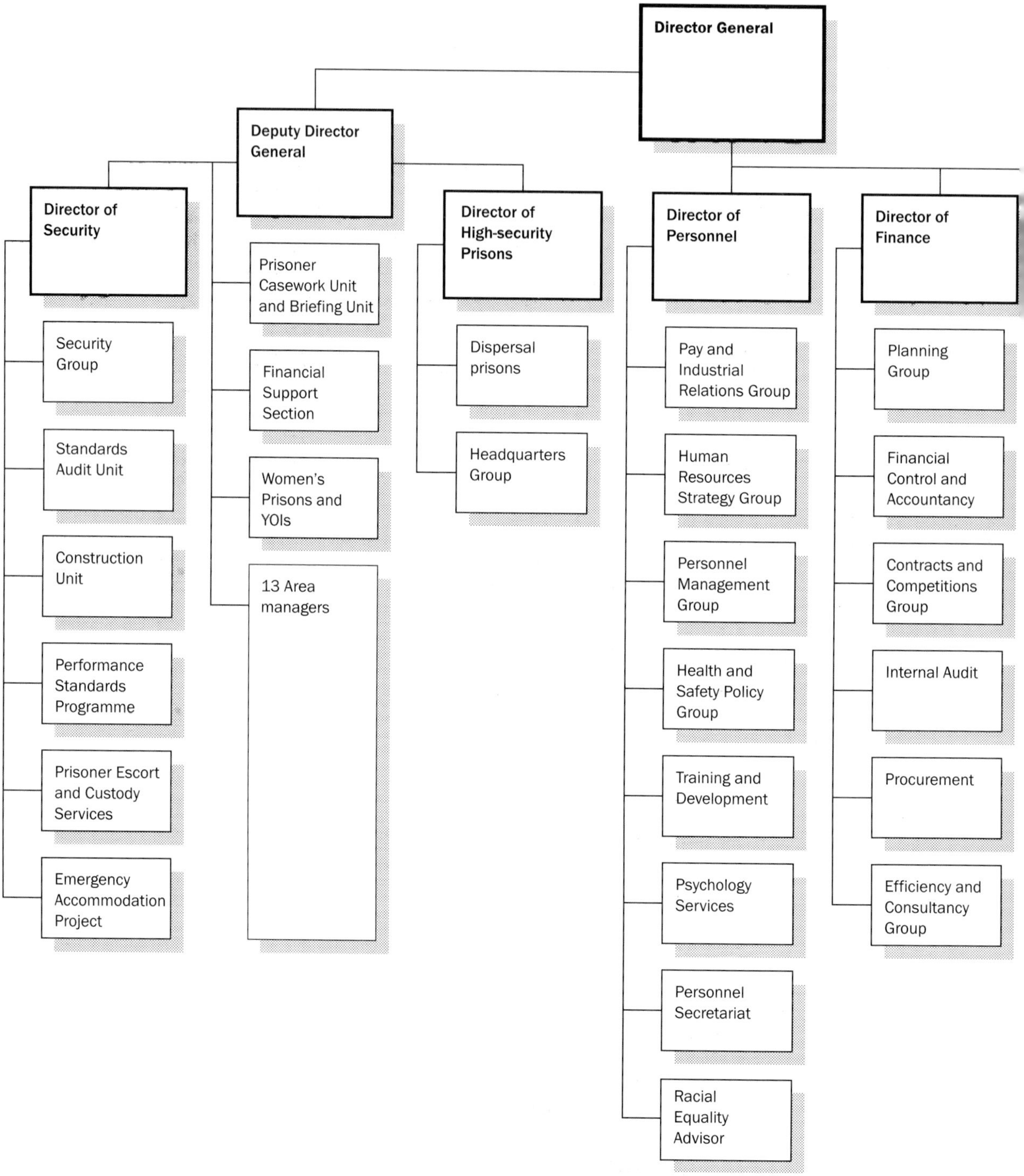

```
                                                          ┌─────────────────┐
                                                          │ Director General│
                                                          └─────────────────┘
                        ┌──────────────────┐
                        │ Deputy Director  │
                        │ General          │
                        └──────────────────┘
┌──────────────┐                              ┌──────────────┐    ┌──────────────┐    ┌──────────────┐
│ Director of  │                              │ Director of  │    │ Director of  │    │ Director of  │
│ Security     │                              │ High-security│    │ Personnel    │    │ Finance      │
└──────────────┘                              │ Prisons      │    └──────────────┘    └──────────────┘
                                              └──────────────┘
```

Director of Security
- Security Group
- Standards Audit Unit
- Construction Unit
- Performance Standards Programme
- Prisoner Escort and Custody Services
- Emergency Accommodation Project

Deputy Director General
- Prisoner Casework Unit and Briefing Unit
- Financial Support Section
- Women's Prisons and YOIs
- 13 Area managers

Director of High-security Prisons
- Dispersal prisons
- Headquarters Group

Director of Personnel
- Pay and Industrial Relations Group
- Human Resources Strategy Group
- Personnel Management Group
- Health and Safety Policy Group
- Training and Development
- Psychology Services
- Personnel Secretariat
- Racial Equality Advisor

Director of Finance
- Planning Group
- Financial Control and Accountancy
- Contracts and Competitions Group
- Internal Audit
- Procurement
- Efficiency and Consultancy Group

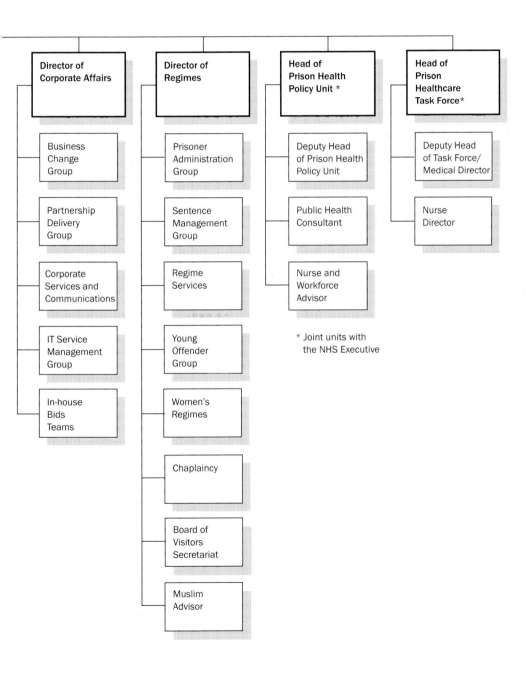

Director of Corporate Affairs

- Business Change Group
- Partnership Delivery Group
- Corporate Services and Communications
- IT Service Management Group
- In-house Bids Teams

Director of Regimes

- Prisoner Administration Group
- Sentence Management Group
- Regime Services
- Young Offender Group
- Women's Regimes
- Chaplaincy
- Board of Visitors Secretariat
- Muslim Advisor

Head of Prison Health Policy Unit *

- Deputy Head of Prison Health Policy Unit
- Public Health Consultant
- Nurse and Workforce Advisor

Head of Prison Healthcare Task Force*

- Deputy Head of Task Force/ Medical Director
- Nurse Director

* Joint units with the NHS Executive

Area structure

The Prison Service has more than 135 prisons of which seven are contractually managed by the private sector. These are a combination of DCMF prisons (designed, constructed, managed and funded by the private sector under the government's Private Finance Initiative (PFI)) and privately managed prisons. Prison Service establishments are divided between thirteen geographical areas, each one having an area manager (North East; Yorkshire and Humberside; East Midlands (North); Lancashire and Cumbria; East Midlands (South); Manchester, Mersey and Cheshire; Eastern; West Midlands; Wales; South West; Thames Valley and Hampshire; Kent, Surrey and Sussex; and London). The exceptions to this are the high-security estate, which has its own director and contains the eight dispersal prisons; and women's prisons and YOIs, comprising fourteen establishments. Area managers report directly to the Deputy Director General and manage governing governors. They are responsible for the implementation of policies, such as a drugs strategy within their area, and they offer support, guidance and advice to governors on myriad matters. Area managers also carry out audit and monitoring functions and have their own support staff.

Prison establishments

> … the Prison Service should aim for a situation where it is appreciated by the Service as a whole, that management (and the framework of controls that have been created) only exist to enable Governors to govern and to provide support for staff, so that both Governors and staff can perform that task as well as possible (Woolf and Tumim 1991, para. 12.73)

Lord Justice Woolf identified in his report how critical it was for the Prison Service to establish the right relationships between 'Headquarters' and establishments. The precise role, size and purpose of Headquarters and its relationship to establishments has historically been a source of tension and confusion. There have been many attempts to clarify the Headquarters–establishment relationship.

The number of types of prisons in England and Wales are significant and varied, as shown in Figure 4.2. 'Local prisons' are those directly serving the courts by holding prisoners on remand, during trial and post-sentence. Once sentenced, prisoners are usually transferred to 'training prisons' which look to offer prisoners personal development through their sentence. Training prisons differ according to their security classification, so, for example, open prisons are for prisoners requiring the least control or security. Prisoners can progressively move from one training prison to another. Adult males form the majority of the population. Two significant groups – young offenders and women – have different needs and so require a separate estate to meet those within the wider prison population. Further, size of prison establishments varies considerably, which affects organisation structure and management style.

Figure 4.2: Prison Service establishments by type

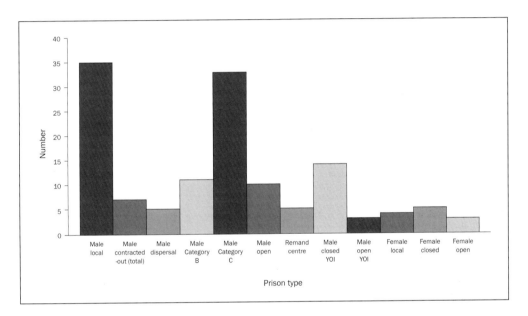

Diverse prisons require a range of organisational structures in order that local needs can be met. While accepting that establishments differ, there are some common structures amongst them. All establishments are likely to have 'functional' managers responsible for 'operations' (the gate, communications, security, prisoner movement, court liaison), 'residential' (throughcare, accommodation routines, sentence management), 'healthcare', 'management services' (financial, personnel), 'regimes' (education, physical education, offending, chaplaincy, behaviour programmes), 'works' (maintenance of prison fabric) and 'secretariat' (planning and casework). This type of organisational structure is similar to management structures in other public and private organisations, and is becoming flatter and less hierarchical. The number of levels, for example, between a prison officer and the governing Governor has reduced over the last five years. Under the Pay and Grading Initiative these will reduce even further as governors are amalgamated with Treasury grades, from the current five to three grades. Management models now are generally less bureaucratic, more account-able and simpler.

Most prisons have a senior management team who, with the governor as the 'Chief Executive', are responsible for the running of the establishment. Examples of 'common' management and policy committees are those dealing with security, suicide awareness, health and safety, and finance. Some of the work/services within prisons are delivered under contract: all education services, prisoner escort services, some catering services, and probation services (delivered under 'service level agreements'). One final unifying factor for all establishments is their accountability – through the governor to area managers and on to the Deputy Director General.

Managing performance

A principled service and good practice

The Prison Service works to a Statement of Purpose, an Aim, two Objectives and six Principles. These are set out in Annex A at the end of this book. They are inte-grated with the wider aims of the criminal justice system and are designed to contribute to public understanding of the Service and to focus staff on the meaning and purpose of the work they carry out.

The Prison Service Objectives are designed to 'provide a framework for the management of the Prison Service to reinforce the Statement of Purpose' (HM Prison Service 1997, p. 55). From these Objectives are drawn performance indica-tors, which allow prison practice to be evaluated internally and on a regular basis by the Home Secretary. The result of these evaluations are also made available to the public. There are 11 Key Performance Indicators (KPIs) at present (see Annex B at the end of this book); others are to be introduced in 2000–01 including literacy and numeracy (which at present is a shadow KPI) and HQ telephone call-response time. It is also likely that there will be future attempts to measure recidivism rates and resettlement jointly with the probation service (Home Office 1998, pp. 16–17).

A lingering criticism since the Woolf Report is that the KPIs are crude and tend to measure quantity rather than quality. For example, the only KPI relating to cost is the one measuring the cost per prison place. The current KPI cost per place is set at £26,208 (HM Prison Service 1998, p. 7). Prisons are measured against this figure without taking account of the different costs of housing certain types of prisoner. In particular, special psychiatric and medical needs may raise the cost per place for some prisoners to as much as £70,000 (the cost could be no less outside prison if the person was to be kept in a psychiatric or ordinary hospital). Within this context it is argued that quality and type of provision of care should be taken into account, as well as the average efficiency target.

In the planning and business year 2000–01 the Prison Service introduced, following a series of pilots, a new measure of performance to all establishments, Key Performance Targets (KPTs). There are 43 of these new measures, which aim to provide a broader and fairer measure of Prison Service performance. Some KPTs are mandatory (for example, number of escapes) and some apply only to certain establishments (for example, protocol for pregnant women). By using a mixture of KPTs the Service hopes to target specific of levels of performance and differentiate between types of establishments.

Staff in the past worked to standards laid down in a variety of documents:

- Standing Orders, which are legally binding;
- a core of Operating Standards established in 1994, which are not legally binding;
- Prison Service Instructions and Instructions to Governors, parts of which may be mandatory; and
- audit baselines, which must be adhered to.

There has been a lack of clarity as a result of the mass of instructions. Internal and independent reviews have highlighted this as a problem for the Service. However, in recent years a significant effort has been made to streamline the standards laid down and to reduce the number of sources providing mandatory instructions. As part of the Performance Standards Programme the Service has combined those mandatory instructions identified as being essential to positive outcomes with other advice and goals into a core set of standards. The first five standards were issued in May 1999; there are a total of 76, covering everything from accommodation, hygiene, parole and training through to video links and visits. The aim of these new standards is to 'bring about an acceptable and consistent level of service delivery by Prison Service staff, and further the achievement of the objectives set for the Prison Service' (HM Prison Service 1999c, p. 4). It is hoped that these new standards will communicate more clearly and succinctly what the Prison Service should aim to deliver and why. They are supported by Prison Service Orders and Instructions that set out the detail of how the standards should be achieved. Further, the standards are checked against key audit baselines, which are an essential part of the new integrated audit system.

The Woolf Report also drew attention to the need for management systems that enable governors to govern and staff to be supported. In this way performance should be maintained to the highest level. Woolf also emphasised the importance of planning documents. The corporate and business planning systems now in use by the Prison Service have developed significantly since his Report. There is now a formal planning system in place throughout the Service. The purpose of the system is to provide a clear direction for the work carried out by the Service (strategic) and to ensure that resources are secured and used efficiently (economic). Plans for the Prison Service are drawn up and approved by ministers in the context of the wider criminal justice system (HM Prison Service 1999b, p. 11). Each year the Director General submits a three-year corporate plan to both ministers and the Strategy Board, which includes strategies, objectives, lists of resources and assets, and efficiency plans.

As establishments are at various stages of development and house different groups of prisoners with myriad needs, so each prison has specific objectives in any period of work. The business planning process comprises the following elements:

Level 1   an establishment overview including financial information, staffing figures, cellular accommodation and bids for capital funding.

Level 2   KPTs against which the establishment and area manager can monitor performance. These are specific to each establishment and are agreed between the area manager and the governor.

Level 3   individual plans for all working groups within an establishment. These reflect work, resources and objectives, and should be filtered up to senior management teams for approval and inclusion in the final planning document.

Individual staff performance and planning records (the Personal Performance and Review System) link into the business planning process. Staff are set SMART objectives (specific, measurable, achievable, realistic and time-bounded), which are clearly linked to the business plan. In this way a common purpose and direction may be maintained within the establishment. Currently, area managers are responsible for approving local business plans. This is an evolving process which aims to synchronise management and financial timetables and to encourage a higher degree of staff involvement, at all levels, in the planning process.

The focus on managerial issues has caused some to argue that the Service has become preoccupied with efficiency for efficiency's sake, and that as a consequence it is in danger of losing sight of its custodial care purpose (Rutherford 1993, p. 26). However, the benefits of having an effective management structure, with realistic and achievable targets that are monitored, can provide a motivated workforce, working to a shared set of objectives. For prisoners, this often provides the best environment for coping with custody and preparing for release. This is largely because there is likely to be greater consistency of practice, which will reduce the chance of aggravating the sense of injustice often felt by those in prison. By maintaining an atmosphere of trust through fairness and consistency it is then possible to deliver constructive regimes most effectively. Indeed, the 1998 Comprehensive Spending Review allocated £660 million to regimes, indicating that the care and rehabilitative aims of the Prison Service were being given equal strategic importance by policy-makers.

The development of prison policy

As an agency whose remit is to carry out the coercive power of the state, the Prison Service must implement policy determined by the government. How it delivers government policy is a matter of prison practice. As specialists in delivery, the Prison Service is in a powerful position to advise government of what is likely to work in terms of meeting the stated purpose and the corporate and business plans at any time. In recognition of this expertise, para. 3.9 of the new agency *Framework Document* states that the Director General is responsible for 'preparing the Prison Service's draft corporate and business plans, including key targets, and submitting them to the Home Secretary for approval' (HM Prison Service 1999b, p. 8).

Practice evolves constantly within the Prison Service. Despite, and as a result of, the legal and statutory framework in which prisons operate, and the nature of the work the Service is committed to, a vast amount of administrative decisions have to be made every day and at every level of the Service. All these decisions will, in one way or another, affect the liberty of an individual or group of prisoners – or staff looking after them, who also have rights that need to be considered. These individual responses drive constant development and adjustments in penal practice to take into account endless variations in human behaviour and circumstance. In this respect the Service stands apart from another business or government agencies.

Within the structure described in this chapter it can be said that there are three main ways in which policy is made and practice develops:

1. as a result of political agendas or top-down decision-making: For example, the current government have made significant reforms to the youth justice system and have created a statutory advisory board to assist in this process. The previous government restricted the release of prisoners on temporary licence by legislating against it, whilst the current government has legislated to

reduce these restrictions. In addition, the Home Secretary can commission independent reports from Her Majesty's Chief Inspector of Prisons. These reports may be thematic, for example covering young offenders or lifers.

2. in response to outside pressure in the form of legal judgements or advice from pressure groups, the public and other interested parties: the Service is constantly in the process of justifying itself to the outside world and regularising its procedures as a result. For example, the Flood judgement (*R.v. Accrington Youth Court and others, ex parte Flood,* 19–22 August 1997) ruled that female sentenced young offenders should not be housed with adult prisoners, and the Service is undergoing a degree of reorganisation to accommodate people in accordance with this judgement. Equally, there was public outcry about the fact that women prisoners were handcuffed when going into hospital to give birth. As a result the Service rethought this practice and issued new instructions to staff escorting pregnant women to hospital.

    Decisions and practice in prisons can be challenged by the law. Within the legal system there is often wide discretion in terms of making specific decisions. The incorporation of the European Convention of Human Rights (ECHR) into domestic law is likely to open the door to wider court scrutiny of prison practice and provoke an additional requirement for the Service to justify its actions. It is also likely that the Convention will extend the boundaries of prisoners' rights which could cause conflicts in some key policy areas, for example adjudications.

3. the Service itself can initiate reviews and make changes in practice: for example, in 1997 the Prison Service Review was commissioned by the then Director General, Richard Tilt. That Review recommended that senior managers be recruited from a wider net. Since 1998 experienced managers have been able to join the Service as governor grades. In addition, the Service can formulate policy, for example the Incentives and Earned Privileges Scheme, which evaluates prisoners' behaviour and progress on addressing offending behaviour and seeks to reward those prisoners who work well in prison.

    Another method of internal review and change is from prisoners themselves, who may initiate change through feedback to prison management or through the request and complaints procedures (see Leech 1999).

    Lastly, there may be external indirect factors that force a change in practice, for example sudden increases in prison population. The difficulties such increases can bring are exacerbated by the impossibility of forecasting what the future level of the population will be, since these are dictated by external sources. Few people could have predicted the unprecedented rise in the prison population in the last four years.

Effective communications

In light of the multiple factors influencing prison practice and decision-making a sophisticated and supportive administrative and communications system is necessary to inform staff of changes in practice, to share best practice and to protect them from a barrage of legal and political challenges. Without good communication, management systems cannot work to their full potential: too many projects may be undertaken and left unfinished; resources may not be properly bid for. It is these sorts of problems that lead many staff to criticise the Prison Service for being reactive rather than proactive. Yet, given the range of internal and external influences on the Prison Service's objectives, this is a largely unavoidable aspect of prison work. Contingency planning is critical. The business planning process is a helpful tool that enables management to manage circumstances and equip staff to deal with the reactive nature of their work. Managers' greatest role is to provide stability and consistency for staff and prisoners in a complex environment.

References

Dunbar, I. and Langdon, A. (1998) *Tough Justice: Sentencing and Penal Policies in the 1990s*, Blackstone Press

HM Prison Service (1997) *Prison Service Review*, The Stationery Office

— (1998) *Annual Report and Accounts 1997–98*, The Stationery Office

— (1999a) *Corporate Plan 1999–2000 to 2001–2002 and Business Plan 1999–2000*, Home Office

— (1999b) *Framework Document*, The Stationery Office

— (1999c) *Prison Service Standards*, Home Office

Home Office (1998) *Joining Forces to Protect the Public: Prisons–Probation*, A consultative document, The Stationery Office

— (1999a) *Home Office Business Plan 1999–2000*, Home Office

— (1999b) *Quinquennial Review of the Prison Service: Prior Options Report*, The Stationery Office

Leech, M. (1999) *The Prisons Handbook*, Winchester: Waterside Press, pp. 234–7

Lewis, D. (1997) *Hidden Agendas: Politics, Law and Disorder*, Hamish Hamilton

Lygo, R. (1991) *Management of the Prison Service*, Home Office

Rutherford, A. (1993) 'Penal policy and prison management', *Prison Service Journal*, No. 90, pp. 26–9

Woolf, Lord Justice and Tumim, Judge S. (1991) *Prison Disturbances April 1990: Report of an Inquiry by the Rt Hon. Lord Justice and His Hon. Judge Stephen Tumim* (The Woolf Report), Cm 1456, HMSO

PRIVATE SECTOR INVOLVEMENT
Colin Edwards

Introduction

> In a democracy grounded on the rule of law and public accountability the enforcement of penal legislation, which includes prisoners deprived of their liberty while waiting trial, should be the undiluted responsibility of the state. It is one thing for private companies to provide services for the prison system but it is an altogether different matter for bodies whose motivation is primarily commercial to have coercive powers over prisoners (Sir Leon Radzinowicz, in a famous letter to *The Times* (in Kent, D. 1998)).

In the late 1980s and early 1990s the uncontrollable rise in the prison population presented the Conservative government with a real problem. A new option began to take shape, reflected in their ideology, with defined needs to increase prison capacity, improve standards and exact greater accountability from those responsible for running the Prison Service. That option was privatisation.

The above quotation reflects the concern expressed by criminologists from many quarters of the academic world, both in this country and internationally, about privatisation. As it has made increasing inroads in the Prison Service, not only with the management and construction of prisons but also with the court escort and transfer of prisoners, so inevitably has the debate about private sector involvement in the Service grown.

Development of the privately managed prison sector

Prisons have been directly managed by government (national or local) in this country since the 19th century. Discussion in the United Kingdom began in the 1980s about the possibility of introducing prisons run by private companies, following the development of private prisons in other countries such as the

Table 5.1: Prison contracts and costs

Contractor	Prison location	Role of prison	Certified normal accommodation (CNA)	Pop. at 30.12.98	Director and Controller	Start/end contract (planned)	Net present value¹/contract price	Cost per place/prisoner	Average per type of prison
Group 4	Wolds Brough, near Hull	Male local	360	396	Director: Dr A. Rose-Quirie Controller: Mr G. Morrison	Started: 6.11.91 Extended: 31.10.96 Expires: 21.3.02	Contract price: £38m over 5 years	£20,606/place £18,572/prisoner	£20,340/place £18,133/prisoner
	Buckley Hall Rochdale, Lancs.	Male Cat. C training	350	379	Director: Mr S. Mitson Controller: Mr D. Pike	Started: 20.12.95 Expires: 30.5.23	Contract price: £30m over 5 years	£16,967/place £15,869/prisoner	£16,594/place £16,248/prisoner
	Altcourse Fazakerley, Merseyside	Male local and remanded YOs	600 500 100	667 573 94	Director: Mr W. MacGowan Controller: Mr M. Constantine	Started: 20.12.95 Expires: 30.5.23	NPV: £247m over 25 years	£247 (NPV) 25 years 600 places = £16,467	No cost per place
Premier Prison Services	Doncaster, South Yorkshire	Male local and remanded YOs	771 346 425	1,026 599 427	Director: Mr K. Rogers Controller: Mr H. Jones	Started: 18.2.94 Expires: 7.8.00 (Invitation to tender: 4.99)	Contract price: £84m over 5 years	£19,475/place £14,094/prisoner	£20,340/place £18,133/prisoner
	Lowdham Grange, Notts.	Male Cat. B training	500	494	Director: Mr R. Tasker Controller: Mr D. Atkins	Started: 7.11.96 Expires: 15.2.23	NPV: £137m over 25 years	£137m (NPV) 25 years 500 places = £10,960	No cost per place
Securicor	Parc Bridgend, South Wales	Male local and YOs	800 500 300	767 545 222	Director: Mr B. Dixon Controller: Ms J. Wallsgrove	Started: 4.1.96 Expires: 14.12.22	NPV: £266m over 25 years	£266m (NPV) 25 years 800 places = £13,300	No cost per place
UK Detention Services	Blakenhurst Redditch, Worcs.	Male local	647	802	Director: Mr P. Siddons Controller: Mr P. Hanglin	Started: 3.10.92 Extended: 16.3.98 Expires: 25.5.01	Contract price: £35m over 3 years	£17,248/place £13,919/prisoner	£20,340/place £18,133/prisoner

¹ The net present value (NPV) is the amount that has to be invested at the start of the contract to fund the expected future cash payments that the Prison Service will be expected to make to the contractor (National Audit Office 1997, p. 57).

Table 5.2: Planned DCMF prisons

Contractor (preferred bidder)	Prison	Location	Start/end contract	NPV	Role of prison	CNA
UK Detention Services	Forest Bank (Agecroft site)	Salford, Greater Manchester	Signed: 1.7.98 Planned start: 1.00 Planned expiry: 12.24	£205m over 25 years	Male local	800
Premier Prison Services	Pucklechurch	Near Bristol	Signed: 29.6.98 Planned start: 10.99 Planned expiry: 9.24	£121m over 25 years	YOI	400
Premier Prison Services	Marchington	Near Uttoxeter, Staffs.	Signed: 7.99 Planned start: early 2001 Planned expiry: 9.25	£240m over 25 years	Male local inc. therapeutic community	800 inc. 200
Group 4	Onley	Near Rugby	Signed: 7.99 Planned start: early 2001 Planned expiry: 9.25	£154m over 25 years	Male Cat. B training	600

United States. The Home Affairs Committee visited the United States, in 1987 and examined facilities operated under contract (city, state or federal) by the Corrections Corporation of America. The Committee cited the possible benefits of cost and speed of delivery, but also the prospect of improvements in the quality of prison conditions. They recommended that the Home Office should conduct an experiment in the contract provision of new remand centres.

In the reply to their report the then Home Secretary, Douglas Hurd, announced that although he was not yet persuaded, he would be publishing a Green Paper on private sector involvement in all aspects of the remand system. However, in March 1989 Mr Hurd announced the government would be promoting legislation to allow the contracting-out of remand prisons to take place, and the authority for this was accordingly included in the 1991 Criminal Justice Act (CJA). The legislation went even further and provided for the enabling powers to be extended to other kinds of prison; such orders were enacted in 1992, allowing the contracting-out of new prisons for sentenced prisoners, and in 1993 allowing the contracting-out of existing prisons.

The first competition opened to the private sector was for the management of a new remand centre being built at Wolds (Humberside). This competition was won by Group 4, and Wolds Remand Prison opened in April 1992. The second competition was won by UK Detention Services and led to the opening of Blakenhurst Prison in May 1993. Tenders were invited in July 1993 for a third competition, won by Premier Prison Services, for the new Doncaster Prison (which opened in June 1994). In September 1993 the government announced a policy of moving towards 10% of prisons (twelve prisons including Wolds, Blakehurst and Doncaster) being run by the private sector through the award of contracts for the design, construction, management and financing of new prisons. In July 1994 Group 4 won the market testing competition for a rebuilt former prison establishment at Buckley Hall (Rochdale), which opened in December 1994. Buckley Hall recently returned to the public sector after a second competition.

The target of 10% of prisons to be privately run has not formally been shelved, but it has been overtaken by events in the form of the present government's sentencing proposals in the Crime (Sentences) Bill.

Accountability

There are two types of privately managed prison. First, the early prisons, for example Wolds, were built by the Prison Service under the then usual methods of procurement and handed over to a private company to manage. By contrast, Parc, and the remaining four due to open by mid-2000, were built under Private Finance Initiative (PFI) arrangements (the capital construction costs and the ongoing operational costs are amortised and repaid to the contractor over the 25-year contract period). If all these prisons are still being run by the private sector in 2000, they will total eleven. The private sector has been shown, through annual studies, to provide value for money – that is, quality services at low cost. The sector also provides an incentive for directly managed prisons to improve their performance. Details of private prison contracts are shown in Table 5.1, and new private prisons in Table 5.2.

Each privately run prison is headed by a director, approved by the Director General of the Prison Service, who is an employee of the contractor as are his staff. The Director is immediately responsible for the management of the prison, subject to a number of constraints. The CJA 1991 (as amended by the Criminal Justice and Public Order Act 1994) provides a framework of safeguards, controls and accountability which must be reflected in order for the contractual process to take place. These are:

1. The presence of a Prison Service Controller (an experienced and senior manager) on site to monitor the contract and to undertake those functions reserved for state servants – that is, to adjudicate on disciplinary charges brought against prisoners and investigate allegations against staff. The Controller is assisted by a Deputy Controller who is also a Crown servant. The Controller is also responsible, except in cases of urgency, for segregation and the use of special control and restraint measures.

2. The same degree of public scrutiny that applies to public sector prisons, namely:
    •   scrutiny by Parliament (through parliamentary questions) and parliamentary Select Committees
    •   a detailed external audit on finance by the National Audit Office and by the Chief Inspector of Prisons, and regular visits by the local community watchdog body, the Board of Visitors;
    •   compliance with the Prison Rules (1952), Key Performance Indicators (KPIs) and most Prison Service Orders and Instructions. (Annual studies have shown that, judged by KPIs, contracted-out prisons perform as well as, and in some cases better than, their closest directly managed counter-parts.)
    •   direct and unfettered access for prisoners to senior Prison Service management, the Prison Ombudsman, the courts (via state-funded legal aid) and Members of Parliament.

3. Vetting by the state of all prisoner custody officers (the equivalent of prison officers at directly managed prisons) who are trained to a Prison Service syllabus.

4. Arrangements for the state to take over all or part of the establishment should it appear that the contractor has lost, or is likely to lose, effective control over a prison.

5. If there are disturbances, arrangements for mutual support between contractually managed and directly managed prisons. (Assistance has also been given by a privately managed prison in dealing with a disturbance at a directly managed prison.)

6. A prohibition on the organisation of strikes among prisoner custody officers (as for prison officers at directly managed prisons).

Additionally, because of the financial provisions contained in the contract, private sector prisons can be (and have been) financially penalised for three reasons: non-compliance with the contract in accordance with a system of performance measurements, the non-availability of places, and overcrowding beyond the permitted level. These sanctions cannot be available in the context of directly managed prisons.

Following the change of government in 1997 the Home Secretary commissioned a review of the policy regarding private sector involvement in prisons. He decided that the Prison Service should be given the opportunity to show that it can offer better value for money than the private sector. The contracts for the management of Doncaster and Buckley Hall Prisons expired in 2000. Bids from the private sector and 'in-house' bids from the Prison Service were invited. (The teams managing the in-house bids are entirely separate from the part of the Prison Service that manages the current prison contracts, with the public service bid being successful at Buckley Hall.)

Concerns

It is essential that ministers and the Prison Service be accountable for everything taking place within the Prison System. It could be suggested that the introduction of private management into prisons weakened the chain of accountability, because prison staff and management in such prisons were accountable primarily to the senior management and the board of their company rather than to the Prison Service and the public. For example, if their operation and performance is commercially confidential, then the public are denied the opportunity to examine what they have done and why. This concern has been echoed by the Prison Governors' Association, who have complained of the difficulty of obtaining information on performance from private prison companies (House of Commons 1997b, p. 49). Furthermore, the existence of a private sector within the prison system weakens accountability for the system as a whole, to the extent that it has meant that particular policies cannot necessarily be implemented consistently in each establishment (Woolf and Tumim 1999, Appendix 14, para. 3.2).

A contrary view to the objections to the principle itself was that it was not the *punishment* that was being privatised or even the **prison** itself (under the contracting-out process), but only the **management** of the prison. Sir David Ramsbotham, Chief Inspector of Prisons, argued in his first annual report that they are 'not private sector prisons but HM Prisons being run on contract for the prison service by a private company' (HM Chief Inspector of Prisons 1996, p. 10). Perhaps more importantly, the different nature of the private prison companies has not led to any difficulties in the actual running of the prisons. Group 4 stated in their annual report that their staff at Wolds and Buckley Hall had not been treated with any less respect by prisoners than were public prison staff; Premier Prison Services reported the same for Doncaster.

If one accepts the general principle of contracting-out, then the question is whether any disadvantages are outweighed by the benefits contracting-out can bring. The overall aim is to improve standards in the quality of provision and make financial savings for the privately managed prisons themselves. Then there is the added benefit of the positive influence that the sector has had on the performance of the remaining publicly managed prisons.

Quality of service provision

There remains difficulty in comparing the performance of any two prisons, particularly in establishing how far like is being compared with like. This is certainly true of the comparisons of privately managed prisons with other prisons within the Prison Service. Among the factors which can make it difficult to compare the quality of provision are such issues as the age of prison buildings and their design, the mix of prisoners between security categories and between those on remand and those convicted, and the extent to which the patterns of activity for which the prison is staffed are disrupted by prison overcrowding. However, these difficulties do not render all comparative assessments impossible. Individual prisons can still be usefully compared with those with which they are most similar, so long as the limitations of the exercise are kept in mind. For the first three privately managed establishments, an attempt has been made to identify the most similar establishments in the rest of the prison system, as part of a Home Office-sponsored study on the savings arising from contracting-out, and comparisons can to some extent therefore be made (Coopers and Lybrand 1996). The closest comparator prisons were identified as Elmley and Holme House (for Blakenhurst); Elmley, Holme House and Birmingham (for Doncastor); and Exeter, Bedford and Cardiff (for Wolds).

There is a consensus between the private prison companies and outside observers that the privately managed prisons had teething troubles. These were evident in the area of control and discipline; a central measure for this is the rate of recorded assaults on staff and inmates. Wolds, in its first year of operation (1992–93) had 27.3 assaults per 100 inmates, while the average for public sector local and remand prisons was 10.8. In Blakenhurst's first year (1993–94) the rate was 33.7 compared to a public sector average of 12.5. Doncaster also recorded 33.7 in its first year (1994–95), compared to a public sector average of 12.3. In each case, performance in the second year was greatly improved, although it did not fall to the levels recorded by those prisons identified as their closest public sector counterparts. Blakenhurst suffered a disturbance in February 1994, and the then Chief Inspector of Prisons (Sir Stephen Tumim) criticised the prison for inadequate control of prisoners in his inspection report.

In response, these problems were partly explained by the private providers. Premier Prisons Services, for example, stated that Doncaster's high rate was due in part to the high proportion of young offenders the prison held, and that the behaviour of these prisoners was, if anything, better at Doncaster than at their previous establishments. UKDS suggested that one of the reasons the assault rate appeared poor at Blakenhurst was because they unlocked their inmates for a larger proportion of the day than did their comparators. The average number of hours spent doing purposeful activity has generally been higher, in some cases by quite substantial amounts. In 1995–96, provisional figures for Blakenhurst were 25 hours per week (closest comparators 19 hours), for Doncaster 24 hours (18 hours) and for Wolds (24 hours).

The Prison Governors' Association, however, reiterates the difficulty in assessing relative performance. Some management information made available by public sector prisons was not available for study from the privately managed prisons. The PGA stated that the 'Association of Governors throughout England and Wales are highly suspicious of what they are told about the performance of private prisons' (House of Commons 1997a). The published study on Wolds Prison (Home Office 1997) argued that the more formal checks on the performance of privately managed prisons needed to be accompanied by a greater openness, about contracts, costs and operating difficulties.

Raw statistics, however comprehensive, can only describe part of the picture. Overall impressions and opinions, now that privately managed prisons have been running for some years, are just as important. The Chief Inspector of Prisons has reported very favourably on Doncaster and Blakenhurst in a recent report listing examples of best practice sent to the Director General of the Prison Service (HM Chief Inspector of Prisons 1998). This was endorsed by Richard Tilt, then Director General.

DCMF prisons

The first four privately managed prisons – Wolds, Blakenhurst, Doncaster and Buckley Hall – were all built within the public sector. However, all subsequent prisons have been designed, constructed, managed and financed in accordance with the PFI. Thus the capital costs incurred in the construction stages of each prison did not rely on taxpayers' money but fell instead on the company that won the contract. There will, however, be an increase in the annual commitments of current expenditure for the whole duration of the entire contract. The potential for savings under DCMF arrangements is greater than those realised by simply contracting-out of prison management. So, too, are the risks, as highlighted by the Prison Governors' Association, who see these arrangements as potentially involving the build up of long-term debt.

The main advantage of DCMF arrangements is the faster rate at which the private sector can bring new prisons into operation, particularly with the current prison population forecasts (the contractor faces financial penalties if the start date is not achieved). Additional benefits are expected from the fact that contractors are able to design the buildings that best suit their methods of operation.

Market testing

Two private prisons have been subject to market testing, that is, putting out to tender the management of an existing prison against a competing bid from within the Prison Service. The first was for Manchester (Strangeways) Prison in 1993, which was won by the in-house Prison Service bid, and the second was for Buckley Hall, won by Group 4, in 1994. The process was then suspended for a period pending legal proceedings instituted by the Prison Officers' Association (POA) but has now resumed with the market testing of Brixton. Derek Lewis, then

A 'quick-build' prefabricated prison wing being erected within the walls of an existing prison. This is an example of the Prison Service accomodation expansion programme.

Director General of the Prison Service, had previously argued for the resumption of the market testing programme so as to develop proper competition and avoid the creation of a series of monopolies instead of a single monopoly, particularly considering existing longer-established prisons.

Management improvements

How far has the development of the private sector led to management improvements more generally, and are these improvements in the quality of programmes or in cost-effectiveness? Both Derek Lewis and Richard Tilt, in giving evidence to the Home Affairs Committee in 1997, took the view that there had been improvements, at least in terms of cost: 'They certainly provide an enormous spur in terms of cost per place because they have demonstrated they can provide a good service at a lower cost' (House of Commons 1997b). As an example they cited the successful in-house bid by the Prison Service for the management of Manchester (Strangeways) Prison. In addition, they noted that the public sector should not fear the private sector as a competitor since it could compete effectively. This has been the experience in the United States, where the existence of a private sector encouraged the public sector to raise levels of performance.

HM Prison Service's partnership approach

The first two DCMF prisons did not open until late 1998; another opened early in 1999. Contracts have been awarded for four more. In May 1998 a Labour government was elected, which, in opposition, was strongly against private prisons. Their stated policy was that imprisonment was a matter for the state, not private companies. When they came to power they commissioned two reviews, one on whether privately managed prisons could be returned to the public sector, and the other on whether private finance could be used to build prisons but they could be managed in the public sector (see Kent 1998).

The first review, about returning private prisons to the public sector, examined various options but concluded that this could not be achieved without losing value for money. The main reason was because the conditions of service for private sector employees are not as generous as those negotiated by the public sector over the years. The same factor (cost differential between private and public sector staff) occurs in the findings of the second review. Another important factor is that there would be insufficient risk transfer to the private sector for a workable PFI arrangement to be reached. There are, in fact, no plans to build any new prisons, either public or private, beyond the current programme. Policy emphasis now is on reducing crime and introducing alternatives to imprisonment, such as the detention curfew and community service.

Cost analysis

There have been a number of studies comparing the costs of private prisons with their closest public sector counterparts which show that the gap between the sectors is getting smaller, but there seems no prospect of this gap closing altogether. However, the Home Secretary has decided that it is right for the public sector to be given another chance to demonstrate whether it can provide better value for money than the private sector. Therefore, when the contract for a 'management only' prison expires an in-house bid from the Prison Service is mounted against private sector companies. Indeed, Buckley Hall was transferred from the private to the public sector following a second market test.

How do privately managed prisons compare against their public sector comparators in outputs as opposed to cost measures? Key Performance Indicators (KPIs) are set for all prisons, and privately managed prisons are subject to them and are measured using the same methodology.

Table 5.3: Cost difference between privately managed prisons and their public sector comparators

1994–95	1995–96	1996–97
13–22%	11–17%	8–15%

The procurement process

The procurement process is dynamic, with procedures being improved in successive DCMF competitions. There was an early lesson learnt at the very beginning of the first competition (Altcourse in Merseyside and Parc in South Wales). The original invitation to tender resulted in non-compliant bids, mainly because the balance of risk transfer was too much in favour of the Prison Service. The contract specification was therefore revised to reflect an allocation of risks acceptable to all parties. Five compliant bids were submitted. Subsequent competitions have been run on the basis of the European Union's negotiated procedure.

The timescale has been tightened since the first competition with the important result for the Prison Service that prisons open earlier, meeting a need that became ever more pressing with the rising prison population. Six months were saved during the second competition (Lowdham Grange in Nottingham) over its predecessor. The key to this success centred primarily on the Prison Service team being unchanged and the same bidding consortia being involved. This body of expertise, evidently absent at the beginning of the DCMF programme, has been built up over the last five years and applies both to the Prison Service and contractors. It can be suggested that the initial aims of the first competitions, building a mature market, have been achieved. The costs inherent in the procurement process have been reduced over time.

Contract templates and compliance

The DCMF contract differs from other institutional PFI projects, such as a hospital or a school, where the core services, provided by doctors and teachers respectively, remain in the public sector. A contract template has evolved through successive DCMF competitions. Although it is fair to state that no one has yet written the perfect contract, when shortcomings have been detected measures have been taken to remedy them when subsequent contracts have been negotiated. Each successive contract thus builds on the experience of the past.

The essence of DCMF contracts is that there have to be risks and rewards to both parties. The contractors wish to make as good a profit as they can, but the Prison Service has to have the means of ensuring that the service provided will function at an agreed level. There are three reasons why payments to contractors can be reduced:

- unavailability of places;
- non-compliance with performance measures; and
- overcrowding.

The payments to contractors are made on the basis of 'available places'. These places are deemed to be available if a number of criteria are met (obtaining the engineer's declaration and regime approval), namely that the cell is physically suitable for occupation and the service required for a prisoner can be provided. Therefore a place is 'available' if it complies with the physical cell requirements and, on a daily basis, with minimum requirements. The minimum requirements include the following:

- full compliance with prison rules;
- provision of washing and sanitary facilities, heating and lighting, meals, bedding, clothes and mail arrangements;
- access to drinking water;
- an hour's exercise per day;
- a cell call system in working order;
- approved level of security and safety in the prison; and
- control of prisoners in general.

Contracts also contain a system whereby any non-compliance with specified performance measures lead to the imposition of predetermined penalty points. The contractor is allowed a quarterly threshold of penalty points up to which no financial penalty is incurred. Once the threshold is exceeded financial penalties are applied up to a limit of 5% of the contract's annual price. Performance points relate to KPIs.

The third way in which payment of fees may be reduced occurs if the contractor holds more than a specified number of prisoners two to a cell for two days or more. However, it should be noted that the Prison Service can and does require a prison to accommodate more than the normal number of prisoners and to provide additional prisoner places. This is also known as 'overcrowding' and does not lead to a reduction in fees.

The mechanisms are in place for penalties simply to ensure that the level of service the prison service requires of the contractor is delivered and that failure to do so on the part of the contractor is penalised. There is a body of thought in the United Kingdom that suggests that the penalties are not severe enough. Recently the Public Accounts Committee of the House of Commons considered the procurement of the first two private prisons and, amongst other deliberations, reported that in their view the 5% limit to the financial penalty for non-compliance with performance measures was too low (1998, para. 34). There must be a balance between the Prison Service's need to obtain a cost-effective deal for the expenditure of taxpayer's money and the contractor's need to make a reasonable profit.

Summary

There are encouraging and positive improvements in the way private sector contracts are drawn up and managed, and in the numerous ways in which the Prison Service has been able to secure better value for money within such contracts over the years. These improvements range from the financial (such as lower rates of wage inflation and higher rates of liquidated damages) to the operational (for example, reducing the opportunity for cell double occupancy without penalty). Another development was made in the contracts for Forest Bank in Merseyside and Pucklechurch near Bristol. 'Benchmarking' was introduced, under which the cost of the operational service can be reviewed after fourteen years. In this way, in the absence of comparable services, the Prison Service can consider whether current provision is likely to represent value for money by reference, amongst other things, to the cost of the provision of custodial services by the public sector.

The concept of agency status and the stimulation of privately managed prisons have undoubtedly introduced a dynamism into what can be remembered as being a uniformly old-fashioned, cumbersome and inefficient structure. There also seems to be a new sense of purpose, which has improved the morale of those who work within the system and even those who are confined by it.

References

Coopers and Lybrand (1996) *Review of Comparative Costs of Privately and Publicly Operated Prisons*, HM Prison Service

Criminal Justice Act 1991, Royal Assent July 1991, entered into force October 1992

HM Chief Inspector of Prisons (1996) *Annual Report 1995–96*, HMSO, p. 10

— (1998) *HMP and HMYOI Doncaster: Report of an Unannounced Short Inspection*, 3–5 November 1998, Home Office, p. 6.

Home Office (1997) *Monitoring and Evaluation of Wolds Remand Prison*, The Stationery Office, p. 58

House of Commons (1997a) *Home Affaires Select Committee, Second Report: The Management of the Prison Service (Public and Private), Vol. 1*, Report, together with the proceedings of the Committee, The Stationery Office, p. lxxi

— (1997b) *Home Affairs Select Committee, Second Report: The Management of the Prison Service (Public and Private), Vol. 2*, Minutes of evidence, The Stationery Office, p. 49

Kent, D. (1998) 'Secure partnerships', *Private Initiative Journal*, (November/ December), pp. 15–18

National Audit Office (1997) *The PFI Contracts for Bridgend and Fazakerly Prisons*, The Stationery Office, p. 57

Public Accounts Committee (1998) *Fifty-seventh Report of the House of Commons Public Accounts Committee: The PFI Contracts for Bridgend and Fazakerley Prisons*, HC 499, The Stationery Office

Woolf, Lord Justice and Tumim, Judge S. (1991) *Prison Disturbances April 1990: Report of an Inquiry by the Rt Hon. Lord Justice Woolf and His Hon. Judge Stephen Tumim* (The Woolf Report), Cm 1456, HMSO, Appendix 14, para. 3.2

6

ETHNIC MINORITIES AND RACE RELATIONS POLICY IN PRISONS

Kevin Leggett

The Prison Service statement on race relations includes the declaration, 'the Prison Service is committed absolutely to a policy of racial equality and to the elimination of discrimination in all aspects of its work' (HM Prison Service 1997, p. 1). The Prison Service shares the belief of the Commission for Racial Equality that 'the most reliable and efficient means of measuring, and then ensuring, the effectiveness of any racial equality policy is to institute the system of ethnic record-keeping and monitoring' (HM Prison Service 1997, p. 10).

Ethnic monitoring of prison populations

With regard to prisoners, ethnic monitoring and analysis covers allocation to accommodation, work and training/education; adjudications; temporary release on licence; segregation; and requests/complaints. Establishments are also asked to consider formal monitoring of allocation/transfer to other prisons, transfers under the Mental Health Act, use of sports facilities, use of the library, mandatory drug-testing and use of the chapel. Any significant racial imbalances that are detected by this analysis can be examined to assess whether there is an acceptable explanation for them, or whether there are indications of direct or indirect discrimination that require corrective action. The keeping of ethnic data does not, in itself, change anything because the data is neutral. It is the analysis of the data and any subsequent action that brings about changes in Prison Service policies, practices and individual behaviour.

Racial equality is an important issue for the Prison Service, both for staff and prisoners. In December 1998, of those staff whose ethnicity is recorded, only 0.5% of governor grades, 2.5% of prison officers and 5.2% of other staff were from non-white ethnic groups. This is in sharp contrast to the prisoner popula-

Two officers work on files in a busy local prison. Prison officers and other staff are drawn from every part of the community.

tion where around 18% are from non-white ethnic groups (HM Prison Service 1999a, p. 32). The Prison Service monitors the following ethnic groups:

- white;
- black (African, Caribbean, other),
- Asian (Indian, Pakistani, Bangladeshi, other);
- Chinese; and
- other.

The statistical breakdown of the prisoner population by ethnic group at the end of March 1999 is shown in Figure 6.1. A considerable proportion of the ethnic minority prison population consists of foreign nationals (29% of males and 49% of females at the end of March 1999). This tends to inflate the proportion of prisoners from ethnic groups as compared with the general population. A better way of comparing the ethnic composition of the prison population with that of the general population would be to exclude those who are not resident in England and Wales from the analysis. Due to a lack of data on the usual place of residence of prisoners, however, British nationality is used instead.

Among male British nationals in the prison population, 86% were white, 10% were black, 2% were south Asian and 2% belonged to Chinese or other ethnic groups. This compares with the general male population of England and Wales

Figure 6.1: Population in prison by main ethnic groups, 31 March 1999

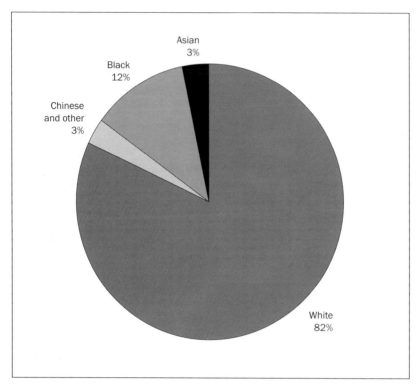

Source: HM Prison Service 1999b, p. 2

(British nationals aged 15–64) of whom 95% were white, 1% were black, 3% were south Asian and 1% belonged to other ethnic groups. For female British nationals in the prison population, 86% were white, 11% were black, 1% were south Asian and 2% belonged to Chinese or other ethnic groups. This compares with the general female population of England and Wales (British nationals aged 15–64) of whom 95% were white, 2% were black, 2% was South Asian and 1% belonged to Chinese or other ethnic groups (HM Prison Service 1999b, p. 2).

The history of race relations policy

The Prison Service first issued specific instructions on race issues in 1981. At that time race relations were seen as a matter that needed consideration, but not necessarily any immediate action. The Service's first Circular Instruction on race relations (CI 28/1981) was designed to help prisons tackle problems if they arose. It set out the following principles:

- good community relations should be based on knowledge and understanding of ethnic minorities;
- all prisoners should believe that they will be treated equally; and
- no prisoner should be allowed to exploit racial differences to his or her advantage.

The circular suggested that if prisons had a significant number of ethnic minority prisoners a race relations liaison officer (RRLO) should be appointed. However, the actual responsibilities of the RRLO were not spelt out until an addendum (CI 27/1982) was published in 1982. This said that the main duties of the RRLO were to:

- be a source of information to prisoners and staff about relevant legislation, instructions and the different ethnic groups in prison;
- develop links with outside community groups;
- help with training; and
- inform the governor of potential or actual problems, suggesting ways of dealing with them.

It was emphasised that race relations were not just a concern for the RRLO but an issue of importance for everyone in prison. A second circular (CI 56/1983) was issued in 1983 and expanded upon the Prison Service's Race Relations Policy Statement. While being built on the principles of the earlier circular, it differed in emphasis by placing clear responsibility for race relations on prison governors. The circular also stressed the need for RRLOs to be appointed at every prison and for them to be sufficiently senior to carry out their responsibilities.

Policy was taken further in a third circular (CI 32/1986). It began with the words:

> The Prison Department is committed absolutely to a policy of racial equality and to the elimination of discrimination in all aspects of the work of the Prison Service. It is also opposed to any display of racial prejudice, either by word or conduct, by any member of the Service in his or her dealings with any other person.

This circular addressed the mechanics of implementing good race relations' practice. Resolutions needed to become integrated in a management framework, so the circular proposed the setting up of a race relations management team (RRMT) to support and raise the profile of the work of the RRLO. Management teams were to assist in the development of local race relations' policy and to devise action plans. Race relations in each prison were to be monitored locally with checklists used on various aspects of the regime, which were later sent to Headquarters.

The Prison Service issued an addendum to the 1986 circular in 1988. This re-emphasised the need to avoid racially offensive remarks and derogatory language in reports. The same year, the Chief Education Officer issued a memorandum to help prison education departments provide a curriculum that was sensitive to different racial and cultural backgrounds, and the prison chaplaincy published the first part of its directory and guide on religious practices in the Prison Service (HM Prison Service 1988).

In 1991, in an effort to bring all the different aspects of race relations policy together, the Prison Service published a comprehensive manual (HM Prison Service 1991). This defined all the different aspects of prison life into separate components, setting out policies for each area, for example residential units, and the steps necessary to implement them. Each category was accompanied by an audit section and an action plan clarifying what was to be done, who should do it and the deadline by when it was to be done. The 1991 manual was widely respected and the Prison Service was seen as one of the first organisations, public or private, to put a comprehensive race relations management structure in place. However, by 1995 the manual was in need of revision. As Richard Tilt, then Director of Regimes, acknowledged in his speech to that year's RRLO's confer-ence: 'The manual is bulky and not always easy to use. Nor is it clear which proce-dures are mandatory and which are recommendatory.' Similarly, the Prison Service statement on race relations was criticised for being directed at prison staff and making no mention of prisoners or visitors. A new manual was published in late 2000.

In 1994 the Criminal Justice Consultative Committee carried out a review of race relations in the Prison Service. The committee was impressed with the efforts made by the Service to address the major issues. However, it recommended that governors should consider inviting representatives from the local Race Equality Council to join the RRMT and that each Board of Visitors should monitor and comment on race relations and the work of the RRMT in their annual report.

In June 1997 a new Prison Service order on race relations was published (PSO 2800). This was based on joint research carried out in 1995 by the Commission for Racial Equality and the Prison Service. It completely revised the instructions and guidance in the 1991 manual. The new statement says:

The Prison Service is committed to racial equality. Improper discrimination on the basis of colour, race, nationality, ethnic or national origins, or religion is unacceptable, as is any racially abusive or insulting language or behaviour on the part of any member of staff, prisoner or visitor, and neither will be tolerated (HM Prison Service 1997, p. 1).

This new statement makes it clear that race relations policy applies to all those who enter prison, including uniformed and civilian staff, visitors and prisoners. As a whole, the new order is an attempt to produce a user-friendly tool that ensures race relations is an integral part of prison administration through the setting of clearly defined, mandatory standards. It is mandatory that the new statement is prominently displayed in all Prison Service establishments.

Policy and practice are now audited against a Prison Service standard which reads:

The Prison Service will have policies and practices which will eliminate improper discrimination. Racially abusive or insulting language or behaviour on the part of any member of staff, prisoner or visitor will not be tolerated (HM Prison Service 1999c, p. 14).

Policy implementation

Implementing the Service's race relations policy must be regarded and conducted as an integral part of the day-to-day responsibility of managers at all levels. Governors find it helpful to be advised by the RRMT, which brings together experience from a number of disciplines. The team should include a representative of each major department of the prison, a member(s) of uniformed staff, the RRLO, the chaplain, a member of the Board of Visitors (as observer) and representatives from local community organisations. They should meet at least quarterly and the chair should be a senior manager. The role of the RRMT is to develop local race relations' strategies, promote racial equality and monitor the prison's performance, endeavouring to become the eyes and ears of the prison on race relations' issues. It provides an overview and plans and monitors related initiatives.

Governors provide the RRMT with clear terms of reference, which might include points such as:

- monitoring the state of race relations in the establishment;
- identifying and discussing general race relations matters;
- promoting staff awareness of and training in race relations matters;

- developing and implementing action plans by reference to the race relations manual, to achieve the objectives of the race relations policies;
- supporting the work of the RRLO; and
- reporting on its work to the governor (HM Prison Service 1997, ch. 3, p. 1).

Each prison carries out ethnic monitoring of all areas of activity. The statistics are compiled and analysed at each of the RRMT meetings. It is also the role of the RRMT to investigate and address any imbalances found. If investigation is necessary, the manager responsible for that area is asked to look into the matter and report. A decision is then made as to the reasons for the imbalance and the action, if any, that should be taken.

Governors have found the advice and assistance of the RRLOs essential in carrying out their responsibilities for implementing service policy. It is important that governors make the appointment of RRLOs with some degree of care. Rank used to be, but is no longer, the key driving factor when selecting people to carry out the duties of a local RRLO. Individuals are comprehensively assessed to ensure that they have the necessary skills and competencies to carry out the role. The job requires an individual who has the confidence of staff and prisoners as well as a certain degree of self-motivation, energy and the ability to withstand criticism. RRLOs have an especially important role to play as a link between prisoners and the RRMT. They act as a source of information for prisoners and, staff, and, when necessary, discuss complaints of a racially sensitive nature with prisoners. The RRLO may be called upon to act to resolve misunderstandings between prisoners and staff and, as a result, may have to report some of these instances to the RRMT and/or the governor for further investigation.

Given the volume of work, assistant RRLOs are often a necessary addition to the structure. Wing-based RRLOs provide an immediate contact if either prisoners or staff experience difficulties. Minor queries or problems are usually addressed at this level, and need go no further; but wing-based RRLOs can act as a link between the RRLO and prisoners.

Training in support of race relations is provided both centrally and locally. All RRLOs attend the race relations' course at one of the Prison Service training colleges. This course lasts two weeks and involves participatory sessions and visits to local places of worship. Attendance at a similar course is now compulsory for all members of the RRMT. All prison staff, uniformed and non-uniformed, must attend the local training sessions that are delivered by the RRLO.

Finally, in 1999, the Prison Service launched the 'Service First' approach, through a national charter. One of the key aims of this document is that the Prison Service

Prisoners discuss the issues of the day with their landing officer. Wing-based RRLOs and landing officers are often best placed to address minor queries, problems or particular issues raised by prisoners.

should ensure that it treats all people fairly, paying particular attention to any special needs. For example, all prisons now cater for a wide range of diets, including halal, kosher, vegan and vegetarian.

The RESPOND initiative

The Prison Service is determined to create an environment in which prisoners and staff can be confident that they will not encounter racial discrimination in any form. A new Prison Service racial equality action programme called RESPOND – Racial Equality for Staff and Prisoners – was launched by the Director General at the Prison Service annual conference in February 1999. The programme is focused on racial equality, but there will be wider benefits accrued in securing equal opportunities for other under-represented groups. The vision statement of the initiative declares:

> The Prison Service represents and serves the whole community. We aim to become more representative of the community and deliver a better service by ensuring equality of opportunity and just treatment for staff and prisoners of all ethnic groups, and by eliminating all forms of discrimination within the Service (HM Prison Service 1999d, p. 2).

The RESPOND initiative came about as a result of the Macpherson Inquiry into the murder of the black teenager Stephen Lawrence, who was killed by a gang of white youths while waiting for a bus in south London in 1993. As a result of this inquiry, targets for the recruitment of black and Asian staff are being set for the fire, immigration, probation and Prison services. The current Home Secretary Jack Straw stated:

> The Macpherson Inquiry quite rightly ensured that the spotlight fell largely on the police. But it is up to all public authorities to challenge racism, improve race equality records and ensure there is a fair representation of ethnic minorities within that organisation. I am determined to ensure the Home Office sets a positive example to others and becomes a beacon of good practice for other parts of the public sector (HM Prison Service 1999a, p. 32).

RESPOND is a free-standing racial equality programme agreed by the Prison Service Management Board. It consists of five main strategies:

- confronting racial harassment and discrimination;
- recruiting ethnic minority staff;
- ensuring fairness in recruitment, appraisal, promotion and selection;
- developing and supporting ethnic minority staff; and
- ensuring equal opportunities for ethnic minority prisoners (HM Prison Service 1999d, p. 3).

Each of the five strategies had outcomes, measures, targets and key actions for 1999–2000. Some of the measures included:

- the appointment of a racial equality advisor;
- the establishment of a recruitment outreach team to assist prisons in the recruitment of ethnic groups;
- the creation of a national ethnic minority network to provide support for ethnic minority staff;
- the review of harassment and discrimination complaints procedures;
- targets for the recruitment, representation by grade and retention of ethnic minorities;
- improvement of racial equality training for senior managers; and
- the regular review of progress by the Prison Service Strategy Board.

In addition, various targets and statistics were monitored and specific measures were implemented, including:

- the number of reported racial incidents;

- the number of complaints;
- the number of recruits from ethnic minorities;
- career progression and retention rates;
- an audit of the selection process;
- race relations monitoring; and
- evaluation of outreach activities (HM Prison Service 1999d, pp. 3–8).

In line with the RESPOND initiative the Prison Service has made a number of new appointments. On 13 September 1999 Judy Clements joined the Prison Service as its first race equality advisor from the Birmingham Partnership for Change where she was Chief Executive (HM Prison Service press release, 21 September 1999). Prior to this, on 7 September 1999, Magsood Ahmed was appointed Muslim advisor to the Prison Service (HM Prison Service press release, 27 October 1999).

Conclusion

We all have a right to live and work in an environment that is free from discrimination, the presence of which can cause stress, anxiety and even illness. It can also lead to tension and conflict, which in a prison environment can affect the maintenance of good order and discipline. We can contribute to eliminating discrimination by challenging racial attitudes, offensive remarks and discriminatory decisions and practices. Prisoners also have obligations and are expected to act in a proper manner. Any alleged acts of racial abuse or harassment against prisoners, staff or visitors is thoroughly investigated and, if proved, dealt with firmly under the appropriate disciplinary procedure. Failure to eliminate discrimination can also be costly in terms of disciplinary cases and legal proceedings brought against the Prison Service, an establishment or even an individual.

The instructions and guidance in the latest order (HM Prison Service 1997) have built on the progress already made by the Prison Service, and indicate the sort of behaviour that is unacceptable and the key role which staff, prisoners and, in particular, managers have to play. The management structures that have been developed provide the framework for effective and consistent implementation of the Prison Service's race relations and minorities policy. These have been strengthened by the introduction of measurable standards, accompanied by mandatory and recommended procedures for their fulfilment. Important aspects of the policy framework include stimulating the development of innovative strategies at local level, the sharing of best practice among establishments, and providing the basis for measuring performance and achievement.

The Prison Service has made great efforts to ensure that prisons adhere to the principles and practices of good race relations. On paper, the Service's policies go further than those of virtually any other organisation, whether in the public or private sector. Furthermore, management structures have been put in place to ensure that the policy is integrated into daily prison life. However, translating policy into practice is not always easy. Although major racial incidents in prison are notable for their absence, and most prisons report little or no racial tension, there are still prisoners, as well as staff, who are not aware of the structures that have been established. RRLOs and the whole RRMT need to be much better known, more active and fully integrated within the lifeblood of the institution as a whole. The new prison order, backed by the RESPOND initiative with its mandatory standards, is designed to address these needs.

References

HM Prison Service (1988) *Religious Practices in the Prison Service*, HM Prison Service

— (1991) *Race Relations Manual*, HMSO

— (1997) *Prison Service Order 2800: Race Relations*, HM Prison Service

— (1999a) *Corporate Plan 1999–2000 to 2001–2002 and Business Plan 1999–2000*, Home Office

— (1999b) *Prison Population Brief for England and Wales*, HM Prison Service

— (1999c) *Prison Service Standards Manual*, HM Prison Service

— (1999d) *RESPOND: Racial Equality for Staff and Prisoners*, HM Prison Service

Press releases
HM Prison Service, 21 September 1999, 'Prison Service disowns racism'

— 27 October 1999, 'Racism to be targeted by changes to Prison Rules'

**PART TWO:
PRISONERS**

THE PRISON POPULATION
Roger Haley

This chapter discusses how and why the prison population has changed over time and especially between 1989 and 1999, a decade that saw steadily reducing population levels transformed into rapidly growing ones. Secondly, it investigates links between the law, crime rates, the amount of court business and the size of the population. Thirdly, it answers the question, 'Who are the prisoners?' Fourthly, it explains how the population is managed; and, finally, it discusses some of the problems faced by the Prison Service when population change has been significantly faster than expected.

In their first-ever report, the Prison Commissioners tell us that there were about 30,000 prisoners in England and Wales in 1879, a figure that represented about 120 prisoners per 100,000 of the general population (Home Office 1998). Between the wars the prison population settled at a little over 10,000, which was about 33 prisoners per 100,000. By 1998 the population had grown to 66,500, representing again about 120 prisoners per 100,000 people. This illustrates one of the problems encountered when attempting to explain prison population changes. It is equally correct to say either that the population has at least doubled in size, or that after a fall it is now no higher than it was 120 years ago – it all depends on how we count it. The statistics used above are the average daily population (ADP) figures for the years referred to. The prison population can also be counted by the number of receptions into prison, which gives us a better – though not perfect – idea of how many different people have been sent to prison over a period. This, too, is usually expressed as an annual figure, and in 1997 there were about 125,400 new receptions received into our prisons (in 1879 there were 186,060 receptions). The figure that is most widely quoted is probably the 'headline' figure, for example 'The prison population on 31 July 1998 was 66,517.'

The term 'prison population' is of little use to researchers or practitioners however, because in reality we are dealing with a number of different populations, and the size of some may be changing at a very different rate to others. They include males and females, remanded and sentenced prisoners, young offenders and adults, as well as juvenile offenders. As some groups may not be held with others (for complex legal and other reasons), the differing growth rates can have profound consequences for the Prison Service, as accommodation has to be continually re-roled to deal with surges in one sector or another.

The criminal justice system and prison population

The **causes** of population fluctuations are complex, but the **determinants** of population fluctuations are simple: the number of people sent to prison and how long they stay there. The length of stay is not solely a matter for the courts. It can be affected by rules relating to time spent in police or prison custody before sentence, or early release schemes such as parole or home detention curfew. We saw above that the number of receptions in 1879 was about 50% higher than in 1997, but that the ADP was about half (Home Office 1998). This is mainly because custodial sentences were far shorter then than now. We do not know precisely the same things about the composition of the population in 1879 as we do about today's population because circumstances, statistical information and social values are very different: varying criteria are measured and commented upon. We know little about young offenders (YOs) or vulnerable prisoners (VPs) in 1879, for example, but know precisely the number of servicemen held in custody. There are two changes we should note here, however. The first is the very large difference in the number and type of receptions. Of 186,060 receptions in 1879 only about 13,000 were remands, with over 143,000 being convicted by the magistrates alone. In 1997, of 125,400 receptions, 75,700 were remands with about 54,000 being convicted. In Victorian times it was far easier to find yourself in prison: there was little opportunity to prepare a defence, but your stay was likely to be a short one. The second change relates to women and is even more marked. The ADP in 1879 was almost the same as in 1997, but the number of receptions of women in 1997 was 8,600 versus 48,600 in 1879. These figures suggest that there has been a marked change in thinking about the use and purpose of imprisonment.

One aim of this chapter is to describe the situation during the past decade or so and to consider some possible explanations. We should expect to find that things at the end of the 20th century were very different to things at the end of the 19th. But during the six years 1992–98 we saw the population rise from 40,600 to 66,500, an increase of 64%. In most respects society changed little over this period, so how are we to explain such a dramatic rise, especially when between 1988 and 1992 the population actually fell by 18% (Home Office 1994).

One might reasonably expect to find that the causes of increases are attributable to rising levels of crime, leading to more business in the courts with more people being punished. In fact this seems not to be the case. During much of the decade (1989–99), recorded crime levels fell (Home Office 1997). Although other measures of crime exist, such as the self-reporting and victim data found in the *British Crime Survey*, it is recorded crime that matters when discussing prison populations. Recorded crime fell each year between 1993 and 1996, while the prison population rose from 45,000 to 55,000. The increases could be explained, in part, if police clear-up rates had improved – that is, a greater proportion of recorded crime was actually solved – but this was not the case (Home Office 1997). Another explanation might be that more cases than before were referred to the courts instead of being dealt with by other means, such as police cautions. This is partially true, as the use of cautions fell from 1992 onwards, but this did not result in more people appearing in court instead. The number of defendants proceeded against at magistrates courts fell each year from 1991 to 1996, by a total of about 4%. The number of guilty findings also fell for most of those years. A similar picture emerges when we look at the amount of business in the Crown Court (Home Office 1997). There is nothing here that explains the increase in the number of people imprisoned. What did increase, however, was the number of cases sentenced at the Crown Court after being heard by the magistrates. In the absence of legislative changes to encourage this behaviour, this suggests a change of mood.

The determinants of population size, as stated earlier, are the number of people sent to prison and their length of stay. If magistrates refer more cases to the Crown Court for sentence, it is almost inevitable that sentence lengths will increase. This is precisely what happened after 1992. This was not solely due to the increase in referrals from magistrates courts however; all courts were becoming more custodially minded, as is evidenced by the custody rate. The custody rate is the proportion of cases that result in a sentence of immediate custody rather than in the award of a non-custodial sentence such as a fine or probation order. Between 1992 and 1996 the custody rate doubled at magistrates courts and rose from 44% to 60% at the Crown Court. It was simultaneous increases in custody rate and sentence length together that fuelled the massive population growth which characterised the prison system from 1992 onwards.

This gives us a deterministic answer, but does not explain **why** the courts began to behave in the way they did. There are two factors that must be mentioned here. The first is legislative change. It is clear that certain laws passed have the aim of sending more people to prison, while others have the aim of reducing imprisonment. This ought to be our answer, but in practice there is little correlation between the enacting of legislation and the expected prison population movement. Two good examples of this are the Bail Act 1976 and the Criminal Justice Act (CJA) 1991. The first was a response to concerns about the number of prisoners held on remand, which by 1975 was believed to be far too high. The remand population fell between 1975 and 1977, but was rising again by the time the law came into force and has continued to rise more or less constantly since then. Similarly, the CJA 1991 was intended to reduce the prison population and was in preparation during a period in which the population was in fact falling. But by the time of implementation in October 1992, the population was again increasing. In both cases the legislation reflected attitudes that existed at a particular time. With the Bail Act, the underpinning assumptions about the use of bail persisted after the passing of the Act but still the remand population grew. With the CJA, attitudes towards imprisonment hardened before the legislation came into force and the population began to grow rapidly. This suggests that factors other than legislation affect the behaviour of the courts.

The attitude of the popular press is one of those factors. Not only does it impact directly on magistrates and judges, but frequently on political leaders who then either accuse the courts of being soft on crime or, at other times, of being unthinking by sentencing too many people to a wasted period of imprisonment. Both of these phases are evident during the decade in question and at other points during the 20th century. In the late 1970s and early 1980s, research suggested that programmes aimed at helping prisoners to avoid crime were a failure. It became the conventional wisdom that prisons were an expensive way of making bad people worse. This was, in part, reflected in the CJA 1991 and the falling population levels between 1988 and 1991. This soon changed, however, as the press and police alike campaigned for tougher action by the courts. Politicians of all persuasions were quick to sense the change in mood and began to echo the comments made in the press. The courts responded to the new situation. In a democracy this can be understood as a legitimate expression of the public will being taken seriously by the authorities. But for this to be acceptable the public needs to be sure of its own mind. Research suggests that there is a great deal of misinformation guiding public thinking. When questioned, members of the public state that they believe that the courts are too lenient. When asked to sentence real cases for themselves, they turn out to be more lenient than the courts actually were. This suggests that the rhetoric to which members of the public are so frequently exposed is misleading them in no small part, yet courts feel obliged to take account of public opinion as expressed in the media.

From 1993, the clamour for tougher justice became synonymous with Michael Howard, the then Home Secretary, and his revisiting of the 'Prison Works' philosophy. It has been suggested that the prison population increase after 1993 was a result of his 'talking up' the population. There is probably some truth in this, but it can be no more than partial. For it to be true, the population would have needed to grow uniformly across all sectors, otherwise other factors were at work. The fact is that the prison population did not grow uniformly at all during the period and the 'talking up theory' cannot explain the sorts of changes discussed below.

Who are the prisoners?

Various types of prisoner comprise the prison population. Figure 7.1 shows the breakdown of the average prison population for 1997.

One feature stands out here: imprisonment most frequently affects males. Of an ADP of 60,540 for 1997, 57,860 were male and, for the most part, young males. Less than 18% of sentenced male prisoners were aged 40 or over. What crimes had they committed?

Figure 7.1: Main components of the prison population: average during 1997

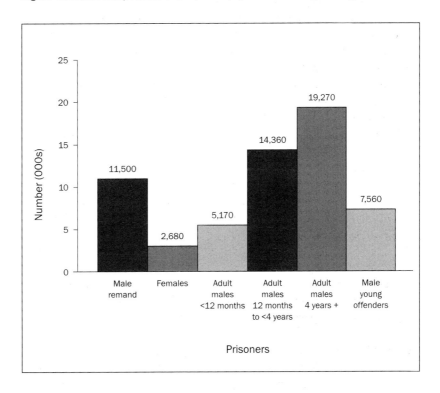

Offence profile

Figure 7.2 shows the offence profile of the adult male prisoner population in 1997. We need to be cautious about what this figure tells us. At first glance it might seem that most offenders go to prison for offences of violence or drugs. If we look at the type and number of offences recorded by individual reception, however, a different picture emerges. Of the total adult male receptions in 1997, 32% fall into the 'other offences' category such as motoring offences, breach of court order or drunkenness, with 22% being sent to prison for theft (Home Office 1998). The reason that Figure 7.2 presents a different picture is that theft and 'other offences' usually attract far shorter sentences than violent ones. So, on any particular day, more people are **sent** to prison for these types of offences, but they make up a smaller proportion of ADP because they are released more quickly.

Figure 7.2: Male prison population under sentence, 1997

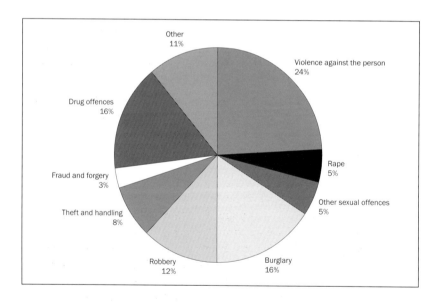

Remand prisoners

Not all prisoners are sentenced, of course, and as we saw in Figure 7.1, on average 11,500 male prisoners were held in custody on remand during 1997. Altogether 12,100 persons – about 20% of ADP – were held on remand. This is a very high proportion for a country that prides itself on a legal system which is based on the principle that a person is presumed innocent until proved guilty. It has caused widespread concern, but that concern is not new, however, as Parliament has made periodic attempts to address the issue. The most recent piece of major legislation reflecting this concern is the Bail Act 1976, which clearly states that remands in custody should be used sparingly. Most, though not quite all legislation since then, has confirmed that principle. Yet attempts to reduce the use of custodial remands have failed. In 1975, when Parliament was sufficiently concerned with the size of the remand population to act, there were 5,500 prisoners held on remand, but by 1997 the figure had more than doubled. The number of receptions of remand prisoners has not, however, risen apace and the chief, although not the only, reason for the increases has been delays within the criminal justice system.

The determinants of the size of the remand population are just the same as for the sentenced one: the number sent to prison and the length of time they stay. We have already seen that the number of remand receptions in 1879 was very low by modern standards and that the remand population has doubled since the Bail Act 1976. Most of that increase occurred between 1976 and 1987, and the rise was fuelled by delays in getting **untried** prisoners into court (Morgan 1989). Since then the situation has changed markedly, with the number of untried prisoners being lower in 1997 than in 1987. The number of prisoners who are classed as **convicted unsentenced** has, conversely, increased by 21,000 receptions per year and added about 2,200 to the ADP. The average time spent in custody for untried prisoners in 1997 was 51 days for men and 36 days for women. Of those convicted and unsentenced males spent an average 37 days in custody and females 30 days.

Age profile

Another way of breaking down the population is by age. In general, sentenced persons under the age of 21 years are kept apart from older prisoners. In practice, prisoners under 21 years of age are normally kept separately at every stage of imprisonment, even if this means in a separate part of an adult establishment. Persons of the same sex aged over 21 can mix together freely, although remand prisoners are generally held separately from those sentenced and cannot be compelled to share a cell with a sentenced prisoner. The age breakdown of the sentenced population is shown in Figures 7.3 and 7.4, male and female populations being shown seperately. They cover the period 1987 to 1997 so that not only a snapshot view is revealed, but trends are shown.

We see that all age groups increased in number from 1992–93 onwards. As a proportion, juvenile numbers increased, the 18–29 age group contracted slightly, while the proportion of prisoners over 30 years of age also grew. This process, known as age bifurcation, has no single cause. The reasons for the increase in the

Figure 7.3: Male population by age range, 1987–97

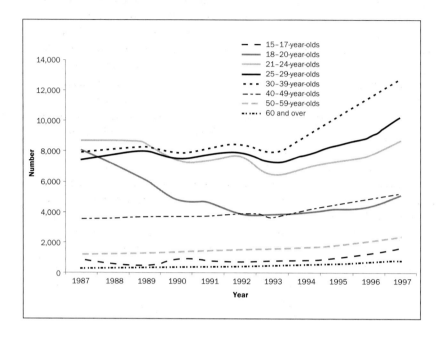

Figure 7.4: Female population by age range, 1987–97

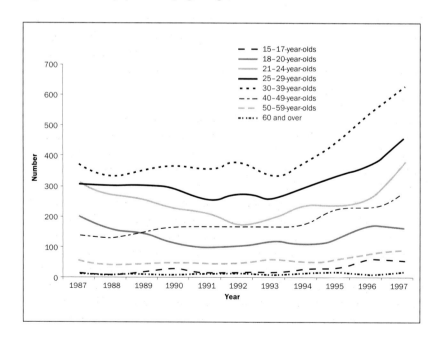

proportion of older prisoners are linked to the increasing number of prisoners serving longer sentences, including life. It is more difficult to explain the juvenile increases, especially as the proportion of young prisoners in general is falling, partly by legislative design and partly because of demographic change. Overall, juvenile numbers more than doubled over the period 1992–97. This increase was preceded by press campaigns about the inability of the law to take action against criminal children, sometimes as young as ten, who were, according to the press reports, terrorising housing estates and town centres. The courts reacted to the campaigns by imprisoning more children, and Parliament responded by doubling the maximum sentence length available to the courts in the case of children. Then, in February 1993, 2-year-old Jamie Bulger was taken from a shopping precinct and battered to death by, as it later proved, two 10-year-old boys. The effect on all sections of society was profound and the change in the size of the prison population mirrored this. There are other reasons why the population overall grew rapidly from this point onwards, but the Bulger case can certainly explain in part why the proportion of juveniles increased so dramatically there-after. The explosion in their numbers was not to abate until five years later, when, with the population at about 2,500 remanded and sentenced juveniles, it stopped almost as suddenly as it had started.

Gender

If it is males who most frequently attract prison sentences, it is women who bore the brunt of the increases from 1991, when they numbered some 1,560, to reach levels in excess of 3,200 by 1999. During this time they rose from representing 3.5% of the total population to 4.4%. Nobody is quite certain why this should be, but a number of theories exist.

Some have argued that the rise in female numbers began when suspended sentences were all but abolished by the CJA 1991 because courts particularly liked suspending sentences for women. When courts lost the power to do this, they responded with sentences of immediate custody rather than non-custodial alternatives. There is some evidence to support this, as the number of suspended sentences passed on women fell from 2,700 in 1992 to just 700 by 1996. Others have argued that the causes are more complex, having more to do with changing attitudes to women as they become more emancipated. History suggests that women may be imprisoned for different reasons to men, and we saw earlier that women used to form a large part of the total of those received into custody but a smaller proportion of ADP. This is because many women were sent to prison for very short periods, often for drunkenness, prostitution or other offences which we would today view rather differently. These crimes have a moral overtone that

Young prisoners talk with one of their wing officers. Some ethnic minorities are massively over-represented in the prison population.

contrasts with those for which men are typically imprisoned and where there is generally an immediately identifiable victim.

Ethnicity

Another way of looking at the prison population in the post-War era is on the grounds of ethnicity. United Kingdom citizens from some ethnic minorities are massively over-represented in prisons. Per 100,000 of their own ethnic group there are over six times as many black prisoners as white, and between 1992 and 1997 they rose from being 10% to 12% of the population overall. Home Office research in 1990 suggested that a black prisoner could expect to receive a sentence 98 days longer than a white male adult convicted in similar circumstances, and there is little evidence that this is because black prisoners committed the more serious offences (Home Office 1990). Of prisoners sentenced for offences of violence against the person, black people make up the smallest of all the ethnic groups, for robbery the highest, and for drug offences they constitute a higher proportion than the white population but a lower proportion than that of other races. These features suggest that discrimination can be found within the criminal justice system.

Management of the prison population and the problem of rapid change

In theory, the management of the prison population is a simple enough process. When remanded, prisoners are held in a prison near the court, known as a local prison. They return there after sentence for assessment, following which they are transferred to a training prison, where they complete their sentence and learn new skills, address their offending behaviour and are prepared for release. Young offenders are held on remand in local prisons but are sent to young offender institutions (YOIs) directly after sentence, where they undergo a similar process. All would be well were it not for:

- prisons being in the wrong place;
- training prisons being perpetually full;
- limited funds being available for rehabilitative programmes; and
- constantly changing ideas about the role and purpose of imprisonment in general, or for specific groups such as juveniles and young adults.

No one in their right mind would today design a prison estate on the model we are faced with as we enter the 21st century, but then the estate never was designed, as such. Traditionally, training prisons were built well away from towns or cities. This probably seemed like a good idea at the time, but the distances that now have to be travelled by visitors, probation staff and members of the legal profession have become a major concern.

Although ideas come and go, there are a number of themes that persist and that have influenced the way in which the Prison Service manages its charges. In particular, prisoners should not be allowed to escape from lawful custody and should experience, during their period of imprisonment, some assistance in developing skills that could help them to live a law-abiding life after release. For these reasons, newly sentenced prisoners have, for years, undergone a process of assessment. At the most fundamental level this was an assessment of the degree of security needed to ensure custody and the skills a prisoner should acquire to enable him or her to find work. As time progressed these assessments became more sophisticated and included other features, such as attendance at programmes designed to address their offending behaviour. Simultaneously, greater attention began to be paid to the overall prison experience and, in particular, such matters as prisoners being locked in their cells with little to do for up to 23 hours each day. Life for prisoners began to change. Life changed for governors and staff too, as managerialism crept in. They found that they had to monitor how time was being spent and were given targets to achieve in such areas as prisoners' time out of cells, purposeful activity or the completion of offending behaviour programmes. As a result, when the population began to mushroom from 1992, everybody was affected.

Population fluctuations cause all sorts of difficulties. Falling populations cause problems as they eventually lead to the need to close prisons on cost grounds, which probably leads to the changing of the role ('re-roling') of other establishments. However, the major difficulty, of course, comes in periods of rapid population growth, as discussed earlier in this chapter and below. At the worst point in the mid-1990s the population was growing in excess of 1,000 each month, the size of a very large prison. During earlier crises the Prison Service had been able to use cells in police stations to supplement prison accommodation. But managerialism brought with it devolved budgets and, instead of payment from a Home Office contingency fund, the Service was faced with having to pay the full cost of police cell use from its own resources. At £120,000 per prisoner held in police cells per year, this, potentially, could have absorbed much of the non-pay running costs available. The leaders of the Prison Service agreed that this was something that could no longer be afforded: police cells were to be avoided at all costs.

In normal times, training prisons declare their vacancies to Headquarters. Local prisons bid for these places and allocations are made on the basis of which local prison has the greatest need to create the spaces needed to handle the business of the courts. Which individual is moved is left to the prison to decide, and the considerations referred to earlier come into play. When population pressures intensify there are insufficient places available in training prisons and prisoners are moved from full local prisons to those with space, on what are called over-crowding drafts. When most prisons are full, overcrowding drafts can be to prisons hundreds of miles away. This is clearly an inconvenience to prisoners and their families and friends, and adversely affects the prisons involved. Some of the prisoners may be in the middle of an education course or one addressing offending behaviour. Staff may need to be diverted from other duties to travel with the prisoners, causing staff reductions in the prison and a consequent closure of some aspects of the regime, leading to more unproductive prisoner time and a failure to achieve prison targets. No one benefits from this, and thus the notion that a period of imprisonment can be of some benefit to a prisoner looks decidedly questionable. At Headquarters, senior staff need to negotiate funding for new accommodation to deal with the problem, other staff need to be drafted in to deal with the management of building programmes, or existing staff are diverted from their main jobs to deal with re-roling and other issues. The desirable is forced to take second place to the exigent.

That, in a nutshell, is the tragedy of prison over-population. For whatever the pros and cons of imprisonment, the processes and activities which could help prisoners to desist from crime will be continually threatened until wiser counsel prevails. We saw at the start of this chapter that in England and Wales the prison population represented 120 persons per 100,000 of the general population in 1997. This was the highest figure in the European Union, double that of the Scandanavian countries and half as many again as much of western Europe (Home Office 1998). They appear to manage their societies with far fewer prisoners.

References

Home Office (1990) *The Prison Population: A Statistical Review,* Home Office/ HMSO

— (1994) *Prison Statistics England and Wales 1993*, Cm 3087, HMSO

— (1997) *Criminal Statistics 1996*, Cm 3764, The Stationery Office

— (1998) *Prison Statistics England and Wales 1997*, Cm 4017, The Stationery Office

— (1999) *Prison Statistics England and Wales 1998*, Cm 4430, The Stationery Office

Morgan, R. (1989) *Remands in Custody: Problems and Prospects in Criminal Law Review*, Butterworths, pp. 481–92

8

HIGH-SECURITY PRISONERS

Peter J. Leonard

History

The long-term imprisonment of serious offenders in modern Britain can trace
its origins to the abolition of transportation. While there are some references to
imprisonment in ancient records these are rare, and when it was used the sentences,
even for quite serious offences, seem to have been quite short by modern standards. A year and a day can be thought of as a fairly typical sentence, with only a
handful of examples of substantially longer terms. Penal thinking of the day, in so
far as it existed at all, set out to right a wrong rather than exact retribution. The law
was, therefore, more likely to demand compensation from offenders by way of
fines or restitution. In very serious cases offenders could, of course, be put to
death, but this wasted valuable labour and could make dependent families a
burden to communities.

In the 17th century, the use of the death penalty was again constrained by
economic factors. The British drive to acquire overseas territories and to found
new colonies created the need for additional workers. The early colonies needed
cheap labour in order to expand and generate revenue for the British Exchequer.
The enslavement of innocent people was one of the options chosen, the other
was to force convicted criminals to work in the far-off lands of the growing
Empire. The inhospitable conditions and dangerous nature of the work frequently
meant transportation was a death sentence in everything but name. At first there
was a fairly loose arrangement by which some prisoners who had been sentenced
to death were allowed to take their chances in the colonies. The exact method of
selection is not entirely clear, and there might have been some choice, but not all
were given the opportunity to go. Those who did were given Crown Pardons
conditional on their working as directed in the colonies. In 1679 this apparently
casual arrangement formally entered the law books, and transportation became
widely used for punishing non-capital offences.

Transportation worked when there were large developing countries willing to accept convict labour. The frailties of the system were apparent, however, when it was interrupted by American independence. Gradually the colonial governments became increasingly concerned at the growing size of the convict and ex-convict population and by 1850 it was clear that Tasmania and the eastern Australian colonies wanted the practice stopped.

Another influential factor was that the late 18th and early 19th centuries were a high point of European penal reform. In Britain, one manifestation of this was a reduction in the number of capital offences. The net result of all this was a growing number of convicts who could not be transported and no plan in place to deal with them. A return to wholesale executions, which had provoked public anger a century earlier, was out of the question, and there were no large colonies willing and able to absorb the numbers involved. The last convict ship sailed from England in 1867 but well before then the Westminster government took the only practical course of action. In 1850 it assumed responsibility for those sentenced to transportation, who could not be shipped abroad, and sought to provide prisons in which to house them. This was a new undertaking for central government because at that time practically all prisons were funded and administered by local authorities. It was also an important development historically because it paved the way for the total **nationalisation** of all English and Welsh prisons 27 years later.

The 20th century saw a substantial growth in the prison population generally and, in its closing decades, the long-term prison population in particular. In 1965 11% of the sentenced average daily population (ADP) was serving four years or more; by 1998 the proportion had risen to 38% (Home Office 1999). There were many reasons for this:

- the number of younger men in the general population;
- sentencing and early release policy;
- lower public tolerance of crime;
- political expediency; and
- improved police methods.

The abolition of the death penalty in the 1960s is sometimes cited as a reason for an escalation in violent crimes, although the evidence for this assertion is flimsy and its continuation would have had little impact on the prison population. Whatever the explanation the fact is the Prison Service found itself dealing with a growing number of, mainly, men with the incentive, skills and resources to escape and endanger the public.

The century had opened amidst the reforming zeal of the report of the Gladstone Committee which paved the way for a progressive penal system (Gladstone 1895). The report led to the 1908 Act which introduced probation, diverting some offenders from prison altogether. For the most serious offenders, however, the Prevention of Crime Act 1908 introduced preventive detention, which is best thought of as an early version of the American 'three strikes and you're out' concept. It was aimed at protecting the public by allowing courts to pass a sentence of between five and ten years **in addition** to the normal sentence on offenders with three previous convictions. While this disposal was rarely used it did put into the prison system a few very-long-sentence prisoners whose security was said to be of great importance. Interestingly, though, for most of the 20th century the Prison Service was not especially preoccupied with security.

A turning-point

The mid-1960s were to prove a major turning-point for the Service in terms of the custody of long-term prisoners. Following the sentencing of the Great Train Robbers and other notorious gangsters there was a growing realisation that prisons were going to have to hold sophisticated and dangerous people for a long time. It also became clear that there was increasing public disquiet about prisons, especially the number of escapes, which the authorities could no longer ignore. The original convict prisons were in no shape to provide the level of security needed because their physical condition had been allowed to deteriorate, prisoners had been given greater freedom of movement, and procedures were not good enough to ensure proper control. The response of the Prison Service was to open a small special security unit inside Leicester Prison, quickly followed by another in Durham Prison, which combined better levels of physical security with rudimentary electronic security devices. Before the effectiveness of these measures could be evaluated, however, George Blake, a spy, and Ronnie Biggs, a train robber, escaped from London prisons. The resulting outcry caused by these and other escapes, led to the appointment of Lord Louis Mountbatten to inquire into prison security. Mountbatten's report was to radically reshape the modern long-term prison system in England and Wales (Mountbatten 1966).

The Mountbatten Report is sometimes misrepresented as being purely about security. What it in fact tried to do was separate the problem of length of sentence from that of dangerousness to the public. It is commonly thought that a prisoner receiving a long sentence must automatically be dangerous to the public and require conditions of the highest security. While this is obviously true in some cases, it is not always so. What Mounbatten did was to recommend the introduction of a system that used information about the level of threat the individual posed to the public, the police or the security of the state to locate the prisoner in one of four security categories. This was to be done regardless of how likely he (it was not applied to women) was to escape. The highest, Category A, should, Mounbatten said, be held in a single fortress-style prison. The lowest, Category D, could be trusted in open prisons. It was reasoned that, freed from the pressing concern of high-security prisoners staff in the lower category establishments would have opportunities to develop positive regimes for all, including some long-sentence prisoners. There would be incentives to encourage good behaviour in all prisons, and in the Category A prison there would be mechanisms to prevent boredom, psychological conditioning and mental deterioration. In the end the fortress prison was not built although, as we shall see, the idea was to re-emerge 30 years later. The categorisation system, together with some recommended procedural and physical security improvements, were implemented and have survived, with a few adaptations, to form the basis of the modern high-security system.

Development of the modern system

High-security units came in for close scrutiny when a committee of the Advisory Council on the Penal System, chaired by Professor Leon Radzinowicz, was asked to look at the regime for maximum-security prisoners (Advisory Council on the Penal System 1968). The committee thought the units were a temporary and most undesirable expedient but acknowledged that relationships between staff and prisoners were good. This helped the members to conclude that maximum security did not have to mean minimum treatment. Having compiled evidence in Britain and abroad, the committee thought that concentrating the highest-escape-risk prisoners together would place a strain on staff, lead to a repressive atmosphere and deny long-term prisoners the facilities they needed. The fact that the United States had closed Alcatraz Prison for economic reasons and chosen not to replace it reinforced the view that concentration was not the way forward. Instead, it was recommended there should be a policy of dispersing Category A prisoners among the Category B populations at several specially equipped and resourced closed training prisons (Advisory Council on the Penal System 1968, paras. 208–10). The recommendations were accepted by the then Home Secretary, James Callaghan, and the policy of dispersing Category A prisoners, although often challenged, has remained in place ever since.

The decision to disperse Category A prisoners around a number of secure prisons, which became known as 'dispersals', was generally welcomed by the press at the time. Informed academics took the more measured view of 'let's wait and see', but the Prison Officers' Association (POA) opposed the policy from the outset. The POA had accepted Mountbatten's recommendation of concentration, believing this would result in the very worst-behaved prisoners being kept in one place. The right physical and staffing resources would enable their effective management. There was also a strong identification with Mountbatten by rank and file prison staff. He had, after all, been a successful naval officer and understood operational matters. The Radzinowicz team, on the other hand, was made up largely of academics who could not claim the same pedigree. The argument ignored the fact, however, that dangerousness to the public did not automatically equate to disruptiveness in prison. The POA, however, stuck to their view and the troubled first decade of the dispersal system almost justified their doing so.

Between October 1969 and June 1983 there were at least ten major disturbances in dispersal prisons. One notable example lasted for four days at Hull Prison at the beginning of September 1976. The Chief Inspector, who carried out the inquiry, believed it was a riot of unprecedented ferocity causing around £0.75m of damage (HM Chief Inspector of Prisons 1997). He did not, however, blame it on dispersal policy or Category A prisoners; instead he thought the prison contained a lot of potentially violent men who had been shown considerable tolerance and conditioned the staff through free and easy relationships. This analysis strikes to the heart of the problems of managing long-term prisons. By their nature they contain some calculating and manipulative prisoners who are willing to use those who are potentially violent to disrupt the establishment. Staff always have to be

Damage caused by prisoners to a prison washroom. Disturbances in prison, while not common, can cause widespread damage that is costly to repair.

on their guard against conditioning and must use security information effectively in order to plan and carry out pre-emptive action.

Another factor contributing to the Hull riot was the curtailment of the regime for prisoners. Whilst this is occasionally unavoidable, lessons about how changes to routine should be managed had been learned at another dispersal prison, Albany, in 1972 (King and Elliott 1997, pp. 295–9). There a quantity of escape equipment had been found and the governor advised that a complete 'lock-up' search of the prison was essential. The staff were briefed to lock up the prisoners, who were given no explanation as to why the normal routine was being interrupted. Prisoners were quiet at first but, as staff applied the rules regarding unauthorised articles with unusual strictness, the prisoners began to smash furniture and set fire to bedding. The disturbance occurred over a Bank Holiday weekend, was widely reported by the press and caused sympathetic action in some other prisons, including one in Scotland. This particular disturbance demonstrates the delicate balance of power that exists in long-term prisons and the need for them to be sensitively managed. It seems likely that giving prisoners a proper explanation for the lock-down and arranging for the better supervision and support of the searching staff would have avoided such serious ramifications.

Following the Albany disturbance the then Home Secretary, Robert Carr, ordered a further review of dispersal policy. This led him to conclude that it would be unsafe to put the prisoners most likely to cause trouble in a single prison. He said that cells would be set aside in some local prisons in which dispersal governors could temporarily locate disruptive prisoners. He also said that two control units would be built to house the most difficult prisoners for longer periods. Using cells in local prisons is a valuable tool for governors who need to move prisoners quickly from dispersal prisons. It can, however, provide nothing more than a short-term expedient. The control units, which might have become part of a longer-term solution, were never opened because there were humanitarian concerns about the physical conditions and the regimes proposed for them.

Secure units?

The problem of difficult prisoners did not, however, go away and in its 1984 report the Control Review Committee attempted to find other solutions. The Committee recommended the establishment of three or four units each offering a different regime. Within this framework of variety and flexibility it was thought troublesome prisoners could be managed and prepared for return to the normal dispersal prison routine. In December 1985, C wing at Parkhurst Prison was opened as a facility for long-term prisoners with both a history of troublesome prison behaviour and psychiatric illness. Two years later units were opened at Lincoln and Hull Prisons. The Lincoln and Parkhurst units have now been replaced by ones at Woodhill and Durham Prisons but the policy remains to provide a variety of regimes in order to meet the different individual needs of very difficult and dangerous prisoners. The objective always is to get prisoners' behaviour to improve so they can leave the units and go back into an ordinary dispersal prison regime as soon as possible. Importantly, the policy is not to run the units as a simplistic, progressive system that would lead to one becoming a place of last resort, which quickly fills up and makes the return of some individuals impossible.

Concerns about control soon gave way to those of security when, in 1987, two Category A prisoners escaped from Gartree Prison. This escape involved the use of a helicopter for the first time in an English prison. The fact that the aircraft was able to overfly parts of the prison, land on the sports field for the twenty seconds or so needed to load its illicit cargo and make off without effective challenge, was proof – if proof were needed – that security at the dispersal prisons was not all that it should be. Twelve months later a secure escort van carrying three Category A and one Category B offenders, was damaged by an internal explosion set off by one of the prisoners. This was clearly part of an escape plot and the van, which remained driveable, diverted to a police station compound and the occupants were secured. These two incidents resulted in a number of improvements in both physical and procedural security throughout the high-security estate. This did much to reassure those concerned about the state of security, especially in the dispersal prisons.

For a while attention was turned to other parts of the prison estate, however in April 1990 there was then the worst riot ever to take place in an English prison. For 25 days prisoners rampaged through Manchester's Strangeways Prison causing both considerable anxiety to the public and extensive physical damage to the establishment. Interestingly, although things were tense for a while, there were no reported serious incidents in other dispersal prisons which could be attributed to the Srangeways riot. This underlines the position often ascribed to dispersal prisoners: they see themselves as distinct from other prisoners and having a different set of interests.

In July 1991 attention again switched back to security when two prisoners on remand for alleged terrorist offences escaped from Brixton Prison using smuggled firearms. This was a shocking event which, although technically not an escape from a dispersal prison, clearly brought into question the efficiency of the whole high-security estate. Around this time the Prison Service was managing needed changes prior to it becoming a 'Next Steps' agency. New managerialist techniques and processes, especially the devolution of responsibilities outward from central Headquarters, were required so that proper accountability through the organisation, in preparation for seeking improved service delivery, could be ensured. It has been argued that this diverted senior managers' attention away from operational matters and allowed them to accept poor physical and procedural security and other shortcomings. Whatever the truth of this criticism, the escapes from Whitemoor and Parkhurst Prisons, three years later were to prove cataclysmic events for the Service. The armed escape from the special security unit at Whitemoor in September 1994 was undoubtedly the worst lapse of professional standards, causing a serious loss of confidence in the Service.

After the helicopter escape from Gartree, Mountbatten's security categories were reviewed. The highest category, A, was further subdivided to target resources better on those prisoners requiring extra security measures. 'Standard escape risk' continued to apply to the majority of Category A prisoners. Those requiring extra vigilance, within the normal dispersal regime, were henceforth categorised as 'high risk'. Those for whom current security intelligence indicated the very highest level of security was needed – and there are very few of these in the system at any one time – were to be categorised as 'exceptional risk' and held in one of the small special security units located in several of the dispersal prisons. These are, in effect, secure prisons within secure prisons, which was why the seriousness of the Whitemoor escape and its embarrassment were so acute. Sir John Woodcock, appointed to enquire into the escape, criticised specific procedures at Whitemoor and pointed to problems in the Prison Service generally, in particular with regard to security (Woodcock 1994). This caused the then Home Secretary, Michael Howard, who accepted all of Woodcock's recommendations, to announce a comprehensive review of security throughout the Service.

As the review team, under General Sir John Learmont, was being established the news broke that three prisoners, two of them Category A, had escaped from Parkhurst Prison. Learmont's terms of reference were immediately extended to include an inquiry into the escape. The report of the Inquiry again raised the question of whether all high-security-risk prisoners should be concentrated in one establishment with Learmont concluding that they should (Learmont 1995). These recommendations were not acted upon but one, which brought the management of the high-security estate under a single director, was.

Following the escapes from Whitemoor and Parkhurst the Service rapidly focused its attention on the need to improve security. Both the Woodcock and Learmont Reports pointed to numerous weaknesses and, even while the latter was being written, radical steps were taken to prevent further high-profile escapes. The resources of the Service were galvanised into action to review physical and

Table 8.1: Numbers of prisoners in the high-security estate, 1999

Prison	Category A			CNA[1] 1999
	Standard risk	High risk	Exceptional risk	
Belmarsh[2]	55	15	–	833
Frankland	117	13	–	558
Full Sutton	158	21	–	602
Long Larton	79	1	–	456
Wakefield	71	1	–	743
Whitemoor	168	14	3	522

[1] CNA = Certified Normal Accommodation, which is the capacity for prisoners of all categories.

[2] Though strictly not a dispersal prison, Belmarsh is part of the Directorate because of its special role.

Source: HM Prison Service 1999

procedural security and a massive investment programme was planned to recruit more staff and install the equipment needed to correct the shortcomings. The effects of this effort were felt in all establishments, but most especially those holding Category A prisoners. The number of local prisons, which contain those awaiting court appearances, authorised to hold provisional Category A prisoners was reduced from over 30 to ten. One of these, Belmarsh, a modern prison with secure access to a court, became an especially important part of the high-security estate, holding those accused of terrorist and other very serious offences, and awaiting trial.

Dispersal prisons: security, regimes and skill

Dispersal prisons are characterised, as was the intention of the Radzinowicz Committee, by a strong emphasis on perimeter security. This means that each has a wall and an inner fence protected by electronic devices, closed-circuit television cameras and floodlights. They are patrolled inside and out by dog teams, and have specially equipped vehicles able to deal speedily with threats to security. All visitors and staff are routinely searched before entering dispersal prisons and there are both targeted (that is, intelligence-informed) and random searches of people leaving. One feature of some dispersal prisoners is that they glean information about staff, regular visitors and their families and then use this to apply pressure

A specially trained operational support grade officer watches activities on a monitor in the prison control room. Most prisons employ closed-circuit security cameras to monitor high-risk arears.

to achieve their illicit ends. Searching, therefore, is done not only to detect those who wilfully traffick with prisoners but also to protect the unwilling victims of prisoner exploitation and threats.

Life inside a dispersal prison is not dramatically different to that in other prisons. Staffing levels are generally higher because of the nature of the population, but not oppressively so. Dispersals have to provide high security but they also have a training function: the aim always is to generate an environment in which this work can be effective. Especially important are the research-based offending behaviour programmes that contribute to the Home Office aim of reducing crime. These subject some of the most dangerous violent and sex offenders to intensive and challenging courses aimed specifically at reducing the chances of them committing further crimes on release. The regimes in dispersal prisons also provide for work, education and some recreational activities in order to promote a balanced lifestyle and assist prisoners to prepare for release. The movement of prisoners between the different activities is carefully controlled and, as a consequence, there is a greater emphasis on searching them than in other types of prison. Staff and prisoners occupy the same physical spaces, mixing together in workshops, classrooms and other areas of association. Because of this staff are able to use interpersonal skills to develop positive relationships with prisoners, which is the most effective way of controlling the difficult dispersal population. More often than not staff are able to defuse potentially dangerous situations before they get out of hand. Great skill and no small amount of courage is required for a member of staff, unarmed and outnumbered, to calm down angry long-term prisoners. It is, however, something that occurs quite often.

Dispersal prisons have undoubtedly been one of the success stories of the Prison Service since 1995. Generally speaking, they are controlled and ordered places providing a positive training environment for long-term prisoners. The potential within them for things to go dramatically wrong will always be extremely high because of the type of prisoners they hold, many of them for a very long time. Their management requires great skill in order that the demands of security are kept in balance with prisoners' needs. Staff have to exercise considerable professionalism to control prisoners with firmness and simultaneously ensure their human rights are not violated. To a great extent this has been achieved and the policy of dispersal vindicated.

References

Advisory Council on the Penal System (1968) *The Regime for Long-term Prisoners in Conditions of Maximum Security* (The Radzinowicz Report), HMSO

Control Review Committee (1984) *Managing the Long-term Prison System*, HMSO

Gladstone, H. (1895) *Report of the Departmental Committee on Prisons* (The Gladstone Report), C 7702, HMSO

HM Chief Inspector of Prisons (1977) *Report of an Inquiry [. . .] into the Cause and Circumstances of the Events at HM Prison Hull During the Period 31st August to 3rd September 1976*, Cm 453 HMSO

HM Prison Service (1999) *Annual Report and Accounts, April 1998 – March 1999*, The Stationery Office

Home Office (1999) *Prison Statistics England and Wales 1998*, Cm 4430, The Stationery Office

King, R.D. and Elliott, K.W. (1977) *Albany: Birth of a Prison – End of an Era*, Routledge & Kegan Paul

Learmont, Gen. Sir J. (1995) *Review of Prison Service Security in England and Wales and the Escape from Parkhurst Prison on Tuesday 3rd January 1995* (The Learmont Inquiry), Cm 3020, HMSO

Mountbatten, Earl (1966) *Report of the Inquiry into Prison Escapes and Security* (The Mountbatten Report), HMSO

Woodcock, Sir J. (1994) *The Escape from Whitemoor Prison on Friday 9th September 1994* (The Woodcock Inquiry), Cm 2741, HMSO

9

LIFE-SENTENCE PRISONERS

Rachel Jones

Background

Life imprisonment is the most severe penal sanction that can be imposed in those countries which either do not have, or do not choose to apply, the death penalty. The European Convention on Human Rights (ECHR) outlaws the death penalty in peacetime and provides that detention after conviction should be by the order of a competent court. The Convention does not refer directly to life-sentence prisoners, but judgements of the European Court of Human Rights have recognised the legitimacy of the sentence. The term 'life sentence', however, is an ambiguous one, which has different meanings in different countries (United Nations 1996, p. 1). Few life sentences mean that the prisoner will be incarcerated for the remainder of his or her life.

Life sentences have a symbolic significance in the mind of the public. They are likely to be regarded as appropriate retributive punishment for those who have committed the most serious crimes. The imposition of a life sentence is often seen as reflecting national opinion on the seriousness of such crimes. One consequence of this symbolic function of the life sentence is that individual prisoners serving life may find their sentence extended or release postponed by the executive in response to public opinion many years after the commission of the original crime. Some researchers have suggested that the treatment of life-sentence prisoners is often the public showcase of political drives to be seen to be tough on crime (Cavadino and Dignan 1997, p. 159).

Life-sentence prisoners are often the subject of much press attention and speculation, which is frequently couched in emotive terms. For example, when the Prison Service was rumoured to be discussing the reintroduction of escorted absences for life-sentence prisoners, the *Daily Express*, under the headline 'Trips to the shops for jail lifers' wrote; 'Murderers and rapists serving life are to be offered shopping trips in an easing of jail rules' (*Daily Express*, 1 November 1997).

Life-sentence prisoners often experience a greater degree of social isolation than other prisoners.

Despite this media interest, however, there are comparatively few studies on life-sentence prisoners and little published material, with the exception of a recently published book by Eric Cullen and Tim Newell, *Murderers and Life Imprisonment* (1999).

Research also indicates that life-sentence prisoners may often experience a far greater degree of isolation from society than other prisoners. Many experience the breakup of relationships and lose family and community contact with the outside world. They are sometimes seen as model prisoners, which is viewed by some as a symptom of their institutionalisation. Prison systems, therefore, look for ways of managing 'lifers' that encourage them to face up to the crimes they have committed and help them to deal with their social dislocation.

The United Nations argues that life sentences should only be imposed on offenders who have committed the most serious crimes, and only when absolutely necessary for the protection of society. It recommends that, wherever possible, prisoners should be involved in the release process and that they should have the right of appeal against decisions made about them. The UN also argues that all prisoners serving life imprisonment should have the eventual possibility of release (United Nations 1996, Annex A).

Offences and sentencing

There has been a sometimes uneven increase in the number of the life-sentence prisoners since 1957 when life imprisonment for some murders was introduced in place of the death penalty. In that year there were 140 prisoners serving life (3% of the sentenced population). This rose to 730 in 1970 (3% of the total prison population); 1,129 in 1975 (3%); 1,584 in 1980 (4%); 2,051 in 1985 (5%); 2,795 in 1990 (8%); and 3,192 in 1994 (9%). Figure 9.1 shows the increase between 1986 and 1998. Although having a lower homicide rate than many of the countries of western Europe, England and Wales has more life-sentence prisoners than that region as a whole (Penal Affairs Consortium 1996, p. 1).

In 1997 in England and Wales there were 738 cases initially reported as homicides, and while 88 of these were later re-recorded as natural or accidental deaths, the total remained the highest total this century. There has been a steady increase in recordable homicides over the past ten years. The overall rise has been 1.7% as compared to 6.9% for all serious crimes. In 1997 the homicide rate was 1.4 per 100,000 in England and Wales (Home Office 1998a, para. 4.1).

Figure 9.1: Population of life-sentence prisoners, 1986–98

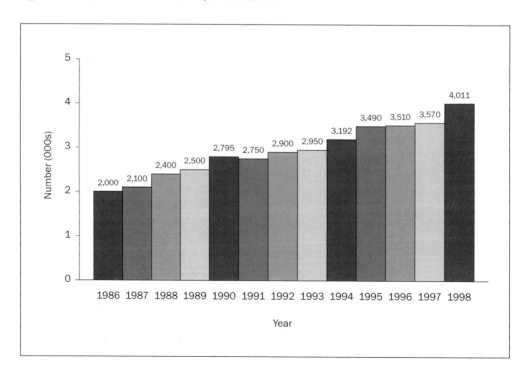

The life sentence is the only sentence available to the courts in the case of a conviction for murder. Thus the homicide and resultant conviction rate directly affects the life-sentence population. In November 1998 there were 4,011 prisoners serving life sentences in England and Wales. Of these, 3,206 were serving sentences of mandatory life and 805 serving discretionary life (Home Office 1998a). Women and young prisoners made up only a small proportion of this number, which reflects their overall numbers in the prison system. Women prisoners, for example, made up only 4.8% of the total prison population. In that year, approximately 7% of women in prison were serving life sentences (120 in 1997), as opposed to 8% of men.

The life sentence is imposed in three different ways in England and Wales, as can be seen from Table 9.1. The mandatory life sentence for murder in England and Wales was substituted for death as the mandatory penalty in some cases of murder by the Homicide Act 1957, and in all murder cases by the Murder (Abolition of the Death Penalty) Act 1965. It represents one of the few cases in sentencing in England and Wales where the discretion of the judge has been confined by statute.

There has been some criticism of the mandatory life sentence in England and Wales. The voluntary organisation Justice suggests that:

- it does not allow a judge to form his or her own opinion of the crime;
- it is inflexible and unfair; and
- does not allow for differentiation between different types of murder (Justice 1996, p. 29).

A number of other arguments have been made for the life sentence to be the maximum and not the mandatory sentence for murder. The report of the Butler Committee on Mentally Abnormal Offenders (1975) pointed out that some offences of manslaughter could be more culpable than some murders with mitigating circumstances. They quoted Lord Kilbrandon in the case of *Hyam* who suggested that, 'It is no longer true, if it ever were true, to say that murder as we now define it is necessarily the most heinous example of unlawful homicide' (Parliamentary All-Party Penal Affairs Group 1987, p. 3). A change to the mandatory life sentence has also been recommended by:

- the Advisory Council on the Penal System (1978);
- the Parliamentary All-Party Penal Affairs Group (1986);
- the House of Lords Select Committee on Murder and Life Imprisonment (1989); and
- the Independent Committee on the Penalty for Homicide, chaired by Lord Case in 1993.

Table 9.1: Imposition of a life sentence in England and Wales

Crimes	Maximum custodial sentence
Murder	**Mandatory life sentences** • Life imprisonment (over 21) • Custody for life (18–21 at the time the offence was committed) • Her Majesty's pleasure (under 18 at the time of the offence)
Manslaughter, attempted murder, armed robbery, arson, rape or other serious sexual offences, kidnapping, wounding with intent, causing an explosion	**Discretionary life sentences** • Life imprisonment (over 21) • Custody for life (18–21 at the time of the offence) • Detention for life (Section 53(2), Children and Young Persons Act 1933) (under 18 at the time of the offence)
Second violent or serious offence committed after 1.10.97 of: murder, manslaughter, wounding or GBH with intent, rape and attempted rape, intercourse with a girl under 13, and various firearms offences	**Automatic life sentence/** **Section 2 discretionary life** Judicial discretion to impose a life sentence under the Criminal Justice Act 1997

Other non-governmental organisations (NGOs) such as the Penal Affairs Consortium continue to argue for a change in both the mandatory sentence itself and the continued involvement of the executive. They argue that the mandatory life sentence produces serious distortions in criminal proceedings as jurors often try to bring in diminished responsibility verdicts to enable the trial judge to show humanity. They suggest that this leads to dubious manslaughter convictions. They put forward the case of the Australian State of Victoria, where the life sentence became discretionary in 1986, and the number of guilty pleas in murder cases increased (Penal Affairs Consortium 1996, p. 5).

Tariff setting

Those in favour of the system counter with the argument that the judgement on the seriousness of the crime is made at the tariff-setting stage, and that any change in the mandatory life sentence would be seen as symptomatic of a government 'going soft' on law and order. In the case of mandatory lifers it is the Home Secretary who decides what the 'tariff' should be. This is the minimum time that the life-sentence prisoner should serve in the interest of retribution and deterrence before he or she is eligible to apply for conditional release. It does not take into account the risk of reoffending or public acceptability, which are both examined at the pre-release stage. In 1984 Leon Britton, then Home Secretary, introduced a minimum qualifying period of twenty years for certain types of murder, including the murder of police and prison officers, terrorist murders, the sexual or sadistic murder of children and murder by firearm in the case of robbery (Maguire et al. 1994).

In 1993, Michael Howard, then Conservative Home Secretary, created a category of 'whole life' prisoners who were informed that they would probably never be released. He put into practice a review for such prisoners after they had served a minimum of 25 years and at five-year intervals thereafter (Cavadino and Dignan 1997, p. 170). Myra Hindley, one of the so-called 'Moors Murderers', is an example of this type of prisoner. In a recent judgement by the Court of Appeal her application for judicial review of the 'whole life' tariff was dismissed. The grounds for appeal were that the tariff had been set retrospectively, and that it left her with no hope of parole. The court held that the fixing of a 'whole life' tariff was not unlawful, but that a fixed tariff could not be increased in the absence of new circumstances. This judgement also affects other 'whole life' tariff prisoners such as Dennis Nilson and Rosemary West. During the ruling Lord Chief Justice Bingham opined that he would prefer a determinate sentence for lifers saying, 'I think, risk apart, that it is not for a man to stigmatise any fellow citizen as irredeemable' (*Independent*, 10 November 1998).

In setting the tariff for mandatory lifers the Home Secretary gives consideration to the recommendation of the trial judge and the Lord Chief Justice, but is not bound by them. The Home Secretary's tariffs have often been higher than the recommendation of the trial judge. Between August 1990 and July 1993, ministers considered 806 mandatory life-sentence tariffs. In 409 cases they set a period that agreed with that of the trial judge, a period that accorded with the Lord Chief Justice in 244 cases, and a period between the recommendations of both in 38 cases. In 112 cases ministers set a period higher than the recommendation of both the trial judge and the Lord Chief Justice. Three prisoners did not receive tariffs as they successfully appealed against conviction before the tariff could be set (Penal Affairs Consortium 1996, p. 6). More recently however, more tariffs have been set within the judicial recommendation. In the nineteen months up to November 1998, twelve out of the 427 tariffs set were above either judicial recommendation.

In 1993, in *R. v. Secretary of State for the Home Department, ex parte Smartt, Pegg, Doody and Pierson*, it was held that mandatory life-sentence prisoners were entitled to be told the recommendations of the judiciary and to make informed representations on the tariff to be set. Prior to this ruling the process was conducted in secret (Maguire et al. 1994, p. 279). Most prisoners were able to estimate their tariff, however, as the first Parole Board review date was set at three years before their tariff expired.

Some problems identified with the tariff-setting process for mandatory lifers have been defined as:

- the involvement of the executive in the person of the Home Secretary;
- the retrospective increase of tariffs;
- the absence of appeal against the tariff; and
- the delay in setting it.

A Home Affairs Select Committee report in December 1995 concluded that the mandatory life sentence should be retained, but that responsibility for setting the tariff and for taking decisions on release should be taken from the hands of the executive: 'It is wrong in principle for the executive (that is, politicians) to have a role in decisions which effectively determine how long a prisoner subject to a mandatory life sentence remains in prison.' They suggested that as ministers set the tariff without hearing the arguments in court, this went against the principles of natural justice (Penal Affairs Consortium 1996, p. 6).

Discretionary life sentencing

Not all life sentences are the result of a conviction for murder, however. In the case of discretionary lifers a judge may impose a life sentence, but is not obliged to do so, if he or she believes that a certain type of crime is serious enough to merit it, or that the offender is a serious danger to the public. The 1997 Criminal Justice Act introduced a new category of discretionary lifers, known as Section 2 discretionaries, where a judge can impose a life sentence for a second serious or violent crime, unless there are exceptional circumstances. The case of *R. v. Kelly*, heard on appeal in the High Court on 5 December 1998, established that it would be very difficult to find grounds for 'exceptional circumstances' except in bizarre cases (Padfield and Percival 1999).

When the proposal to introduce this second discretionary life sentence was made in 1995, critics argued that it, along with new compulsory minimum sentences for burglars and repeat sex offenders, might raise the prison population by as many as 28,000 if fully implemented. A dramatic rise has not occurred to date and the new sentence has only been imposed in a small number of cases. Critics continue to use the example from the United States where the 'three strikes and you're out' legislation has caused the prison population to rise. Further, they point to Jerry Williams, a US citizen, who in 1995 was sentenced to life for stealing a slice of pizza, as an example of the compulsory 'strikes and out' policy gone wrong (Cavadino and Dignan 1997, p. 174). Mr Williams was later freed on appeal.

Discretionary life-sentence prisoners make up only a small part of the overall life-sentence population. The percentage of prisoners serving discretionary life sentences was under 20% of the total life-sentence prisoner population in 1996 (Home Office 1998b, p. 114). Figures 9.2 and 9.3 give a breakdown of the offences committed by female and male life-sentence prisoners.

Figure 9.2: Population of female life-sentence prisoners by offence, 1996

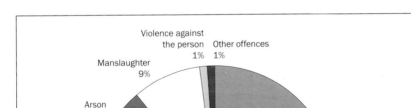

Figure 9.3: Population of male life-sentence prisoners by offence, 1996

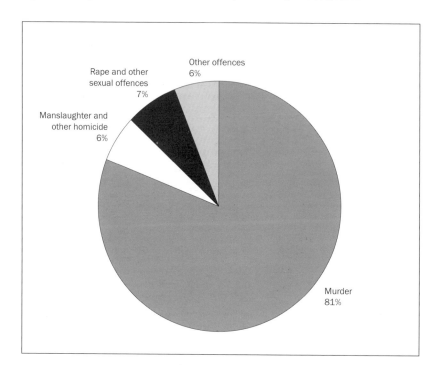

In discretionary and Section 2 cases the tariff-setting procedures are different from those for mandatory lifers. In these cases 'tariff' is used to describe the relevant part of the sentence determined by the trial judge to reflect the seriousness of the offence, that should be served in the interests of retribution and deterrence. This is set in open court at the time of sentencing. Both the sentence and the tariff can be subject to appeal, in accordance with the Criminal Justice Act 1993 and a Practice Direction issued by the Lord Chief Justice in 1993. In England and Wales it is expected that there will be a number of appeals against the automatic life sentence under the European Convention on Human Rights, while the specified period set to be served can be relatively low.

Prison practice

In England and Wales all life-sentence prisoners, while having a managerial input from the establishment level, are also centrally managed for some important functions by the Lifer Review Unit (LRU) – responsible for tariff setting for mandatory lifers and the review process for all lifers, and by the Lifer Management

Unit (LMU) – which handles management and allocation. Both are based in London.

Life-sentence prisoners are initially allocated to some kind of closed establishment, sometimes depending on a needs assessment. A male life-sentence prisoner will remain in a local prison until space is found for him at one of the main centres – Gartree, Long Lartin, Wakefield, Wormwood Scrubs and Brixton (in the case of shorter-term lifers). He will then be transferred there and be held usually for three to four years in Category A or B conditions. Gartree is an all-lifer prison for main centre and Category B prisoners; Kingston is an all-lifer Category B prison. In other establishments lifers are either integrated into the main prisoner population or held in separate wings. This practice allows for a comprehensive assessment of the life-sentence prisoner and the drawing up of a detailed sentence-management plan.

Most female prisoners serving life are classified as suitable for either open or closed conditions (unless classified as Category A) but all female lifers will go to a closed establishment at the start of their sentence. Although they will be held in a local prison to begin with, due to the small number of establishments holding women prisoners, this prison will often not be 'local' to the prisoner herself (HM Chief Inspector of Prisons 1997, p. 17). There are two main centres for women lifers, at Durham and Bulwood Hall Prisons. There are four defined second-stage establishments. Like their male counterparts, women lifers will spend about three years in the main centre.

For male young offenders serving life or its equivalent there are four long-term young offender institutions (YOIs), equivalent to the adult main centre: Aylesbury, Castington, Moorlands and Swinfen Hall. Those who start their sentence under the age of 18 will normally remain in the childcare system until transfer to the prison system at 18, and must be transferred to the adult system before their 22nd birthday. Lifers under the age of 18 may be held in YOIs if they are assessed as requiring this type of accommodation and supervision. A training plan will be drawn up at the main centre equivalent and this will be confirmed at the six-month stage. It covers personal training and remedial needs, including the concerns and risks that need to be dealt with, as well as the means of dealing with them.

Lifers with mental disorders remain subject to their life sentence upon any transfer to a special hospital, but they will not be recategorised or considered for release until transferred back into the custody of the Prison Service, the Mental Health Act taking precedence over the Criminal Justice Act.

Managing the life sentence

The sentence management system is central to decisions made about prisoners, and this is particularly true of those serving life. The process of planning the life sentence is begun at the main centre with a risk assessment, which identifies the needs of the prisoner through an examination of factors such as offence history; family and background; employment history; specific offence-related risk factors such as anger, drink and drugs; as well as reports from the police, probation services and the courts. Contributions will also come from within the establishment, for example from the education department, psychiatrist, medical officer or chaplain. From this the life-sentence plan will be drawn up, recording the risk factors, needs and offending behaviour to be addressed and the means of addressing them. A prisoner with a particular addiction problem, for example, will therefore be enabled to tackle it by allocation to a suitable prison establishment. The prisoner is closely involved in this process with his personal officer, who is a basic grade prison officer.

The life-sentence plan has three parts:

- the initial assessment, completed within three months of arriving at the main centre;
- the review of evidence for predicted risk behaviour; and
- the pre-transfer report and final review reports.

The sentence plan includes an assessment of risk based on both qualitative and quantitative analysis and, with the assistance of a computer, a risk predictor. The overriding consideration in the process of risk assessment is the protection of the public. In terms of prison categorisation, the assessment is based on the likelihood of a prisoner making an effort to escape, and the consequent risk to the public if he or she were to do so. The process, therefore, concentrates on factors that might threaten public safety such as criminal history and lifestyle.

While the initial plan is drawn up at the main centre, and the prisoner starts work on his objectives there, it is designed to be a 'live' document that will travel with the prisoner for the whole of his or her time in custody. A 'typical' male life-sentence prisoner will go through nearly all the different categories of prison in the system: local prison on remand and immediately post-sentence, the main centre, a Category B training prison or a dispersal or both, a Category C prison and, normally not more than three years from the first Parole Board review, a Category D resettlement prison or a pre-release hostel. Particular needs for lifers will be addressed at a defined time in a specified prison. For example, all lifers who have committed a sexual offence are assessed at an early stage for the sex offender treatment programme and, if found suitable, will proceed straight from the main centre to an establishment that offers this. Much of a lifer's offending behaviour work will be started in a Category B prison, and he may be held in one or more Category B prisons. He will have to show significant progress before a move to Category C conditions. Once transferred to Category C, the offence-related work continues but the focus changes towards preparation for release on licence. The period in Category C conditions also provides facilities for supervised outside activities. In a Category D prison the purpose of the stay is to test the lifer in more challenging conditions before the move to a pre-release employment scheme or a resettlement prison prior to release. The sentence-management process is, therefore, fundamental to what a lifer may do during his or her sentence.

Most courses identified for lifers are related to their offence and personal problems, for example alcohol and drugs awareness and treatment, anger control, offending behaviour, or reasoning and thinking skills. The Prison Service is moving towards a system of accredited courses that are delivered uniformly throughout the system (see Chapter 18). Few of the offence-related courses are lifer-specific, but usually there is priority given to lifers. There are also pre-release courses. These are of particular importance since, as noted earlier, life-sentence prisoners often experience a high degree of isolation from the rest of society.

All convicted prisoners in England and Wales are required to work (see Chapter 17). Work opportunities vary, but there are workshops and other work available in all lifer establishments. Many of these opportunities are linked to educational and vocational qualifications. Lifers have the same educational opportunities as other prisoners, with a large variety available at all ability levels.

Reviewing progress

Authority for progress throughout the system is given at different stages by different parts of the organisation. If a lifer is a Category A prisoner then his move to Category B will be on the authority of the Prison Service security committee. The move from a Category B to C prison is decided by the LMU. Any move to an open prison must be recommended by the Parole Board and is subject to ministerial approval.

During this process, which is not automatic, a life-sentence prisoner may be subject to the following types of review:

- an annual internal review by the lifer board within the prison;
- a review for Category A prisoners;

- an interim F75 (lifer sentence plan) review requested by the Parole Board and the LMU every three years;
- a Parole Board review;
- an automatic ten-year review by ministers; and
- a ministerial review at the 25-year point of 'whole life' tariffs and at five-year intervals thereafter.

A number of reports will be compiled for each review, containing contributions from prison staff, instructors, teachers and medical staff as well as the home probation officer. These reports are intended to concentrate on the degree to which the lifer has addressed his or her offending behaviour or other targets identified in the sentence plan. Each prison has a governor grade, responsible for life-sentence prisoners, who co-ordinates such reports and is often the first point of contact for Headquarters staff. Unsatisfactory reports can mean that the lifer will not move to a lower category, and it is possible that some lifers will never progress to an open prison.

A risk and individual assessment will also be conducted on the prisoner if he or she applies for a period of temporary release on licence. These licences might allow a lifer to work outside a prison or attend external rehabilitation meetings. (They should not be confused with the life licence, which is discussed below.) In

A review board examining a prisoner's progress within the establishment. In attendance are a governor grade and staff from the prisoner's wing, including his personal officer.

the case of temporary release, the majority of applications will come from lifers in open prisons. Eligibility is calculated as follows:

- those with a provisional release date can apply for all the different types of licence (compassionate, facility and resettlement) after a minimum of four months in an open prison, and having completed supervised outside activities; and
- those in open conditions without a provisional release date may apply for a facility or compassionate licence after six months, and a resettlement licence after nine months.

Temporary licence applications are considered within the prison at a board chaired by a governor grade, and first applications must be approved by Prison Service Headquarters. Release on licence can assist lifers in making the transition back into their community and family.

Release and recall

A life sentence is wholly indeterminate: there is no entitlement to release. Prisoners may, however, be considered for release on life licence. In the case of mandatory lifers, release may only be authorised by the Home Secretary on the recommendation of the Parole Board, and after consultation with the Lord Chief Justice and the trial judge, if available. The Home Secretary is not obliged, however, to follow the Parole Board's recommendation. In recent years the number of release applications made by mandatory lifers but rejected by the Home Secretary has risen. The probability of a life-sentence prisoner being released after a positive review dropped from 1:3 in 1980 to 1:5 in 1997 (Cavadino and Dignan 1997, p. 195).

The procedure for the release of discretionary lifers is different. After the prisoner has served the 'relevant part' recommended by the trial judge, he or she can require the Home Secretary to refer the case to a discretionary lifer panel (DLP) under the remit of the Parole Board. This procedure was introduced by the Criminal Justice Act (CJA) 1991 for discretionary lifers and extended by the Crime (Sentences) Act 1997 to cover those sentenced to automatic life sentences under Section 2 of the former Act and to detainees at Her Majesty's pleasure. This panel then assesses whether it is necessary for the protection of the public for the prisoner to remain confined. If the DLP determines it is not necessary, it can direct the Home Secretary to release the prisoner on licence. Decisions are made by a majority of the panel and are recorded in writing, with reasons. The Home

Secretary has no power in these circumstances to reject the recommendation of the Parole Board.

In all cases, life-sentence prisoners will not be released until they satisfy the Parole Board and the Home Secretary (mandatory lifers) that they pose no risk to the public. Release procedures for lifers under 21 are the same as for adults.

The Home Secretary's release of mandatory lifers is usually subject to their spending a 6–9-month period in a pre-release employment-scheme hostel or a resettlement prison. To go there, mandatory lifers must have a provisional release date. Discretionary lifers may also be placed in either of these for a final period of testing before release is determined by a DLP. The purpose of the pre-release employment scheme is to:

- pose an important final test of the prisoner's suitability for release; and
- provide an opportunity for the lifer to readjust to normal life in the community and undertake or gain regular employment.

These schemes may be administered from a prison establishment or a hostel attached to a prison, with its own warden and liaison officer. Both will report on the lifer's progress to Prison Service Headquarters via the prison governor. Lifers can be returned to prison at any time during this period.

A prisoner practices his skills in machinery manufacture. The Prison Service aims to provide prisoners with employment skills that can be applied on release.

The average time spent in prison by lifers has risen over the years, and the average time to first release has more than doubled since 1940. Time served varies considerably. For those lifers received into custody between 1965 and 1983, 50% were still in custody 13 years after reception. Of those received between 1965 and 1976, 17% had not been released by the end of 1996, and had thus served at least 20 years. For those received by 1975 the median period before release on life licence was normally between 10 and 12 years. For those received between 1976 and 1980 this had increased to 14–16 years. The average time served by life-sentence prisoners has increased from 11.1 years in 1986 to 14.3 years in 1997 (Home Office 1998b, p. 117). Figure 9.4 illustrates the increase in the number of life-sentence prisoners by time served under sentence from 1975 to 1996.

Once a life-sentence prisoner has been released on a life licence he or she remains subject to that licence until death. All life-sentence prisoners have a supervising officer from the probation service, who reports on any progress made to Prison Service's Headquarters at pre-arranged intervals. The life-sentence prisoner will have had regular contact with the probation service, both inside and outside prison, during his or her sentence. The Prison and probation services work closely together in these cases so that informed assessments can be made, particularly in terms of risk. Lifers will have a number of conditions attached to their life licence. At the beginning the main ones will be regular contact with the probation service and regular residence at an approved address, but they could also include attendance at drug or alcohol rehabilitation meetings, etc. The conditions of

Figure 9.4: Population of life-sentence prisoners by time served under sentence

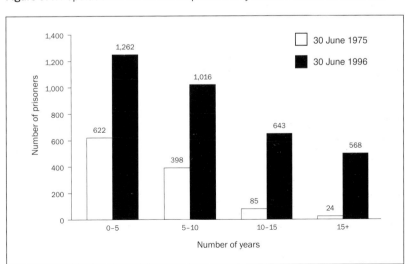

supervision may be cancelled after four years if all is well, on the authority of Prison Service Headquarters, but there will still be some contact with the supervising officer.

The life licensee remains subject to recall to prison at any time. This may be done on the recommendation of the Parole Board, but under Section 39(2) of the CJA 1991 the Home Secretary can also recall a lifer to custody without prior consultation. If a lifer is recalled then he or she must be immediately returned to prison and informed of the reason for recall. Recall may be based on drug or alcohol misuse, or because of a change in behaviour that gives cause for believing that the lifer would be a risk to the public. It may be authorised on the grounds of increased risk only, so it is not dependent on the life licensee having committed a criminal offence (Home Office 1998b, p. 118).

In all cases a review will be carried out by the Parole Board to decide whether the prisoner should remain in custody for the protection of the public. For mandatory lifers, if immediate re-release is not ordered, then the Home Secretary decides when the case should next be referred to the Parole Board. Any further applications for release on licence are then considered by him or her. In the case of discretionary lifers, a DLP will review applications in accordance with statutory requirements if immediate re-release is not ordered.

There have been some criticisms levied at the recall process, namely:

* the absence of a statutory test, the delay in reassessment; and
* the conditions for the re-release of mandatory lifers.

Others argue that since the crimes that have been committed to warrant the life sentence are so serious, recall procedures should be flexible enough to address the question of increased risk at an early stage (Justice 1996, p. 75). Comparatively few lifers go on to commit further serious crimes after release on licence. In England and Wales, only 9% of lifers released between 1972 and 1993 were reconvicted of a standard list offence within two years (Home Office 1998a, p. 118).

As HM Chief Inspectors of Prisons and Probation concluded in their 1999 review of life-sentence prisoners:

> The importance of work with lifers must be acknowledged due to the gravity of the offences, the lifelong consequences for victims and their families, the indeterminate nature of the sentence for lifers and the sense of responsibility experienced by staff working with them (HM Chief Inspector of Prisons 1999, p. 7).

Tables 9.2, 9.3 and 9.4 show the number and percentage of lifers sentenced, in prison and on supervision in the community in 1998. This relatively small percentage of the prison community garners both a raised level of public interest and a high degree of responsibility for those in the Service who deal with them.

Table 9.2: Life-sentence cases in lifer prisons (number and percentages of total), February 1998

	Male		Female		Total	
	No.	%	No.	%	No.	%
Mandatory						
Category A	216	6.2	2	0.1	218	6.3
Other categories	2,216	63.3	97	2.8	2,313	66.1
Total mandatory	**2,432**	**69.5**	**99**	**2.9**	**2,531**	**72.4**
Discretionary						
Category A	107	3.1	1	0.0	108	3.1
Other categories	472	13.5	15	0.4	487	13.9
Total discretionary	**579**	**16.6**	**16**	**0.4**	**595**	**17.0**
Detention during HMP and other sentenced as young person (under 21)						
Category A	13	0.4	0	0.0	13	0.4
Other categories	352	10.0	12	0.3	364	10.3
Total	**365**	**10.4**	**12**	**0.3**	**377**	**10.7**
Total life-sentence prisoners in lifer prisoners						
Category A	336	9.6	3	0.1	339	9.7
Other categories	3,040	86.8	124	3.5	3,164	90.3
Total	**3,376**	**96.4**	**127**	**3.6**	**3,503**	**100.0**

Source: HM Chief Inspector of Prisons 1999

Table 9.3: Life-sentence prisoners in local prisons (percentages of total), March 1998

	Male	Female	Total
Provisional Category A	4.1	0.0	4.1
Other categories	85.7	10.2	95.9
Total	**89.8**	**10.2**	**100.0**

Source: HM Chief Inspector of Prisons 1999

Table 9.4: Life-sentence cases subject to supervision in the community (percentages of total), February 1998

	Male	Female	Total
Adult mandatory	60.6	3.6	64.2
Adult discretionary	15.3	0.5	15.8
Detention during HMP and other sentenced as young person (under 21)	19.8	0.2	20.0
Total life-sentence cases currently subject to supervision	**95.7**	**4.3**	**100.0**

Source: HM Chief Inspector of Prisons 1999

References

Cavadino, M. and Dignan, J. (1997) *The Penal System: An Introduction*, Sage

Cullen, E. and Newell, T. (1999) *Murderers and Life Imprisonment*, Winchester: Waterside Press

HM Chief Inspector of Prisons (1997) *Women in Prison: A Thematic Review*, Home Office/Stationery Office

— (1999) *Lifers: A Joint Thematic Review by HM Inspectorates of Prisons and Probation*, Home Office/The Stationery Office

Home Office (1998a) *Statistical Bulletin: Criminal Statistics 1996/7*, HMSO

— (1998b) *Statistical Bulletin: Prison Statistics in England and Wales 1996*, HMSO

Justice (1996) *Sentenced to Life: Reform of the Law and Procedure for those Sentenced to Life Imprisonment*, Justice

Maguire, M., Morgan, R. and Reiner, R. (eds) (1994) *The Oxford Handbook of Criminology*, (2nd edition), Oxford: Clarendon Press

Padfield, N. and Percival, R. (eds) (1999) *Archbold News*, (February), Sweet and Maxwell

Parliamentary All-Party Penal Affairs Group (1987) *Life Sentence Prisoners*, Home Office/The Stationery Office

Penal Affairs Consortium (1996) *The Mandatory Life Sentence: Submissions by the PAC to the House of Commons Home Affairs Committee in December 1994 and January 1996*, PAC

United Nations (1996) *The Life Sentence: Report of the Criminal Justice Branch of UNOV*, Geneva: United Nations

Newspaper articles
Daily Express (1 November 1997) 'Trips to the shops for jail lifers'

Independent (10 November 1998) law report

The author gratefully acknowledges the assistance offered by the Prison Service Lifer Management Unit in the writing of this article. Any errors are the responsibility of the author.

10

WOMEN IN PRISON
Sally Swift

Women represent only a small minority of the prison population, and this is true on both a global and a national scale. At January 2000, in England and Wales, there were 3,240 female prisoners, which represented 5.1% of the prison population. Such relatively small numbers create problems both for imprisoned women and for those responsible for their care. There are also difficulties caused by the fact that imprisoned women have a different profile to that of men. Their profile is comprised of offences, length of sentence, previous history of imprisonment, responsibilities before and after imprisonment and a number of other related issues. For example, there are comparatively fewer woman in the youngest and oldest age groups, as compared to men.

Incarcerated women – facts and figures

While the numbers of incarcerated women represent a small percentage of the overall prison population that percentage has rapidly increased. The average annual female population in 1991 was 1,559 (3.5% of the total population) but by 1998 this had risen to 3,110 (4.8%), an increase of 99% in seven years (Home Office 1999). This rise has meant that there has had to be a corresponding increase in the number of female prisons: from nine in 1994 to twelve in 1999. There is no even geographical spread and some women, despite there being more prisons, will continue to be held many miles from their home area. The long-term trend also seems to indicate that the female population will continue to rise.

The main offences for which women are **received** into prison are theft and handling (38%), drugs (17%) and violence against the person (11%). However, because of differences in sentence lengths, patterns of offences for the population differs from that of receptions. The largest group amongst the sentenced population is for drug offences (35%), with violent offences representing 19% and theft and handling 17%. These statistics are rather different compared to the persistent image of prisons housing women who have mainly defaulted on fines or were shoplifters. Indeed, the numbers of fine-defaulters continues to diminish, with the average daily population (ADP) being only five in the first half of 1998.

Women are less likely to be remanded in custody during proceedings at magistrates courts; however, this partly reflects the differences in the types of offences they commit. Amongst those who are remanded, 69% will either receive a community sentence or be discharged; only 31% will receive a custodial sentence (Home Office 1998). Fines and custody are less likely to be the disposal for women, for example women shoplifters are less likely to receive a custodial sentence than comparable men. However, because the range of penalties is narrower, some women end up with a less severe sentence while others will get a more severe one (Home Office 1997). Women do serve shorter sentences than men, with 71% of women in 1997 serving sentences of up to one year in length.

A higher percentage of incarcerated women, 20%, are African or Afro-Caribbean, with 45% of that group being foreign nationals (Home Office 1998). These women are mostly convicted of drug-related offences and help to account for some of the increase in the number of drug offences committed by women of all origins. The previous drug histories of men and women are also different. Mandatory drug tests within prison have shown that more women (6%) than men (4.9%) test positive for opiates, the comparable figures for benzodiazepines being 6% for women and 1.2% for men. Women are also much less likely to be cannabis users than men. These figures probably are indicative of the different patterns of drug use and misuse by women in the community.

Perhaps the most marked contrast between men and women in prison relates to childcare. Less than 25% of women reported that their children were being cared for by their spouse or partner, compared to 90% of men (HM Chief Inspector of Prisons 1997). Women also want to keep up family involvement during their time in prison and to continue their parental duties. This is often made more difficult by distance from home and is a particular problem for women serving life sentences. Such problems of keeping in contact with their children are exacerbated by the relative decline in the use of temporary release for women. While there has been an overall increase in the use of temporary release of 53% since 1993, the number of temporary releases for women has declined by 21%. This reflects a change in the rules regarding the use of temporary release and highlights how policy changes that are introduced to deal with perceived problems with male prisoners may have a different effect on female prisoners (a point that is examined in more detail later in this chapter).

Historical context

There have always been women in prison but until the early years of the 19th century there were few, if any, separate prisons for women. There were some exceptions and probably the first purpose-built prison for women was the Spinhuis in Amsterdam, which was opened in 1645. Over the entrance was carved the salutation:

> Fear not! I do not exact vengeance for evil, but compel you to be good.
> My hand is stern but my heart is kind.

However, for the majority of women, being in prison meant incarceration in a local prison, sharing unbelievably squalid accommodation with male prisoners and being guarded by male staff. This led, almost inevitably, to the sexual exploitation of the imprisoned women. Zedner (1994) cites the example of the Indiana State Prison in the United States, where women prisoners were forced into prostitution to provide sexual services for the male guards. Similarly, in 1829 at the central prison in Montpellier, France, several women were found to be pregnant in spite of having been in captivity for more than a year. In addition, women often had to endure much worse conditions than their male counterparts. For example, Canadian female prisoners in the late 19th century were kept altogether in one large open attic of the men's penitentiary in Kingston, Ontario, disdained as lazy and a disgrace to their sex (Faith 1993). Male prisoners at that time often had single cells.

Women convicted of more serious crimes and sentenced to transportation were often assumed to be prostitutes, or perhaps this was used to justify the sexual abuse that they suffered at the hands of male prisoners and the crew on board the ships taking them to the colonies. The treatment that women transportees received on arrival was often little better. Women were not free to refuse offers of employment and the so-called factory at Parramatta in New South Wales, to which newly arrived females were sent, quickly became a sort of brothel and marriage mart (Zedner 1994).

Improvement and 'reforms'

The intervention of middle-class women, such as Elizabeth Fry, brought about a relative improvement in the conditions for imprisoned women in England and Wales. There was also a certain amount of impetus for reform from those responsible for running prisons, who had realised that something needed to be done to resolve the scandal of prison pregnancies. Combined efforts resulted in the segregation of male and female prisoners: the Gaol Act 1823 (passed in England) required that men and women be held separately. Furthermore, women prisoners were to be looked after by female guards. Similar legislation was passed in other countries at around the same time. Unfortunately, the number of prisons made available specifically for women remained small, so the majority of places provided were in separate wings of male prisons. In some prisons this has remained the situation until recently, although Durham Prison is now the only establishment where women still occupy wings within a male prison, while Winchester and Highpoint Prisons hold women in separate areas.

Another relevant factor in this consideration of prison reform is the pedestal upon which Victorian men wished to place women. Although the position of working-class women, from whose ranks the majority of incarcerated women were drawn, was different to that of their more cosseted middle-class sisters, they still were expected to fit into the Victorian ideal of woman as wife and mother. Reformers were quite clear that the purpose of prison was to re-educate women into those values of femininity that they had lost – or, more probably, never acquired – so that they would be fit to fulfil their role in society as wives, mothers and domestic servants. Elizabeth Fry and her sisters saw themselves as examples to which incarcerated women would be able to aspire. Unfortunately, some of the incarcerated women seemed unable to appreciate this principle and continued to behave as they had always done. Indeed, over time Elizabeth Fry's work with incarcerated women became more focused on what Carlen (1998) refers to as a 'technology of reform', involving constant surveillance, the erasure of individuality and strict programmes of discipline. While this concern for control over the lives of those incarcerated was also a feature of male prisons, the form that it took in women's prisons could be said to be even more oppressive because women were being policed not just as individuals who had broken the law, but also as women who had become unfeminine.

While the desire for the separation of men and women showed some recognition of the differences between them it did so in a paternalistic way, to protect vulnerable women both from men and from themselves. However, because the system overall was run by men, and because women remained the minority of prisoners, there was a failure to recognise that the particular needs of women might require a different type of institution. Incarcerated women were still accommodated in a system designed and run primarily for men. As Carlen (1998) expresses it: 'Prison administrators and reformers, as well as many prison campaigners, have perennially found it difficult to think of women prisoners as being anything other than not men.' Prisons, in common with other total institutions, are, in general, run at the level of the lowest common denominator: it is difficult to make exceptions for minorities. While women have a higher rate of offences against discipline than men, they rarely indulge in acts of concerted indiscipline – the last major riot at a women's prison took place at Bullwood Hall in the mid-1970s. Thus, this relative passivity meant that incarcerated women were often overlooked, and this, in turn, affected the way that policy developed within the Prison Service. Policy formulation in relation to security and temporary release focused more on the requirements of the male population and took little account of the distinct needs of women prisoners.

The introduction of the incentives and earned privileges scheme was one example of catering for the majority of prisoners, and governors of women's prisons were left to make what sense of it they could. There was no consideration of women's childcare requirements or the need for flexibility in granting temporary release until the very last stages of policy preparation, when it was almost too late to change anything. This situation is now changing, following the creation of the Women's Policy Group at Prison Service Headquarters, but as yet there are few proposals to look at existing policy to see where changes could and should be made to make them more women-friendly. Governors of women's prisons receive no specific training for working with women and it is only recently that one area manager has been given responsibility for all female establishments.

Regimes for incarcerated women

Similar problems have affected the development of meaningful regimes for incarcerated women. Early regimes in the late 19th and early 20th centuries were geared towards domesticity and those skills seen as appropriate for women:

> They worked in association on rough sewing, bag-making, knitting, cooking, baking, and, of course, cleaning and laundering. At Brixton the laundry employed a hundred women in a large-scale enterprise, washing for convicts at Millbank and Pentonville prisons as well as for themselves. Considered to have failed in their natural role as wife and mother, the women were given a second opportunity to develop feminine attributes in the exercise of domestic service (Zedner 1994, p. 192).

Little changed until the 1970s when vocational courses were introduced for women prisoners. Where industrial work was supplied for women in prison it tended to be 'suitable' light work such as assembling and packing small toys, electrical fittings or cardboard boxes. In the 1960s, Holloway Prison was renowned for its jam factory. In a similar vein, training courses for women tended to concentrate on housewifery and maternal skills. The only vocational training course for female borstal trainees at Bullwood Hall in the 1970s and 1980s was in home economics.

It must, of course, be remembered that, until the Equal Opportunities Act 1976, women's prisons continued to be staffed solely by women. While policy continued to be made by Headquarters, female prison staff were left to get on with the job without too much interference from the centre. Many of these women in senior positions had come into prison work from other forms of social work and brought with them the sense of vocation which, for career women of earlier generations, had been essential. They carried with them, consciously or unconsciously, the role-model ideals of Fry and her cohorts and this was reflected in the way that they managed their establishments. Miss Elsie Hooker, governor of East Sutton Park from the late 1940s until 1964, ran her establishment very much as a public school. Staff were expected to centre their social life around the prison and to involve prisoners in any outings to the cinema. She also held open days and encouraged old girls to return to show off husbands and children. A Girl Guide troop for prisoners was in operation. It all sounds very strange now but it was not uncommon in its day.

The problem with this maternalistic approach was that it could not cope with those who could not or would not accept that domesticity and passivity were their lot in life. There was little or no knowledge of issues such as sexual abuse to which a very high percentage of women prisoners had been subjected, and which for many may have been a factor in their offending. There was little or no help for lesbian women for whom the prospect of settling down with a husband and family was not an option. There was little recognition of woman's capacity for violence and of the help needed to cope with this. What did happen was that women in prison became medicalised. If it was difficult to accept that some women were bad then it was easier to redefine them as mad. The majority of women prisoners were considered to be in need of some kind of psychiatric assistance. This was the underlying assumption behind the plans for the redevelopment of Holloway in the late 1960s:

> In 1968 the then Home Secretary announced that it was intended to reshape the whole prison system for the custodial treatment of female offenders and that, as part of this comprehensive change, Holloway Prison was to be completely redeveloped. A central feature of this development was to be provision of comprehensive medical, psychiatric and general hospital facilities for the whole of the women's prison service (Home Office 1985).

In more recent years there has been a continued fragmentation of the female estate, in terms of regime development and a lack of central strategy. Alongside this, there has been an increasing debate about the imprisonment of women, however much of that debate still has been framed by the fact that women exist within a Prison Service dominated by men. Changing the types of institutions in which women are held and what happens to them in those institutions has been difficult, because the debate has often been hijacked by the argument that reformers are seeking to be soft on women. It has been difficult to centre the debate around the differences that exist between men and women who offend. Nevertheless, the fact that the debate is taking place at all is a hopeful sign, and it has led to some changes in official thinking about incarcerated women.

There is an increasing awareness that women in prison need a much wider range of courses and educational and training opportunities than were traditionally offered. There is also a growing recognition of the particular problems of incarcerated women and the need to address some of those issues in specific ways that are appropriate to them as women. It is no longer sufficient merely to make minor adjustments to something prepared for male prisoners and hope it will fit. Work has begun on designing offending behaviour programmes specifically for women, on looking at the age mix within prisons, and on providing properly designed programmes for female young offenders. It is hoped that all of these initiatives will contribute to the debate about what purpose should be served by imprisoning women, and will continue to raise the profile of incarcerated women.

References

Carlen, P. (1998) *Sledgehammer: Women's Imprisonment at the Millennium*, Macmillan

Faith, K. (1993) *Unruly Women: The Politics of Confinement and Resistance*, Vancouver: Press Gang

HM Chief Inspector of Prisons (1997) *Women in Prison: A Thematic Review*, Home Office/The Stationery Office

Home Office (1985) *HM Prison Holloway, Report by Chief Inspector of Prisons*, Home Office

— (1997) *Understanding the Sentencing of Women*, Home Office Research Study 170, Home Office

— (1998) *Prison Statistics England and Wales 1997*, Cm 4017, The Stationery Office

— (1999) *Prison Statistics England and Wales 1998*, Cm 4430, The Stationery Office

Zedner, L. (1994) *Women, Crime and Custody in Victorian England*, Oxford: Clarendon Press

11

YOUNG PEOPLE
Zoë Ashmore

Society has a right to expect that young people for whom custody is unavoidable should be held safely, made to confront their behaviour, provided with opportunities for constructive activity, including reparation, encouraged to change and prepared for release to a life without crime (HM Chief Inspectorate of Prisons 1997, p. 69).

Archbishop William Temple once commented that no one is a criminal and nothing else. This must be particularly true of those young men and women in prison who are still maturing physically, socially, emotionally and psychologically. This chapter describes who those young people are and how the Prison Service approaches their custody and care.

At the outset, it is helpful to acknowledge the lack of clarity and consistency in distinguishing young people from adults. While 18 is now the age of majority it is not until offenders are 21 that they are sentenced to custody by the courts as an adult. Conversely, while the law in many other respects regards the under-18-year-old as a child, the 15-year-old boy remanded into custody must be held by law in an establishment designated as a prison (rather than in a young offender institution, YOI), operating under adult Prison Rules.

The Prison Service is now endeavoring to discharge its twofold duty (of keeping someone in custody and helping to prevent re-offending) by distinguishing the needs of individuals within two groups of young people: the under-18-year-olds (that is, those aged 15–17 years, who are sometimes referred to as juveniles), and the 18–20-year-olds (who are sometimes referred to as young adults). This approach is driven principally by the government's commitment to reform the youth justice system (which relates to those aged under 18) in furtherance of its policy of being tough on crime and its causes. This chapter identifies the typical characteristics of young offenders and the factors connected with youth offending. It outlines the legislative framework, the characteristics of young people in custody and the type of conditions and regimes they experience.

Legislative framework

A summary of the custodial sentences available for juveniles and young offenders and where they can be served is given in Table 11.1. There are several custodial sentences for under-21-year-olds which can be served in different types of custody, and for those aged under 18 the sentences have recently been revised and came into force on 1 April 2000. A useful account of the legislative framework can be found in *Introduction to Youth Justice* (Gordon et al. 1999).

Table 11.1: Custodial sentences for young offenders and juveniles

Sentence	Age group	Rationale and sentence length	Where sentences can be served
Section 53 CYPA 1933	10–17	Convicted of a murder or a serious crime which, for an adult, would carry a sentence of at least 14 years: Section 53(1) is the equivalent of a life sentence; Section 53(2) is a determinate sentence of any length	Local authority secure unit, YTC Prison Service establishment (YOI or juvenile establishment)
Detention in a YOI	18–20	Upper limit to sentence length is the same as for adults	YOI
Custody for life	18–20	For offences for which an adult must or could be sentenced to life	YOI
Detention and Training Order (DTO)	10–17	The length of sentence imposed can be for periods of 4, 6, 8, 10, 12, 18 and 24 months only	Secure training centre (STC), Prison Service establishment (YOI or juvenile establishment), local authority secure unit, YTC

The objectives and philosophies of local authority secure accommodation and youth training centres (YTCs) versus those of YOIs are essentially different. Many young offenders receive inadequate information about the differences and are ill-prepared for the move to a YOI. The result is that they find the transition into their new environment fraught with difficulties (Castro-Spokes 1998). Boswell (1991, p. 23) concludes that the Section 53 sentence is characterised by lack of information, confusion and uncertainty.

Remand in custody

It is common for all those in prison to be regarded as convicted criminals. In fact, approximately 25% of their number are unconvicted and therefore innocent, being held on remand pending trial or sentence. For many young offenders their first experience of prison custody will be on remand while they wait for their charges to be processed through court. The remand process is slow and, as described by the Audit Commission (1996, p. 10), costly. The Commission discovered that over one-third of those remanded in custody and subsequently found guilty did not receive a custodial sentence. *The Thematic Review* (HM Chief Inspector of Prisons 1997) found that sentenced young male offenders had been on remand for an average of three months, but one had spent two years on remand before being sentenced. In 1996, it took an average 131 days to deal with a young offender from offence to completion. Not surprisingly the government is concerned about the delays in dealing with young offenders (Home Office 1997, p. 25). It made a manifesto pledge to reduce by half the time it takes to deal with a young offender from arrest to sentence.

Holding a young person on remand in prison custody can also have a high human cost. Too often the regime is impoverished because these establishments focus on meeting the needs of the court but provide little more than the bare essentials: food, fresh air and visits. In order to ensure that they are close to the court at which their cases are to be heard, some young people are held in adult remand establishments. In addition, time spent on remand is a stressful and uncertain period as young offenders worry about their impending court case and adjust to prison life. The periods passed in cells give young offenders the opportunity to brood about their problems and some are unable to cope. In a study of suicide and self-harm by young people carried out by the Trust for the Study of Adolescence, young people on remand were found to be a particularly vulnerable group (Lyon 1998).

Who are the young offenders?

Facts and figures

Twenty-six per cent of known offenders are under 18 (Audit Commission 1996). There were 11,800 young people in prison at the end of June 1998, a figure that is comprised of 11,411 young males and 389 females; of these 8,521 were sentenced young offenders and 3,279 were held on remand (Home Office 1998). The peak age of known offending by young males has risen from 15 to 18 years over the last decade, and for young females it is 14 (HM Chief Inspector of Prisons 1997). Morgan (1997, p. 1157) found that there is a substantial over-representation of ethnic minorities in the prison population (17% of male prisoners and 24% of female prisoners) and the proportion is greater among young adult prisoners.

Prisoners are overwhelmingly young, male, socially and economically disadvantaged, repetitive property offenders (Morgan 1997, p. 1151). There is evidence that the prevalence of offending differs for different age groups for males and females. Property offences (excluding fraud and theft from work) are most prevalent among 18–21-year-old males, and expressive and violent offences predominate among 14–17-year-old males (Graham and Bowling 1995). This is reflected in the prison population. In June 1998, 2,216 out of 8,521 (26%) were serving sentences for burglary (Home Office 1999). Robbery accounted for 1,909 (23%) and violence against the person and sexual offences for 1,761 (22%). Theft and handling offences accounted for 809 (10%) of the young prisoners' sentences and drugs offences rose from 393 in September 1997 to 457 a year later, a rise of over 16%. Robbery offences increased over the same period by 6% (up 108) (Home Office 1998).

Female young offenders accounted for only 3.6% of the total sentenced young offender population in 1998. However, this was the highest number of female young offenders there had been since 1980. Theft and handling stolen goods form the majority of offences committed by young females: 87% of offences for 10–14-year-olds and 74% for 14–18-year-olds. Violence against the person accounts for 7% of the 10–14-year-olds and 12% of the 14–18-year-olds' offences (Newburn 1997).

Education and employment

Young people who truant or experience exclusion from school are more likely to offend. Forty-two per cent of offenders of school age who are sentenced in the

A group of young male prisoners in the exercise yard ouside their wing. Prisoners today are overwhelmingly young, male, socially and economically disadvantaged repetitive property offenders.

youth court have been excluded from school, while another 23% truant significantly (Audit Commission 1996, p. 21), compared to 3% of the general population. Negative experiences of school are commonly related by young prisoners. Repeated incidents of fighting, bullying, stealing or drug-taking can lead to their exclusion. Once excluded, they mix with peers who are either older or in a similar situation to themselves, and young offenders admit that they can be influenced to offend by their peers (HM Chief Inspector of Prisons 1997). It is easy to become involved in the abuse of alcohol or drugs as they find themselves with little constructive activity to fill their day.

In the general population under 25, only 11% left school before the age of 16 but for male prisoners, 40% had left by this age (Home Office 1991). Two-thirds fail to gain educational qualifications and the same proportion are unemployed before being sent to custody. For young female prisoners, only 15% had any past experience of paid work (HM Chief Inspector of Prisons 1997). Many have difficulty reading and writing and their vocabulary in spoken English may be limited.

For some young offenders, the taboo associated with basic education classes in prison is difficult to overcome. Innovative methods of delivery are being developed to make it easier for young people to engage positively in learning. An example of this is the training of physical education officers in the delivery of basic skills. Practical courses such as cookery, computer studies and music are

Young prisoners learning computer skills which will equip them for employment on release.

very popular, as are vocational qualifications. Forty-five per cent of young female prisoners at Holloway Prison expressed an interest in learning about handling finances and 30% in learning cookery (HM Prison Service 1998). Certificates of achievement are highly valued by young offenders, several of whom have never experienced success. Many gain educational and vocational achievements which they believed were beyond their reach, before coming into custody.

Threats from within and without

Substance misuse

The use of drugs and alcohol is prevalent among young offenders. Seventy per cent of those interviewed by the Audit Commission said that they took drugs and over half said that prior to coming into custody they got drunk at least once a week (Audit Commission 1996, p. 27). Almost a quarter of young male prisoners had been under the influence of alcohol at the time of their offence and up to a quarter claimed a current or past drug problem (HM Chief Inspector of Prisons 1997). Staff working with young offenders would most probably view these numbers, high as they are, as an underestimate.

It is difficult to completely stop drugs coming into prison in spite of search procedures, supervision by staff, the use of drugs dogs and closed-circuit television. Young prisoners who are trying to keep away from drugs may choose to be visited by close family members only and so not put themselves at risk from their peers outside, who may attempt to bring in drugs on a visit.

Bullying

Bullying is characteristic of adolescent behaviour. It is not always conscious exploitation, rather a feature of growing up among young people. Bullying is a significant threat to the maintenance of a secure and well-ordered environment and is often related to drug-trafficking. In the prison staff booklet *Bullying in Prison: A Strategy to Beat It* (Prison Service 1993), using threats to persuade young offenders receiving visits to bring in drugs is listed as one of the forms that bullying can take. It can also include assault, verbal abuse or forcing others to hand over their possessions, particularly tobacco and other goods which they may have bought from the prison shop from their weekly earnings (about £5). Bullying can become an insidious problem, especially when it contributes to low self-esteem. Self harm attempts can be triggered by it and staff need to be sensitive and well trained to detect and counter bullying behaviour (HM Chief Inspector of Prisons 1997, p. 25). To tackle bullying, establishments need a clear anti-bullying strategy that addresses how to measure the problem, change the climate, improve supervision, support the victim and challenge the bully.

Suicide and self-harm

The rising number of suicides among young people is of concern and prison staff are very aware of the vulnerability of many young offenders. Some young people will try to injure themselves using razor blades, glass or any other available materials. Suicide-attempters have suffered more severe disadvantage, violence and family problems in their histories, and their contact with criminal justice agencies and Social Services is more frequent. They also find prison life more difficult in almost every respect (Liebling 1995). The hallmarks of vulnerability in young people at risk of suicide or self-harm are listed by Lyon (1998) as:

- experience of loss;
- isolation;
- lack of support;
- low self-esteem;
- a sense of powerlessness/helplessness; and
- an uncertain future.

Other groups of prisoners who may be at particular risk are the psychiatrically ill, long-sentenced prisoners, poor copers and those leaving care (Liebling and Krarup 1993; Liebling 1995; Lyon 1998).

Fifty-one per cent of suicides in all types of prisons occurred in the first three months of sentence after the prisoner had been sentenced (Liebling 1992). Four young offenders, aged 15 and 16, committed suicide in prison between 1990 and 1992. In the three years 1996–98, when the number of under-18-year-olds was 70–80% higher than in 1990–92, a total of four young people took their lives.

Working with young people who self-injure, swallow items or attempt suicide is a challenge for prison staff, and the systems in place aim to provide extra individualised care to those who are at risk of suicide or self injury. Staff from different disciplines will support the young person through the crisis period. In addition, the work of the Samaritans in training young prisoners to act as listeners for others in custody, for example, is invaluable.

Families and care

The childhood experiences of the majority of young prisoners have been far from ideal. New prison staff, who may not be aware of this fact, are often struck by the overwhelming catalogue of events and failure by authorities in the backgrounds of young prisoners. The problems preceding offending can be detected from an early age and yet the opportunities for prevention have been missed with many young prisoners. Harsh or erratic parental discipline; cruel, passive or neglecting parental attitudes; poor supervision; and parental conflict (all measured at age 8) predicted later juvenile convictions (West and Farrington 1973). Seventeen per cent of young prisoners admit to having suffered violent, sexual or emotional abuse (HM Chief Inspector of Prisons 1997), and again, this is probably an under-estimate as many find it difficult to trust adults sufficiently to disclose these incidents. In a longitudinal study of 400 London males, the Cambridge Study (Farrington 1997) – the results of which are concordant with similar studies in North America, Scandinavia and New Zealand – the reliable predictors of delinquency were:

- poor parental supervision;
- parental conflict;
- an antisocial parent;
- a young mother;
- large family size;
- low family income; and
- coming from a broken home.

Numerous other studies cited by Farrington confirm a link between family factors and offending.

As many as 38% of young prisoners under 21 have had experience of local authority care (Home Office 1991). This figure is all the more revealing when it is compared with the experience of the general population (whether under 21 or not) which is only 2 %. Lyon (1998) finds that young people in care try to live independently at 17 or 18 years old, which contrasts sharply with the rest of the population who are now not leaving home, on average, until they are 23 years old. Young women leaving care at 18 are pregnant or have a child already (Lyon 1998, p. 23). In a study of the characteristics of 39 teenage girls at Holloway Prison, Rutherford and Seneviratne (1998) summarise their findings by concluding that:

> The frequent descriptions of childhood deprivation, physical and sexual abuse, and placements in care all contribute to a picture of disturbed teenagers with poor coping skills, who lead chaotic lives characterised by substance abuse, offending and homelessness.

In summary, young prisoners are those whose life experiences have included turmoil and disruption, much of it compounded by misuse of drugs or alcohol, increased by poor educational experiences and lack of qualifications, and followed by poor employment histories. As if all this was not enough, their experience of family life is, at best, unlikely to have been positive and has more usually been abusive, leading to local authority care.

Regimes

In determining what type of regimes should be provided, governors have been constrained in recent years by budgetary pressures. Before that, the absence of a belief that prison can do anything more than incapacitate by depriving someone of their liberty led to a reduction in regimes. Thus, too easily, regimes could become merely institutional provision to meet basic needs (food, healthcare, visits and exercise). Research has now established what helps young people in custody most to tackle their offending behaviour. This body of research is generally referred to as 'what works'. It forms the basis of the Prison Service's evidence-based approach to constructing regimes that give new life to its rehabilitative duty. 'What works' highlights the importance of the following features of positive and purposeful regimes for young people in custody:

- a clear set of aims and objectives;
- well-selected, well-trained, well-motivated and well-managed staff;
- activities (or interventions) designed to tackle offending behaviour by targeting individual needs;
- activities that provide and develop employable skills;
- strong throughcare arrangements which ensure that post-release supervision and support is carefully planned;
- environments in which young people feel safe, particularly from being bullied; and
- regimes which foster positive links and good relationships between young people and their families.

The Prison Service's objective to establish regimes based on the 'what works' principles has been led by the development of offending behaviour programmes (see Chapter 18). These are based upon the rigorous provision of tightly structured courses designed specifically to tackle the thinking behind offending. Each course that runs in a prison establishment must be properly accredited, which is an ongoing process of quality assurance. While good regimes are built upon 'what works' principles, the best establishments also recognise the characteristics of adolescent behaviour, offering practical arrangements for promoting good behaviour, and pastoral care and welfare arrangements.

Maintaining a safe and secure environment also comes directly from the 'what works' research. Custodial institutions are complex places in which some very sensitive and complex issues are explored, and the dynamics that influence the behaviour and attitude of all who work and live in them cannot be reduced to a few stand-alone factors. Neither staff nor young people can work effectively unless they feel safe and secure. Safety is not just about the absence of assaults, for example (although the absence of assaults goes a long way to making establishments safer places); it is also about the presence of appropriate caring and supportive mechanisms, and about humans being conscious and tireless in the furtherance of clear aims and objectives. Above all, the provision of a full, purposeful and active day; and arrangements that promote, recognise and reward good behaviour, rather than just identifying and punishing the bad, are probably two of the most important elements in maintaining a safe and secure environment.

The reform of the youth justice system

One of the central features of the government's reform of the youth justice system is the establishment in statute of its principal aim. Section 37 of the Crime and Disorder Act 1998 states simply that the aim of the youth justice system is to prevent offending by children and young persons. Section 37(2) of the Act imposes a duty upon all persons and bodies carrying out functions in relation to the youth justice system to have regard to that aim. The most significant developments in the Prison Service in respect of this aim, which came into force on 30 September 1998, are:

- the creation of an estate in which almost all under-18-year-olds offenders will be held;
- the introduction of new regime standards for under-18-year-olds;
- the creation of three units for the detention of those sentenced under Section 53 of the Children and Young Persons Act 1933; and
- consideration of the best arrangements for 18–20-year-olds once the under-18-year-olds are held and cared for entirely separately.

Overarching each of these developments is the Youth Justice Board (YJB), a non-departmental government body established by Section 41 of the Crime and Disorder Act 1998. Its responsibilities include:

- monitoring the operation of the youth justice system and youth justice services;
- advising the Secretary of State on this and on the setting of national standards for the provision of youth justice services and custodial accommodation;
- advising on how the principal aim of the youth justice system might most effectively be pursued; and,
- identifying, promoting and making grants for the development of good practice.

The existence of the YJB has, and will continue to have, a profound effect on the way the Prison Service goes about its duties, as the Director General indicates in Chapter 27. Although its role is advisory, the YJB has a commanding influence by virtue of its unique statutory position overseeing the entire workings of the youth justice system. Its influence is already being felt in the work the Prison Service is doing to establish a separate estate for under-18-year-olds and in the drawing up of new regime standards for under-18s. Finally, and most importantly for the longer term, the YJB is planning to take on a commissioning/purchasing role which would see it determining how much and what sort of new secure accommodation for under-18-year-olds is required and where it should be sited. Presently, the Prison Service provides approximately 90% of all secure accommodation for this age group. The YJB could decide in the longer term to contract to providers other than the Prison Service, whose accommodation is, on the whole, too large for the purpose.

Central to the delivery of the new standards is effective interagency co-operation, the introduction of a new custodial sentence for under-18-year-olds (the Detention and Training Order (DTO)) and a commitment to make the custody of young people a positive and purposeful experience.

In many respects, determining the regime standards was not difficult. There is much in them which common sense, humanity and good management dictate. The challenge comes in delivering real differences in a service whose past culture embraced incarceration and the security and control aspects of custody rather than the caring and rehabilitative ones. The new regime standards are founded upon four key features:

- the importance of the role of staff;
- the enablement of the development of the individual young person;
- the maintenance of a safe and secure environment; and,
- the prevention of re-offending.

Staff selection, training and support (in its broadest sense) underpins changes in the culture and ethos of any establishment. Without empowering staff to take a more constructive, involved and fulfilling role, little will be achieved.

Rigorous assessment of every young person's needs, abilities and aptitude underpins their purposeful custody. By the time a young person is received into custody a number of assessments will already have been made. It is crucial that effective arrangements for interagency co-operation exist so that information previously collected and insights already gleaned may be exchanged. The assessments form the basis upon which sentence plans (including the time a young person is in custody and when they are supervised following their release) will be drawn up.

Lastly, the new regime standards are founded upon activities which are designed and have been proved to help prevent offending. Mention has already been made of the current work to establish offending behaviour programmes which focus upon the particular needs of young offenders. The programmes are a key aspect of a young offender's sentence plan.

Of course, effective regimes are about more than key features and important elements: ultimately, they will only demonstrate their effectiveness by making collective sense – the sum must be greater than its parts. The art of working with young people in custody involves having an innate sympathy for them. It requires patience, strength of character and a stubborn belief in individuals of whom much of the rest of society has given up on. As Sir Alexander Paterson, the great Prison Commissioner, commented, 'We are dealing with hard facts and cannot afford to be soft; on the other hand, we are dealing with human beings and cannot afford to give up hope' (Paterson 1951).

References

Audit Commission (1996) *Misspent Youth: Young People and Crime*, Audit Commission for Local Authorities/NHS

Boswell, G. (1991) *Waiting for Change: An Exploration of the Experiences and Needs of Section 53 Offenders*, The Prince's Trust

Castro-Spokes, M. (1998) 'Section 53 offenders: their needs reconsidered', unpublished M.Sc. dissertation, Loughborough University

Farrington, D.P. (1997) 'Human development and criminal careers', in M. Maguire, R. Morgan and R. Reiner (eds), *The Oxford Handbook of Criminology*, (2nd edition), Oxford: Clarendon Press

Gordon, W., Cuddy, P. and Black, J. (1999) *Introduction to Youth Justice*, Winchester: Waterside Press

Graham, J. and Bowling, B. (1995) *Young People and Crime*, HMSO

HM Chief Inspector of Prisons (1997) *Young Prisoners: A Thematic Review by HM Chief Inspector of Prisons for England and Wales*, Home Office

HM Prison Service (1993) *Bullying in Prison: A Strategy to Beat It*, Home Office

— (1998) 'Younger prisoners at Holloway: profile and background', unpublished internal paper, HMP and YOI Holloway: Psychology Unit

Home Office (1991) *The National Prison Survey*, HMSO

— (1997) *No More Excuses: A New Approach to Tackling Youth Crime in England and Wales*, HMSO

— (1998) *Young Prisoners Monitor*, Research, Development and Statistics Directorate, Home Office

— (1999) *Prison Statistics England and Wales 1998*, Cm 4430, The Stationery Office

Liebling, A. (1992) *Suicide in Prison*, Routledge & Kegan Paul

— (1995) 'Vulnerability and prison suicide', *British Journal of Criminology*, Vol. 35, No. 2

— and Krarup, H. (1993) *Suicide Attempts in Male Prisons*, Home Office

Lyon, J. (1998) 'Growing up in prison', in S. Hayman (ed.), *The Forgotten Children: Young People in Prison*, ISTD

Morgan, R. (1997) 'Imprisonment: current concerns and a brief history since 1945', in M. Maguire, R. Morgan and R. Reiner (eds), *The Oxford Handbook of Criminology*, (2nd edition), Oxford: Clarendon Press

Newburn, T. (1997) 'Youth, crime and justice', in M. Maguire, R. Morgan and R. Reiner (eds), *The Oxford Handbook of Criminology*, (2nd edition), Oxford: Clarendon Press

Paterson, A. (1951) *Paterson on Prisons*, Friedrick Muller

Rutherford, H. and Seneviratne, S. (1998) 'Characteristics of teenage female offenders', unpublished internal paper, HMP and YOI Holloway

West, D. and Farrington, D. (1973) *Who Became Delinquent?*, Heinemann

PART THREE: PEOPLE WHO WORK IN PRISONS

PRISON SERVICE STAFF

Shane Bryans

The most valuable asset

Prisons function effectively because of the staff who work within them. While a governor may be 'the most important individual influence on what a prison is like' (West 1997, p. 32), nothing could be achieved without able, well-motivated and competent staff. As has been pointed out elsewhere, the staff who work in a prison do so for 'a variety of reasons with a variety of intentions', (West 1997, p. 43). Some do it simply for the money or because it is a 'job for life'. The vast majority do it to protect the public, whether by maintaining appropriate security to keep people inside, or something more aspirational like reforming or rehabilitating prisoners.

> … the staff of the Prison Service are its most valuable asset. They are the means by which the great majority of services to prisoners are delivered. They are directly responsible for the custody and safe-keeping of prisoners, for their fair treatment and care (Home Office 1991a, p. 35).

This chapter gives an account of the various staff who work in prisons and at Prison Service Headquarters. It discusses the biggest group of staff in the Prison Service, prison officer grades, plus the contribution of other groups of staff including administrative, instructor and industrial grades. (The work of governors and healthcare staff is explored in later chapters.) Critical elements of the Prison Service Human Resource Management Strategy are then discussed including:

- the core competency framework;
- leadership charter;
- staff culture;
- equality of opportunity;
- conduct and discipline;

- staff care and welfare; and
- industrial relations.

Within each prison are to be found governors, uniformed officers, administrative and specialist staff including psychologists, instructors, nurses, doctors and chaplains. In addition to these directly employed staff there are probation officers and teachers whose services are provided under contract with local probation committees and education colleges. Table 12.1 shows the breakdown of directly employed staff by specialism.

Table 12.1: Total Prison Service staff, January 2000

Specialism	Number	Percentage of total staff
Senior administrative grades	79	0.2
Governor grades	1,080	2.6
Administrative grades	5,602	13.0
Uniformed grades	29,814	68.5
Chaplains	217	0.5
Medical officers and nurses	1,246	2.9
Psychologists	476	1.0
Instructors, farm and technical staff	4,981	11.15
Total	**43,495**	

Prison officers

Prison officers, senior officers and principal officers together with the operational support grade (OSG) form by far the largest group of staff in any prison. If the prison is to function correctly the uniformed staff must be well managed, their morale maintained and their talents harnessed into productive activity. Prison officers perform many tasks within a prison. Some work in areas such as the gate, control room, searching, security and operations. Other prison officers work in specialist areas, once they have received appropriate training, including physical education, works, dog patrol, healthcare and as workshop instructors. However, the majority of officers work as discipline staff, responsible for the core work of dealing with prisoners on residential wings. The OSG staff provide a number of support functions, where they are not responsible for prisoners. These tasks include the gate, control room, vehicle escort, canteen and visits. Senior officers are a supervisory grade who are responsible for the work of prison officers and OSGs. The principal officer is the most senior uniformed grade and manages a specific department, wing or function. The grade structure, gender breakdown and the maximum pay scales for prison officer grades is shown in Table 12.2.

Table 12.2: Uniformed staff, December 1998

Grade	Number	Percentage female	Maximum pay 1998 (£)
OSG	4,684	24	13,987
Prison officer	18,927	15	20,843
Senior officer	3,743	8	22,570
Principal officer	1,202	7	24,643
Total	**28,556**	**15**	

Applicants to be prison officers are subject to a comprehensive Job Simulation Assessment Centre (JSAC) selection procedure provided that they meet the application criteria of a minimum education requirement (five GCSEs, including English and Maths, or the equivalent) and pass a competence-based questionnaire. The JSAC procedure comprises a series of simulation exercises and a report-writing exercise (Roden 1997, p. 36). The exercises cover a number of skills areas: calming, making a complaint, taking criticism, giving constructive criticism, dealing with requests for help, listening with a purpose, and written/analytical skills. Successful applicants who do well on the JSAC procedure then attend the prison officer initial training (POINT) course (see Chapter 14) prior to taking up a post at the prison to which they originally applied. Since 1989 it has been possible for female officers to work in male establishments and vice versa.

Prison officers have a very considerable influence on the daily lives of prisoners as Stern (1987, p. 76) has pointed out:

> The prison staff are at the very centre of any discussions about change or improvement in the prison system. They see prisoners every day, talk to them, listen to their complaints and problems and help [them], or ignore them, as the case may be. They, and not prison administrators, determine the atmosphere of a prison, the level of day-to-day fairness and freedom from

harassment that prevails. They decide whether well-intentioned reforms will be carried through or subverted.

Prison officers are critical to maintaining the security of an institution, as well as ensuring that the daily routine occurs and that effective offending behaviour programmes take place. Little research has been done on the history and development of the variously called 'dubsman', 'turnkey', 'warder' or 'officer'; the notable exceptions being Thomas (1972) and Coyle (1991).

A useful categorisation of the work of prison officers was formulated by Lombardo (1981). He categorised prison officer's work as involving human services, order maintenance, security, supervision and rule enforcement. 'Human services' encompass a range of issues from counselling prisoners on problems, and ensuring prisoners get food and clothes, to identifying and dealing with self-destructive behaviour by prisoners. 'Order maintenance' refers to a policing function that staff are expected to fulfil to prevent fights, gambling, homosexual and other activities which are against the Prison Rules. Vagg has described this function as 'keeping the inmates safe from manipulation, intimidation and assault by others' (Vagg 1994, p. 87). 'Security' involves officers preventing escapes by watching and counting prisoners and searching. Lombardo describes 'supervision' as a making certain that prisoners are ready to do whatever they are supposed to do, or be wherever they are supposed to be, at the appointed time. In addition, it involves ensuring that cleaning and food distribution takes place efficiently and effectively. Lastly 'rule enforcement' encompasses both placing prisoners on report for breaking the rules and detecting illicit activity.

Lord Justice Woolf outlined his view of the role of the modern prison officer in his report on the riot at Manchester Prison:

> Management must make clear to staff that in a modern prison service, the role of the prison officer must not be confined to the unlocking of cells. It should be a skilled professional role within a disciplined service. It should involve constructive care of the prisoners. It should involve preparing them to return to the community in ways which will make it less likely that they will re-offend (Woolf and Tumin 1991, para. 13.9).

Attempts have been made in many areas to enlarge the prison officer's job (extending it horizontally by adding tasks and increasing the variety of work) and to enrich it (enhancing it vertically by adding higher-level, more stimulating and challenging work). In addition, less skilled work, which does not require the expertise of prison officers, is sometimes contracted out to civilian staff or OSGs. However, prison officers are still required to do the basic routine custodial work:

A prison officer unlocks a cell for a prisoner's breakfast call.

they continue to do the locking and unlocking, walking the landings and serving meals to prisoners. The systematic approach to these tasks ensures security and control in prison establishments and thus will remain a key part of prison officers' work.

And yet, in addition to the physical security (walls, locks, bars, fences, cameras, and in some places, dogs), it is now accepted that 'dynamic security' plays a vital role in maintaining order and preventing escapes (see Chapter 20). Dynamic security involves officers interacting with prisoners, occupying them in purposeful activity and helping prisoners to face up to their offending behaviour. The officer's job is to know about and be in control of activity, not just to observe it. The main emphasis of dynamic security is on **active** supervision, in place of more passive surveillance. Direct supervision of prisoners, by prison officers mixing and talking with them, has occurred for many years in some prisons, but it is only recently that officers have become involved in therapy work.

The use of prison officers to help deliver professional treatment and development programmes is one example of prison officers acquiring and applying new skills. By facilitating group sessions with prisoners, prison officers aim to help them confront the excuses that they often construct for their behaviour, create understanding and sympathy for their victims, and learn how to avoid offending behaviour in the future. This new work – in the past, the preserve of social workers and psychologists – is demanding and challenging but rewarding. Prison officers are now involved in numerous programmes including those aimed at sex offenders, anger management, bullying prevention strategies, suicide prevention, and countering alcohol and drugs misuse.

Prison officers are taking the lead in sentence planning for prisoners. Personal officer schemes have been introduced, where a named officer is linked with a small group of prisoners to help them with institutional adjustment and through-care. The officer helps the prisoner to identify what work he or she will do in prison, what offending behaviour needs to be addressed, and what developmental needs he or she may have. Officers also run pre-release and development schemes that help prisoners prepare for their return to the community. These schemes focus on life skills, especially in relation to accommodation, employment and family relationships. Such work requires a high level of skill and dedication, given the reluctance of many prisoners to get involved in sentence planning.

Politicians have also recognised the roles and skills which prison staff now have to exhibit:

> It is not so much the variety of tasks that have to be performed which makes it so demanding, but combining and sometimes switching them from one to another as operational circumstances demand – exerting discipline while exercising support, ensuring physical security while preparing for freedom. The officer who is trained to be involved in treatment programmes, to be sensitive and a good listener, has also been trained to be ready to deal with a disturbance. So it takes courage, initiative and imagination to be an effective prison officer, as well as interpersonal skills (Lloyd 1993).

A recent review of the literature on staff–prisoner relationships summarised the job of the prison officer as being to:

- maintain secure custody, in a context where people are held in confinement against their will;
- provide prisoners with care and with humanity;
- provide prisoners with opportunities to address their offending behaviour; and
- assist with day-to-day management in the complex organisational environment of the prison (Liebling and Price 1998, p. 3).

While prison officers often describe themselves as having no authority to make decisions, in reality, as Vagg points out, 'they had and used various means to exercise control over the daily work and to reach some accommodation with inmates' (1994, p. 93). Despite the hierarchy and regulations to be found in prisons, prison officers exercise an enormous amount of discretion, for example: answering cell buzzers quickly or slowly, addressing prisoners formally or informally, abiding by or ignoring some minor rules, including or omitting small pieces of information from verbal and written reports to senior staff, in the thoroughness of searches, the speed of unlocking prisoners for exercise or association, and whether to place a prisoner on report for breaking a rule of the prison.

The existence and use of discretion was highlighted by Liebling and Price, who found that 'there is consensus amongst prison staff that their work consists mainly of "grey areas" with small areas of clarity, despite the existence of an increasing number of rules and regulation.' (1998, p. 4). They point out that the diversity of circumstances encountered in prison make the use of discretion both inevitable and necessary, but that there are 'no explicit principles and guidelines to aid staff in the exercise of the (largely underestimated) discretion they hold' (p. 4).

The academic view of prison officers' approach to change varies dramatically. On the one hand officers have been regarded as dinosaurs resisting change at every opportunity: 'All too often in the past, attempts to liberalize the prison systems have been obstructed and frustrated by the actions and prejudices of basic grade officers fearful of losing their "authority" and "control"' (Cavadino and Dignan 1997, p. 135). Other academics have rejected 'the commonplace view of prison officers as a body of people who, at every opportunity, set themselves against the liberal and progressive policy changes proposed by those responsible for managing the Service' and concluded that 'prison officers are often less reactionary, and prison governors and administrators less progressive, than that caricature supposes' (Sparks et al. 1996, p. 137).

Chaplains

There have been chaplains in prisons since Parliament gave authority for their appointment to the old county jails in 1773. The role of the chaplain has changed over the years, but their presence in every prison is still recognised by law. Chaplains, like governors, are appointed by statute. Section 7(1) of the Prison Act 1952 states that 'every prison shall have . . . a chaplain'. The Act goes on to state in Section 7(4) that 'the chaplain and any assistant chaplain shall be a clergyman of the Church of England' and in Section 9(2) that the chaplain 'shall not officiate in the prison except under the authority of a licence from the Bishop'. The Act also allows the Secretary of State to 'require the appointment of a minister' of another denomination where the number of prisoners who belong to a religious denomination other than the Church of England merits it.

A prison chaplain has an informal discussion with a prisoner. Each chaplain fulfils their minimum statutory duties in his or her own way.

Chaplains are appointed and paid by the Prison Service like other members of staff. However, they also need the authority of their churches to carry out their work, and they have responsibility to the local bishop or church leader. Chaplains are often licensed or authorised to carry out their prison work at a special service in the prison chapel.

Certain statutory duties for chaplains are laid out in the Prison Rules. Section II of Prison Rules 1964 specifies that: 'The chaplain or prison minister of a prison shall interview every prisoner . . .' This interview varies from a brief greeting to a longer chat, depending on the chaplain. The purpose of the interview is to check on the prisoner's welfare. Chaplains must also visit daily those who are sick, under restraint or undergoing cellular confinement. They conduct worship services, run classes and discussion groups of various kinds and visit prisoners in their cells. Each chaplain fulfils these minimum requirements in his or her own way, ministering to those in need or at a point of crisis, seeking to make it possible for there to be growth in the faith for individuals and groups, and exploring ways of contributing to the overall health of the establishment.

The Prison Service is committed to observing the rights of all prisoners to practise their religion. Visiting ministers from non-Christian faiths are appointed to each prison to cater for the needs of their members. These ministers are appointed by the governor and supported by the chaplaincy team. Over recent years chaplaincy teams have become ecumenical in outlook and practice. Statutory duties are now shared with other Christian denominations, mainly Methodist and Roman Catholic. This ecumenical approach is fully supported by the various church bodies that make ministers and priests available to serve in the Prison Service chaplaincy and was recently acknowledged by the organisation 'The Churches Together in England' (1998). Such recognition is seen as expressing full approval of and confidence in the ecumenical ministry of the Prison Service chaplaincy.

Chaplains have been recognised for the variety of skills and talents that they can bring to an establishment over and above their ministerial role. These skills are often put to good use by including the chaplain in: senior management teams, race relations work, suicide awareness, offending behaviour programmes, throughcare; drug awareness and sex offender treatment programmes, Prison Visitors' schemes and many other groups within the prison. Chaplains also develop links with volunteer groups, Prison Fellowship, local faith communities and a number of agencies that are working in the criminal justice system. In addition many chaplains play a full part in the welfare and care of staff.

Today, prison chaplains are seen as professional and skilful practitioners who are able to minister and manage the very particular needs of prisoners and prison staff. Although they have many new skills and talents to share with the prison community they still remain guardians of the Gospel and give a 'greater common witness to Christ' by their unique position within the prison system.

Specialist staff

The Prison Service employs highly qualified professional staff to undertake specialist work in prisons. These might include psychologists, teachers and probation officers who have often received many years of professional vocational training prior to working for the Prison Service. They have their own professional bodies, to whom they are accountable, which in turn have their own codes of ethics.

Prison psychologists can be used in forensic, clinical and occupational roles. In an article titled 'What do Psychologists do?' Cynthia McDougall, Head of Prison Service Psychology outlined the psychology statement of purpose:

Prison Service psychology supports the Prison Service statement of purpose and its staff by applying sound psychological principles and high professional standards to: the delivery of agreed organisational objectives;

the understanding of individuals at the organisations; the design of strategies for change; the evaluation of effectiveness (McDougall 1992, p. 30).

Psychologists undertake individual casework with prisoners; design, run and evaluate offending behaviour programmes; and help governors to govern prisons more effectively. Psychologists are increasingly being used to help manage institutional change, analyse the behaviour of groups within prisons and produce management data on the functioning of regime activities. They also lead the research planning departments in some prisons.

Prison education underwent a major change in 1993 following the passing of the Further and Higher Education Act 1992. It was decided that thenceforth, education services would be bought directly from education suppliers selected by competitive tender rather than the local education authority. This in itself was in line with wider government policies outlined in the *Competing for Quality* White Paper. The result of the exercise has been to allow governors greater flexibility in the use of education, and more responsive programmes. Employment of more part-time teachers has enabled the contractors to respond to the changing needs of the prisoner population very quickly. Governors have been able to vary their contracts to increase or decrease the number of education hours, depending on demand and budget availability.

In terms of their role within the criminal justice system, the professional group most closely linked to prison staff are probation officers. Since 1966, probation services have seconded staff to work in prison establishments in their area. Initially, this was as welfare officers, taking over a role held by a voluntary agency. These posts were funded centrally so there was little financial control and varying degrees of management accountability for the tasks seconded staff performed. Added to this, at that time there was a tension between the purpose of probation services and their position in prison establishments.

The probation staff who work in prisons do so under an agreement between the governor and the chief probation officer of the local probation area. This agreement had its genesis in Instruction to Governors 30/1993 (HM Prison Service 1993b) which was a result of the White Paper *Custody, Care and Justice* (Home Office 1991a). The White Paper emphasised the importance of close co-operation and good understanding between the Prison and probation services. The framework document was to be used by governors as the basis for determining and implementing more effective local arrangements for the delivery of throughcare work, to formulate a throughcare business and development plan, and to agree the seconded probation officer complement. By 1 April 1994 this 'agreement' had been converted by Instruction to Governors 31/1993 into a 'new style contract between Chief Probation Officers and Governors' (p. 1). The managerialist nature of the contract – with the inclusion of budget estimates, performance indicators, specific inputs required from the probation service and management responsibilities – made explicit the nature of the service provision relationship between the governor and probation service.

The situation that emerged was that at a local level governors and chief probation officers were thrust into a purchaser – provider relationship that neither side was prepared for. The lack of clarity and consistency regarding the contribution of probation staff to prison establishments led to a sudden cutting of posts and some souring of relations (James 1997). In 1995 there was a tightening-up of procedures for releasing prisoners on temporary licence, putting more emphasis on assessing and managing the potential risks prisoners posed to the public (HM Prison Service 1995). During 1995–96 there was a review of sentence planning arrangements, and improvements introduced in 1997 also gave a high priority to risk assessments (HM Prison Service 1997c). The relaunch of both these processes recognised and valued the contribution of probation staff to risk assessment, improving the ability of prison managers to make informed decisions. It was during this period that HM Inspectorate of Probation, considered the work of probation departments located in prisons (Home Office 1996). In the summary the report concluded:

> Inspectors found many examples of good practice and imaginative and creative work by prison probation staff. The inspection showed them making a major contribution to throughcare work including the rehabilitation of offenders, sentence planning and the assessment and management of risk and dangerousness. Such work sometimes had to take place in adverse circumstances brought about by the security demands of the institution, the pressures on other prison staff and the poor physical conditions.

Since then, much has been done locally and nationally to define the contribution to prisoner throughcare that probation staff should make in prison. Prison Service Instruction 74/1997 recognises the contribution of probation staff as essential to:

- risk assessment;
- sentence management and planning;
- confronting offending behaviour;
- accredited offending behaviour programmes;
- maintaining community links/family ties; and
- inmate development programmes (HM Prison Service, 1997a).

Following the Prisons–Probation Review in 1997–98, the relationship between the services is becoming increasingly close. One chief probation officer is already working in the Prison Service and one governor is on secondment to a probation service.

Administrative, instructor and industrial grade staff

After uniformed staff, the largest group of staff are the administrative, instructor and industrial grades. The administrative grades provide a full complement of administrative and clerical support for prisons. The finance function deals with budget management, procurement and cashiers; and most prisons also have a personnel and administration function. The latter deals with human resources, the discipline/custody office, records, training, health and safety, canteen and stores. This group of staff often receives little attention and recognition, but the smooth running of each prison depends crucially on the efficiency of the administrative machinery. With the devolution of finance and personnel matters to prisons the expertise required by the administrative staff has greatly increased. Today, staff who work in the personnel function are expected to study for an Institute of Personnel and Development qualification, and those in finance for an accounting qualification.

Industrial grades include works department craftsmen, plant attendants and estate staff. The work carried out by members of the industrial staff includes participating in new building projects and building maintenance work, and the cultivation of farms and gardens of varying sizes. They are employed to run prison workshops and vocational training courses. Instructors are often highly qualified in their own profession and train prisoners to a standard similar to that found in colleges of education and apprenticeships outside of prison. Their work, involving supervising and training prisoners, is covered in Chapter 17.

A large number of administrative grades, and a few governor grades and specialists, work at Prison Service Headquarters. Their work is primarily to do with policy formulation, monitoring establishment performance and providing advice and guidance to establishments. Some Headquarters administrative staff move freely between jobs in the Prison Service and in the Home Office. Chapter 4 provides a more detailed exploration of the work of the staff who work at Headquarters.

Core competence framework (CCF)

The Prison Service, like other civil service executive agencies, was encouraged to develop a competence framework as part of a broader review of pay and grading arrangements. The White Paper *Development and Training for Civil Servants* (Chancellor of the Duchy of Lancaster 1996) pointed out that competence frameworks were one of the developments that aided professionalism within the civil service as they enabled job requirements to be better defined. They help staff to apply for posts that match their skills and potential, and enable skills deficits to be identified by individuals and managers.

Following extensive consultation and piloting a set of twelve competences, grouped around four themes or 'clusters', was found to be required at all levels in the Prison Service (Bryans 1998, p. 30). Unlike the Home Office, the Prison Service core competence framework (CCF) does not have competences identified for each managerial level, but instead is a framework of twelve competences applicable to all staff in the Service. The twelve competences are shown in Table 12.3. Each of the twelve competences is defined by means of three overarching phrases (known as 'descriptors'), supplemented by a number of performance indicators. For example, the three descriptors for 'team-building/liaison' are: 'Is able to get people to work well together'; 'Gains understanding of the need for trust and co-operation to achieve effective working'; and 'Can reconcile conflict and build group identity'.

Table 12.3: The Prison Service core competence framework

Custodial skills	Systematic and procedural skills
• Security awareness	• Adopting a systematic approach
• Concern for prisoner care	• Planning and reviewing
• Rehabilitation orientation	• Organising and empowering
Innovative and informing skills	**Interpersonal skills**
• Communicating clearly	• Team-playing/networking
• Problem-solving/continuous improvement	• Team-building/liaison
• Leadership and decision-making	• Motivation and commitment

One of the four clusters in the CCF addresses organisation-specific competences: security awareness, concern for prisoner care and rehabilitation orientation. These were included to reinforce the Prison Service's purpose, vision, goals and values. The remaining nine competences are applicable to both the public and private sectors and are to be found in many competence frameworks. The CCF now informs the Prison Service's recruitment, selection, promotion assessment and development processes (Greenbury 1998, p. 14). It is integrated with, and designed to assist the delivery of, other Prison Service strategies and processes.

The CCF profile for each post can be used for a number of purposes (Roden 1998, p. 43). For example, individuals can be assessed against the CCF job profile as part of the appraisal system. A four-level marking system is used: 'yet to demonstrate required competence'; 'competence demonstrated in some areas of work'; 'competence demonstrated in all areas of work'; and 'demonstrates competence required for jobs at next level'. This forms the basis for a structured dialogue between individuals and their line manager about their performance, which in turn brings greater focus, clarity and objectivity to the appraisal system. The gap between demonstrated and desired competences as shown in the CCF profile then becomes the subject of the individual's development plan for the following year. The Prison Service's Training and Development division has mapped its courses against the CCF. Individuals can pinpoint the competence that needs developing and identify which courses or development opportunity is most suited to their needs (see Chapter 14).

The CCF profile is also used by assessment centres, promotion boards and the recruitment process to assess people's competences against the competences identified as being required. Jobs and promotion/selection board opportunities are now advertised with a job specification containing a competence profile. Applicants and their manager are asked to indicate how well the individual meets the competence profile and give some recent examples where the specified behaviours have been demonstrated. As job competence profiles are readily available, people wishing to apply for other positions (horizontally or vertically) can easily identify the competence required in those posts. They can then see if they meet the competences and apply for the post, or identify competences that they need to develop prior to applying.

The CCF forms an integral part of the Prison Service's cultural change strategy. Desired behaviours are being clearly identified and staff assessed against them. The staff who demonstrate the desired behaviours are being selected for key jobs and/or promotion. Staff who do not demonstrate them are being encouraged, once the shortfall is identified, to develop the required competences through training and development. Since the launch of the CCF in autumn 1997 there has been general acceptance that the twelve competences are an accurate reflection of the required behaviours that contribute to first-class performance in the Prison Service.

The leadership charter

The core competence that has received most attention is leadership. Few organisations take leadership seriously enough to actually articulate its role within a given structure and their views on what makes for good leadership (Bryans and Walford 1998, p. 12). The Prison Service Review recommended that the Prison Service draw up a leadership charter to clarify what leadership in the Prison Service means in reality (HM Prison Service 1997b, para. 12.10). The Prison Service responded by launching a bespoke leadership charter in late 1998. It made clear that leadership was not just something that should be demonstrated at Director General level but that senior and principal officers must demonstrate team leadership, functional heads must be operational leaders and governors have strategic leadership. The leadership charter is shown in Figure 12.1.

Staff culture

The concept of culture as it is viewed in organisational studies, is derived from social anthropology and refers to a community's way of life, including shared values and symbols. The term 'prison culture' is often used by researchers and commentators on the prison system when, in reality, they are referring to **prisoner** culture, that is, the culture amongst the prisoners themselves. As any sociologist would point out, a prison is made up of many subcultures of which 'prisoner culture' is only one. Academics have neglected staff culture and have assumed that a prison's culture is largely that of the prisoners' alone. However, prison culture is the sum of **all** the subcultures within it, including the various staff subcultures.

Staff culture can be described as the signs, symbols, myths, rituals and common patterns of behaviour ('the way we do things around here') found amongst a group of people. This particular group will have shared values, common beliefs and attitudes. Some of these will be observable and conscious; others not. From this definition it is clear that there is no homogeneity in prison staff culture: different groups of staff have different cultures. Some staff subcultures are much stronger than others because of the level of staff turnover, the closeness of the working relationship and the operating environment within a workplace. The

Figure 12.1: Prison Service leadership charter

A framework for leadership in the Prison Service

Vision
Leaders
- provide a clear vision which is consistent with the Prison Service purpose, vision, goals, and values, and captures the imagination;
- describe their vision in effective ways and in ways that demonstrate personal commitment;
- translate their vision into strategic and measurable goals; and
- encourage, direct and influence others to follow a consistent direction or set of goals.

Commitment
Leaders
- consistently demonstrate their personal commitment to the vision through appropriate allocation of resources and through their own behaviour; and
- enthuse the team in committing staff to the vision and continuous change/improvement.

A leader creates the developing Prison Service culture by emphasising behaviours under the headings:

People
Leaders
- encourage open and honest communications between individuals and teams in an atmosphere of trust and mutual support;
- communicate by a wide variety of means while placing a particular emphasis on face-to-face interaction;
- recognise and seek to develop the potential in others;
- are aware of the impact of their own behaviour on others;
- coach staff and give opportunity for self-development/learning;
- set realistic personal objectives and priorities;
- emphasise team and individual goals and priorities;
- are committed to equality of opportunity;

- adapt their leadership style to needs and circumstances;
- give praise and recognition where appropriate;
- demonstrate support and care for colleagues and maintain appropriate confidentiality; and
- work towards bringing out the best in people, but also ensuring that deviant behaviour is not rewarded.

Organisational performance

Leaders:
- provide a clear direction;
- encourage a pro-active and forward-thinking approach;
- set the highest standards;
- maintain morale, cohesion and commitment;
- are flexible in initiating change; and
- explore working partnerships with other groups and organisations in order to facilitate change.

Personal contribution

Leaders:
- seek opportunities to demonstrate Prison Service values;
- act as role models by displaying high personal levels of competence, judgement, caring, authenticity and integrity;
- empower staff to allow them freedom to release their creativity, drive and energies;
- inspire confidence by being self-assured, decisive and creating a good impression;
- demonstrate self-discipline, loyalty and readiness to accept responsibility;
- are highly motivated to achieve;
- learn from mistakes;
- are accessible and visible;
- communicate with the right people in the right way;
- seek input and listen carefully;
- show humility and compassion; and
- develop and maintain a team.

prison officer subculture is generally accepted as being particularly strong compared to the probation officer subculture, for example.

Where a strong subculture exists it tends to be learnt in an indirect manner through the work environment and can overcome any management 'cultural indoctrination' which takes place during initial training and induction. However, to focus on the example above, 'prison officer culture has not received serious attention in prison research' (Liebling and Price 1998, p. 4). Prison staff have developed their own principles as 'working cultures'. Liebling and Price point out that each prison – even each wing of a prison – tends to have its own 'ethos' or 'way' which can represent differences in the exercise of discretion. For example, some wings are very disciplinary and rule-based, whereas in others staff respond to prisoners' needs in a more flexible and responsive way.

There is a growing body of research which suggests that cultures can be viewed as a 'controllable variable' and that they can be manipulated and managed to ensure improved organisational performance. Research has shown that 'a prison system cannot expect to change its culture overnight, nor through a statement or order from the top, changing the way in which people act requires involvement, consultation, motivation and commitment' (Jones 1998, p. 33). An example of this, at the national level, is the Director General's determined aim to 'move towards a partnership-based relationship with the Trade Unions' (HM Prison Service 1999, p. 32).

Equality of opportunity

Equality of opportunity is one of the values set out in the Prison Service's set of Principles (see Annex A at the end of this book). In seeking to realise its Vision and to live by its Principles, the Prison Service is committed to equality of opportunity and the elimination of discrimination on improper grounds. The Prison Service policy is within the broader Home Office policy of equal opportunities, which is outlined below:

> The Home Office has a policy of equality of opportunity for all its staff, which has been agreed with the Home Office Trade Union side. The only factors which are relevant for employment and advancement are the individual's ability, qualification and suitability for the work or post in question. The Department is committed to the principle that all Home Office staff are given an equal opportunity for training, development and advancement so that they can contribute to the Department's work to the full extent of their abilities and enjoy the full benefits of that contribution. The Department

therefore takes decisions about its own staff and applicants for employment on the basis of evidence about performance and potential. It takes specific steps to promote equality of opportunity and to guard against discrimination [whether direct or indirect, conscious or unconscious] on grounds of ethnic origin, religious belief, sex, sexual orientation, disability or any other irrelevant factor (Home Office 1991b).

This has been translated into the Prison Service's Principle to 'Promote equality of opportunity for all and combat discrimination whenever it occurs.'

The Prison Service, like other employers, has a duty – created by the Sex Discrimination Acts 1975 and 1986, the Race Relations Act 1976 and the Disability Discrimination Act 1995 – to prevent discrimination and harassment. In an attempt to eradicate discriminational harassment the executive committee of the Prisons Board and Prison Service trade unions worked together to produce a guidance document entitled *Combating Harassment and Discrimination*, which was launched in July 1996 (HM Prison Service, 1996a). The guidance contains comprehensive information and advice about the law on harassment and discrimination; definitions and examples of unacceptable conduct; responsibilities of staff and managers; and the processes for making and dealing with complaints. It goes on to specify that all managers should:

- encourage a working environment that welcomes diversity and is supportive of all staff;
- ensure that they and their staff are aware of the Service's commitment to equal opportunities and of the standards of behaviour expected of management and staff;
- ensure that potentially offensive material is not displayed or circulated in the workplace;
- take prompt action, before any complaint is made, to tackle unacceptable language or behaviour; and
- be alert to signs that all may not be well within their team (p. 2).

In order to ensure a more effective implementation of the Prison Service's equal opportunities policies, governors were required, in 1996, to identify an equal opportunities officer for their prison and to arrange for all managers to receive one day's training on managing equal opportunities. Further, all staff were to receive one day's training on combating sexual and racial harassment.

Despite the existence of policy statements and guidance documents the Prison Service still has a less than impressive record on equal opportunities. Currently, women account for only 26% of all staff employed, and 12% of uniformed staff.

Ethnic minority staff account for only 3% of all Prison Staff compared to 7% in the UK workforce. There are only just over a hundred staff working in the Prison Service recorded as having a disability, representing just 0.02% of all staff employed (HM Prison Service 2000). Table 12.4 shows female and ethnic minority representation in the Prison Service.

Table 12.4: Prison Service staff by gender and ethnic background, January 2000

Specialism	Number	Percentage female	Percentage ethnic minorities
Senior administrative grades	79	18	Not known
Governor grades	1,080	14	1
Administrative grades	5,602	74	5
Uniformed grades	29,814	12	2
Chaplains	217	23	1
Medical officers and nurses	1,246	69	13
Psychologists	476	83	3
Instructors, farm and technical	4,981	16	1
Total	**43,495**	**26**	**3**

Source: HM Prison Service 2000

The Prison Service has made it clear that it is determined to create an environment in which prisoners and staff can be confident that they will not encounter discrimination in any form. A new racial equality action programme (called RESPOND – Racial Equality for Staff and Prisoners) was launched in February 1999 (see Chapter 6). Although the programme is focused on racial equality it is hoped that there will be wider benefits in securing equal opportunities for other under-represented groups.

The programme involves the appointment of a racial equality advisor, national support and help with recruitment campaigns, and training on equal opportunities. The Prison Service has set itself a very challenging target of achieving 7% ethnic minority representation in its workforce by 2007.

Conduct and discipline

The disciplinary arrangements for Prison Service staff were reviewed following Sir Raymond Lygo's recommendation that there should be a single set of arrangements for all staff in the Service (Lygo 1991). An extensive consultation exercise took place with trade unions, and the Advisory Conciliation and Arbitration Service (ACAS) was fully involved in the process. The new disciplinary arrangements, which were consistent with employment law and ACAS guidance, took effect from 1 July 1993 and were published that same year (HM Prison Service 1993a). The new code of discipline covered all Prison Service grades, made clear the responsibility for discipline of line managers, and set down timetables for completing each stage of the process. It provided for a single disciplinary hearing in the majority of cases, which would be conducted by the governor or head of division.

All members of staff were given a personal copy of the new code which made clear the high standards expected of Prison Service staff. The Introduction states:

> All members of the Prison Service are expected to observe certain standards of conduct. Indeed a positive commitment on the part of members of the Prison Service to those standards of conduct and strict adherence to them are fundamental to the successful performance of the duties and responsibilities of the Service. Any failure to meet them undermines the work of the Service.

> The commitment to upholding standards of conduct in the Prison Service must, therefore, be underpinned by disciplinary procedures which provide a fair method of dealing with alleged misconduct. This document sets out the standards of conduct expected of staff and goes on to detail in the code of discipline below the procedure for taking disciplinary action when conduct falls below that standard. The primary objective is to ensure that standards are maintained and to encourage improvement in individual conduct (p. 1).

The key features of the new arrangements are:

- Employers and managers must act in a way which an objective observer would consider reasonable.
- All disciplinary matters must be handled as quickly as possible, at various stages in the process; specific timetables are included.
- Wherever possible, informal guidance or counselling should be regarded as the most appropriate way of encouraging a member of staff to improve their conduct; only if this is not appropriate should there be a recourse to formal disciplinary action.

- The code introduces new disciplinary warnings and penalties. The most common response to proven misconduct will generally be a formal disciplinary warning (oral, written and final written). Other penalties range from financial restitution to dismissal.
- The code must be applied in a non-discriminatory fashion.
- All disciplinary matters must be handled with discretion and confidence.
- There is clear line management responsibility for disciplinary action.
- Members of staff must be informed of a case against them and allowed to state their case and to challenge any evidence.
- A member of staff may be assisted by a colleague or trade union representative at all times.
- No member of staff will be dismissed for a first breach of discipline except in the case of gross misconduct.
- There is a right of appeal against any disciplinary decision or penalty.

The governor, or Head of Group at Headquarters, is responsible for deciding whether to take formal disciplinary action and for conducting disciplinary hearings for all staff in their prison. An exception to this latter point is if he or she is the line manager of the person under investigation, or the person being investigated is less than two substantive grades below that of the governor/Head of Group. In the latter case a senior manager from another establishment will be asked to conduct the hearing. The standard of proof required at the hearing is that required for all employment matters, namely 'the balance of probabilities'.

Staff care and welfare

The Prison Service staff care and welfare service (SCWS) was created in January 1994 when the Prison Service separated itself from the main Home Office staff welfare service, bringing it and the post-incident care provisions under one organisation. The purpose of the SCWS is to provide an advice, information and counselling service to promote the well-being of all Prison Service staff. The SCWS is part of the Personnel Directorate and as such it covers a range of issues including:

- staff sickness due to illnesses, stress, anxiety, depression or incident at work;
- bereavement;
- relationship problems;
- financial problems;
- dependency on alcohol, drugs or gambling;
- harassment;
- workplace problems;

- transfers and postings on promotion where compelling compassionate grounds exist;
- disciplinary matters, where individuals require support and advice; and
- accommodation problems.

The task of the SCWS is to help staff address and overcome barriers which stand in the way of effective working and to help ensure that staff at all levels are able to make the maximum possible contribution to the efficient and effective working of the Prison Service. It has the specific responsibility of providing a post-incident care service, locally through care teams and nationally through in-service counsellors.

Welfare officers provide a confidential, independent advice and information service about work-related or personal problems and may be contacted directly by staff. The only time a welfare officer will override confidentiality is in the case of a gross breach of the code of discipline or of the law. It is important that the staff welfare service should not be seen as an arm of management, otherwise the bond of trust between staff and their welfare officer will be broken.

A good welfare service is one in which there is understanding and co-operation right from the earliest stages amongst managers, personnel sections, trade unions, the welfare officers and, most importantly, staff themselves. With this understanding and co-operation difficulties can be recognised when they first arise, whether they stem from personal, working or other situations. By providing appropriate help at the right time, the SCWS enables the problem to be speedily overcome and the individual to become a happier and more effective person at work.

Industrial relations

The Prison Service *Framework Document* (HM Prison Service 1993b), which established the Service as an agency, made it clear that the Director General was responsible for ensuring good industrial relations (IR) within the Prison Service. More recently, the 1996–99 corporate plan indicated that one of the main steps to be taken to strengthen staff effectiveness (strategic aim 9 of the Service) was to 'work with trade unions towards an improved industrial relations climate' (HM Prison Service 1996b).

The legal framework for Prison Service IR is contained in a number of Acts of Parliament. The first of these is the Trade Union and Labour Relations (Consolidation) Act 1992, which deals with the definition of trade unions, the certification of independent trade unions, the disclosure of information in collective bargaining, non-discrimination against officials, what is meant by 'lawful' industrial action, the role of ACAS, and the various codes of practice. The second is the Trade Union Reform and Employment Rights Act 1993, which addresses the question of facilities for trade union members. The third is the European Rights Act 1996, which clarifies various health and safety matters. (A useful history of IR in the Prison Service is to be found in Bryans and Wilson (1998, ch. 4).

The Prison Service *Framework Document* reiterated that the Service would continue to operate Whitley arrangement. Governors are required to adhere to a number of agreements in their interactions with unions and staff associations at a local level. The key ones are the IR policy statement, local Whitley committees and the procedural agreement with the Prison Officers' Association (POA).

The term 'Whitleyism' is the name given to the long-established system of collective bargaining between management and unions in the civil service. It had its origins in a 1916 report on relations between employers and employees by the Rt Hon. John Whitley, which recommended ways of improving IR in the United Kingdom following years of industrial unrest. The civil service set up a Whitley Council in 1919, followed by the Home Office setting up its own Whitley Council in 1921. The three general objectives of Whitley Councils, as set down in their constitutions are:

- to secure the greatest measure of co-operation between employers and the general body of staff, with a view to increased efficiency combined with the well-being of staff;
- to provide machinery for dealing with grievances generally; and
- to bring together the experience and different points of view of employers and staff regarding conditions of service.

Governors of the larger prisons were required in 1973 to introduce local Whitley committees. This was later extended to all Prison Service establishments. The instruction provided information and guidelines on the setting-up and operation of local Whitley committees, and included a model constitution. Representatives of all recognised Whitley trade unions are entitled to sit on a committee which should consist of the governor and not more than thirteen members, six appointed by the governor and seven by the trade union side.

The Prison Service involves trade unions and staff associations in a number of ways including 'provision of information', both by regular written communication and by oral briefings; 'consultations', where issues and proposals are raised and views sought which management then consider; 'negotiations', involving collective bargaining on pay and conditions issues or otherwise conferring with a view to reaching agreement; and 'participation', where both sides work together on a project to generate ideas or proposals to develop a shared commitment. One example of such involvement includes the Health and Safety (Consultation with Employees) Regulations 1996 which require consultations where any workplace measures may substantially affect employees' health and safety.

The IR situation in the Prison Service was changed dramatically by, and improved following, the Criminal Justice and Public Order Act (CJPO)1994. The Act, which received Royal Assent on 3 November 1994, put IR on a sound legal footing by:

- applying to prison officers and other Prison Service staff who have the powers of a constable the same employment rights as other Crown servants. The bodies representing these staff were given the status and immunities of independent trade unions (Section 126);
- maintaining the position that it is unlawful to induce governors, prison officers and/or prisoner custody officers to withhold their services or commit a breach of discipline. For this purpose a 'breach of discipline' means a contravention of Prison Rules or, in the case of governors and prison officers, the code of conduct and discipline in the Prison Service. If inducements occur and loss results, the Secretary of State may take legal action against the person(s) so inducing those staff for damages (Section 127); and
- enabling the Secretary of State, after consulting relevant representative organisations and others, to make regulations establishing new procedures to determine the pay and pay-related conditions of governors and prison officers affected by the provisions of Section 127 (Section 28).

The executive committee of the Prisons Board and the POA national executive committee issued a joint statement in April 1996 following an IR workshop with ACAS. The workshop agreed some simple machinery to examine ways to improve the framework within which they did business. The work fell within four areas:

- the need to establish and work within a clear framework for IR. That framework must include the values to which both sides are committed;
- the obligations on officials to conduct IR effectively, and the scope for joint training;
- the IR machinery required; and
- the most effective communications required, especially in view of the ever-changing climate of the Prison Service.

The joint statement concluded by stating that the Prison Service and the POA 'want to build on that [excellent work already being done] as the basis for moving industrial relations forward in a more equitable, positive and constructive way' (HM Prison Service 1996c, p. 1).

Recognising staff performance

The Prison Service is committed to the Investors in People strategy as a means of achieving its business goals through the motivation and skills of its staff. It aims to meet the government's targets and to achieve Investors in People accreditation for all prisons and Headquarters by the target date of 1 April 2000. The Staff Ideas scheme that operates in the Prison Service aims to encourage and award staff for their extremely valuable ideas both at establishment level and centrally. It offers staff the opportunity to influence policy and practice throughout the Prison Service by submitting their ideas for improvement and greater cost-effectiveness. Over 150 ideas were received centrally during 1997–98. Awards by the Butler Trust are also made to staff who have achieved much more than their jobs require of them. The annual awards for outstanding achievements are presented by the Trust's patron, the Princess Royal.

Two officers checking detailed points. Prison staff are encouraged to contribute ideas that may influence both local and national prison policy.

The effectiveness of our prisons, and the quality of life for the people held in them, will primarily depend on the attitude, ability and energy of all those who work in our prisons. Prison staff are too often stereotyped as either buffoons from *Porridge* and other television comedies, or as the sadists who seem to work in prisons in the eyes of Hollywood. The Prison Service, like all organisations, contains a very small minority of staff who abuse their power. However, the vast majority of staff act with humanity, decency and compassion in their daily work.

References

Bryans, S. (1998) 'Competency behind bars', *Competency*, Vol. 5, No. 4, pp. 30–3

— and Walford, J. (1998) 'Leadership in the Prison Service', *Prison Service Journal*, No. 119, pp. 10–13

— and Wilson, D. (1998) *The Prison Governor: Theory and Practice*, HMP Leyhill: Prison Service Journal Publications

Cavadino, M. and Dignan, J. (1997) *The Penal System: An Introduction*, Sage

Chancellor of the Duchy of Lancaster (1996) *Development and Training for Civil Servants: A Framework for Action*, Cm 3321, HMSO

Churches Together in England (1998) *Constitutional Guidlelines for a Local Ecumenical Partnership*, CTE

Coyle, A. (1991) *Inside: Rethinking Scotland's Prisons*, Edinburgh: Scottish Child

Criminal Justice and Public Order Act (1994), Royal Assent 3 November 1994

Greenbury, B. (1998) 'The practical application of the Prison Service Core Competence Framework', *Prison Service Journal*, No. 115, pp. 14–16

HM Prison Service (1993a) *Conduct and Discipline in the Prison Service: A Guide for Staff*, Notice to Staff 65/1993, HM Prison Service

— (1993b) *National Framework for the Throughcare of Offenders in Custody to the Completion of Supervision in the Community*, Home Office

— (1995) *Release on Temporary Licence*, Instructions to Governors 36/1995, Home Office

— (1996a) *Combating Harassment and Discrimination*, Notice to Staff 23/1996, HM Prison Service

— (1996b) *Corporate Plan 1996–1999*, HM Prison Service

— (1996c) *Prison Service Executive Committee and Prison Officers' Association National Executive Committee Joint Statement on Industrial Relations*, HM Prison Service

— (1997a) *Effective Implementation of Throughcare*, Prison Service Instruction 74/1997, Home Office

— (1997b) *Prison Service Review*, Home Office

— (1997c) *Sentence Management and Planning: An Operational Guide for the Prison and Probation Services*, Home Office

— (1999) *Business Plan 1999–2000* in *Corporate Plan 1999–2000 to 2001–2002 and Business Plan 1999–2000*, Home Office

— (2000) *HR Planning-Diversity Statistics*, HM Prison Service

Home Office (1991a) *Custody, Care and Justice: The Way Ahead for the Prison Service in England and Wales*, Cm 1647, HMSO

— (1991b) *Equal Opportunities in the Home Office*, Home Office Notice 158/1991

— (1996) *The Work of Prison Probation Departments: Report of a Thematic Inspection*

James, S. (1997) 'Probation in prison: post-devolution of budgets', *VISTA*, Vol. 3, No. 2, pp. 141–47

Jones, R. (1998) *Enabling Prison Staff to Cope with Organisational and Cultural Change*, International Centre for Prison Studies

Liebling, A. and Price, D. (1998) 'Staff-prisoner relationships', *Prison Service Journal*, No. 120, pp. 3–6

Lloyd, P. (1993) *The Changing Role of the Prison Officer*, Rugby: HM Prison Service Library

Lombardo, L. (1981) *Guards Imprisoned: Correctional Officers at Work*, New York: Elsevier

Lygo, R. (1991) *Management of the Prison Service*, Home Office

McDougall, C. (1992) 'What do psychologists do?', *Perspectives on Prison*, HMSO

Roden, C. (1997) 'Prison officer recruitment and promotion', *Prison Service Journal*, No. 113, pp. 33–8

— (1998) 'The Prison Service Core Competence Framework', *Prison Service Journal*, No. 116, pp. 43–4

Sparks, R., Bottoms A. and Hay, W. (1996) *Prisons and the Problem of Order*, Oxford: Clarendon Press

Stern, V. (1987) *Bricks of Shame: Britain's Prisons*, Harmondsworth: Penguin

Thomas, J.E. (1972) *The English Prison Officer Since 1850: A Study in Conflict*, Routledge & Kegan Paul

Vagg, J. (1994) *Prison Systems: A Comparative Study*, Oxford University Press

West, T. (1997) *Prisons of Promise*, Winchester: Waterside Press

Woolf, Lord Justice and Tumim, Judge S. (1991) *Prison Disturbances April 1990: Report of an Inquiry by the Rt Hon. Lord Justice Woolf and His Hon. Judge Stephen Tumim* (The Woolf Report), Cm 1456, HMSO

PRISON GOVERNORS
Bill Abbott and Shane Bryans

Introduction

Prisons are unique institutions. The governors who run them need to be resilient and knowledgeable people with a wide range of skills. The governor must provide both staff and prisoners with strong professional leadership that enables the establishment and the Service as a whole to deliver objectives set by ministers. It is for this reason that the role of the governor has been described as the most important in the Prison Service. This point was highlighted in the most recent review of the Prison Service in England and Wales:

> Prisons remain very hierarchial and almost feudal. There is a strong dependency on the role and person of the Governor. Research has shown that a well-run prison runs more than anything else on the skill and approach of the Governor … The key managerial role in the Prison Service is that of Governor (HM Prison Service 1997, paras. 9.14, 10.9).

The role of the prison governor has received little attention from researchers and academics, unlike prisoners who have been the subject of much academic interest. The role of the warden in American penitentiaries, however, has received some attention from researchers. They have found that the warden's managerial style is the most salient determinant of whether prisons are safe, orderly, clean and capable of providing inmates' amenities (DiIulio 1987); 'Wardens are important actors in the Correctional arena, and they warrant far more study than they have received to date' (Cullen et al. 1993, p. 70); and 'the key to the conditions and general climate of any prison is the warden' (Peak 1995, p. 269).

One recent book (Bryans and Wilson 1998) has gone some way to open up the role and the world of the governor. The role is a challenging one that requires personal commitment and the ability to deal effectively with competing demands. The governor is required to maximise the use of resources to protect the public and reduce crime. As the work is accomplished with and through people, many of the skills needed are those associated with general management. However, the role goes further: the governor must appreciate the political sensitivities and public concerns surrounding prisons and understand the sometimes volatile or fragile nature of prison culture. Occasionally, the role requires calmness and courage in the face of violent disorder or other incidents such as a death in custody. It has been pointed out elsewhere that in addition to creating the ethos and shaping the regime of their prison, governors exercise immense power over the individual, on behalf of the state (Bryans 2000). Prisoners can be segregated, transferred, confined to their cells, strip-searched, refused physical contact with their families, sentenced to 'additional days' and released temporarily by the governor.

This chapter considers governors' recruitment, their legal status, key elements of their work, the finer points of their role and some of the tensions and authority boundaries encountered when governing a prison.

Background

Each of the 135 prisons in England and Wales has a governor or, in the case of contracted-out prisons, a director. The rank of the governor will depend on the size and complexity of the establishment: maximum security 'dispersal' prisons and large local remand prisons have a senior governor who will be a governor grade 1; the majority of other prisons will be governed by a governor grade 2; and smaller prisons will have a governor grade 3 as governor. In addition to the governor, a number of other governor grades will work in a prison. These other governor grades will be heads of a function (custody, regimes, activities, works) or heads of departments (residential, operations, security, throughcare). The exact number of governor grades and their ranks will vary and be agreed between the establishment's governor and his or her line manager (the area manager). The breakdown of governor grades, their number, maximum pay and gender is shown in Table 13.1.

Recruitment

There are four routes to becoming a governor grade. The main route is on promotion from the rank of principal officer, the most senior uniformed grade. Existing principal officers who have demonstrated the necessary competences to become a governor grade are recommended by their line manager and attend a Job Simulation Assessment Centre (JSAC). If successful, new governors attend

Table 13.1: Governor grades, January 2000

Grade	Number	Percentage female	Maximum pay (£)
1	41	7	55,510
2	72	14	49,939
3	139	19	43,026
4	311	15	36,956
5	517	12	33,102
Total	**1,080**	**14**	

a two-week new governor 5 course and apply for vacancies anywhere in the country. The accelerated promotion scheme (APS) is the second route and is aimed at graduates and exceptional Prison Service staff of any rank. The scheme provides members with a wide range of experience and training and gives them the opportunity to reach senior management in less than five years. The third route is the direct entry scheme aimed at experienced managers from inside and outside the Prison Service. Applicants must have at least five years' management experience in a dynamic people-orientated organisation. The final route of entry is the cross-hierarchical move scheme which is aimed at existing civil servants. The target recruits in this case are talented staff in other occupational groups who are skilled individuals, have a flair for managing people and are seeking to develop and further their careers within an operational setting.

Applicants for all the schemes undertake written tests, attend a JSAC and are the subject of an extended interview process. Successful candidates who have no experience as prison officers are required to undertake prison officer training (see Chapter 14) and then to spend a period as a prison officer. On completion of the period in uniform they then undertake a prison management course and normally achieve accreditation 12–24 months later, to governor grade 5.

Promotion from one governor grade to the next depends on developing the requisite competences, skills and knowledge; favourable recommendations from line management; and attendance at assessment centres. Promotion to an in-charge governor post requires experience in a number of different types of prisons, attendance on a variety of courses and, in most cases, experience as a deputy governor.

Legal status and authority

The Prison Act 1952 is the baseline authority for the Prison Service and governors. The Act itself is a consolidation measure and reflects the values of its day. It spends more time defining the role and the authority of the chaplain than of the governor. The Prison Act recognised the role of the Secretary of State, the Prison Commission, the governor, medical officer, chaplain and officers. By 1963 the Prison Commission was abolished and nothing was put in its place. Therefore, the Prison Act 1952 does not recognise the Director General, the current Prison Service Management Board or the area managers, who manage governors.

Governors are vested with formal authority and status by virtue of the Prison Act 1952. They are appointed by the Secretary of State under Section 7 of the Act and are, therefore, holders of a statutory office. Governors also hold the office of constable (*R. v. Secretary of State for Home Office, ex parte Benwell* [1985] QB 554). As the holder of the office of governor incumbents exercise powers delegated by the Home Secretary, as well as their own statutory powers. The legal framework is developed in the Prison Rules and in Prison Service Orders (PSO) and Instructions. Governors have the freedom to use their legitimate authority without being unlawfully constrained or fettered. PSO and Instructions empower and direct governors to undertake certain tasks and duties which contribute to their formal authority and status. Governors are required to ensure that the requirements of Prison Rules, other statutory obligations and line management are met.

It is the Secretary of State who has the responsibility for the administration of prisons under the Prison Act 1952 and it is the policies of the Secretary of State that determine how prisoners are dealt with. The warrant of the court, on whose authority the prisoner is sent to custody, is addressed to the governor, however, and requires the governor either to produce the remand prisoner back to court or to keep the convicted prisoner in custody for the time determined. The prisoner is in the legal custody of the governor, who is accountable to the court. Curiously, the courts do not tend to hold governors to account when they fail to produce or hold a prisoner because of escape. Govenors are also accountable to the Secretary of State through line management.

Duties and competences

The job description for governors outlines what tasks and duties they are expected to undertake. It includes a number of key elements, grouped under three management headings: the business, staff and prisoners, and 'boundaries' (that is, the interface between the prison and Headquarters, other organisations, the community or the media). It covers managerial duties such as:

- achieving Key Performance Indicators (KPIs);
- ensuring financial control mechanisms are in place;
- implementing a self-audit system;
- testing contingency plans;
- providing constructive regimes;
- fostering positive and effective public relations; and
- working constructively with outside agencies.

Other prison-specific areas are also covered:

- maintaining order and discipline;
- providing constructive regimes; and
- anticipating, responding to and managing the concerns of the Board of Visitors.

The job of governing prisons is becoming increasingly complex and demanding. The recent review of the Prison Service described the role as 'that of general manager, but with a significant professional component which relates to managing prisons and managing staff and, most critically, managing the interface between the two … there is also a political dimension in relation to the wider Prison Service, Ministers and other stakeholders and representing those interests back to the prison'. (HM Prison Service 1997, p. 99).

In a recent survey, a group of 31 governors identified motivation and commitment, leadership and decision-making, and organising and empowering as the most important competences which a governor needs to govern effectively (Bryans 1998). In addition to these behavioural competences, governors require underpinning knowledge and skills if they are going to demonstrate competence. A recent paper argues that governors need to be able to demonstrate competence in four distinct areas: general management, public sector management, incident command and prison management (Bryans 2000). The paper makes clear that:

> The incident command, general management and public sector management competences have to be contextualised to reflect the penal setting. However, prison management competence is more than being able to undertake these tasks in a prison. It also involves more than the acquisition of prison-specific technical knowledge and skills, such as how to conduct adjudications, undertake risk assessments and authorise release on temporary licence (p. 25).

A prison governor has to balance issues of custody, care and change before reaching a decision about a prisoner's wing location.

One of the key facets of prison management competence is the ability to balance security, control and justice in prison. A study of governing suggested a number of other areas which make up prison management competence:

> Governors must be able to craft prison culture (both prison subculture and prisoner subculture); blend elements of legitimacy-based control (humane regime, justice and fair treatment) with elements of situational control (management, design and manipulation of the prison environment); … maintain a highly visible profile in the prison; demonstrate clear values and beliefs in order to demonstrate what is and is not acceptable behaviour; exercise power and decision-making based on a firm moral foundation; effectively channel extreme emotions and feelings of prisoners and manage culture, relational and discretionary elements of the prison environment (Bryans and Wilson 1998, p. 54).

The Prison Service Review, which took place in 1997, identified similar elements, including dealing with difficult prisoners, guarding against staff abusing their power, ensuring that staff exercise their authority legitimately and fairly, and maintaining a proper balance between the legitimate expectations of staff on the one hand and prisoners on the other (HM Prison Service 1997, p. 96). In addition to these elements, governors must increasingly manage the tensions associated with resource allocation. They also have an important representational role – to prisoners and staff, as well as to the wider community. They need to manage boundaries effectively. Politicians, Headquarters, area managers, the public, pressure groups and other criminal justice agencies all expect governors to do certain things in a certain way and at a certain time. The governor is the only person who has an overview of the entire prison community, who must skilfully manage emotions within the prison and, at the same time, focus outside of its walls onto the wider community.

Managing in a complex environment

The concept of tensions and authority boundaries within the role of governor takes us to the core of its managerial dynamic. The essential governing task is to manage the prison in accordance with ministerial policy and instructions from Headquarters. At first sight, that appears a simple managerial task but in reality it is highly complex. The complexity arises from a Prison Service Statement of Purpose that can be seen as contradictory; from a perceived failure of the Service to define the role of the governor in recent times; from a lack of line management accountability enshrined in law; from a mix of perceptions about a governor's power projected onto the role by Headquarters, prison staff, the public and prisoners; and from the dynamic between emotion and reason within the Service and, more importantly, within a prison. This dynamic is one of the most important elements in effectively governing a prison.

The Statement of Purpose reads: 'Her Majesty's Prison Service serves the public by keeping in custody those committed by the courts. Our duty is to look after them with humanity and help them lead law-abiding and useful lives upon release.' The two sentences are inherently contradictory – humane treatment is often at odds with the concept of secure custody. Currently, there is an understanding that the task of the governor is to balance the tension between the two statements. In effect, the declared Statement of Purpose creates this tension and requires the governor to exercise discretion and authority to resolve it on a case-by-case basis.

There is an ongoing debate about the extent of the governor's discretion and the power which line management can exercise. For example, if the Secretary of State or an area manager were to decide that to reduce the presence of drugs in a prison the governor hearing an adjudication should be told to set the maximum punishment of added days for the offence, they would be acting unlawfully by fettering the governor's discretion. Adjudications are a judicial process and subject to judicial review but, along with punishments, they are measures that contribute to the control and stability of a prison. The governor could argue that to ensure control he or she must retain the discretion to decide punishments, which is inherent in the wording of the Prison Rule 50, which reads: 'If he or she finds the prisoner guilty of an offence against discipline, the governor may [subject to Rule 52 of these rules] impose one or more of the following punishments … '. There are times when a wise governor will consider the question of how much punishment a prisoner can take at any one time. Levels of punishment are about control and security but they are also about listening with compassion to a defence, and mitigation.

Effective governing

A governor must not only manage the tensions inherent in the Prison Service's current organisational structure, but also the prison establishment itself. The greater the success of the latter, the less the tensions of Prison Service organisation will impinge on the prison establishment.

Within a prison there are prisoners, various types of staff and their representatives. Each group will have different perceptions as to how much authority a governor actually has and how he or she should exercise it in any given situation. Tension arises when these varying groups present an issue but seek different solutions. A simple illustration is in the unstated question to a new governor, 'Are you for the staff or for the prisoners?' The answer 'for both' – in that he or she represents particular values – can be confusing. A series of decisions may indicate the answer to the question, but lack of time might thwart a resolution: a governor's reputation can be made or lost within days of taking up the post.

Typically, tension occurs within a prison between prisoners and staff. In taking up the management of a prison, the governor should ensure a positive relationship with his or her senior managers; they in turn should reflect the same relationship with their own staff. The next task is to ensure that staff care for one another. This factor may be the key to a successful prison and point to the overall health of a prison. From this the staff are more likely to develop positive relationships with prisoners. However, governing is more than management through a formal structure of command. The representational element in the role is essential and requires a high degree of visibility. That visibility allows both staff and prisoners to project onto the governor their concerns and expectations. The role of governor represents the human values of the prison; he or she mirrors moral values, safe custody, a caring environment. However, such high visibility can create tensions between a governor and managers, who may see the governor providing access for personal and direct lobbying by prisoners, which challenges managers' own authority. Such a situation can be managed by putting informal applications into formal structures, but there are occasions when the informal application will need to succeed. The tension between formal and informal structures and between a command and a representational role are always present.

Because the relationships across and within a prison are complex rather than singular, there is a need to manage the tensions between the formal and informal. The reality is that people, including managers, want each issue or decision to be addressed in their own particular context. There is more difficulty when a single issue has implications for a series of other complex ones or, indeed, structures. But if the focus remains on individual people then the interactive dynamics of emotion, concern and care remain as determinant factors. There is a skilful art in saying 'no'. Many prisoners will press a concern until they see the governor – at which point they will accept 'no'. This is an aspect of the representational role the governor holds, and often control is influenced by the quality or accessibility of the governor to key prisoners. Ultimately the aim is to create and maintain a controlled atmosphere that is relaxed and which respects people as people, whether they are staff or prisoners.

The managerial and representational role requires time management. Paperwork can be delegated, the representational role cannot; and yet in job descriptions time management is rarely, if ever, referred to. There is something within the representational role that suggests it is most effectively done outside the core management day. A governor who is available in the evenings, at times when prisoners are on association, will be seen as visibly present. Equally, staff put great store on seeing the governor in the prison during unsocial hours. For them, there is something about the leader being willing to share the domestic difficulty of unsocial hours and of understanding the prison world over the 24-hours' experience. At such times the focus of the role is in relationships with people and much of the discussion will be about relationships, about interests and hobbies – less about penal practice and theory.

Balancing reason and emotion

Within a prison there is also tension between reason and emotion. The relationships between prisoners and prison staff are complex and yet very little research has been done on those relationships. Prisoners do not want to be in prison. They tend to be people who act out their emotions rather than sit down and reason them through. In many cases, their criminal acts were actions born of emotion rather than reason. The pressures of imprisonment tend to heighten emotional stresses. One minute prison officers are a listening ear for a depressed prisoner, the next moment they may be faced with a very angry and threatening prisoner, and the next they might be required to wear protective clothing to deal with a major disorder. This changing role is a difficult one to manage and prisoners are continually challenging it, continually trying to push the boundaries outwards. It is the prison officer who is hourly trying to reconcile the tension created by the Statement of Purposes, between security and humanity. The task is difficult enough if seen as a purely rational debate, but when the emotions of people also have to be managed it becomes increasingly complex. When judgements go wrong it is usually because the force of emotion has overwhelmed the balance of reason.

The governor, as manager, is continually balancing reason and emotion. There are times when the level of emotion is so high it appears as if the prisoners are acting out the emotions of the staff. Given the complexity and closeness of their working relationship perhaps we should not be too surprised by this. However, it presents a very difficult tension to manage and one which can be dangerous to control if it goes too far. In judging issues of atmosphere and control the governor must be in touch with the emotions within the prison and must be continually working to influence them.

Headquarters often presents itself as the rational face of the Prison Service and individual prisons as the emotional face of the organisation. There are times when several changing policies emerge from Headquarters and their cumulative impact is only understood when they converge for implementation on the governor's desk. The governor has to manage the tension between policy and implementation or, put another way, between reason and emotion.

The Prison Service KPIs all measure outputs within a prison. The danger is that they measure rational output and ignore emotional feeling. Two prisons can achieve KPI scores but only one might riot. That disturbance may have something to do with judgements about individual issues, about personal respect, about how roles are allowed to be taken up or about how much freedom people – staff and prisoners – are given to interpret their own role. If the role of governor is approached creatively and human emotions are managed well, staff will reflect this back onto prisoners who will also work to control and change their emotions. The atmosphere of the prison – the mix of reason, of policy, of emotion, of acting-out – will then be relaxed but controlled, safe and secure.

Louis XIV claimed he was the state, 'L'etat c'est moi'. The governor is the prison; the prison is the governor. Any tensions presented are focused in on the governor as the key person in the prison. The task of the governor is to manage and absorb those tensions and act them out creatively with interpersonal skills. The demands of the task also require governors to manage the balance between reason and emotion within themselves, and to have a strong framework of philosophy from which to draw support.

References

Bryans, S. (1998) 'Managing or governing?', unpublished lecture to the Senior Command course, Rugby: HM Prison Service Library

— (2000) 'Governing prisons: an analysis of who is governing prisons and the competencies which they require to govern effectively', *Howard Journal*, Vol. 39, No. 1, pp. 14–29

— and Wilson, D. (1998) *The Prison Governor: Theory and Practice*, HMP Leyhill: Prison Service Journal Publications

Cullen, F., La Tessa, E., Burton, V. and Lombardo, L. (1993) 'The correctional orientation of prison wardens', *Criminology*, Vol. 31, No. 1, pp. 69–92

DiIulio, J. (1987) *Governing Prisons: A Comparative Study of Correctional Management*, New York: Freedom Press

HM Prison Service (1997) *Prison Service Review*, Home Office

Peak, K. (1995) *Justice Administration: Police Courts and Correctional Management*, Englewood Cliffs, NJ: Prentice Hall

THE TRAINING AND DEVELOPMENT OF PRISON SERVICE STAFF

Steve Lowden

The Prison Service is an organisation of mammoth complexity, employing over 40,000 staff whose roles range from doctors to dog handlers, caterers to architects, prison officers and management staff to chaplains. Numerous government reports have commented upon the considerable range of knowledge and skills necessary for staff to perform their roles effectively. Consequently, the Prison Service now offers its staff the most comprehensive range of management and leadership training available in the public sector. The training and development of all groups of staff – ensuring they are able to fulfil their true potential and contribute positively to the work of the Prison Service – resulted in the Prison Service offering over 4,000 different training and development courses in 1998. In the financial year 1997–98 there were 304,000 training days achieved by its staff.

The national training plan

A national training plan was introduced in 1996 to provide an overview of the training offered to Prison Service staff and to support a Key Performance Indicator (KPI9) for staff training (HM Prison Service 1996). It is produced annually, at the start of the financial year, and enables Prison Service managers to plan their staff training needs over the ensuing twelve months. The national training plan and the KPI are agreed by the Prison Service Management Board before being issued, and copies of the plan are sent to all prisons, area managers, staff associations, central services and the wider criminal justice system. Establishments are provided with resources to release staff for training (and to cover sick and annual leave) through a proportionate addition to their staff budgets (the 'non-effective' addition).

The national training plan contains information on all the courses offered, their duration, the staff required or eligible to undertake the training, and the classification of each course. All courses are classified as either 'mandatory' or 'discretionary' (when they are at the discretion of the line manager). Mandatory courses include training that must be repeated annually. Mandatory training per member of staff in 1997–98 averaged three days. For recording purposes, each course is given a code. All establishments are required to show the volume and types of training they have completed, on a monthly basis. This information is collated centrally by the Training Policy Unit and provides an overview of the training achieved and enables outstanding training requirements to be assessed. The Prison Service Standards Audit Unit also examines prison establishments' training monitoring records and these details are made available to the Prison Board.

The Prison Service in England and Wales demonstrated its commitment to staff training by introducing in 1996 a specific KPI for it, which measures the volume of training achieved by Prison Service staff. Table 14.1 shows that in 1996–97 the Service almost achieved its KPI target of six days per staff member. In 1997–98, due mainly to the high volume of Prison Officer Initial Training (which accounted for 21% of the total training), it managed to surpass its set target.

Table 14.1: Staff training targets, 1996–97 to 1998–99

Year	Target days per staff member	Days achieved per staff member
1996–97	6	5.4
1997–98	6	7.8
1998–99	6.5	7.8

Source: HM Prison Service 1999

The national training plan sets out what the Prison Service must do to ensure that it meets the staff training KPI and seeks to achieve this by establishing the volume of training the Service needs. It estimates the number of training days needed in each area of mandatory training, and this in turn enables prisons and central services to develop a local training plan by identifying those required to receive, or who might benefit from, a particular type of training.

Delivering training to the Prison Service

The comprehensive range of training and the geographical spread of Prison Service staff throughout England and Wales results in training being delivered by a number of different parts of the Service, the main ones being Headquarters, prison establishments themselves and the Prison Service training service (PSTS). In the case of Headquarters, the training delivered is specialist in nature, reflecting the responsibilities of specific parts of the organisation. For example, the Directorate of Healthcare (DHC) contracts with external bodies to deliver medical training to doctors and nurses. It is required to deliver such training within its budget bids and manage all aspects of the training including the design, specification, delivery, quality assurance and evaluation. In December 1998, DHC training resulted in nine doctors working in the Prison Service being awarded the diploma in prison medicine.

Every prison has a training manager, who is responsible for organising the local training plan, and a number of staff trainers, who organise and deliver training in how to organise and deliver training for their colleagues. This arrangement means that staff receive training at their own workplace so that they are able to resume their normal work duties quickly, thus minimising disruption to the prison. Some governors have opted for staff spending one afternoon each month undergoing some form of training within their workplace while the prison runs on a restricted regime. Prisons usually have a dedicated classroom for staff training, a range of distance-learning materials and, increasingly, videos and CD-ROMS. The content of many of the local courses is laid down nationally but quality assurance, monitoring and evaluation is a local responsibility and some courses are modified to suit local demands.

The biggest single provider of training and development for the Prison Service is the PSTS, which is part of the Personnel Directorate. The head of PSTS reports directly to the Personnel Director, who is a member of the Prison Service Management Board. The head of PSTS is supported by a number of functional heads including:

- Head of training policy – responsible for the development of PSTS strategy and determining the Prison Service's training requirements;
- Head of national training units – responsible for delivering courses and consultancy to prisons in a specific geographical area;
- Head of management and specialist training – responsible for the development and delivery of management, leadership, personnel, chaplaincy and finance training opportunities;

- Head of operational training – responsible for the development and delivery of Prison Service-specific training: control and restraint, dog handling, security, incident control, etc.; and
- Head of prison officer induction training (POINT) – responsible for the development and delivery of induction and basic initial training for new prison officer recruits.

The main responsibilities of PSTS are to determine strategic training and development needs across the Prison Service and to provide training/developmental opportunities, directly or under contract, which meet those needs. To achieve this, PSTS employs 260 members of staff in fourteen locations. A number of (local) prison training managers and other prison staff may develop a level of expertise in a given area so that they are used, with the permission of their governors, by the PSTS to deliver training. Ordinarily they work in prisons, but are temporarily attached to PSTS to deliver some courses and are referred to as 'associate trainers'. In 1998–99 PSTS had an annual budget of around £15 million of which just under half was deployed on staff salaries.

PSTS has four residential colleges: Newbold Revel, which specialises in management and some operational training; Aberford Road and Love Lane in Wakefield, where the vast majority of prison officer induction training (POINT) takes place; and Clayton Hall, at the National Sports Centre in Lilleshall, which specialises in physical education. Collectively these colleges can accommodate over 600 people per night. Figure 14.1 also shows the seven training units that are strategically sited throughout England and Wales. These units work directly with prisons in their region by:

- seeking to respond directly to their training needs;
- supporting them in developing and delivering local training plans; and
- ensuring they are aware of new national training initiatives that may impact upon their staff.

Training units do not have residential facilities and so a large proportion of their courses are short, lasting one day. Currently, about 20% of PSTS events are organised by training units, which are normally managed by a governor grade 4, and held locally in or near prisons. By their actions, PSTS training units are helping the Prison Service to develop the infrastructure of a 'learning organisation'.

During 1997–98 PSTS delivered 180,000 days of training and trained 1,500 new prison officers. Overall 29,500 staff received some form of training from them. This ranged from control and restraint training to catering, rugby coaching and

Figure 14.1: PSTS site locations

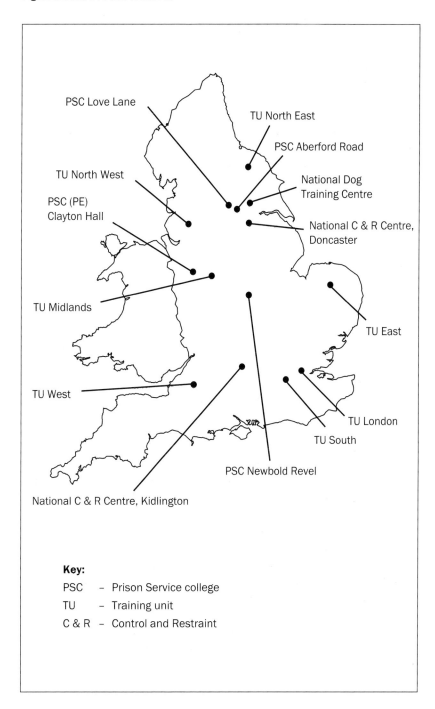

PSC Love Lane

TU North East

PSC Aberford Road

TU North West

National Dog Training Centre

PSC (PE) Clayton Hall

National C & R Centre, Doncaster

TU Midlands

TU East

TU West

TU London

TU South

PSC Newbold Revel

National C & R Centre, Kidlington

Key:

PSC   – Prison Service college

TU   – Training unit

C & R – Control and Restraint

certificates in management. Altogether over 400 different courses were offered, which reflects the complexity of the tasks that Prison Service staff perform.

Training new recruits

Prison officer initial training (POINT)

While prison officers are recruited by the prisons they are going to work in, they are all trained by PSTS, using nationally agreed criteria. This ensures that all newly recruited prison officers receive the same standard of training. The number of prison officers recruited has varied considerably since 1995 when there was a virtual recruitment freeze as the Service introduced a voluntary early retirement scheme (VERSE) to encourage targeted staff nearing retirement age to leave. In 1997 and 1998 around 1,500 new officers a year were recruited as the Prison Service attempted to train new staff to accommodate the rapidly rising prisoner population.

The POINT course is an eleven-week sandwich course consisting of eight weeks of residential training, usually at one of the Wakefield colleges, in two blocks of four weeks each. Prior to attending the course new entrants spend a week in their own prison observing work practices and they return to their prison in weeks 6 and 11 of the course to consolidate and consider how they will apply their newly gained knowledge in their workplace. The course also has a number of 'streaming days' which are designed to give extra information and guidance to students who are going to work in a particular type of prison, including those housing female prisoners, young offenders or maximum-security prisoners. During 1998, male and female students were equally represented.

Sessions on searching cells and prisoners, handcuffing, radio skills, suicide prevention, first aid, and basic control and restraint training are included in the POINT course. Each student needs to pass written exams, in weeks 5 and 10, and practical exams to gain a certificate of competence that enables them to work as a prison officer. In 1998, approximately 9% of students starting the POINT course either resigned or failed the course. All new recruits who pass are registered for the National Vocational Qualification (NVQ) level 2 in custodial care and the vast majority continue to work towards this award back at their establishment.

Fast-track schemes

Accelerated promotion scheme (APS)

The accelerated promotion scheme (APS) was started in 1988 and is designed for graduates; it also gives selected non-graduate Prison Service staff an opportunity to reach senior management positions in less than five years. All new recruits to the Prison Service undertake POINT and a variety of training courses and work placements designed to provide them with a comprehensive understanding of how the Prison Service and prisons work. The APS supports students up to the point when they reach their national assessment for governor grade 4 posts.

Direct entry scheme

The direct entry scheme gives managers with at least five years' experience of working in a dynamic people-orientated organisation, or existing Prison Service staff who have passed their probationary period, direct entry into the Prison Service at governor grade 5 training level. Successful applicants receive an intensive four-week period of initial POINT, work for eight weeks in uniform as a prison officer and complete an eight-week prison management course. Participants in the scheme serve a 12-month probationary period, followed by the achievement of formal accreditation approximately 12–18 months after joining the scheme. Once accredited to governor grade 5, career progression is through the normal promotion assessments.

Cross-hierarchical move scheme – for existing civil servants

This scheme enables established civil servants, from higher executive officer to grade 6 and equivalent grades, to develop their careers within the operational setting of the Prison Service. The majority of scheme members are appointed to governor grade 5 level but can be appointed at governor grade 4 or, exceptionally, governor grade 3. Successful applicants receive an intensive four-week period of initial POINT, work for eight weeks in uniform as a prison officer and complete an eight-week prison management course. Participants should achieve formal accreditation to governor grade 5 within 6–10 months of joining the scheme and can take up a full-time appointment at the level offered, at either governor grade 5, 4 or 3.

Operational training

Most operational training undertaken by Prison Service staff, including control and restraint, security and regime training, has been developed as a result of recommendations in government reports. These courses are usually mandatory for staff and are constantly reviewed to ensure they meet changing needs, demands and new legislation. PSTS expects to deliver to the Prison Service in the region of 58,000 days of operational training each year.

Operational training is delivered by PSTS in a variety of locations, including specialist sites at the National Control and Restraint Centres at Doncaster and Kidlington, near Oxford, which have replica prison buildings. Courses run from these centres aim to prepare staff to respond to a serious incident in an establishment and to operate as part of a team in riot situations. Simulated incidents are enacted to ensure that the training offered has a high degree of realism. In addition, the training staff at these centres are a national resource, available to respond to a prison establishment's call where an incident is occurring. The National Dog School, located near Doncaster, is a further specialist site. It provides training for prison dogs and their handlers in searching techniques including searches for drugs, firearms and explosives. The school also offers training for dog handlers involved in patrol work in prisons.

A prison dog undergoing training for guarding the perimeter of a high-security prison.

The operational courses offered include the incident command course, which was developed as a direct response to the Woolf Report (Woolf and Tumim 1991) and aims to prepare senior managers for their roles in incident control. The dedicated search team course was a recommendation of the Woodcock Report (1994) and is a one-week course aimed at those staff who are to be deployed as part of an establishment's dedicated search team (Category A establishments only). Course participants are introduced to new and sophisticated equipment that will assist them in their search operations. The X-ray machines and metal detector search techniques course aims to familiarise staff with techniques for searching people and baggage using those devices and portals (door frame-shaped detectors, often seen in use at airports) to identify weapons and explosives. Special secure units accommodate some of the most dangerous prisoners in the prison system and the special secure unit course has been designed to equip staff with the necessary knowledge and skill to maintain effective security and control in such units. Learning about the effective use of support mechanisms, course participants are given an overview of terrorist and criminal organisations, including command structures and the resources available to them. PSTS also runs a course for those working in closed supervision centres, which aims to give staff the appropriate skills and knowledge to deal effectively with the highly disruptive prisoners housed in thoses centres.

Management training

The Prison Service offers a wide range of management courses for its staff and in 1998 committed over £2.5 million pounds in each of the following three years specifically for management training. This initiative was in response to a need identified in the Prison Service Review (1997), and provides 24 new management training schemes. PSTS have developed contracts with further education colleges, the Open University, Financial Times Management, in association with Nottingham Trent University and Cambridge University, to deliver bespoke management courses for prison staff.

The certificate in supervisory management is a course designed for first-line supervisors and those aspiring to such roles. It explores aspects of controlling resources, information analysis, recruitment procedures, improving individual and team performance and an introduction to quality management. Participants need to successfully complete eight assessments and a project to be awarded the certificate by the Institute of Management. In 1998 over 700 Prison Service staff enrolled for this course.

The capable manager for the Prison Service course, developed by the Open University Business School (OUBS) and PSTS, is open to middle managers, from executive officer through to senior executive officer and governor grade 4. It is a customised version of the OUBS capable manager course and provides Prison Service staff with the opportunity to gain a professional qualification in management. The course covers a wide range of topics within the four key roles of management: people, operations and marketing, information and finance. Course participants apply general management concepts to the Prison Service and deepen their understanding of some critical issues facing the Service. Successful completion of this one-year course leads to the award of the Open University's professional certificate in management. The Prison Service is the largest single customer for this course, with over 500 students enrolling on it in 1998. Over 85% of all students who have enrolled so far have passed the course.

In 1999, 120 places on a post-graduate diploma course in management studies – organised by Financial Times Management in association with Nottingham Trent University – were made available to middle managers, at higher executive and senior executive officer and governor grades 3 to 5. Staff who have also successfully gained the Open University's professional certificate in management, but have not reached the specified grades, are also eligible to apply. Although postgraduate diplomas are normally only available to individuals holding a degree, Prison Service staff without a degree are able to apply. Prior work experience is taken into account when selecting candidates for the course.

Senior Prison Service managers at governor grade 3 and senior executive officers' level and above also have the opportunity to apply for a diploma/Master's degree in applied criminology and management at the University of Cambridge. The diploma focuses on four core subject areas: strategic leadership, understanding how prisons work, the criminal justice and legal context, and criminal behaviour. Assessment for the diploma is by successful completion of a total of three essays based on any three of the modules. Students who successfully gain the diploma can go forward for the Master's degree. To be successful, candidates need to complete a module and assignment on applied criminology research, a 3,000-word assignment on the subject area not covered in the assessment of the diploma, and a further 18,000-word assignment.

All the management courses outlined above have residential elements, classroom teaching, distance-learning material provided by the contracted supplier and assignments needing to be successfully completed by the student to achieve the nationally recognised qualification. It is envisaged by the Prison Service Management Board that staff will, by completing such courses, have a deeper understanding of organisational and managerial issues and will thus be more able to examine and improve their own managerial practices.

National training organisations (NTOs)

National training organisations (NTOs) are a major government training initiative aimed at developing and enhancing the qualifications of the United Kingdom's work-force. By December 1998 over 80 NTOs had been formed. The Prison Service is a leading member of the custodial care NTO and will influence the qualification structure and content for all custodial training.

The Prison Service is just one part of the criminal justice system and works closely with staff from the probation, police and court services. Throughout 1998 a working group of staff from the Prison and probation services explored how a common infrastructure for staff management, development and accredited courses could be established between the two services. Planned work includes a functional mapping project to identify common and interrelating staff functions across prisons and NVQs across the services. Some of this work is being delivered in co-operation with the community justice and custodial care NTOs working together to share their expertise.

Developing into a 'learning organisation'

The Prison Service, as has been demonstrated, has a flexible approach to training, offering a comprehensive range of training opportunities in the workplace, colleges and universities. This flexible approach, using Prison Service and external suppliers, creates an element of choice for staff who want or need to avail themselves of training and development opportunities. By utilising videos, CD-ROMS and distance-learning materials students have the opportunity to learn at their own pace and often in a location of their choosing. Such training options enable prison staff to absorb new information, raise their self-awareness and skills, and transfer their newly gained learning into their workplace. They thereby, further develop their own competence in the work environment and consequently their value to the Prison Service, and aid the Service to become a 'learning organisation'. A learning organisation facilitates the learning of all its staff and consciously and wilfully transforms itself and its context.

Evaluating training

One of the greatest challenges for those who organise training, whether in the public or private sector, is to be able to demonstrate the impact that training received has had on staff. All training opportunities should enable staff to transfer their newly developed skills, behaviour or knowledge back into the workplace and make a measurable impact, a significant difference.

Evaluating the impact specific training courses have on individuals and workplace practices is notoriously difficult. PSTS is developing its capacity to evaluate the training courses it offers by asking all course participants to complete an end-of-course questionnaire, which gives an indication of how useful, or not, a person found the training. Participants on some courses also receive a questionnaire after they have been back in the workplace for a period of months and have been able to use and personally evaluate their newly gained knowledge. A questionnaire is also sent to line managers asking whether there has been a discernable, measurable change in performance as a result of the training received. The development of a comprehensive strategy to evaluate Prison Service training and to feed the results back into the organisation is a major but attainable challenge.

Developing new courses

Developing a comprehensive evaluation strategy enables training to be modified in response to the feedback received from previous course participants and ensures that it is totally relevant to the needs of new participants. New training courses are developed, or current ones modified in the light of:

- Prison Service initiatives (for example, developing comprehensive Prison Service drug strategy will have major training implications);
- new legislation;
- Inspectorate of Prisons' Reports, which show that there are training deficiencies;
- Prison Service Instructions and Orders;
- staff association comments; and
- the trainers themselves, who develop considerable technical expertise in delivering courses and so can see how they might improve that delivery.

To aid a 'continuous improvement' philosophy, in 1998 PSTS introduced a programme board to oversee and co-ordinate the development of new training courses and provide a quality-control mechanism for existing ones. Through development and modification of existing courses it is possible to examine the portfolio of training opportunities offered to the Prison Service and to prioritise the organisation's training needs. This scrutiny is particularly important if new training initiatives are to be met within current budget provision. Courses continue to take place which incorporate the new Prison Service core competency framework (CCF). Further research will be pursued into the viability of grouping together operational courses, including adjudication and incident command courses, to achieve a recognised, externally validated qualification for governors. As governors normally take such courses throughout their Prison Service career, such action will help underpin the philosophy of lifetime learning. At the same time it recognises the fact that prison managers discharge both managerial and operational functions.

References

HM Prison Service (1996) *National Training Plan*, HM Prison Service

— (1997) *Prison Service Review*, Home Office

— (1999) *Annual Reports and Accounts April 1998 – March 1999*, The Stationery Office

Woodcock, Sir J. (1994) *The Escape from Whitemoor Prison on Friday 9th September 1994* (The Woodcock Inquiry), Cm 2741, HMSO

Woolf, Lord Justice and Tumim, Judge S. (1991) *Prison Disturbances April 1990: Report of an Inquiry by the Rt Hon. Lord Justice Woolf and His Hon. Judge Stephen Tumim* (The Woolf Report), Cm 1456, HMSO

15

A PRISON OFFICER'S PERSPECTIVE

Gareth Sands and Charlotte Rendle

Introduction

Somewhere in the middle of the main course comes the inevitable but so far politely skirted question: 'So, what line are you in?'

Then the dilemma:. 'Oh, I'm a civil servant' comes quickly to mind. Or, 'I'm in security' perhaps. But these are only delaying tactics. Ultimately I have to confess, 'I work for the Prison Service.'

'Pardon?' Perhaps they misheard.

Again, slightly louder, 'I work for the Prison Service.' Or sometimes the shock tactic: 'I'm a screw.'

Typically, a stunned silence ensues as the inquirer immediately regrets the question and realises that the boundaries of the usual career comfort zones have been exceeded. Slowly at first, ('wow – that's … er, unusual …') then with increasing confidence, the hackneyed questions come: 'Aren't you scared?' Or, 'Do you 'look after' anyone famous in your prison?' Very soon the questioning descends to the wisecracks: 'Well, at least it's a secure job', or another favourite, 'Any escapes lately?'

Invariably, the attention of the whole table becomes focused, bringing with it the familiar feeling of becoming the object of interest again. Above all, what most people seem to want to know is: Why would you want to do that? Why would you want to earn your living locking up human beings?

Preconceptions about prisons and the people who work in them range from Fletch in *Porridge* to the shaking walls of *Prisoner Cell Block H*. If stretched, people's imagination might range to a recent news story, the escape or release of a particularly high-profile prisoner or the proposal of a new prison, all too close to their home. In fact, the average person knows very little about the behind-the-wall workings of our penal establishments or what is involved in the work of a typical prison officer. Indeed, the Prison Service has been described as the 'Invisible Man', remaining unseen and unconsidered until disaster strikes: escapes, sentence calculation dilemmas or suicides. Similarly, for most newly recruited prison officers, training college and the two subsequent observation weeks often provide the first insight into life in the Prison Service and the unique culture of prison environment. Such first impressions are largely dependent upon the particular prison chosen to work in. Any ideals about the Prison Service as an organisation – where individuals are able to make a real difference in a challenging, fulfilling and thought-provoking environment – are destroyed or affirmed according to the environment and culture of a particular establishment, underlying the sheer diversity contained among all of the prisons in England and Wales.

Apart from the 'hidden' aspect of prisons, another source of public misunderstanding about the Prison Service springs from the way in which prisoners themselves are popularly visualised. At best, this may be as deranged but largely harmless lunatics; at worse, as psychotic and dangerous semi-alien beings with no capacity for any kind of finer human feeling. Some prisoners may be like this, but they are very few. First and foremost, prisoners are people, human beings. They are not the identical clones of television images nor the repulsive projections of nightmares but a diverse collection of individuals. Like any group of people there will be a wide spectrum of personalities, dispositions and abilities. There will be some prisoners who are more likeable than others and those whose particular officers will relate to better than others. There are some with whom prison staff will develop close relationships and some who will cause problem after problem. Some prisoners will be serving a first, one-off sentence; many will return to prison again and again. They will have families, who they will miss and worry about, and issues to come to terms with relating to their crimes and incarceration. Often, individual prisoners are people you would not believe capable of committing the crimes for which they are serving prison sentences.

Similarly, there is no such thing as a typical prison officer. The circumstances from which they come to the Prison Service are as varied as the establishments in which they will work. Traditionally, becoming a prison officer stands out as one of the 'natural' choices following time in the armed forces, and it is perhaps to the mental image of ex-squaddy that most people refer when trying to visualise a prison officer. Yet the kind of people recruited into the Service has altered significantly in recent years. The profession now recruits an incredibly wide range of personnel, sometimes attracted by the security of the job or the starting salary. This very diversity and richness of backgrounds and skills creates a wealth of

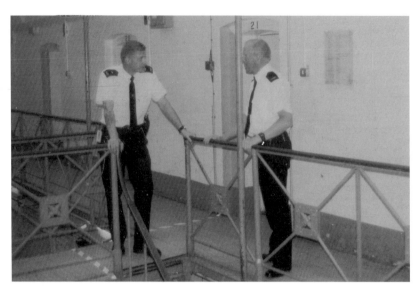

A senior officer receives a briefing from a member of his staff on the latest wing events. Prison officers are recruited from diverse backgrounds and offer a wide range of experience.

experience within the Prison Service which, if managed effectively, can help drive the Service effectively through the 21st century.

Daily life 'inside'

The job of a prison officer stretches far beyond the conventional image of turning keys and counting prisoners. Perhaps the simplest way of understanding the role is to list all the tasks performed by people in society every day; then acknowledge that most of these rituals also take place in some form inside prisons. Prisoners eat, receive mail, have haircuts, go to work, make phone calls, see visitors, use the library, visit sick relatives, have families and experience both good and bad days. In fact, a prison is a microcosm of society behind a wall. All of the activities embraced by these phrases – and many more – are managed, encouraged and supervised day-to-day by prison officers. Frontline prison staff, through their belief, determination and discernment, do have the ability to impact upon the often complex lives of inmates, shaping their behaviour and helping to fulfil the Service's Statement of Purpose 'to look after [prisoners] with humanity and help them lead law-abiding and useful lives in custody and after release'. But this is far from being a straightforward process and any preconceptions about the Prison Service providing an easy career option are soon dispelled. The prison environment uniquely exposes staff to many difficult and dangerous situations, in

Part Three – People who work in prisons

the face of which they are required to cope sensitively and appropriately, diffusing conflict and remaining confident and calm.

Many prison officers work in local prisons that serve the courts and the community in a given area and house a diverse population of remand, convicted and sentenced prisoners. A typical prison officer's day in such a prison starts at about 7.30 a.m. with roll-check and the unlocking of any inmates who might be required in reception to be taken to court for trial or sentencing, discharge, or transfer to another establishment. (Reception is not, as its name might suggest, a comfortable lobby area with potted palms, magazines and piped music, but one of the most frenetic, chaotic, noisy and, for some reason, normally the smallest areas of an establishment.) Meanwhile, back on the wing the other inmates are unlocked in a 'controlled manner' for breakfast. This can be a volatile time – your average burglar will be the first to admit that he is 'not really a morning person'. Porridge with the consistency of cement and toast with the properties of rubber are among the stereotypes more correctly associated with a prison and therefore perhaps not much of an incentive. 'Treatments' or 'sick parade' soon follow, when the National Health Service performs one of its more amazing but less well-known feats of diagnosing and prescribing for the minor ailments of perhaps upwards of a hundred prisoners (the numbers are always higher in summer) within an incredibly short time-frame.

Next comes preparation for movement to various prisoner activities. In itself, co-ordinating mass movement to and from all possible destinations around the establishment presents most prisons with a logistical nightmare. The net result typically resembles organised chaos, resolved only when the incessant process of collecting and collating inmate numbers has confirmed that all prisoners are accounted for. Activities traditionally fall under the headings of education or work. A renewed interest in 'constructive regimes' is widening the definitions of such terms, but education still consists predominantly of lessons in basic numeracy and literacy while work is usually focused around specific workshops or the cleaning and routine maintenance of the prison's fabric. Nominal wages are earned through such participation. Other prisoners, normally in open conditions, might venture beyond the prison gates in their own cars to outside work locations. This is in preparation for release under resettlement licence entitlements. However, while convicted prisoners are legally required to work there are rarely sufficient openings for 'full employment', and those who remain unemployed will spend most of the day behind their cell doors.

When prisoners are thus duly dispatched wing staff can begin their daily chores. Accommodation fabric checks (AFCs) have to be completed on all cells – a check for evidence of unauthorised articles, illegal substances, escape attempts, etc.

Exercise (normally 30 minutes to an hour a day, weather permitting) will have to be supervised, and mail and newspapers are to be handed out. When these tasks are completed there is always plenty more work to be done. Cell searches have to attain target figures; various items of paperwork must be completed including complex sentence-planning documents, observation books, suicide-watch logs and individual history sheets. There is also the ceaseless round of responding to cell bells – ostensibly for use in emergencies only but in reality used mainly for prisoners' trivial requests or demands, or merely as an expression of frustration.

Lunchtime sees most prisoners coming back to their wings for roll-check and food, followed by a return to work or association. Afternoons and dinnertime typically have the same pattern and are normally followed by evening association: inmates are allowed out of their cells to watch television, socialise with others, or play pool, table tennis or table football. Finally, the day is concluded with 'bang-up', prison slang for the nightly ritualistic game of chasing prisoners around land-ings, trying to achieve the correct number and identity of individuals in each cell. Prisoners, however, normally have other ideas and do their best to foil the staff's attempts by protesting an urgent need to collect hot water from the landing boilers or purloining tobacco and magazines from neighbours. After yet another roll-check (but not the last one of the night) a prison officer's day ends. But he or she will not have long to recover, for a 9 p.m. finish is invariably followed by a 7.30 a.m. start.

Relationships with prisoners and with management

Prison 'culture' becomes a central and troublesome issue when 'them and us' lines are drawn, a conflict situation that has dominated, historically, staff–prisoner relationships. One of the first pieces of advice traditionally given to any new prison officer before the first day on the landings, reflecting the cultural evolution of several centuries, is 'Just remember, whatever they ask, the answer's no.' If a prisoner then dares to question such an answer, he or she might expect to elicit a reply such as, 'What part of no don't you understand?' While the attitude signified by such a riposte might serve to provide the desired quiet life in the short term, frustrations build and positive relations are often fractured. Yet the key factor in achieving a positive and vital prison culture is the quality of relationships within the institution. Surely the most critical relationship within prison walls is that which exists between prison officers and prisoners.

At their most extreme, such relationships can either create or obstruct occupa-tional or educational achievement, cause or prevent suicide attempts, or motivate the address of victim or family issues. The role of frontline staff in addressing an issue such as individual low self-esteem – at the root of so much offending behaviour – is invaluable. With their 'captive audience', prison staff have the capacity to aid the reconstruction of self-image to a more positive one, reinforcing strong role models and thus breaking the potential cycle of deprivation and the impact of a negative self-fulfilling prophecy. In Young Offender Institutions (YOIs) particularly, even the toughest of prison officers has the capacity to be, and often is, the father or mother figure many juveniles never had. Many find in this role a level of job satisfaction that goes far beyond that which might be expected of somebody who, in the public imagination, simply turns keys and closes doors for a living.

Prison officers also play a vital role in upholding the concept of the seamless sentence, with its ideals of the prisoner receiving planned and consistent attention from the moment of imprisonment until the expiry of their licence in the community. It is therefore crucial that the prison officer avoids any judgemental attitudes and feelings of superiority. Rather, a position of empathy and compassion should be adopted towards prisoners who, while having their liberty curtailed, deserve the basic rights of humanity and should be recognised as being more than simply a name or number.

Another crucial interaction within the Prison Service, perhaps better described as a 'divide' rather than a 'relationship', is that between prison officers and prison

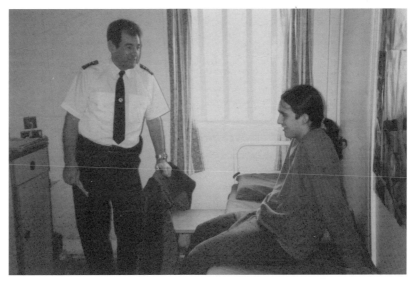

A wing principal officer in informal conversation with a young prisoner. The role of frontline staff in addressing prisoners' welfare is a key factor in achieving a positive and vital prison culture.

management. These divisions, often as culturally entrenched as those between prisoners and staff, are perpetuated and exacerbated by the continuous problem of communication breakdown in the Prison Service. Word of mouth and media interpretations of policy and change frustrate staff at all levels. Therefore, as dedication and perseverance remain vital to the success of a prison establishment, staff must be kept well informed of change, be encouraged to demonstrate initiative and versatility, and be granted greater recognition and reward for outstanding effort. This involves leadership, highlighted in the Prison Service Review (1997) by its claim that 'a well-run prison turns more than anything else on the skill and approach of the Governor'. The management of prison culture through particular styles of leadership or specific values therefore involves managing through symbolic means and organisational rites. However, while this might be fine in theory, in practice there is often discontent amongst uniformed staff, with claims that management are unsympathetic to their requirements and demands, and that more consideration is given to prisoner needs than to those of staff. Such claims do not help to narrow the officer–management divide.

Meanwhile, one of the hardest cultural issues to crack is the popular projections onto and stereotypes of the Prison Service by society, for which the media must accept the greatest share of responsibility. Images of the Prison Service are rarely positive or indeed accurate as the 'News of the Screws' details the latest scandals. Certainly the media do not take pride in the Prison Service, and cynicism about the resulting public image hampers prison staff who, despite talent and dedication, can be forgiven for losing a certain self-confidence and self-respect. It will take more than a public relations drive to overturn such a negative image.

The future

Opinions amongst prison officers remain mixed over reducing re-offending, recidivism and the manipulation of statistics at local and Headquarters levels. The recent drive to work more closely with our criminal justice partners, and the fashionable move towards radical approaches to criminality such as restorative justice, have also attracted their fair share of criticism, both internally and externally. This situation parallels attempts by the Prison Service to break down divisions within it in order that greater co-operation and clarity of direction can be achieved. The next decade will no doubt witness continual fine-tuning of Prison Service practice and policy with the introduction of many new measures. These include attempts at an improved transition for prisoners into the community through electronic tagging while further easing the pressure of prison overcrowding. Therefore, while Prison Service management undergoes significant changes, prison officers are increasingly being encouraged to use their own initiative and drive to find solutions to problems and difficulties within an environment that provides numerous opportunities for vision and change.

In order to take advantage of such opportunities, the process of change should begin by shaping individuals' rites, values, beliefs and attitudes. If the Prison Service is to achieve its desired level of progression and change well into the 21st century, human resource/personnel management and training must form a central plank within the process in an attempt to overcome problems of resistance to change. However, this approach can be seen in some organisations as a smokescreen for the pursuit of anti-unionism. Despite evident division and fear of upheaval, a certain cohesion can often evolve within an organisation when a goal of culture change is sought and driven by strategic direction and business demands rather than being change for the sake of change. The Prison Service must gain and maintain a clear sense of direction when recognising the need to balance security, control, care and rehabilitation.

As the Prison Service experiences major policy changes and upheaval, the culture that has for so long been axiomatic to the Service – that has been both an anchor of stability amidst turmoil and a rope around the neck of innovative change – is inevitably up for grabs. The Prison Service should seize the opportunity that has arisen to evolve a progressive, non-stereotypical culture within the many relationship permutations among prison officers, prison managers and prisoners.

In reminding us that almost all prisoners will one day return to participate fully in our community, Andrew Coyle writes: 'If they are not to come out more bitter than when they went in and more likely to commit further crime, they must be encouraged to develop a sense of personal worth and a realisation that they can contribute to the community, that they are valued human beings' (Coyle 1994, p. 132). If there is one individual who above all others can facilitate this transition and instil a renewed sense of community membership, personal responsibility and self-belief it is the prison officer.

References

HM Prison Service (1997) *Prison Service Review*, Home Office, p. 125

Coyle, A. (1994) 'My brother's keeper: relationships in prison', in E. Burnside and J. Barnard (eds), *Relational Justice: Repairing the Breach*, Winchester: Waterside Press

16

A GOVERNOR'S PERSPECTIVE

David Godfrey

Then and now

As an undergraduate at a Scottish university in the late 1960s I intended to apply to join the probation service, but the university careers service suggested that I should visit a couple of prisons before entirely ruling out a career in the Prison Service instead. My first visit was to an open borstal based in a castle on the banks of the Tay. My impression was that the governor there – a charming man – spent much of his time in the pleasant occupations of a semi-retired country gentleman. We admired the view from the battlements, the manicured gardens and the spit-and-polished accommodation; the prisoners we spoke to seemed cheerful and busy: I was most favourably impressed. A subsequent visit to Perth Prison showed me another side of the Scottish Prison Service as it then was: long rows of sullen prisoners hand-sewing mailbags; hard-faced officers imposing rigid discipline; a pervading stink of sweat, urine and stale food in the wings; and a party of prisoners collecting up 'parcels' that had been thrown from windows by prisoners who preferred not to spend long hours sharing a cell with buckets of their own and their cell mates' excrement until 'slopping out' time. Subsequent visits to English institutions revealed similar contrasts. Exeter was (and is) an overcrowded Victorian local prison, and the then governor, Colin Honey (subsequently a much-respected regional director), left me in no doubt about the difficulties of providing decent conditions and reformative opportunities. However, Wetherby borstal, where I spent a fortnight, was an open borstal with a regime that struck me as making a genuine effort to help its young prisoners and to treat them humanely.

I applied to join the English Prison Service as an assistant governor (AG) and attended an interview in London, where the panel noted with interest that I was a psychology student and seemed to think this would be an advantage, though their conception of psychology bore no relation to mine. I was accepted. As one of the members of the selection panel was then governor of Wakefield Prison, and I would be at the Prison Service College in Wakefield for training, I rather cheekily asked him for a job to fill the time between leaving college and starting the course for newly joined AGs. The chief officer was not, I surmise, pleased by my appointment as a temporary officer and took care that I was kept well away from the prisoners. He sent me to work at the south gate, where the job entailed searching lorries and escorting them within the prison. I was under the jaundiced eye of a long-serving senior officer who had spent his entire service at Wakefield and who regarded AGs, especially young, idealistic ones from college, with deep suspicion. His attitude was not unusual among uniformed staff at that time.

There were about 50 of us on the assistant governors' course, including two women (whose postings were limited to establishments for women) and only one member of an ethnic minority group. Nearly all were 'direct entrants' rather than ex-officers. We had no idea where we were eventually going to work – in a prison with concerns about accommodating ever-increasing numbers of prisoners, maintaining security and control, and trying to alleviate conditions for prisoners; or in a borstal with anxieties about the dilution of the original training concept as pressure of numbers brought earlier release. The underlying ethos of AGs in both kinds of institution was grounded in social work values and the emphasis was on trying to reform offenders. Our training was largely academic and theoretical: we read books, wrote essays and participated (with varying degrees of enthusiasm) in group discussions. Only near the end of our eight-month training course were we given a clue to our final posting. It was assumed that on completion of the course we would obediently go wherever we were sent – and we did.

I started as a housemaster at an open borstal where my time was devoted almost exclusively to the concerns of the 60 or so trainees under my care. Management, strategic planning, budgeting and cost-efficiency did not feature in our lexicon. Our approach to reformative treatment, education and training was, in retrospect, crudely amateurish, but we were deeply committed to our mission. Our sanguine view of our work was severely shaken by the emergence of the new 'critical criminology' in the 1970s, with its clear-eyed view of what was 'really' going on in custodial institutions. Furthermore, prisoners in the 1970s increasingly demonstrated their dissatisfaction with their situation. Whatever we might have **intended** prison regimes to achieve, prisoners were telling us in good round terms that their experience of imprisonment was of inhumane conditions, injustice and neglect. There were several serious riots. Developing methods of preventing and containing disorder became a new priority.

Another growing concern was industrial relations. Assistant governors in general, and borstal housemasters in particular, worked long and unsocial hours for modest pay, and considered it a duty, if not a privilege. Prison officers, becoming increasingly militant, also worked long hours in some establishments but were compensated by overtime pay at multiple rates. Between the two groups of staff lay wide differences in values and conceptions of how prisons ought to be run. The power of the officers to bring the system to immediate crisis by declining to work overtime had created timid management, and it is now widely acknowledged (though it was hotly denied at the time) that some outrageous practices had been allowed to develop. The notion that AGs 'managed' officers in most establishments would have been considered risible: AGs dealt with prisoners.

The contrast between the late 1960s and the late 1990s is in many ways striking. The borstal system has long since been abolished, and the type of open establishment that first beguiled me is now a rarity. There have been no repeats of the major riots of the 1970s and 1980s, and those disturbances that have occurred have been much better handled. Specific programmes to address offending behaviour have been developed and their effectiveness evaluated. Prison conditions are in some ways much improved, with overcrowding limited to 'doubling' rather than 'trebling' the occupation of cells designed for one. Escapes have been reduced to about one-tenth of their previous number in the past few years. The rank structure has changed and governor grades now manage staff and their work much more closely. There is much sharper definition of what the Prison Service should be doing, and recognition of the importance of monitoring what is being done, what it achieves and what it costs. The emphasis in training now reflects this shift towards accountable management, budgetary control, value for money and audited performance.

The process leading to this transformation was complex. It included the identification in 1984 of the tasks of Prison Service establishments so that governors could begin to be held accountable for the performance of their prisons. Almost unbelievably, this was the first time anyone had tried to define what each prison should be doing. Probably the single greatest step was the Fresh Start initiative of 1987, which abolished overtime for officer grades, greatly increased basic pay, eliminated most of the wasteful practices of the past, introduced a modern team-based approach, encouraged staff to move out of official quarters into their own houses, amalgamated the chief officer ranks into the governor grades and enhanced promotion prospects for officers.

From a governor's viewpoint, this transformation was accompanied by new demands. Value for money had to be demonstrated, which meant that activities, their costs and outputs had to be constantly monitored. At the same time, the introduction of information technology (IT) meant that Headquarters was able to keep a much closer check on what individual prisons were doing. The flow of paper from Headquarters to prisons became a blizzard – more than a hundred new Instructions every year in addition to papers giving advice and information. Governors found themselves with much less time for 'management by walking about'. Many of the new Instructions seem to have been drafted with little consideration of the pressures on those who must implement them: some are positive masterpieces of needless complexity. Although Headquarters undoubtedly regards itself as a resource to them, I fear many governors view it not as a source of help, guidance and support but as one of unreasonable demands, arbitrary decisions and needless complexities.

Political opportunism versus values

The building programme of the 1980s opened up the prospect that prison accommodation would at last be sufficient for the population, especially as the benign influence of a succession of liberal-minded Home Secretaries had slowed the rate of population increase. Although the Strangeways riot in 1990 came as a sharp reminder that prisons are always vulnerable, the Woolf Report which followed it (Woolf and Tumim 1991) set an agenda that appealed to many in the Prison Service, and recovery from the trauma of the riot was quick. Woolf made twelve central recommendations which, taken together, seemed to offer an attractive vision of what the Prison Service should be like in the 21st century. Given the air of optimism in the early 1990s, the trough into which many governors' morale plunged in the middle of this decade requires an explanation beyond their sadness that some crucial elements of Woolf were shelved in response to resumed population pressure. The concern from 1993 onwards shown by many governors may be explained in terms of both **what** was done and **how** it was done, which may be related respectively to the **goals** and the **values** of the Prison Service.

The 'tough' rhetoric adopted by Kenneth Clarke as Home Secretary drove up the prison population at an unprecedented rate, bringing renewed overcrowding and deteriorating conditions, for example by necessitating the accommodation of prisoners further from their homes. It was followed by even tougher rhetoric from his successor Michael Howard, to which was added a policy of greater punitiveness in regimes – for example by curtailing prisoners' opportunities to spend periods out of the prison for compassionate, educational or resettlement purposes. This 'decent but austere' approach came at a time when we were finding the provision of 'decency' difficult and 'austerity' was widely seen within the Prison Service as unnecessary and motivated by party political populism. However, governors, as civil servants, recognise that the Home Secretary is entitled to change policies and our duty is to apply them diligently, even if we think them ill-advised.

More damaging to the morale of governors was the ministerial reaction to the escapes from Whitemoor (1994) and Parkhurst (1995) Prisons. This brings us to the issue of **how** the Prison Service should do its work and the essential **values** to which it should subscribe. Wisely, when the values of the Prison Service were promulgated in April 1993, 'integrity' was placed first. This was appropriate because prisons are inescapably punitive institutions: even when they are well managed, people suffer in them. When they are badly managed, prisoners – whose power is curtailed by their situation – are vulnerable to neglect and abuse by staff and by each other. For that reason it is especially important that prisons should be managed at all levels with absolute integrity.

In the aftermath of the Whitemoor and Parkhurst escapes the governors of both prisons were sacrificed. The treatment of John Marriott, late governor of Parkhurst, was seen as especially unfair: he was removed from office at short notice so that a characteristically 'tough' statement could be made in the House of Commons. This was perceived by many governors as entirely inconsistent with the integrity and commitment to staff that ought to be fundamental in the Prison Service. It was deeply resented. When Derek Lewis, the Director General, was also sacked on the day of publication of Learmont's Inquiry into prison security in 1995 this was seen as a further instance of ministerial self-interest taking precedence over appropriate values.

Some unresolved issues

Punishment or reformative treatment?

The vulnerability of the Prison Service to shifts in the priority accorded to security, control, reformative treatment and resettlement is heightened by our lack of confidence about the fundamental purpose of imprisonment. It might seem strange that the issue of purpose remains controversial, given the long history of imprisonment. The Statement of Purpose says:

> Her Majesty's Prison Service serves the public by keeping in custody those committed by the courts. Our duty is to look after them with humanity and help them lead law-abiding and useful lives in custody and after release.

Talking to prisoners leaves no doubt that custody is experienced by nearly all of them as punitive, so the punitive element is clearly inescapable, but how is it to be balanced against the demands of humanity, reformative treatment and resettlement?

Part of the difficulty is that the courts are not required to specify their intentions when passing sentences so that the relative importance of punishment, compensation to the victim, reform of the offender and protection of the public remains in most cases unclear. This unresolved issue has more than theoretical significance since it underlies many of the daily dilemmas confronted by governors. What is the right balance in a prison regime between work and education? What priority should be given to the treatment of addicted prisoners compared with the detection and punishment of illicit drug-taking? How much risk is acceptable in giving prisoners periods of resettlement leave before final release? The answers to such questions depend largely on whether imprisonment is intended to punish in proportion to the harm done or risked by the offender, or whether it is intended to equip the offender for a law-abiding life in future. If both objectives are to be pursued, by what principles are we to judge their priority?

Balancing demands and resources

Throughout the past 50 years the prison population in England and Wales has been rising, leading to persistent overcrowding, and this seems to have been unrelated to fluctuations in crime. The massive building programme of the 1980s was intended to restore the balance between demand (mostly a matter of prisoner numbers) and resources (mostly a matter of available accommodation). However, the 'tough' rhetoric of the mid-1990s led to an unprecedented rise in the prison population, amounting to a 50 % increase in five years (Learmont 1995, p. 149), and plunged the Prison Service once more into overcrowding and all the associated problems. In our more optimistic and reflective moods we discuss the kinds of institutions we would **like** to be running, but an honest answer to the fundamental question, 'What kind of business are we in?' would admit that we succeed mostly in terms of custody and punishment. Reformative treatment, humanity, decency and justice remain largely unrealised ambitions.

The reality is that we are still requiring many prisoners to eat their meals in a cell that is also a lavatory. In the case of shared cells, it is also a shared lavatory with only the sketchiest provision for privacy. In some cases bullies and their potential victims are locked up together. It seems unlikely that this will change until the population pressure has been brought under control, which would require us to regulate the size of the prison population to match available resources, rather than regarding population growth as akin to a force of nature in the face of which we are helpless.

Overcrowding impinges on constructive activities as well as on living conditions. Unless we can provide interesting things for prisoners to do out of their cells –

bearing in mind that many of them are unable to enjoy reading and have no taste for radio listening beyond pop music – it is inescapably true that some will continue to bully the vulnerable, damage themselves or the prison, or lapse into boredom and despair during long periods of lock-up. Despite the efforts of the listeners (prisoners trained by the Samaritans to offer a support service in prison for suicidal or despairing inmates), the number of suicides seems likely to continue to rise unless regimes can be improved.

Looking to the future

The population pressure remains intense, the provision of more capacity fast enough to keep up with demand is difficult, prison regimes are deteriorating and industrial relations are again fraught. As has been noted, none of this is unfamiliar. It remains to be seen what will be the long-term effect of the introduction of home detention curfew ('electronic tagging'). Although this initiative has been described as offering benefits in terms of resettlement, a cynic would see it as merely the latest in a long line of measures designed to create a breathing space in the battle against overcrowding without appearing 'soft on crime'. It is unlikely to offer more than a palliative. In the longer term, we need legislation to prohibit prison overcrowding, and a system to increase remission when the population outstrips the available accommodation. The fact that no such legislation has been proposed, even at times of gross overcrowding, illustrates the allure of 'tough' talk and the political unattractiveness of being perceived as 'soft on criminals'.

During my 30 years in the Prison Service we have made enormous gains in efficiency, but the latest round of budget cuts will be difficult. It is not obvious to me how further substantial efficiency savings can be made in the typical public sector prison. I suspect that this latest round of budget cuts will result in further deterioration in regimes, most of the available improvements in efficiency already having been implemented over the past ten years. On the other hand, the provision of additional funding for regime development under the comprehensive spending review is welcome. In addition, the belated introduction of in-cell television might prove to be a useful further incentive to good behaviour, as well as ameliorating prison conditions.

I fear that unrealistic expectations have been raised about the latest range of programmes aimed at reducing re-offending. It would be a pity if they were used to justify even greater use of custodial sentences, like the borstal system in its heyday. More interesting would be the effect of paying prisoners much more than the current £6 a week – on condition that they worked much harder – so that they would be able to leave prison with a modest sum in cash. I suspect this might have a greater effect on reducing re-conviction rates than any other single initiative.

Finally, I am confident of one thing at least: to the extent that it is possible to distinguish 'good' from 'bad' prisons, much of the difference will continue to be due to the influence of the governor. I have been privileged to know among my colleagues some people of great humanity, commitment and courage – Peter Kitteridge CBE and the late John Marriott spring to mind. I am proud to have worked with them in the Prison Service. On my better days, I still believe that we are capable of doing more good than harm to the damaged, needy, neglected young men who comprise the bulk of the prison population.

References

Learmont, Gen. Sir J. (1995) *Review of Prison Service Security in England and Wales and the Escape from Parkhurst Prison on Tuesday 3rd January 1995* (The Learmont Inquiry), Cm 3020, HMSO

Woolf, Lord Justice and Tumim, Judge S. (1991) *Prison Disturbances April 1990: Report of an Inquiry by the Rt Hon. Lord Justice Woolf and His Hon. Judge Stephen Tumim* (The Woolf Report), Cm 1456, HMSO

PART FOUR:
WHAT HAPPENS IN
PRISONS

REGIMES
Robert Young

Constructive regimes

Over the years there has been a lively debate, which is still going on, about the purposes of imprisonment. At one end of the scale there is the top-security, all-electronic, high-technology escape-proof Alcatraz for professional criminals, terrorists and spies, and at the other a warm, if spartan, refuge for homeless, root-less alcoholics where at least they get regular meals and medical care (Stern 1989). There is no doubt that prisons serve a variety of purposes. Some commentators argue that prison should be used only to punish criminals. Others insist that its main purpose is to deter individuals in prison from committing further crimes after they are released, as well as to deter those who might be inclined to commit crime. Another suggestion is that people are sent to prison to be reformed or rehabilitated. That is to say, during the time they are in prison they will come to realise that committing crime is wrong and they will learn skills that will help them to lead a law-abiding life when they are released.

Deprivation of liberty is a punishment in itself and prisons have no mandate to inflict further punishment on the prisoner. On the contrary, prisoners should be encouraged to use their time in prison to learn new skills, to improve their education and health, to reform themselves and prepare for eventual release (Coyle 1999, unpublished lecture).

In this chapter we re-visit the questions: What is prison for? What can and should prisons do with, and for, those entrusted to their care? We look at the work of the Regimes Directorate, which was formed in 1997, and, in particular the importance of work, physical education and education, in the rehabilitative process.

A number of themes and causes underpinned the creation of the Regimes Directorate. All were concerned with the goal of giving regimes a higher profile, with policy and practice development being taken forward in a more organised and co-ordinated way. These were:

- a desire to balance appropriate and understandable concerns about security with regime development;
- recognition by the Prison Service itself that there was a need for a more organised, systematic approach to policy and practice development in this area, building on the considerable knowledge, experience and achievements in the field;
- a growing body of research available about 'what works' with offenders, which still needs to be taken into account in policy and practice development;
- the 1997 Conservative government manifesto commitment to constructive regimes as a means to improve public protection;
- the Inspectorate articulating the need for greater focus on regimes; and
- the Prison Service Review (1997) recommending its creation.

The Regimes Directorate brought together in one place a range of functions that underpin regime development (see Figure 4.1 on pp. 44–5). Its creation signified a higher profile for regimes generally, such as more attention being given to issues related to women prisoners, (their own policy unit with an assistant director was established). Greater attention was also given to adult male regimes with the setting up of the regimes policy unit within the Adult Male Prisoner Lifer Group.

The policy behind constructive regimes

So what is the policy framework for constructive regimes? The policy must be fundamentally about public protection, as the government has been pursuing a clear manifesto commitment to constructive regimes as a means of ensuring better public protection by reducing re-offending.

Constructive regimes work best when they are founded in prison communities that are safe, fair and responsible. Prisoners and staff will gain the most from relationships that are based on respect and freedom from fear. External security must be effective, but within the prison there must be incentives to reward decent and tolerant behaviour. The considerable efforts being made by the Prison Service to tackle bullying, drug-dealing and violence within prisons are critical in maintaining such a safe environment. Everyone who works in a prison will also be familiar with how crucial fairness is. Fair dealing with prisoners must extend to the minutiae of everyday existence. Discipline and punishment must be seen to be the consequence of due process. It is right and proper that prisoners should have external avenues of appeal, which work well; and that there should be independent and rigorous inspection of prisons, as they have to be seen to be in the vanguard of tackling discrimination. Responsible communities in prisons will be those where prisoners are constantly expected to make choices and have some control over their own affairs. Challenging prisoners to take responsibility for their own lives is not comfortable for them or for staff, but it is part of what makes the best prisons work. This entails reminding prisoners of their responsibilities and providing them with opportunities to meet those where practical. It involves rewarding trustworthiness, and encouraging and helping prisoners plan and prepare for their release.

Building on this foundation, constructive regimes must:

- focus on release and life in the community following release;
- draw upon evidence of 'what works' in reducing re-offending;
- challenge attitudes that lead to crime;
- focus on 'needs' rather than 'wants'; and
- offer prisoners opportunities to choose not to re-offend, and be effective in supporting that choice.

The key is to focus on release and life in the community following release, acknowledging that all but a tiny number of prisoners will be released back into the community, and that prisons have to prepare for this as soon as someone comes into custody. Concern with public protection, of course, is not new for the Prison Service – it is very familiar with the issues and challenges of assessing, reducing and managing risk. Although the Services knowledge and experience in this area has been developing in many ways, there is still much to do to draw on and apply research about how to be more effective in pursuing it. Developing 'constructive regimes' and 'resettlement' are two sides of the same coin. The Prison Service cannot pursue the objectives of public protection and effective resettlement in isolation: it has to work very closely with the Probation Service.

Reducing re-offending

There are 'course junkies' – prisoners who attend any course going, whether they need it or not; prisoners who pursue education classes rather than tackle their offending behaviour; or prisoners who want to work in the higher-paid workshop or work out in the gym, just to avoid anything which tackles the problems they will face in the community. Each of these types of prisoner should be challenged to consider their future post-release. Focusing on needs rather than wants requires that sound systems are in place to assess the needs of prisoners, including those needs related to their offending. The revised model of sentence management has improved the assessment of prisoners, but the system certainly has potential that is not being fully used.

Fortunately, there are more sophisticated approaches being developed. In the latter part of 1998 work was under way to develop a joint assessment tool with the probation service, a tool geared to assessing the risk of re-conviction and an individual's criminogenic needs (that is, their criminal and offence-related behaviour/needs). A focus on needs rather than wants requires some major and often uncomfortable shifts at a number of levels. Staff have to say 'no' to prisoners who are constantly avoiding addressing the reason that they are in custody. Prisons need to ensure they have an integrated approach, making sure that assessments of prisoners impact on decisions about what prisoners do.

There is research that points to what is effective in reducing re-offending: for whom, when and how; also our understanding about what can make some people worse. It is also helping to shape areas of policy and practice, including the need to focus on improving the employability of offenders and the importance of addressing their basic educational needs. Accredited offending behaviour programmes are also based on this research.

In spite of the introduction of the revised model of sentence management, in many establishments sentence planning and allocation to work, education/physical education, training or offending behaviour programmes are still separate processes. Some practices will need to change if reducing offending really is the key way forward. In particular, prisons will need to ensure that they do not have a pay policy that works against prisoners attending education, or offending behaviour courses. In addition, incentive schemes should not work against prisoners addressing their needs. Sentence planning needs to be programmed properly to timetabled activities, so that, for example, prisoners address their education, health or offending behaviour needs before they are allowed into enhanced-pay workshops. It also means that some provisions may need to be changed, for example giving priority to providing basic and key skills education. Finally, the potential of the regime activities provided should be maximised, so that the right activities are available to the right people at the right time.

Prisons have to ensure that they offer prisoners opportunities to choose not to re-offend, and must be effective in supporting that choice. Opportunities should include:

- education in basic skills;
- training and meaningful work;
- planning for employment;

- offending behaviour programmes targeted at those who can benefit from them;
- planning for accommodation outside prison;
- help in tackling substance abuse;
- focusing on criminogenic factors; and
- concentrating on activities and programmes that make a difference.

Much of the recent success in regime quality and delivery has been made possible because of efficiency measures. Until recently, prisons have not been particularly good at directing regime provision towards reducing offending behaviour, though the progress which has undoubtedly been made recently in this area has been most significant. Incidents of prisoner idleness were common because there was no focused and integrated approach towards how prisoners' time or prison resources could best be utilised. The level of apathy also threatened internal order.

Many historical problems still have to be addressed: there is a clear imbalance between the level and types of regimes that operate in different prisons; there has been an uneven investment across the estate; and there are still many older Victorian prisons, that are limited in the type and volume of activities which they can accommodate. In the 1980s there was no devolution of budgets nor methodology by which the cost of activities could be measured. In 1997, prison regions had been competing rather than co-ordinating with each other for additional resources. At Headquarters, staff working with different regime activities never met. It is only in the late 1990s that regime specialists began to talk to each other and identify with the concept of integrated delivery.

Although there is a clear perception about what is good for prisoners, there has to be a method by which the effectiveness of these activities can be measured and their value for money defended. The development of accredited programmes, effective financial/budgetry systems and the piloting of a costing system all will help in this respect. The regime activity-costing exercise aims to create an efficiency yardstick and will inform value for money considerations.

Constructive regimes, therefore, should demonstrate effectiveness and value for money. Increasingly, there is a need to evaluate the effect of investment on regimes. Evaluating that impact on re-offending patterns and criminogenic factors is becoming central as more funds are invested and there is greater accountability for the investment. Obviously this has to be seen in the context of the realities of establishment life, and balancing the demands of the prison with those of its prisoners. However, increasingly, regimes need to be examined and questions asked. For example, Table 17.1 details the range of costs of education classes per student hour together with the average class-size range. Certainly, one should ask whether low class sizes give value for money, or, indeed, why class sizes are low at all, except for remedial education.

Table 17.1: Adult male education – facts and figures, 8 December 1998

	Range
Cost per student hour	£2.21 – £6.46
Average class size	6.65 – 9.95
Unit costs (spend per prisoner per month)	£31.30 – £66.67

Source: Education Services, Prison Service Headquarters

So how is the goal of reducing re-offending to be realised? It is essential that prisons have a good picture of where they are now, what they are providing in regimes and resettlement and how this provision is managed so that developing policy and practice is well-informed and based in realities. Staff should be encouraged to learn from existing good practice and build on their achievements. A great deal of work has been going on to bring together information from different sources such as regime monitoring, Key Performance Indicator (KPI) data and the standards audit. The close associations between different policy and regime areas is reflected in the revised Headquarters structure, which supports such working between different parts of the directorate. Integrating courses, work and other schemes, monitoring the results and sharing information will help prisons to offer prisoners opportunities to change their offending behaviour and improve their resettlement outcomes.

Work and training within prisons

Employment is the single most significant factor in reducing the likelihood of re-offending. Calls for increased opportunities in work activity are common within much of the contemporary prison literature (see for example; Council of Europe 1991; Simon and Corbett 1996). Since 1991, the development of work and work-related training in prisons for sentenced prisoners has been a prominent feature of Prison Service policy, following the emphasis in the White Paper *Custody, Care and Justice* that 'work should have a central place in the life of the prison' (Home Office 1991, para. 7.25). Individual prisons endeavour to create as realistic a working environment as possible within the many constraints of security and custody. Co-ordinated by the Headquarters group Enterprises and Activity

A female prisoner undertakes the practical aspect of an NVQ course in hairdressing. Prisoners participate in training and education courses as part of rehablilitative regimes.

Services, full-time work experience and training is provided within prisons for up to 12,000 prisoners. This does not include the number on vocational training courses such as painting and decorating, bricklaying or hairdressing, nor does it include those on the many accredited physical education programmes, or those following education courses.

Many prisoners have been unemployed prior to their prison sentence. Most have limited skills, and poor education and work records. The time that they spend on initial assessment is very often the first time they have ever received any advice concerning employment and training. Considerable time, therefore, is needed to encourage and motivate such prisoners. The employment needs of prisoners are complex. They cannot be treated separately from problems stemming from their offending behaviour, their attitude to work and their past training and work experience. For this reason, employment guidance should be integrated with the other support provided in prison. Many prisoners do not consider their employment prospects until the time of their release, which means that they do not always use their time in prison as effectively as they could. The formal sentence management procedures introduced by the Prison Service aim to ensure that this takes place on a more structured basis.

In terms of the Service's Statement of Purpose, work not only enables prisoners to lead useful lives while in custody, it also provides inmates with experience that will help them to lead law-abiding and useful lives after release. Convicted prisoners have to attend work as part of the Prison Rules. The time prisoners spend in work each week is shown in Figure 17.1. Training in prisons should enable prisoners serving more than 12 months to spend 25% of their time in an industrial activity. All prisoners engaged in such an activity should undertake certified training. Good-quality, properly focused work in prisons can offer experience, skills and, increasingly, recognised qualifications, which will be useful in future employment.

Figure 17.1: Average weekly hours that prisoners work, April–October 1998

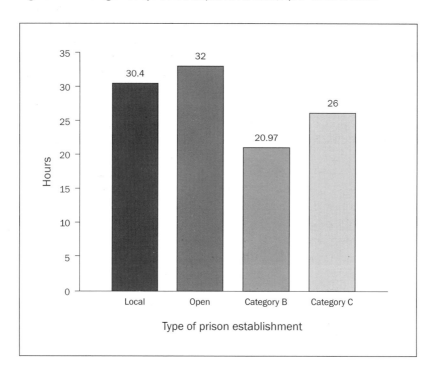

Keeping prisoners occupied helps towards the maintenance of control and aids rehabilitation by instilling the work ethic. Helping prisoners develop the work ethic is important as it involves time-keeping and team work, leadership, organising pay and time-sheets, and administration. To enable the experience to be as realistic as possible, targets are set and monitored for all jobs. Identifying a prisoner's needs should be undertaken as part of their sentence planning. Key workers can then be recruited to their posts through job club adverts and applications, making the process mirror what goes on outside prison.

Work also contributes to the operation of the earned privileges scheme as well as KPI 5: purposeful activity; and KPI 8: cost per prisoner place (see Annex B). The policy on prisoners' pay is currently being revised by the Prison Service to reflect the new Prison Service Management Board's priorities surrounding constructive regimes, the Board's commitment to setting individual and appropriate targets for prisoners through the sentence plan and the reward system, set out in the incentives and earned privileges scheme. Except where prisoners are participating in 'working out' schemes (full- or part-time employment in the community outside prisons), prisoners' pay structures are not intended to reflect rates of pay in the community; they are viewed more as a token payment to encourage participation in the regime and support and reward achievement of sentence and/or learning plan targets. The minimum payment is £3.50 per week, but for prisons operating a differential regime of basic, standard or enhanced, payment is according to the incentive level (basic £5.50, standard £8.75, and enhanced £10.75; a bonus of £2.50 can be earned for measured output over and above the standard required).

As a regime activity, work is relatively inexpensive. The public purse also benefits as Prison Service industries and farms produce £58 million worth of goods and produce each year. The sales policy for the Prison Service is that commercial work undertaken within prisons should not be at the expense of private sector business or employment in the United Kingdom. This is achieved by not dominating any particular market sector, realistic pricing and by undertaking work that would otherwise not be available in the United Kingdom, for example import substitution. This can be assisted by ensuring that the internal production is expanded to cover value-for-money requirements. Goods and services are offered at a fair market price, which recovers direct costs plus a contribution to necessary overheads. For work in prisons to be effective, governors must ensure that the agreed resourced employment places in their workshops are filled and that the net working hours are 31–35 per week, with productivity to at least 60% of commercial standards. This ensures that the work experience and tempo is as realistic as possible in comparison with outside industry.

So how effective are prison industries and farms? Robert Fulton, then Head of Enterprise and Activity Services, visited prisons in Germany in February 1995, accompanied by Ursula Smart (a senior lecturer and prison researcher at Thames Valley University). They established that although it was thought by some that German prisoners worked harder, did better-quality work, were better paid than UK prisoners and that, as a result, German prison industries made substantial profits, their own conclusions put the comparison into a rather different perspective (Smart and Reynolds 1996). Calculated on a like-for-like basis, they did not see anything which would have led them to think that German prison enterprise costs were significantly lower than ours. German prison industries have many

For some offenders, prison employment consists of working on prison farms.

positive and interesting features, from which we can learn, but they do no better than we do on the whole. Both countries have competently managed prison industries and the similarities are more significant than the differences.

The Purposeful Activity Expansion Scheme (PAES)

Aim 4 of the Home Office's Corporate and Business Plan for 1999–2002 is: 'effective execution of the sentences of the courts so as to reduce re-offending and protect the public' (Home Office 1999). There are a number of key projects that the Prison Service must deliver to achieve significant progress on Aim 4 and they are the major challenges and priorities for change over the planning period. The Purposeful Activity Expansion Scheme (PAES), which initially started as the Workshop Expansion Scheme in 1996, is one of those key projects. This initiative is a three-year pilot project involving 24 establishments, acting as 'pathfinders' for the rest of the Service. It aims to find ways of increasing the level of purposeful activity within a fully integrated regime while maximising the opportunities to reduce the risk of re-offending. In a letter to area managers and heads of groups and services in May 1999, the new Director of Regimes wrote:

> PAES has been designed to provide practical help and assistance to establish-
> ments in developing constructive regimes which address offending behaviour,

improve educational and work skills, and promote law-abiding behaviour in custody and after release.

The PAES project is also an important strand of the Prison Service's second objective in the Corporate and Business Plan: the delivery of basic skills accreditation, accredited offending behaviour programmes, and the provision of integrated regimes in which work complements and supports action to reduce re-offending. PAES builds on the achievements and learning of the Workshop Expansion Scheme, but adopts a broader approach in relation to a wider range of regime activity. The key themes of PAES are shown in Table 17.2.

The broader objectives of PAES are supported by multidisciplinary staffing of the central project team (based at Headquarters), which is seen as important to the successful integration of activities (Mcallister et al. 1994). Representatives to the central team are gleaned from education, PE advisory services, the Offending Behaviour Policy Unit and other relevant policy groups. The wider remit is also reflected in the content and approach of the team's work with establishments and in amended frameworks for individual prisons to use to analyse their regime and plans for its development.

The Workshop Expansion Scheme had provided the impetus for establishments to make some fundamental and positive changes, for example in relation to the core day and the organisation of activities. Expanding that scheme's brief enables PAES to be applied to some equally challenging areas, for example setting priorities in education provision and the provision of offending behaviour programmes, as well as accredited physical education programmes aimed at reducing offending behaviour. The PAES project will complement and inform the work already being done on funds allocation for activities that contribute to the objective of constructive regimes which have a positive impact on reducing the risk of re-offending. It should also inform the development of regime standards generally.

While work experience is at the core of the regime, other needs must also be met. Where prisoners' needs for education, training or physical fitness are paramount, then they should be encouraged to address them and to engage in whatever programme is relevant and potentially helpful. In some cases these may be full-time programmes, which will need to be fitted into the sentence at the most appropriate time.

Physical Education (PE) programmes provide the opportunity for prisoners to develop and to maintain their standard of physical fitness whether it be for medical or for recreational purposes. They also offer the opportunity for employment within prison, as well as training, coaching and nationally accredited awards.

Table 17.2: The Purposeful Activity Expansion Scheme

Principles
- to maximise the potential of an increasing range of activities that contribute to reducing the risk of re-offending
- an increasing amount of purposeful activity should accord as closely as possible with 'what works' criteria
- to show a commitment to evaluating or demonstrating effectiveness
- to maintain a balanced and integrated regime
- to maximise the use of resources and achieve value for money

Objectives
- to increase purposeful activity to 30 hours per week

Work
- employment places to meet agreed workshop resourced employment places
- net working hours to increase to 31–35 per week
- productivity and/or qualifications obtained in workshops to increase

Education/physical education (PE)
- for those assessed as requiring it, increase the take-up/completion of basic education programmes
- increase the proportion of prisoners who have a learning plan (integrated with a sentence plan) for those eligible
- increase the proportion of PE which meets the criteria for constructive PE to reduce the risk of re-offending

Offending behaviour
- increase the number of accredited offending behaviour programme completions

Resettlement
- increase the amount of evaluated work to:
  - improve prisoners' employability
  - help prisoners maintain/secure appropriate accommodation

Most prisons have a gymnasium where professionally trained staff teach a wide range of sporting activities. PE programmes offer employment opportunities within prison and play an important role in relieving tensions.

The employability outcomes for prisoners are improved through PE by offering teaching, mentoring, the development of working habits, specific awards and attitude-shaping skills. PE provides a number of certified skills that are appropriate to a range of working environments. In a unique way it can, and does, instil a positive sense of purpose by providing a sporting context into which offending behaviour programmes can be set. PE also plays an important role in relieving tensions within what in some older establishments can be a very claustrophobic environment.

Other subjects do not lend themselves to full-time learning and are more appropriately dealt with by arrangements that mirror those for day-release in the community, such as time away from normal employment to attend necessary education or training programmes. Part-time arrangements of this sort can be very effective in meeting prisoners' needs, as well as allowing the benefits of education to be shared more widely among prisoners.

Foundation skills

Lifelong learning is at the heart of government policy. The clear priority is to improve the basic skills of the national labour force. Many people who have been unemployed for some time missed out on foundation skills earlier in their lives.

That is why full-time education and training are central to all four options of the Labour government's New Deal for young people aged 18–24 (the other three options are employment, environmental task forces and voluntary sector work). For some, primarily those without NVQ level 2 or equivalent, the route to employability will lie in full-time education and training. The government's aims were made explicit in the Green Paper *The Learning Age* (DfEE 1998) and in the 1997 DfEE consultative document *Targets for our Future*. On offenders, the Green Paper says:

> For many adult offenders, learning provides a second chance. Education and training will form a fuller part of the new constructive regimes in prisons, to which the Government attaches great importance. They will also be an important element of the closer working relationships we want to see between prison and probation. We want, wherever possible, to prepare people serving prison sentences for jobs when they are released (p. 22).

It is vital that these aims are embedded within the Prison Service and that education policy and practice in establishments reflects these priorities.

The governments national targets for education and training, devised in conjunction with the CBI, were originally launched in 1991 and later revised in 1995. *Targets for Our Future* further revised these targets in line with government policy. There are currently six targets:

Foundation Target 1   By age 19, 85% of young people to achieve five GCSEs at grade C or above, or an intermediate GNVQ or an NVQ at level 2.

Foundation Target 2   By age 19, 75% of young people to achieve level 2 competence in communication, numeracy and IT; and 35% to achieve level 3 competence in these key skills by age 21.

Foundation Target 3   By age 21, 60% of young people to achieve two GCSE A levels, or an advanced GNVQ or an NVQ at level 3.

Lifetime Target 1   Sixty per cent of the workforce to be qualified to NVQ level 3, advanced GNVQ or two GCSE A levels.

Lifetime Target 2   Thirty per cent of the workforce to have a vocational, professional, management or academic qualification at NVQ level 4 or above.

Lifetime Target 3   Seventy per cent of all organisations employing 200 or more employees and 35% of those employing 50 or more to be recognised as an Investor in People. All lifetime targets are to be measured in stages.

It is important that the Prison Service reflects and supports the government's policy and contributes to meeting the national targets through its education and training programmes for adult prisoners and young offenders. Why? Because while only 20% of the general population have basic skill deficiencies, the proportion among the prison population is much higher: 60% of prisoners have literacy skills below level 1 and 75% have numeracy skills below level 1. The Basic Skills Agency estimates this gives prisoners access to only four out of every hundred jobs. In view of this, improving prisoners' basic and key skills must be a priority for prison education.

The results of the comprehensive spending review (CSR), where funds have been allocated for a specific programme delivery, will strengthen and enhance education and PE in prisons within the policy framework. Priorities for CSR allocations include improving basic and key skills, focusing on young offenders, and improving impoverished regimes. Overall, the impact on adult prisoners and young offenders is that:

- by 2001, 50% of unsentenced and 90% of sentenced prisoners will have a learning plan as part of their sentence plan, or induction assessment for non-sentence plan prisoners;
- by 2001, 50% of prisoners with six months or more to serve of their sentence in custody will achieve level 2 competence in basic skills; and

All prisoners are encouraged to improve their literacy and numeracy skills while incarcerated.

- prisoners who enrol on a distance-learning course, including Open University courses, will have achieved accreditation in key skills at level 2. There is no time limit for this.

Governors will, over time, need to re-order their education provision. This should not impact on staff resources since contractors deliver education programmes in establishments and monitoring of the contract is undertaken by education advisors based within the Regimes Directorate. The annual amount spent on education each year throughout the Prison Service is about £35 million but as education provision is contracted out it allows governors to be flexible, using the funds to provide not only formal education but also, for example, diagnostic testing for planning purposes. Education contracts enable governors to adjust the amount and type of education provision they buy, according to their needs. Regimes in some establishments may change significantly as part-time education, combined with work and accredited PE programmes, become more common. Thus, education should consequently be available to more prisoners.

After release

Unemployment, particularly long-term unemployment, has always been a serious problem among offenders. The ex-offender's need for assistance – in terms of housing and employment – is far greater now than it was ten or twenty years ago. In the past, the ex-offender's problem lay in holding down a job rather than in obtaining one. While in most cases sufficient rented accommodation existed for them to be able to find somewhere to live, currently the difficulties faced are very considerable indeed. Neither possession of a job nor having somewhere to live is necessarily going to rehabilitate anyone but, without either of these, an ex-offender's chance of 'going straight' will be greatly reduced.

Ex-prisoners, particularly, face many difficulties in finding work, yet getting a job is important, if not crucial, for the successful resettlement of offenders and the prevention of crime. Research shows that unemployed ex-offenders are more likely to re-offend, and to receive another custodial sentence, than ex-prisoners who manage to get a job on release (Farrington 1994). A job offers money, identity, status and opportunities to develop abilities, contribute to society and grow out of crime. Staff in the Prison Service, and probation officers based in prisons, recognise the importance of preparing offenders for employment upon release, and they provide support and various practical options to help them. Probation officers in the field, local job centres and voluntary agencies such as the National Association for the Care and Resettlement of Offenders (NACRO) and the Apex Trust also contribute to the resettlement effort.

Real punishment for offenders who have been sentenced to imprisonment begins when they are released from custody. The true test of a prison system is what happens to offenders when they come out of prison. Both of these comments serve to remind all who are concerned with the treatment of offenders that imprisonment cannot be regarded as a self-contained episode; nor can the Prison Service operate in isolation. The task calls for interest, understanding and acceptance on the part of all members of the community (Home Office 1999, p. 64).

References

Council of Europe (1991) *Education in Prison*, Strasbourg: COE

Coyle, A. (1999) unpublished lecture at the International Centre for Prison Studies, King's College, London

Department for Education and Employment (1997) *Targets for our Future*, HMSO

— (1998) *The Learning Age*, HMSO

Farrington, D. (1994) *Psychological Explanations of Crime*, International Library of Criminology

Home Office (1991) *Custody Care and Justice: The Way Ahead for the Prison Service in England and Wales*, Cm 1647, HMSO

— (1999) *Annual Report of the Probation Service 1999*, The Stationery Office

Mcallister, M., Bottomley, A. and Liebling, A. (1994) *From Custody to Community: Throughcare for Young Offenders*, Aldershot: Avebury

Simon, F. and Corbett, C. (1996) *An Evaluation of Prison Work and Training*, Uxbridge: Centre for Criminal Justice Research, Brunel University

Smart, U. and Reynolds, J. (1996) *Prison Policy and Practice: Selected Papers from 35 Years of the Prison Service Journal*, PSJ

Stern, V. (1989) *Bricks of Shame: Britain's Prisons*, Penguin

18

ADDRESSING OFFENDING BEHAVIOUR
Neil S.D. Beales

The Prison Service Statement of Purpose is a clear message of intent for all staff working within the Service. This chapter examines the work of the Service within the context of the second part of the Statement: 'Our duty is to look after them with humanity and help them lead law-abiding and useful lives in custody and after release.' It looks in detail at some of the programmes designed to help prisoners address their offending behaviour, and considers work with those suffering drug and alcohol problems.

The need for offending behaviour programmes

It is now generally accepted that a term of imprisonment is not only meant to be punitive but also rehabilitative. In the vast majority of cases those who are currently serving sentences in prison will be released back into the community. The Prison Service is duty bound, while offenders are in custody, to explore every avenue and exhaust every resource to ensure that an offender is returned to society better prepared to take their place as a responsible, law-abiding citizen. This is more than a duty for some staff, it is a moral obligation.

Crime and its causes have been described as a disease, a cancer that society must work hard to eradicate. All too often, however, the public – fuelled by some parts of the media – seems to want to lock criminals away and forget about them. That is, in the long run, a damaging and short-sighted position. If crime is a disease then it could be treated as such. Hospitals do not just warehouse their patients hoping that they will get better. They investigate, diagnose and treat. They continuously look for new ways to treat new illnesses and seek out better methods of detection and prevention, which inevitably leads to improved lives for their customers. Of course, this is only an analogy; prison is not a panacea for the ills of society, but it can play a key role in helping people to live law-abiding and useful lives.

Many of the prisoners in Britain's prisons have been damaged and abused, and have not had the opportunities to try out a different type of lifestyle. Many come from disturbed backgrounds and have had little or no education. Illiteracy and poor coping mechanisms characterise the lives of many offenders, especially those under 21. Drug addiction and alcohol dependence is a large factor in the crime equation, particularly crimes of violence. Without the ability to break the cycle, many offenders will find themselves back in prison.

The Prison Service has committed itself to helping prisoners address their offending behaviour. This is measured through Key Performance Indicators (KPIs) and Key Performance Targets (KPTs). KPIs and KPTs both refer only to accredited programmes and indeed, as will be seen later, there has been a move away from non-accredited courses within the Service. The KPI on offending behaviour (KPI 7) requires a certain number of course completions, of which a set percentage are programmes for sex offenders (see Annex B). Targets are set by each governor, in agreement with the area manager, and are driven centrally by the number of completions required at a national level. This is designed to rise each year. The 1998–99 national target for offending behaviour programmes was 3,000 completions, of which 680 should be sex offender treatment programmes (SOTP). In 1999–2000, the aim is for 3,600 completions, of which 700 should be sex offender programmes (HM Prison Service 1999, p. 37). Table 18.1 shows performance against previous targets.

Offending behaviour programmes are a cornerstone of the Prison Service's *Corporate and Business Plan*. The plans over the next three years (to 2002) include examining the particular needs of women and young offenders and developing

Table 18.1: KPI performance on accredited offending behaviour programmes, 1996–98

Year	Accredited course completions		Sex offenders treatment courses completions	
	Target no.	Actual no.	Target no.	Actual no.
1996–97	1,300	1,373	650	663
1997–98	2,200	2,240	670	671

Source: HM Prison Service 1999, p. 37

tailor-made accredited programmes to address their specific needs. There is currently a body of research being completed on the criminogenic needs of women (HM Prison Service 1999, p. 23). In his Foreword to the *Corporate and Business Plan for 1999–2002*, the Director General Martin Narey announced that around £226 million of additional money over three years would be used to develop constructive regimes for prisoners, addressing offending behaviour, education and drug abuse (p. 4).

Delivering the programmes

Many prisoners have been through a 'needs analysis' during the pre-sentence report stage of their trial. Some have spent time on remand and had access to evaluation or, indeed, programmes, prior to conviction. Once convicted, all prisoners receive a sentence plan as part of the sentence management system and it is this that will guide their sentence and determine the types of programmes in which they should take part (see Chapter 23). The sentence management system is subject to regular review, both in custody and afterwards, and all departments within the prison will have an input into the process.

Delivery of programmes is a multi-disciplinary effort. Apart from dealing with offending behaviour on an *ad hoc* basis through daily interaction, prison officers work with a mixture of staff drawn from areas such as probation, education, psychology and the prison chaplaincy to deliver programmes to prisoners. In spite of this joint effort, it is important that the core role played by prison officers and others be recognised and maintained. The Chief Inspector of Prisons highlighted this in his thematic review of young offenders:

> Many Young Offender Institutions initially involved specialist departments in setting up and providing offending behaviour programmes, but cost-cutting has meant, in some cases, a reduction in their input. There is every reason why suitably selected and trained Prison Officers should be involved in delivering offending behaviour programmes; the best of them already do so in their daily interaction with young people in custody, which amounts to informal offending behaviour work. It is, however, a sign of poor management as well as being demotivating and unfair to staff, to assign them to a major role in delivering normal offending behaviour programmes without equipping them to do so effectively. Some of the best examples we found of offending behaviour programmes, as in the adult system, involved a productive partnership between several departments (HM Chief Inspectors of Prisons 1997, para. 4.78).

A multidisciplinary group of staff discuss offending behaviour issues with prisoners.

Key players

The Offending Behaviour Programmes Unit (OBPU)

This is based at Headquarters and has overall responsibility for all offending behaviour programmes. Their role is to support and monitor establishments' programme delivery.

Treatment manager

Normally a senior or higher psychologist who has tutored at least two courses, the treatment manager is responsible for programme and assessment integrity. He or she provides supervision and advice to tutors and recruits prisoners for programmes.

Programme manager

This person is accountable for the overall management of a programme and would normally be a governor grade. Practical arrangements for the programme, such as availability of facilities and of offenders, is also a key task. He or she works in close concert with the treatment manager to ensure that the programme is consistent and properly delivered.

Throughcare manager

This post is usually held by a senior probation officer. The key tasks of this role are to ensure effective communication with outside probation staff and to chair course reviews.

Tutors

Drawn from a range of disciplines, tutors deliver programmes and carry out assessments of their effectiveness. In order to be selected as a tutor, candidates undergo a series of tests, both written and oral, to ensure that they have the personal qualities necessary for tutoring. Once past this stage, candidates are sent on a three-day work skills training course. If this stage is also completed successfully candidates progress to tutor training. Tutors are supervised by the treatment manager, who advises on treatment integrity and training, and offers further advice and support.

Offenders

Whilst many offenders might benefit from a specific course, some do not have the cognitive deficiencies that a particular programme addresses. Research from Canada has indicated that programmes are less successful with certain groups of offenders, particularly high-risk acquisitive offenders (Offending Behaviour Programmes Unit 1999, p. 19). Therefore, there are two stages of prisoner selection:

- risk assessment, where prisoners are assessed for course suitability based on their offence record; and
- needs assessment, where prisoners are individually interviewed to assess in-depth their cognitive skills and whether they have any deficiencies in those areas.

Certain offenders will not be able to attend a programme if they do not speak English, have a very low IQ, or have an acute psychotic illness, either at present or at the time of the offence.

Programmes in current use

Prisoners are not a homogenous group, so each person has specific needs. The nature of most prison establishments, however, means that the majority of programmes are delivered in a group setting. There are a large number of programmes being delivered within the Prison Service that are designed to address the cause of prisoners' offending behaviour. The range of programmes in current use includes:

- anger management;
- substance abuse;
- alcohol awareness;
- assertiveness skills;
- sex offender treatment (SOT);
- victim awareness;
- lapse/relapse;
- therapeutic community (TC);
- cognitive skills;
- one-to-one counselling; and
- robbery rehabilitation.

Abundant research carried out over the last twenty years has concentrated on offending behaviour programmes and assessing 'what works'. It has been suggested by Hayman (1996, p. 22) that effective programmes are those which:

- are targeted at individuals with a high level of recidivism;
- focus on appropriate criminogenic needs;
- are delivered using cognitive behavioural techniques;
- are multi-modal, that is, they recognise the variety of offenders' problems; and
- maintain programme integrity.

Cognitive skills programmes are based on the premise that anti-social behaviour can be explained in terms of faulty thinking or reasoning and a general lack of cognitive skills (Offending Behaviour Programmes Unit 1999, p. 6). Linda Blud, principal psychologist with the Prison Service Programme Development Unit, describes cognitive skills programmes as follows:

> Cognitive skills programmes focus on the faulty thinking patterns which typify the strategies many offenders use to solve problems, make decisions and react to situations in their environments. So, in effect, the programmes are about teaching new ways of thinking (Blud 1996, p. 23).

During 1993–94 the Prison Service introduced two cognitive skills programmes into prisons. One was the reasoning and rehabilitation programme (R and R), which was already in use by the probation service. This programme was developed and is used by the Canadian Correctional Service (Offending Behaviour Programmes Unit 1999, p. 6). It is designed to address the main areas of faulty thinking, six of which were identified by Ross and Fabiano (1985):

1. lack of self-control;
2. concrete thinking;
3. rigid thinking;
4. problems with interpersonal problem solving, which leads to problems in four other areas:
    *   problem recognition
    *   thinking of alternatives
    *   consequential thinking
    *   means – end reasoning
5. egocentricity; and
6. critical reasoning.

The R and R programme is comprised of 35–36 sessions in total, but there are also two preparatory sessions and an evaluation session built into the course. The modules include:

*   problem-solving;
*   creative thinking;
*   critical reasoning;
*   management of emotions;
*   social skills;
*   value enhancement; and
*   negotiation skills.

The Prison Service has also developed an in-house thinking skills programme. There are twenty sessions in this programme, plus preparation and assessment time. Currently, the thinking skills course does not include some elements that are viewed as crucial to interpersonal problem-solving: the implementation skills, which include social skills, assertiveness and negotiation. There are, however, plans to extend the programme to include these skills.

The emphasis in cognitive skills training is on programme, not content. It is not about changing what the offender thinks, but helping them to think effectively. There is no guarantee, however, that teaching someone how to think means they will always use those skills effectively. The other important component of such

Prisoners are encouraged to address their offending behaviour through participation in accredited offending behaviour programmes.

courses therefore, is 'empathy value negotiation', which encourages offenders to put their new-found skills into use.

Both Prison Service programmes are designed to be fun as well as educational: There are games, puzzles and reasoning exercises – all designed to appeal to the offender. Motivation is kept to a maximum, and session lengths are limited to two hours so as not to lose concentration and focus. The sessions are carefully sequenced to ensure that new skills are introduced only after prerequisite ones have been taught and practised. Finally, the exercises are designed so that one session builds on another.

Programme accreditation

To count as a programme completion against the KPI target already described, there are two criteria:

- the programme must be accredited; and
- the site running the course must be delivering it to the correct standard.

To gain accreditation, a programme must fulfil ten criteria laid down by the accreditation panel. This is an independent body, made up of experts in the field, run as a joint venture with the probation service. The criteria are:

1. Explicit, empirically based model of change: There should be an explicit model of how the programme works.
2. Targeting criminogenic needs: The programme must be designed to best target the factors linked to the offending of the target group.
3. Responsivity principle: The methods used to target the criminogenic factors should be those to which the participants are most responsive.
4. Effective methods: Programmes should employ methods that consistently work with offenders.
5. Skills-orientated: Programmes should teach skills that will make it easier to avoid criminal activities and to engage successfully in legitimate ones.
6. Range of offence factors: There is a need to address the full range of offence-related factors in an integrated and mutually reinforcing way.
7. Dose: The amounts, intensity, sequencing and spacing of treatment should be related to the seriousness and persistence of offending.
8. Throughcare: Progress made in prison needs to be reinforced and strengthened by rehabilitative effort in the community.
9. Ongoing monitoring: Programmes should have a built-in commitment to monitoring their operation.
10. Ongoing evaluation: They should also have a commitment to ongoing evaluation (Offending Behaviour Programmes Unit 1999, p. 28).

In spite of the large range of programmes currently on offer to offenders, only the following Prison Service programmes are accredited:

- SOTP;
- reasoning and rehabilitation;
- Maguire's thinking skills;
- A Wing at HMP Grendon (TC) (see Chapter 19); and
- thinking skills.

Throughcare

In order for offending behaviour programmes delivered by the Prison Service to be fully effective, the progress made by an offender must be carried out and monitored within the community. Measures must, therefore, be put in place to ensure effective liaison with outside agencies such as the probation service. This includes notifying the supervising probation officer that an offender has begun a course and inviting him or her to attend a course review. It also includes the preparation of a post-course report. Copies of this report, which is compiled by the tutors under the supervision of the treatment manager, are provided to the prisoner, the supervising probation officer, the sentence management officer, the sentence management file and OBPU.

One month after the completion of a programme a course review is held to record the offender's progress during the programme. This is attended by a range of people and is accorded a high priority. Further objectives may be set for the offender during this review. Within a year of completion each offender should be interviewed again to identify whether they have met their objectives (Offending Behaviour Programmes Unit 1999, p. 11).

Drugs programmes and policy

A large percentage of crime in the United Kingdom is drug-related. Home Office research in five locations found that nearly half of those offenders who admitted to using drugs said that their use was connected to their offending (Prison Service Order 1999, p. 1). There are a large number of drug users within prison. Research indicates that the peak age for drug misuse among prisoners is 23 (HM Prison Service 1998, p. 6). Provision for programmes tackling drugs misuse was not always consistent across the estate however, and a Department of Health report in 1996 found that there was a need for a wider range of programmes. In addition, the lack of after-care in the community undermines treatment programmes in prison.

In 1998 the government published *Tackling Drugs to Build a Better Britain*, its ten-year strategy for tackling drug misuse (Home Office 1998). In the light of this publication, the Prison Service reviewed its 1995 strategy document *Drug Misuse in Prison* and produced *Tackling Drugs in Prison* (HM Prison Service, 1998). This sought to balance and focus efforts on drug misuse within prisons, and link them to work in the community under the four main principles of the government's strategy:

1. to help young people to resist drug misuse in order to achieve their full potential in society;
2. to protect our communities from drug-related anti-social and criminal behaviour;
3. to enable people with drug problems to overcome them and live healthy and crime-free lives; and
4. to stifle the availability of drugs on our streets.

Prison policy and strategy

The Prison Service has made considerable advances in its efforts to deal with drug problems, although it is recognised that there is still a long way to go before prisons and prisoners are drug-free. Figure 18.1 shows the overall reduction in the number of positive drug tests between 1996 and 1999 (HM Prison Service 1999, p. 24).

The Prison Service has allocated some £76 million of CSR funds to drugs work over the period 1999–2002, and has made the problem of tackling drug misuse one of its key strategic priorities. To measure achievement it has assigned a number of KPIs and KPTs to the drugs issue. There are two KPIs relating to the number of drug tests that are carried out under the mandatory drug-testing scheme, and one relating to the percentage of those tests that prove positive (see Annex B). The national target for 1999–2000 is 18.5% positive tests. The Service has also introduced two new KPTs relating to drug misuse. These are:

Figure 18.1: Positive drug-testing rate in prisons in England and Wales, 1996–99

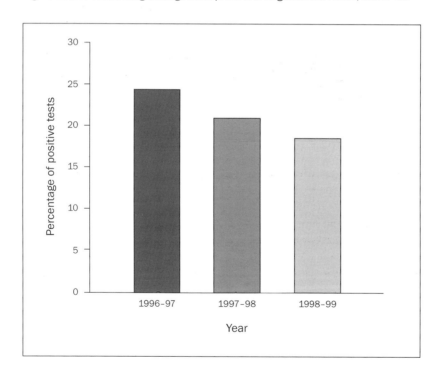

1. to increase the participation of problem drug misusers in drug treatment programmes, which have a positive impact on health and crime, by 66% by 2005, and by 100% by 2008; and

2. to reduce access to all drugs amongst young people (under 25 years) significantly – particularly those drugs that cause the most harm, heroin and cocaine – by 25% by 2005 and by 50% by 2008.

In addition, the Service aims to give all prisoners access to a voluntary testing programme by April 2001 (HM Prison Service 1999, p. 35).

Each prison is required to have its own local drug strategy and a multi-disciplinary team to take the strategy forward. These strategies plan action for each establishment under a series of broad headings, such as:

Reduction of movement and supply   Security measures should be designed to reduce the entry of drugs into the prison, and their movement around it once they are in. These include the use of drug detection dogs, cameras in visits rooms, fixed furniture and the use of intelligence systems to manage information about drug smuggling. Some prisons have introduced confidential phone lines which people can use to supply information about drugs. They also include new measures, recently introduced, to take action against visitors who smuggle drugs, including banning them from visits and putting prisoners on closed (no contact) visits.

Mandatory drugs-testing   Each prison is required to produce a strategy for testing a set percentage of its population each month. Prisons holding less than 400 prisoners are required to test 10% of the population, prisons holding over that number must test 5%. Of these tests, 14% must be carried out at weekends (Prison Service Order 3601). There is also a programme of mandatory frequent testing for those found guilty of using Class A drugs while in prison.

Education, support and advice   There is no point in implementing one of these strategies without the others. In reducing supply and movement a prison can create a climate of fear, if the means are not there for prisoners to deal with their drugs problems. Ultimately, the best method for tackling drugs misuse is to stem the need for drugs. This approach takes time and careful support, and is certainly not as easy as it sounds.

Effective drugs programmes

There are a number of different drug programmes being run in prisons. These include long-term residential projects like those run by outside agencies and non-governmental organisations (NGOs) such as RAPT (Rehabilitation of Addicted Prisoners Trust, who run an effective twelve-step programme in several prisons); and short-term interventions such as lapse/relapse and drug awareness. There are also detoxification programmes, that are targeted at remand prisoners who may come off the streets into prison with a high-level drug addiction. The Service also recognises alcohol problems and provides alcohol interventions for prisoners.

The cognitive skills base can also be used to design effective drug and alcohol programmes. There are eight guiding principles for designing effective alcohol interventions:

- Programmes should be based on theory, so that organisers have a sound rationale for what they are doing.
- Interventions should address offenders' criminogenic needs, that is, the reasons why they offended.
- High-risk offenders should be targeted so that maximum change may be effected.
- Structured cognitive-based programmes have been shown to work best.
- Programmes should be matched to offenders' needs.
- Services should continue into the community, with liaison between the prison and community workers.
- The effectiveness of interventions should be evaluated.
- There should be organisational support for programmes in terms of resources, staff training and monitoring progress.

A reorganisation of delivery has occurred that aims to ensure consistency across the estate **and** when prisoners return to the community. This initiative is known as CARAT (counselling, assessment, referral, advice and throughcare). It has been recognised within the Prison Service that a multi-agency approach to drugs work is necessary, as no one agency can deal with all the problems that arise. The CARAT provision is intended to overcome this problem. Its structure is illustrated in Figure 18.2. The purpose of CARAT services is to ensure effective delivery of drugs programmes in a timely and resource-efficient way. The provision is delivered on a contracted-out basis with each Prison Service area having its own contract. Two essential features are the way that provision acts as a bridge into the community and the post-release support to promote successful transfer (Prison Service Order 1999, p. 1).

The Prison Service aims to provide a comprehensive package of services to enable prisoners to address all aspects of their offending behaviour. Prisoners' needs are often complex and require multi-layered intervention. The Service

Figure 18.2: CARAT service structure

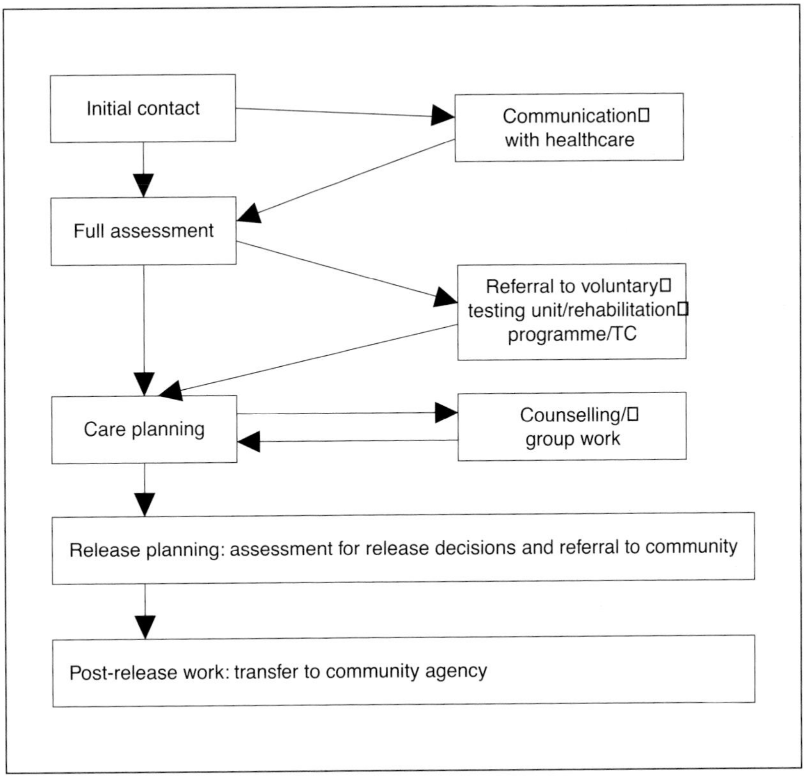

continues to work in partnership with outside agencies such as the probation service to ensure that the package offered is comprehensive and that support continues after the prisoner is released into the community.

References

Blud, L. (1996) 'Cognitive skills programmes in prisons', in S. Hayman (ed.) *What Works with Young Offenders*, Institute for the Study and Treatment of Deliquents

Hayman, S. (ed.) (1996) *What Works with Young Offenders*, Institute for the Study and Treatment of Deliquents

HM Chief Inspector of Prisons (1997) *Young Prisoners: A Thematic Review by HM Chief Inspector of Prisons for England and Wales*, Home Office

HM Prison Service (1998) *Tackling Drugs in Prison: The Prison Service Drug Strategy*, HMSO

— (1999) *Corporate Plan 1999–2000 to 2001–2002 and Business Plan 1999–2000*, Home Office

Home Office (1998) *Tackling Drugs to Build a Better Britain*, HMSO

Offending Behaviour Programmes Unit (1999) *Manager's Manual for Cognitive Skills Programmes*, HM Prison Service

Ross, R. and Fabiano, E. (1985) *Time to Think: A Cognitive Model of Delinquency*, Johnson City, TN: Institute of Social Science and Arts

THERAPEUTIC COMMUNITIES IN PRISON

Jim Gomersall

Summary

This chapter gives an introduction to the history of therapeutic communities (TCs) and explores their inherent values and principles and their place in the prison system. There is a summary of the efficacy of this form of treatment and of the regenerated enthusiasm and possibilities that lie ahead for future development. The chapter is not intended to be an academic exploration of the ideology nor of the outcomes of therapy. Contained within is an argument that prison therapeutic communities, though sharing the majority of characteristics of a non-prison TC, are different enough through necessity to be classed as a separate and successful therapeutic community model. There is some discussion about the vulnerability of small therapeutic units within a conventional establishment. Finally, the chapter has been written using practical experience in prison settings of group working, therapeutic community facility management and, latterly, from experience gained through membership and support of the staff team at Grendon Prison, the best-known and most established TC in a prison setting.

What is a therapeutic community?

There is acknowledged debate about the term 'therapeutic community'. One author (Kennard 1998) has concisely said that this term can be used in either a general or specific way, and that in general terms any institution that is trying to improve the lot of its inmates by offering productive and responsible work and opportunities for participation in the day-to-day running of the institution may call itself a therapeutic community. The term has often been used by institutions to describe a change-over from a non-therapeutic approach to a new and caring operation. An example of this can perhaps be seen in the change that has taken place in the sphere of mental health during the transition from closed mental hospitals to secure units and treatment in the community. This is a basis for the general use of the term, but for a more detailed definition we must look first at the history of TCs.

Psychiatrist and psychoanalyst Tom Main is said to have first used the expression 'therapeutic community' in England during 1946 when describing work undertaken in Birmingham with soldiers suffering from war neuroses. Maxwell Jones developed the notion of therapeutic communities initially working with soldiers during and after the Second World War, then with the so-called work-shy (funded by the Ministry of Labour), but primarily for what he did at Belmont, later renamed the Henderson Hospital. Over the decade that followed a distinctive TC model grew primarily associated with the work of Maxwell Jones (see Jones, M. 1952; 1968). The main features of this model were the reduction of official hierarchies and the sharing of power by staff and patients in the running of the community and in the treatment of residents. In effect, the residents became auxiliary therapists. This rationale allowed experimentation with behavioural change, gave therapists the opportunity to examine and understand patients' behaviour towards each other, and began to shift the responsibility for recovery from the physician to the patient.

The beginnings of the confusion over what constituted the 'model' for a therapeutic community can be found when we consider the work in California of Charles Dederich. Kennard (1998) describes Dederich as an ex-alcoholic who had been an ardent member of Alcoholics Anonymous. Being dissatisfied with the imposed limitations of that body, he founded an organisation called Synanon in 1959. Here ex-alcoholics and ex-drug addicts lived together and helped each other to stay drug- and alcohol-free. The basic principles were open and honest communication, and confrontation about anything and everything. Emotion-based defences were demolished in verbally aggressive and zealous encounter groups known as the 'Synanon Game'. There were fundamental differences between the Dederich model and the British (Jones) version, and one of these was that Synanon, and other communities that followed its lead, were run by ex-addicts for ex-addicts. They distrusted psychiatrists and psychologists, seeing them as having little to offer. Additionally, the organisational structures were radically different: Synanon's steeply graded staff and residents hierarchy – where decisions were made at the top and obeyed at the bottom, and failure at either end meant confrontation in the encounter group – can be compared with that formed in English therapeutic communities, where doctors and nurses were beginning to share decisions with patients and were moving towards a less formal and more democratic approach.

What has been described above has formed the basis for what appears to be a consensus of opinion that there are two primary forms of TC. The first is 'democratic' along the lines of the work of Maxwell Jones; the second is a 'hierarchical' or concept-based (drug/alcohol abuse, etc.) TC, using the Dederich model. In spite of the differences, some analysts have found common themes in the basic values and principles in effect. Kennard (1998) has identified a common set of principles that apply:

- a homely, communal and informal atmosphere – this does not imply that informality should indicate that the atmosphere is relaxed, indeed quite the reverse can often be the case;
- regular group meetings held in central areas for the purpose of information sharing, building a sense of cohesion, open and public shared decision-making, sharing of thoughts and ideas (and feedback on them) and applying pressure to members who are causing concern in attitude or behaviour;
- members share the work of maintaining and running the community, thus teaching a collective approach, building necessary skills for self-sufficiency, raising interpersonal skill deficiencies and social responsibility; and
- community members act as supplementary therapists, commenting on and influencing each other's behaviour and attitudes, and this role is acknowledged and supported by staff. With this last function comes a greater or lesser degree of decision-sharing with staff, depending on the democratic/hierarchical balance in that particular community.

There are, in addition to these key principles, a common set of values to which a therapeutic community may adhere. These consist of an acceptance that most people's difficulties arise from their relations with other people, that therapy is a learning process and that the 'patient' is an active participant in his or her treatment. The therapeutic process may necessitate some basic equalities for members, which includes professional and non-professional staff and therapists. These basic equalities would also include a recognition that there are qualities and deficiencies in the personalities of both groups. Finally, to a visitor, there would be a sense of a 'closed shop' with a fundamental unquestioning belief in the worth of the therapeutic community from permanent members. The targeted therapeutic ethos is probably best encapsulated by Roberts (1997) who has said that a therapeutic community is a consciously designed social environment and programme within a residential or day unit in which the social and group process is harnessed with therapeutic intent.

Intent and outcomes

The previous section looked at how TCs originated and how they can have some common attributes, principles and values. We now examine the purpose and some of the work that has been done to study the end product of this therapeutic process.

What then is the purpose of the TC in prison? Farrington (1997), after many years of research and evaluation of data, has shown that there can be a pattern to the development of an individual's criminal activities and general anti-social behaviour over a considerable time-scale. In many cases, it is possible to predict further criminal activities based on the history of the individual and his or her age and environment. Farrington's findings have illustrated examples of the causation and continuance of the cycle of offending and why, in many cases, this escalates before reduction or cessation through maturation. Following exploration into causative factors and their interrelationship, common strands were found to be the links between physical and social environment, learned behaviour, habit, modelling and decision-making. People develop personalities as a result of learned behaviour through interaction with others, but especially their parents or guardians and peers.

The cognitive development of an individual effectively results from learning to think in a particular way. This being the case, there is the possibility that what has been learned can be modified and a new set of values and cognitive skills developed that enable the individual to function inside accepted societal parameters. The therapeutic community offers people the opportunity to experiment, to expose and deal with problematic social interactions in a safe arena. It permits a learning environment where people can live and work together within a setting of social analysis. This therapeutic process is geared towards insight and a greater level of self-awareness resulting from the confrontation of unacceptable or disordered behaviour. Put simply, the environment in which the residents and staff operate is safe, caring and supportive of positive change; this in turn permits the individual to disclose inner thoughts and feelings, allows other members of the community to respond honestly to those thoughts and feelings, and then allows the individual to reflect and hopefully modify behaviour as a result of this learning.

Having briefly outlined the rationale behind this form of therapy, it is equally important that an examination of real therapeutic outcomes is undertaken. Here we will focus primarily on the work of TCs in prisons.

There has been much research into the efficacy of both concept-based and democratic therapeutic communities, and for good reason. Therapeutic communities seem, at first glance, to be relatively costly to operate when compared to some other forms of treatment. The public have a right to expect that the proportion of their taxes which is spent on what may outwardly appear to be an expensive commodity is providing value for money. Research has, in essence, taken two forms, the first of which compares changes to cognitions, feelings and social skills before, during or after treatment with others who have not undergone treatment. Lees et al. (1999) describe this as 'in-treatment' and 'post-treatment' outcome studies respectively. The second form, and this seems to have gained most attention within the criminal justice system, is a comparison between the average re-conviction rates of those who have undergone therapy in prison with those who have not – this is a specific form of post-treatment outcome study. The diversity of the available literature can be imagined when these research studies are further broken down into those that have been conducted on concept-based and those on democratic models, and then further sub-divided into those involving secure and those involving non-secure facilities. Of the studies conducted some stand out as indicating very positive outcomes, either for the ability to socialise to a greater extent and therefore better integrate into society (Newton 1998), or for lowered levels of re-conviction or both (Cullen 1993; Marshall 1997). Some other studies have suggested that this form of therapy may have little or no effect in some circumstances (Gunn et al. 1978). Others have indicated that in some cases the effects may be negative or even that some types of personality disorder may be made worse by this treatment (Harris et al. 1994).

Therapeutic communities: the prison 'model'

In the United Kingdom, the prison TC 'model' has been in place for the past 35 years at Grendon Prison. Because of the nature of imprisonment there are some fundamental differences between the Maxwell Jones-type TCs run in prisons and those outside. These differences have been acknowledged by Rawlings (1998) who has explained that in prisons, the key workers in the communities are often prison officers with therapeutic skills (under the direction of a therapist), not professional therapists or psychiatrically trained staff. For these officers, the needs of the community have to be balanced with the needs of security and control. This dichotomy of work ethic can cause conflict between the therapeutic ideal and the regular and expected duties that prison officers perform. This conflict could potentially be exacerbated by a lack of understanding of these dynamics by therapists and prison managers. Because of the dual purpose, it could be surmised that rather than undergo a futile attempt to force a prison TC into a true Maxwell Jones model, more can be effected by accepting that the models that exist are similar but different in form.

The difference in form can be seen clearly when we revisit the most widely known finding in Rapoport's (1960) research into the fundamentals of non-prison-based TCs. Four principles were proposed that have since become synonymous with 'democratic therapeutic' communities.

Democratisation   Every member of the community (that is, all residents and staff) should share equally in exercising of power in decision-making about community affairs.

Permissiveness   All members should tolerate in one another a wide degree of behaviour that might be distressing or seem deviant by ordinary standards.

Communalism   There should be tight-knit, intimate sets of relationships, with sharing of amenities (dining room, etc.), use of first names and free communication.

Reality confrontation   Residents should be continuously presented with interpretations of their behaviour as it is seen by others in order to counteract their tendency to distort, deny or withdraw from their difficulties in getting on with others.

It will be obvious that to one degree or another some of these principles do not sit easily in a secure, closed prison setting because of the enforced nature of residency (though prisoners must volunteer for treatment in a prison TC) and the primary statutory requirement of the establishment which is to ensure custody and maintain control.

If prison TCs do not operate in the same way as those outside of this setting, can they be justified? Leaving the evidence of re-conviction studies to one side for the time being, it has been noted by several writers that during and following therapy there is a reduction in personal and interpersonal violence (Cullen 1994; MacKenzie 1997) and that an improvement in institutional behaviour occurs (Sleap 1979; Cooke 1989; Genders and Player 1995). In simple terms, this should mean that as a result of being a part of a TC environment, prisoners – a relatively high proportion of whom have been clinically diagnosed as having personality disorders – behave better not only in the TC but after transfer into the mainstream prison system. Disruptive prisoners become more manageable and therefore become less costly to contain. Further evidence of positive changes in personality have been shown in the works of Newton (1973), Gunn et al. (1978) and Miller (1982). Each research project demonstrated clear indications of reduced levels of hostility, depression, neuroticism, anxiety and introversion, plus improved attitudes to authority figures and a greater acceptance of responsibility for personal behaviour from those prisoners who had undergone therapy.

Moving on to evidence of impact on anti-social and offending behaviour post-discharge, research by Cullen (1993) showed that 33% of men released from Grendon Prison between 1984 and 1989 were re-convicted within two years, compared with 42–47% of adult males released from the general prison population in the same period. Marshall (1997) has recently shown that there is evidence that the prison TC model should be included in the 'what works' side of the intervention equation. His research examined the re-conviction rates of over 700 prisoners who went to Grendon for therapy during a four-year period compared with 142 other prisoners who had applied for Grendon but did not go. He further compared the study group with more than 1,400 prisoners from the general prison population with similar characteristics in terms of offence, sentence length and age. His findings have shown that prisoners who go to Grendon initially present a higher risk of re-offending than the general prison population, but that those who underwent therapy at Grendon had lower re-conviction rates than would have been anticipated had they not gone to Grendon. One of the most significant findings was that time spent in therapy was related to lower re-conviction rates for prisoners who stayed for longer periods. Prisoners who stayed at Grendon for 18 months showed reductions in re-conviction rates of around one-fifth to one-quarter. This massive project supported the conclusions previously drawn by Cullen (1993), who said that there is a relationship between time in therapy and rates of reconviction (with 18 months appearing to be the threshold for greatest improvement). There is a further positive effect for those who leave the TC directly and under parole supervision.

This has been but a précis of some of the differences that prison-based therapeutic communities present and the positive results that have been shown through research and evaluation. However, some would postulate that this is still not enough and that the TC approach should be augmented by supplementary therapies, a multi-modal approach, to further tackle the propensity for anti-social and offending behaviour.

Multi-modal – the way forward?

Palmer (1996) has explored the possibilities associated with a multi-modal approach. He said that programmes that reflect certain combinations of elements may have considerably more relevance to clients, and in that sense more power, than any of those elements alone. If there is a case for a multi-modal form of intervention, it could be strongly argued, however, that as the TC is a holistic form of therapy other forms of treatment may damage the approach by diverting the patient from the primary therapy. To illustrate this point Rawlings (1998) has deduced that as patients are often working with difficult and painful issues it could be held that too much structure or too many extra activities may be used to defend against the pain which must be experienced if progress is to be made. Also, people need time to work through the things they are learning; consequently, spare time is deliberately built into democratic TC timetables as a therapeutic device. Nevertheless, it is common practice in concept-based TCs, and growing practice in Maxwell Jones-type TCs, to offer a range of additional therapeutic opportunities, such as relapse prevention, education and creative therapies. There is often tension between the introduction of structured activities and the need for 'spare' therapeutic time. Further research into this controversy could be of considerable value.

Programme effectiveness

In addition to the push for a multi-modal approach there is a further and justifiable thrust for programme integrity; in other words, that the stated aims are met and are linked to the methods used. This requires adequate staff training, resources and support; an agreed plan for monitoring and evaluation; and accurate, auditable records of activities. Hollin (1995) stressed the importance of programme integrity, citing examples of failure as a direct consequence of programme drift, reversal and lack of proper assessment and audit practices. McGuire (1995) has found that there is no single, outstanding approach guaranteed to work as a means of reducing recidivism. However, McGuire's work, drawn from the findings of several other researchers, has shown that there are a number of principles concerning the design and assembly of effective interventions that can be identified. These are listed in brief below.

Risk classification   Individuals identified as a higher risk receive more intensive intervention, less for lower risk.

Criminogenic needs   This means the separation of problems or features that contribute or support re-offending from those that do not, and the targeting of these for intervention.

Responsivity   This involves matching worker's styles with client learning needs. Generally, most offenders require active, participatory non-didactic methods.

Community base On balance, community-based programmes have been identified as having more effective outcomes, but this does not imply dismissal of institution-based work.

Treatment modality More effective programmes are found to be those:

1. recognising the variety of offenders' problems (multi-modal);
2. with contents and methods that are skills-and coping-strategy-oriented; and
3. drawn from behavioural, cognitive or cognitive-behavioural sources.
   Cognitive behavioural approaches should seek to:
   - address the prime characteristics of offenders
   - reduce impulsivity – thought before action
   - enable the consideration of consequences of actions for self and others, and
   - develop coping strategies and alternatives to offending.

Working TCs in the Prison Service

Prison TCs have waxed and waned over the years and the site locations and numbers have fluctuated. Keeping up with recent growth has proved difficult but it is important to recognise those that are extant at the time of writing. For interest, there follows a shortened list of therapeutic communities that are already established and functioning in the prison estate. It is regretted that there is not enough space to include those TCs under development.

1. The Chiltern Unit therapeutic community was opened in a new healthcare centre at HMYOI Aylesbury in 1997 but was re-located in a residential wing early in 1999. It is a Maxwell Jones-type TC facilitated by a multi-disciplinary team and holding up to 18 young men. This is the only fully functioning 'democratic' young offender programme at the present time.
2. HMP Channings Wood has a concept-based TC that opened in 1996. The unit has 80+ beds and is run in conjunction with the Association for the Prevention of Addiction (Clarke 1997).
3. The Albatross Unit at HMYOI Feltham was established in 1989 as a Maxwell Jones-type TC for young offenders. It is now in a state of suspension pending a decision on its future (Fowler 1997).
4. The GTC unit at HMP Gartree opened in 1993 and treats life-sentenced prisoners during the early part of their sentences. Again, it is a Maxwell Jones-type TC (Rawlings 1998).
5. HMP Grendon opened in 1963 and houses 240 prisoners. The prison is divided into six wings, five of which are relatively independent TCs with 40 or

so residents in each, plus a smaller assessment and preparation wing for 25. There is a community staff team consisting of a lead therapist, a psychologist, a probation officer, senior prison officers and prison officers working within a multidisciplinary ethic. A sixth TC within the prison is planned for the near future. This is the only dedicated TC prison in the prisons' estate (Genders and Player 1995; Cullen 1997). It achieved offending behaviour programme accreditation in 1999, the first prison TC to do so.

6. HMP Holme House runs a concept-based TC with 65 beds. The unit opened in 1996 and is run in partnership with the Phoenix Trust.

7. A concept-based community is established at HMYOI Portland as a partnership between Yedall Manor and Bridges of America (Clarke 1997).

8. HMP Wayland has a concept-based TC that opened in 1995.

9. The Max Glatt Centre at HMP Wormwood Scrubs, opened in 1972 and holds 20+ prisoners. Originally set up as a concept-based TC (for addictions), it now functions as a multi-modal Maxwell Jones-type community treating personality disordered offenders and those with a history of violence, including life-sentence prisoners and sex offenders (Jones, L. 1997).

Difficulties and developments within established prison TCs

There have been some casualties over the years since the first TC was established at Grendon Prison in 1963. These include a unit in HMYOI Glen Parva (MacKenzie 1997) and, in Scotland, the TC-type unit at Barlinnie Prison (Cooke 1997). Why did they close? It may well be that each was an island within the host establishment and as a result not treated as a part of the whole, not supported by off-unit management through lack of understanding or because they just did not fit in with the majority need. Rawlings (1998) explains that small TC units in prisons tend to be relatively short-lived, possibly because of the consistent difficulties of maintaining therapeutic programme integrity inside a discipline environment. Small units either become too isolated from the host institution or are not separate enough. Despite this, the self-contained Max Glatt Centre at Wormwood Scrubs has survived since its inception in 1972 and is still going strong; as is the Gartree TC, which has been running for over five years.

Of late there has been an increase in interest in the organisation and development of TCs within the Prison Service. The Regimes Directorate at Prison Service Headquarters has been given a central co-ordination role for established and further enterprises. There are plans underway for a TC unit to be included in a new prison to be built at Marchington, Staffordshire; also for concept-based communities to be incorporated into the regimes of several prisons; and there is ongoing discussion about the need for a TC for women prisoners. The last follows an experiment abandoned some years ago at Holloway (Madden et al. 1994) and is long overdue because, despite evidence that women could benefit from Maxwell Jones-type therapeutic communities, there are no such prison facilities for women in Britain (Rawlings 1998).

Currently, there appears to be a renewal of interest in and a degree of support from Headquarters for the possibility of further development of TCs in prisons. This may have come about because of a re-focusing on the need to develop a policy framework and supporting standards and guidance for constructive regimes for offenders. It may also demonstrate the beginnings of a more integrated approach within the criminal justice system in pursuit of the goal of better public protection. However, it has also been particularly prompted by the work of therapists, prison officers, psychologists, probation officers and other workers who have continued to dedicate their time to the good of others. In so doing, they have produced the very positive results that have been identified by committed researchers, only some of whom are cited in this text.

The last twenty years have been difficult for prison-based TCs but now that they are beginning to be accepted as part of a national drive towards effective offending behaviour - programmes, with the advent of formalised accreditation to ensure programme integrity and the potential benefits of multi-modal approaches – the future may be more positive.

References

Clarke, D. (1997) 'Therapeutic communities for drug misusers', *Prison Service Journal*, No. 111, pp. 78–96

Cooke, D. (1989) 'Containing violent prisoners', *British Journal of Criminology*, Vol. 29, No. 2, pp. 129–43

— (1997) 'Barlinnie Special Unit: the rise and fall of a therapeutic experiment', in E. Cullen, L. Jones and R. Woodward (eds), *Therapeutic Communities for Offenders*, Chichester: John Wiley & Sons

Cullen, E. (1993) 'The Grendon reconviction study, part one', *Prison Service Journal*, No. 90, pp. 35–7

— (1994) 'Grendon: the therapeutic community that works', *Therapeutic Communities*, Vol. 15, No. 4

— (1997) 'Can a prison be a therapeutic community?: the Grendon template', in
E. Cullen, L. Jones and R. Woodward (eds), *Therapeutic Communities for Offenders*,
Chichester: John Wiley & Sons

Farrington, D.P. (1997) 'Human development and criminal careers', in
M. Maguire, R. Morgan and R. Reiner (eds), *The Oxford Handbook of Criminology*,
(2nd edition), Oxford: Clarendon Press

Fowler, A. (1997) 'Feltham's Albatross Unit', *Prison Service Journal*, No. 111,
pp.12–13

Genders, E. and Player, E. (1995) *Grendon: A Study of a Therapeutic Prison*, Oxford:
Clarendon Press

Gunn, J., Robertson, G., Dell, S. and Way, C. (1978) *Psychiatric Aspects of
Imprisonment*, Academic Press

Harris, G., Rice, M. and Cormier, C. (1994) 'Psychopaths: is a therapeutic community therapeutic?' *Therapeutic Communities*, Vol. 15, No. 4

Hollin, C.R. (1995) 'The meaning and implications of "programme integrity"', in
J. McGuire (ed.), *What Works: Reducing Re-offending*, Chichester: John Wiley & Sons

Jones, L. (1997) 'Developing models for managing treatment integrity and efficacy in a prison-based TC: the Max Glatt Centre', in E. Cullen, L. Jones and R.
Woodward (eds), *Therapeutic Communities for Offenders*, Chichester: John Wiley & Sons

Jones, M. (1952) *Social Psychiatry: A Stude of Therapeutic Communitie*s, Tavistock

— (1968) *Social Psychiatry in Practice: The Idea of a Therapeutic Community*,
Harmondsworth: Penguin

Kennard, D. (1998) *An Introduction to Therapeutic Communities*, Jessica Kingsley

Lees, J., Manning, N. and Rawlings, B. (1999) 'Therapeutic community effectiveness: a systematic international review of therapeutic community treatment for
people with personality disorders and mentally disordered offenders', York: NHS
Centre for Review and Dissemination, University of York

MacKenzie, J. (1997) 'Glen Parva therapeutic community – an obituary', *Prison
Service Journal*, No. 111, p. 26

Madden, T., Swinton, M. and Gunn, J. (1994) 'Therapeutic community treatment: a survey of unmet need among sentenced prisoners', *Therapeutic Communities*, Vol. 15, No. 4, pp. 229–36

Marshall, P. (1997) 'A reconviction study of HMP Grendon therapeutic community', *Research Findings No. 53*, Home Office

McGuire, J. (ed.) (1995) *What Works: Reducing Re-offending*, Chichester: John Wiley & Sons

Miller, Q. (1982) *Preliminary Consideration of Psychological Test/Retest Scores and their Bearing on Criminal Reconviction*, Grendon Psychology Unit series D, report D13, HMP Grendon

Newton, M. (1973) *Reconviction after Treatment at Grendon*, Chief Psychologist Report Series D, No. 1, Home Office

— (1998) 'Changes in the measures of personality, hostility and locus of control during residence in a prison therapeutic community', *Legal and Criminal Psychology*, Vol. 3, pp. 209–23

Palmer, T. (1996) 'Programmatic and non-programmatic aspects of successful intervention', in A. Harland (ed.), *Choosing Correctional Options that Work*, Sage

Rapoport, R. (1960) *The Community as Doctor*, Tavistock

Rawlings, B. (1998) *Research on Therapeutic Communities in Prisons: A Review of the Literature*, HM Prison Service

Roberts, J. (1997) 'How to recognise a therapeutic community', *Prison Service Journal*, No. 111, pp. 4–7

Sleap, H. (1979) *Goal Attainment Scaling: An Introduction and Some Limited Findings*, Grendon Psychology Unit series B, HMP Grendon

20

MAINTAINING SECURITY AND ORDER
Ed Tullett

Introduction

Lack of security, control issues and a defensible system of prison justice have been at the heart of some highly public debates, the outcomes of which have had a considerable impact on the Prison Service. Riots and disturbances in prisons during the 1980s culminated in the 1990 riot at Manchester (Strangeways) prison. The consequent inquiry by Lord Justice Woolf (Woolf and Tumim 1991) resulted in wide-ranging change for the Service. Similarly, the escapes from Whitemoor and Parkhurst Prisons in 1994 and 1995 resulted in the Woodcock and Learmont Reports and a further concentration on the prevention of escapes. Finally, from 1976 to the early 1990s there was an increasing willingness by the courts to intervene in the conduct of prison adjudications. These are quasi-judicial internal prison hearings, normally conducted by a prison's governor, into an alleged disciplinary offence by a prisoner. Woolf suggested that if the adjudication system is not perceived to be fair and just, prisoners are more likely to riot or cause a disturbance. Thus the courts' intervention during this period effectively reformed the way in which adjudications are carried out. Some of these events meant that the Prison Service has had to learn some painful lessons over the years, but in some ways the responses to these crises have brought about a significant modernisation in the way the important service of protecting the public (while delivering services to prisoners) is carried out.

Definitions

'Custody' and 'order' are not easy terms to unravel. They are often mixed up with words like 'security' and 'control', which are often interchangeable, not least in the Prison Service. The title of this chapter is derived from the definitions given at a 1995 Cropwood Conference by Sir Richard Tilt, former Director General of the Prison Service, when he was Director of Security:

custody refers to containment of prisoners within the prison perimeter, and ... *security* is the arrangement by which this is achieved. If we assume that *order* refers to the absence of disruption, then *control* is the means by which staff can achieve order.

Security is a term that can also encompass 'safety'. It can also include activities that do not, on the face of it, have much to do with preventing escapes, for example preventing drugs coming into prisons. Generally, however, it seems to be accepted that security is about preventing escapes. 'Order' is more problematic. For some (Sparks et al. 1996, pp. 70–9, 118–26) order is 'more inclusive'. It is 'any long-standing pattern of social relations (characterised by a minimum level of respect for persons) in which the expectations that participants have of one another are commonly met, though not necessarily without contestation'. These writers define control similarly to Richard Tilt, as a means of achieving order, although they emphasise the use of routines to get to this end.

Security

An escape can happen when a prisoner overcomes the physical barriers of a closed, walled and fenced establishment. The need for secure prisons to protect the public seems to be self-evident. But in the early 1990s the Prison Service tolerated a far higher number of prisoners at large than at present (see Table 20.1). The onset of agency status and the highly public and embarrassing escapes from Whitemoor in September 1994 and Parkhurst in January 1995 contributed towards a systematic focusing of effort and resources towards cutting the escape rate to an 'acceptable' level.

Since 1995 the Prison Service Key Performance Indicators (KPIs) have measured the number of escapes from custody. The current KPI is 'to ensure that there are no Category A escapes and to ensure that the number of escapes from prisons, expressed as a proportion of the average prison population, is lower than 0.05%' (HM Prison Service 1999). The number of escapes from inside prison establishments between 1992–93 and 1997–98 have fallen from 232 to 23, a reduction of 90% (HM Prison Service 1999, p. 17). Prison Service experience suggests that preventing escapes does indeed help to maintain public confidence in the criminal justice system. It means that prison governors can carry out the direction of the courts, and – crucially – allows prison staff to carry out the second part of the Statement of Purpose: 'help [prisoners] lead law-abiding lives ... after release'.

Table 20.1: Escapes from prisons and escorts, 1992–98

Year	Number of escapes		
	From prisons	From escorts	Total
1992–93	232	115	347
1993–94	171	125	296
1994–95	151	66	217
1995–96	52	70	122
1996–97	33	98	131
1997–98	23	82	105

Source: HM Prison Service (1999), Annex 2

What does security consist of?

Security is 'special measures – physical, practical and procedural – to prevent escapes and to ensure that prisoners remain in custody' (Liebling 1997, p. 45). For convicted prisoners these measures begin when they are classified into categories, depending upon risk. They are then allocated to appropriate prisons. Once in prison, security depends on the interaction of the following elements, some of which, like searching, are directly applied to prisoners; others, like perimeter systems, will only come into play if a prisoner attempts to escape. These elements are physical security, procedural security, and 'dynamic' security.

Categorisation and prison allocation

In Lord Mountbatten's report into the escape of George Blake in 1966, he recommended the Prison Service adopt a system of categorisation of prisoners. This is an early form of risk assessment. Adult male prisoners are classified into one of four security categories, from A to D, which aim to ensure that prisoners are sent to prisons with an appropriate level of security. The Service believes it is important to categorise correctly: too high a category would be unjustified on grounds of humanity and cost; too low would be unjustified because the public would not receive adequate protection. There is, however, evidence that some prisoners are placed in more secure jails for control reasons, and the Service is considering whether categorisation should only ever be decided on the basis of escape risk. The existing categories are defined as follows:

Category A   These prisoners are those who would be highly dangerous to the public, the police or the security of the state, and for whom escape must be made impossible.

Category B   This category is for those prisoners who do not require the highest security conditions but for whom escape must be made very difficult.

Category C   These are prisoners who cannot be trusted in open conditions but who lack the will or resources to make a determined escape attempt.

Category D   This denotes prisoners who can be trusted in open conditions.

Prisoners held on remand, female and young prisoners may be categorised A (or restricted status) but otherwise are not categorised. (There are too few female and young prisoners to designate them by category and thus keep them close to their homes.) Those convicted of or accused of serious offences such as terrorism, serious drugs offences, violent or sexual offences are likely to be identified as Category A. This category contains three subdivisions, according to the risk of escape: standard, high and exceptional. Exceptional and high-risk prisoners are likely to be important members of criminal gangs with substantial outside resources which could be used to aid escape. Exceptional-risk prisoners are held in maximum security special secure units.

Remand prisoners are unclassified but are normally treated as Category B prisoners. This is because the risk they pose is usually an unquantifiable one at this stage. Remand prisoners stay in the local prison near to the court trying them. Local prisons apply security conditions appropriate for Category B prisoners. Remanded Category A prisoners are held in one of twelve specially designed or adapted Category A prisons that service all the courts in England and Wales.

Once convicted, prisoners are allocated a prison according to their category. Category A prisoners will be sent to one of six dispersal prisons, which are designed to hold all Category A prisoners. Dispersal prisons are so called because Category A prisoners are dispersed among the Category B population rather than concentrated in one maximum security prison (see Chapter 8). Category B prisoners will remain at their local prison if on a short sentence, or go to a dispersal or another closed training prison. Category C prisoners are sent to closed training prisons with fewer physical security standards. Category D prisoners are allocated to open training prisons with no physical barriers against escape.

Given the small number of them, women and young prisoners are allocated either to closed or open conditions. The Prison Service is currently working on proposals for a more systematic way of categorising women and young prisoners.

Physical security

Perhaps the biggest difference between prisons in England and Wales and most other prison systems is that staff do not use firearms as a security or control measure, either on the perimeter or inside the prison. Physical security systems must take this into account, as must design principles that minimise the possibility of escape. These are set out in the Prison Service *Briefing Guides*, which set the standard for new prisons. Existing prisons are upgraded to the standards when resources allow.

Most Category A and B prisoners live in specially reinforced cells, which should take at least 24 hours to break out of. Many Category C prisoners are held in cells that take at least 12 hours to break out of. Category D prisoners are not held in cells but in dormitories or rooms to which they may or may not have the keys. Young prisoners and women are held in a combination of cells or dormitories.

Other physical security measures include X-ray machines, wands and portals for detecting metal; systems for detecting explosives; and biometric entry systems for visitors, to ensure that prisoners do not escape by posing as visitors. All of these systems are deployed in prisons holding Category A prisoners. In Category B or C prisons, this equipment may be used as local management see fit, depending upon local risks and circumstances.

Procedural security

Clearly none of the physical systems described above would stop escapes on their own. Prison staff are needed to operate and to complement them. All prisons will have a number of security procedures, required to ensure the security of each prison is operable and at the right level. Since the Whitemoor and Parkhurst escapes the need for regular audits, independent of line management, has been recognised.

Procedural security systems are set out in the Prison Service *Security Manual* (HM Prison Service 1997), which was rewritten following the Whitemoor and Parkhurst escapes. The new *Manual* aims to maximise compliance with national security standards but acknowledges that the Prison Service consists of diverse establishments with often dissimilar geography, designs and functions. Within adherence to national standards, it gives governors the flexibility to make sensible day-to-day security decisions. Thus the *Manual* sets out the core minimum standards that must be followed by each category of prison and in each part of the prison. Governors then produce local standards to buttress the national standards. Together, these local and national standards amount to an auditable procedural security document for each prison.

Security procedures cover the spectrum of prison activities, for example:

- lock and key security;
- security at night;
- intelligence, police liaison;
- security of vehicles;
- accountability;
- risk assessment of prisoners going to work or outside hospital;
- escort security; and
- the security of departments of the prison – the gate, visits, reception and healthcare centre.

It is difficult to pick out any aspect of these procedures and say that one is more important than another. Clearly they all have their part to play in ensuring the security of the prison. Three important aids to security, however, are described below in more detail: searching, the use of restraints, and prisoner accountability.

Searching   This is done of people (prisoners, visitors and staff), objects (property, equipment) or areas (cells, workshops, visiting rooms, the chapel, etc.). It is an effective way of finding contraband (weapons, drugs or other illicit items) and of deterring the smuggling into prison of such items. Each prison has a written policy that sets out who is searched and when, together with a schedule of searching targets for all areas of the prison. Category A prisons will have a high level of searching and will employ dedicated searching teams who carry out regular and frequent searches.

Prison Rule 41 authorises personal searches of prisoners, stipulating that:

- prisoners must be searched each time they enter the prison and afterwards, as the governor or Secretary of State directs;
- strip searches may only be carried out by prison officers;
- officers must be of the same sex as the subject; and
- a search must be carried out in as seemly a manner as is consistent with finding anything concealed.

Staff may use reasonable force to effect a lawful search. Three types of personal search are authorised: strip, rub-down and pat-down searches. A strip search is a full search of clothing and the external parts of the body. At no time is the subject fully naked. Prisoners are generally strip-searched each time they are received into prison or leave prison on an outside escort. Prisoners are also strip-searched when their cell is searched, when they submit to a mandatory drug test, or if a prison officer has grounds for suspicion. Visitors and staff may only be strip-searched if there are reasonable grounds to suspect that they are smuggling contraband and then only on the authority of prison management.

A full rub-down search involves rubbing down the clothing of the subject except for the breast (of women) and groin areas. The hair and inside the mouth and nostrils are checked (though not touched). Shoes are also removed and the feet are checked. A pat-down search is the same as a rub-down search except that it is less thorough. It also does not include the front and back of the torso, nor footwear. Domestic visitors entering a prison holding Category A prisoners should be subject to a full rub-down search. Official visitors entering prisons holding Category A prisoners are subject to a modified rub-down search (this is a rub-down search except for the search of hair, mouth, nostrils and feet). For other prisons the level and number of searches is a matter for the governor depending upon local circumstances and needs.

Restraints   Escorting prisoners between prisons and courts, hospitals or other prisons is a time when security is vulnerable. Officers are authorised to use restraints on these occasions by Prison Rule 46(6) (YOI Rule 49(6)) which says that approved restraints may be used for safe custody. With the exception of Category A escorts, all escorts to court are contracted out, and the law allows authorised employees of private contractors to restrain prisoners on escort. Approved restraints are handcuffs and escort chains, which are single cuffs linked by a long chain. The latter are usually used to allow prisoners who require restraint to use the toilet with a measure of privacy.

Prisoner accountability   Prisoners must be in certain places at certain times. Every day, prisoners will be at work, education, at court, on home leave, being transferred to another prison, have been released or have come into prison for the first time. Keeping track of them is all-important, especially when one considers that they are being incarcerated against their will. All prisons, therefore, have systems for regular and irregular checking to ensure that the number of prisoners on the roll is correct. Landing staff must know the numbers on their landing. All prisons undertake roll-checks, which take place before the prison is locked up at night and just before morning unlock as well as at breakfast, lunch and dinnertime.

An officer checks that handcuffs are secure before prisoners are transferred to another prison.

A prison officer undertakes a roll-check to ensure that the prisoner is safe and secure in his cell.

Prisons will also undertake random checks to ensure that during the day prisoners are exactly where they should be.

'Dynamic' security

This term was coined by Ian Dunbar, a former Director of Inmate Administration, and it is the third element of our security system. It is not a procedure nor is it a piece of physical kit. The concept has been developed over the years and essentially it is about a way of working that relies on the traditional strengths of the Prison Service – that of relationships with prisoners, keeping prisoners occupied, 'knowing what is going on', and ensuring that staff play their correct role. 'Good' relationships with prisoners will mean that prisoners talk to staff. In the course of such exchanges information will be received and given. Prisoners will let staff know what is going on, and this is essential for good intelligence as well as for maintaining a benign atmosphere. Prisoners may be less likely to escape or riot if they see officers as human beings. Keeping prisoners occupied is an obvious way of ensuring that they do not have time on their hands to make or plan mischief. Again , 'knowing what is going on' bears directly on talking to prisoners and communicating with staff to ensure that security (and incidentally, order) is maintained. Finally, staff must keep within 'role'. To some extent this means that they must keep their distance. Becoming too close to prisoners brings the danger of conditioning; staff should be 'friendly, not friends' with prisoners. Given that we also expect staff to maintain 'good' relationships with prisoners it is important that managers are very clear about what is expected of staff to avoid 'good' relationships spilling over into inappropriate relationships.

Discussion

Rightly or wrongly, public confidence in prisons is measured by how many escapes – especially high-security escapes – are prevented. Until the escape of George Blake in 1966 it is probably safe to say that the public was not concerned overmuch about the level of escapes. But the outcry following Blake's escape concentrated the minds of prison officials and the result was a system of categorisation for all prisoners and dispersal prisons (described in Chapter 8) for high-category prisoners. This was a very effective policy for 30 years and relatively few high-security prisoners escaped over that period.

In the 1960s policy on security procedures emphasised perimeter security (Home Office 1969, p. 81, para. 200), with the hope that 'that greater security does not involve the placing of greater restrictions on the activities and movement of prisoners' (p. 82, para. 202). Little or no mention was made of intelligence, searching or the use of force. Policy had developed in the 1970s: mention was made of the improvements to cell fabric, CCTV, police and prison contingency plans, and training (Home Office 1975, p. 123, para. 213). In 1975 the concern was that 'the imposition of more stringent security precautions can be detrimental to the treatment and training of prisoners' (para. 214). In the 1990s as much weight was given to internal security procedures.

All this needs to be put in perspective, however. The in-depth intrusive security feared by commentators is to be found at a very small number of high-security prisons, but the new *Security Manual* (HM Prison Service 1997) provides for a graduated security approach for different categories of prison, with fewer and less intrusive procedures being applied at lower categories of prison. All but two closed women's prisons and two closed YOIs must apply no more than Category C security procedures, which are the lowest applicable in the closed prison estate. Risk assessments have been introduced (and are being developed) to decide whether some procedures should be initiated and to what degree. Internal security procedures exist in all prisons but they need not overly restrict the provision of effective education and offending behaviour programmes; indeed, good security provides the foundation for such programmes. These issues are discussed at length in *Security, Justice and Order in Prison* (Liebling 1997), one of the few publications where academics and practitioners discuss frankly and at length some of the dilemmas posed by prison security.

Order

Order is the absence of disruption and it is achieved through control. Roy King (Liebling 1997, p. 46) distinguishes between security and control risk decisions. The former are 'essentially exogenous to the prison', that is, they are based on information (information about the crime from the courts and police) which is in the public domain. By contrast, 'control risk decisions are essentially endogenous to the prison system' and such decisions are often made on the basis of information that is known only to the prison system. King drew the conclusion that security decisions are likely to be more easily justifiable than control decisions and as such present more difficult questions of legitimacy for administrators and the courts. To this end the definitions of control are more wide-ranging than security, which is reasonably self-contained. This is possibly exemplified by the fact that while there is a *Security Manual* there is no separate Control or Order Manual.

This section is in three parts. The first looks at recent innovations in design and practice used to prevent serious disorder in prisons. The second covers the maintenance of day-to-day control, including adjudications. The last considers administrative means of keeping order.

Preventing serious disturbances

Mass disorder in the Prison Service has occurred relatively recently. From the 1930 Dartmoor riot to the riot at Parkhurst in 1969 there were remarkably few disturbances in prisons in England and Wales. But in the following two decades, culminating in the 1990 riot at Manchester Prison, riots and disturbances became depressingly familiar on the penal scene (Liebling 1997, p. 4).

Reasons advanced by those investigating riots differed. The 1976 Hull riot was especially ferocious and the Chief Inspector of Prisons was asked to investigate. He found a number of causal factors and recommended an administrative review of the dispersal estate, including staffing levels, contingency plans and training. He emphasised the importance of the control room in incidents and recommended that the Service take action to prevent prisoners using slates on roofs. His view was that the Service should move cautiously towards a more balanced regime where treatment did not compromise security (HM Chief Inspector of Prisons 1977). The Woolf Report, which followed the Manchester riot, reached the well-known conclusion that stability in our prisons rested on getting the balance right amongst security, control and justice. He recommended a range of improvements in physical conditions, the reduction of overcrowding, reduced powers of punishment, and more effective channels of complaint for prisoners.

Over the years the Service has markedly improved its response to disturbances. All prisons now have officers trained in riot-control techniques, and who can be drafted in to help any prison in response to an incident. One of the most import-ant innovations has been the creation of a secure roof area, accessible only by staff. A C and R (control and restraint) staircase allows staff access to all levels of the accommodation in case of emergency. Other significant innovations are the fitting of gates with overriding locks that help prevent the spread of disturbances, the replacement of slate roofs with steel, and, in some prisons, the splitting of wings to make any disturbance easier to control.

The Service seeks to apply the general lessons learned from each Inquiry in order to prevent the next serious disturbance. Yet it is not enough to rely on physical barriers or riot-control techniques, however effective or sophisticated. Governors must attempt to prevent disturbances beginning in the first place by appropriately balancing security, control and justice. Governors must also know 'what really goes on in the prison subculture and in dealings between prisoners and staff'

A senior officer supervises staff equipped with control and restraint equipment as they prepare to enter the cell of a prisoner armed with a knife.

(Liebling 1997, p. 16). This must be supplemented by clear, realistic and fair standards of acceptable behaviour. Accommodation and food must be efficiently delivered, and routines and procedures justifiable and predictable. The role of Headquarters is to provide policy frameworks and advice to make it easier for governors to carry out these tasks.

Adjudications: purpose and procedure

The White Paper *Custody, Care and Justice* (Home Office 1991) stated that 'All institutions … require means of enforcing their rules and procedures and effective sanctions for those who disobey.' As well as protecting the public from prisoners escaping from custody, the prison authorities must maintain internal order so that everybody who lives and works in the prison can feel safe and secure. Prisoners need to be protected from bullying and assaults, and able to participate fully in the regime. Staff must be free to go anywhere in the prison and be able to exert (legitimate) authority without fear of threats, harassment or assault wherever they are in the establishment.

Until 1976 the courts took no interest in the dispensing of justice in prisons in spite of a long-standing principle that prisons were subject to the courts. Boards of Visitors who carried out adjudications into the most serious cases of indiscipline could take unlimited remission from prisoners. (In 1976, a third of a prison sentence was 'remitted' for good behaviour.) Governors' adjudications were rarely appealed or overturned. This changed with the landmark case of *R. v. Board of Visitors of Hull Prison, ex parte St Germain*. This ruling allowed the courts thenceforth to set aside the findings of Boards of Visitors. The judicial review of many cases over the 1980s pushed and pummelled the system of adjudications into its current shape. (For a full account of the use of judicial review and prison adjudications see Loughlin and Quinn (1993).)

The *Prison Disciplinary Manual* (HM Prison Service 1995) says that the purpose of adjudications is to help maintain order, control, discipline and a safe environment; and to ensure that the use of authority in the establishment is lawful, reasonable and fair. Staff invoke the formal system as a last resort, and it is preferable for both prisoners and staff members to resolve any disputes informally. If, however, staff believe that a prisoner has committed one of the disciplinary offences set out in Rule 47 of the Prison Rules (YOI Rule 50), then a prisoner may be subject to a prison adjudication. Adjudications are quasi-judicial hearings run by a prison governor or, in a private prison, a Home Office-appointed controller (often, though not always, a serving prison governor). The adjudicator must inquire into a report of alleged events and establish beyond reasonable doubt whether a breach of Prison Rule 47 or YOI Rule 50 has occurred. Over 100,000 adjudications take place each year.

The process begins when an officer formally charges the prisoner with an alleged offence against the disciplinary code set out in Prison Rule 47 (YOI Rule 50). This formal charge must be laid within 48 hours of the offence being discovered and at least two hours before the adjudication is to begin. Staff must do their best to ensure that the prisoner understands the charge and if necessary provide him or her with writing materials. They should also supply a note of the adjudication procedure to the prisoner.

On the day of the adjudication the prison medical officer must declare that the prisoner is fit to undergo an adjudication and serve a period of up to fourteen days cellular confinement. At the adjudication the prisoner must be allowed to sit at a table, have writing materials and have access to the *Prison Disciplinary Manual* (HM Prison 1995). The prisoner must be asked if he or she understands the charge and if he or she has had enough time in which to answer it. The prisoner will be asked if he or she requires additional help (including legal assistance). The governor must fully consider any such request against the following criteria:

- the seriousness of the charge and the potential penalty;
- the likelihood that difficult points of law will arise;

A prisoner charged with a breach of Prison Rules is given the opportunity to hear the evidence and present a defence against the charge during an adjudication.

- procedural difficulties, such as the inability of prisoners to trace and interview witnesses in advance;
- the need for reasonable speed in deciding cases;
- the prisoner's capacity to present his or her own case; and
- the need for fairness between prisoners, and between prisoners and prison officers.

Boards of Visitors have not conducted adjudications since 1993. This role is limited to trained and authorised governors. The adjudicator's role differs from that of a judge or magistrate since he or she must ascertain the facts and question, in a spirit of impartial inquiry, the reporting officer, the accused and any witnesses. Unlike the courts, the governor's hearing is not an adversarial one. Governor are masters (or mistresses) of their own procedures: they can call witnesses or not; require or dispense with the presence of lawyers. They preside over inquisitorial hearings, and must conduct a full inquiry to find out what happened. For the purposes of the adjudication the governor is not regarded as a member of Prison Service line management.

It is for the governor to run the hearing subject to the principle of adherence to the rules of natural justice. These are essentially:

- that there must be no suggestion of bias;
- the governor must not act as a judge in his or her own cause;
- the governor must hear each case afresh (that is, must not decide guilt on the basis of what is already known about the prisoner and must demonstrate that steps have been taken to prevent this);
- prisoners must hear and challenge what is alleged against them; and
- reasons must be given for decisions.

The standard of proof is that of beyond reasonable doubt. If a prisoner is found guilty, the governor will then hear a report of the prisoner's behaviour and will give the prisoner a chance to challenge it.

Administrative ways of controlling behaviour

One of the important policy frameworks to help maintain control is a structured system of rewards and punishments. The Prison Service launched an incentives and earned privileges scheme in 1995, which set out a national framework for incentives based on prisoners' behaviour and willingness to co-operate. It told governors to develop local schemes that would set out criteria for earning and losing privileges linked to levels of regimes. Typically, prisoners will start on a 'standard' regime with middling access to cash, visits and association. Those who misbehave will be placed on a 'basic' level of minimum entitlements, often with no association and with the minimum cash and visits entitlements. Examples of misbehaviour are bullying, assaults and use of drugs. Those who behave well will enjoy 'enhanced' privileges with more access to association, private cash, visits and access to TV. Examples of good behaviour are keeping to the expected rules and routines of the institution, showing respect to staff, and good performance in education or work.

A range of powers is available to respond to individuals whose behaviour is unacceptable in anti-social or violent ways. Prison Rule 43 (YOI Rule 46) allows governors to remove a prisoner from their usual location 'where it appears desirable for the maintenance of good order or discipline or in his own interests'. The governor's power to segregate lasts for three days, but can be extended for up to a month by the Board of Visitors or a representative of the Secretary of State. While the power can be used to keep vulnerable prisoners apart from others, its use as a punishment is unlawful. Prisoners must normally be given reasons for their segregation.

Issues surrounding control

The use of force

To effect lawful orders prison staff are entitled to use force, but 'no more force than is necessary shall be used' (Prison Rule 47(1)). Over the years the Prison Service has developed techniques of control and restraint with the intention of minimising the threat of injury when coercing prisoners. Staff may also use restraints including handcuffs and, for those exhibiting prolonged violent behaviour, a body belt. The use of force is clearly a highly sensitive area and there have been occasions when it is alleged that staff have used more force than is necessary. Nevertheless, the Prison Service believe that staff must be allowed to use reasonable force if they are to do the job expected of them by the public. The Service is constantly reviewing its procedures and policy on the use of force to ensure that lessons are learned and that injury to prisoners and staff is kept to a minimum.

Exercise of discretion

Members of the public are entitled to ask why there is a control problem in prisons. The Prison Service is a command and control organisation: why don't staff just tell prisoners what to do? This is a very difficult question to answer satisfactorily. Prisoners have human rights and must be treated fairly and in accordance with recognised standards. Those standards will change as expectations change in line with what happens in the outside world. Also, staff are vastly outnumbered by prisoners who can, if they put their minds to it, do much damage to prisons and staff. There must be an 'accommodation' between the coercive power of the state and the inmates of its prisons.

There is a set of common conditions that heighten the discretionary power of public sector authorities and these are: 'intense political conflict over what [the organisation] does and [pressure to] provide satisfactory solutions to intractable social problems [while faced with] immense difficulties in rationalizing organisational decision-making' (Gilbert 1997, p. 50). The Prison Service fits this model very well.

Liebling and Price (1998) show that there are few rules covering staff–prisoner relationships. Prison Rule 2 exhorts staff to influence prisoners through their own leadership and example, to enlist prisoners' willing co-operation, and to encourage their self respect and sense of personal responsibility. For such an important yet vague rule, very little material exists for the guidance of staff

(Liebling and Price 1998, p. 6) This is echoed by Gilbert (1997, p. 56) about the United States, who notes that only one manual exists (by the Arizona Department of Corrections) that addresses the interpersonal skills required by staff. In the Prison Service, interpersonal skills training is given during the first six weeks of prison officer training; after that staff must pick up whatever they can while working on the job.

There may be drawbacks for staff even when using their discretion successfully. Both Gilbert (1997) and Liebling and Price (1998) note that the skills and knowledge work of prison officers has been undervalued. This can leave officers in difficulties. Gilbert (p. 61) found that:

> On the one hand, if their decisions turn out well, no one really cares. On the other hand, if their decisions turn out badly, officers may be disciplined or terminated.

Liebling and Price (p. 142) show that differences in practice between prisons can lead to petty injustices. More seriously, prison statistics for 1998 show that male black prisoners have an adjudication rate which is 27% higher than male white prisoners and, on average, male black prisoners received a higher number of punishments per disciplinary offence than white prisoners (Home Office 1999 paras. 8.6 and 8.10). Yet it is entirely discretionary for officers to put prisoners on report, and the level of punishment is down to governors.

In Morgan's survey of imprisonment (1997, p. 1164) he takes a generally gloomy view of discretion, with the courts unable to improve prison conditions and prison staff undermined by the daily reality of the 'negotiated settlements which take place between officers and prisoners'. The Chief Inspector of Prisons takes a similarly pessimistic view in his 1996–97 Annual Report calling for more consistency: '… consistency of treatment is essential …' (Home Office 1998, p. 3). An ex-prisoner, John Hoskison, described his view of the exercise of discretion as follows:

> The rules in Wandsworth were not the problem. They were all understandable. It was the way they were enforced that led to the extreme bitterness felt by all inmates (Hoskison 1998, p. 92).

Achieving control in prisons is multi-faceted, relying on a continuum of resources. These range from the physical measures to written procedures to the personalities on a wing. It is also inextricably tied up with the wider treatment of prisoners: humane and equitable treatment has an enormous part to play in our prison system if control is to be maintained. The extensive discussion of discretion indicates that there is a need for the Service to develop its work on 'relationships' and to build a more structured system of discretionary decision-making that is as consistent and transparent as possible.

References

Gilbert, M. (1997) 'The illusion of structure: a critique of the classical model of organisation and the discretionary power of correctional officers', *Criminal Justice Review*, (Spring), Vol. 22, pp. 49–62

HM Chief Inspector of Prisons (1977) *Report of an Inquiry [...] into the Cause and Circumstances of the Events at HM Prison Hull During the Period 31st August to 3rd September 1976*, CM 435, HMSO

HM Prison Service (1995) *Prison Disciplinary Manual*, Home Office

— (1997) *Security Manual*, Home Office

— (1999) *Corporate Plan 1999–2000 to 2001–2002 and Business Plan 1999–2000*, Home Office

Home Office (1969) *People in Prison (England and Wales)*, White Paper, HMSO

— (1975) *Prisons and the Prisoner: The Work of the Prison Service in England and Wales*, HMSO

— (1991) *Custody, Care and Justice: The Way Ahead for the Prison Service in England and Wales*, Cm 1647, HMSO

— (1998) *Annual Report of HM Chief Inspector of Prisons for England and Wales 1996–97*, The Stationery Office

— (1999) *Prison Statistics for England and Wales 1998*, Cm 4430, The Stationery Office

Hoskison, J. (1998) *Inside: One Man's Experience of Prison*, John Murray

Learmont, Gen. Sir J. (1995) *Review of Prison Service Security in England and Wales and the Escape from Parkhurst Prison on Tuesday 3rd January 1995* (The Learmont Inquiry), Cm 3020, HMSO

Liebling, A. (ed.) (1997) *Security, Justice and Order in Prison: Developing Perspectives*, University of Cambridge, Institute of Criminology

— and Price, D. (1998) 'Staff–prisoner relationships', *Prison Service Journal*, No. 120, pp. 3–6

Loughlin, M. and Quinn, P. (1993) 'Prisons rules and courts: a study in administrative law', *Modern Law Review*, Vol. 56, pp. 497–527

Morgan, R. (1997) 'Imprisonment: current concerns and a brief history since 1945', in M. Maguire, R. Morgan and R. Reiner (eds), *The Oxford Handbook of Criminology*, (2nd edition), Oxford: Clarendon Press

The Prison Rules 1999, Statutory Instrument 1999, no. 728.

Sparks, R., Bottoms A. and Hay, W. (1996) *Prisons and the Problem of Order*, Oxford: Clarendon Press

Woodcock, Sir J. (1994) *The Escape from Whitemoor Prison on Friday 9th September 1994* (The Woodcock Inquiry), Cm 2741, HMSO

Woolf, Lord Justice and Tumim, Judge S. (1991) *Prison Disturbances April 1990: Report of an Inquiry by the Rt Hon. Lord Justice Woolf and His Hon. Judge Stephen Tumim* (The Woolf Report), Cm 1456, HMSO

21

HEALTHCARE IN PRISON

Yvonne Wilmott and Vicky Foot

Introduction

> Partisan is our great curse. We too readily assume that everything has two
> sides and that it is our duty to be on one side or the other.

The World Health Organisation defines health as a total sense of physical, mental
and psychological well-being – a very wide remit, beyond the potential of health
services alone to deliver. There is not one item of healthcare in prisons that can be
delivered without the co-operation of the prison but conversely, prison governors
cannot discharge their duty of care to prisoners without full involvement of
healthcare services.

At the time of writing, the healthcare service for prisoners is undergoing a
process of review and reconsideration. In November 1996 Her Majesty's Chief
Inspector of Prisons, Sir David Ramsbotham, published his first thematic review,
entitled *Patient or Prisoner?* (HMCIP 1996). In this paper, he proposed that the
NHS should take over responsibility for the provision of primary healthcare in
prisons. In due course, ministers agreed the establishment of a joint NHS/Prison
Service working group on the delivery of prison healthcare. Its remit was to
consider not only the Chief Inspector's proposals but the whole organisational
structure and process of prison healthcare provision.

This chapter presents the reader with a description of prison healthcare as it
existed in 1998. The chapter concludes with a position statement on the outcome
of the 1998 joint report by the NHS/Prison Service working group, which will
provide the foundation for healthcare in prisons into the 21st century.

The legal background

The statutory provision of healthcare services to prisoners is a long-standing tradition. Medical staff have figured in the history of prisons since the 18th century.

> In 1774 an Act was passed 'for preserving the health of prisoners in gaol' and under that Act local justices were obliged 'to appoint an experienced surgeon or apothecary'. The surgeon or apothecary was required to be resident and have no practice outside the prison. Thus began the Prison Medical Service … (Smith 1984)

The most recent primary legislation is still that contained in the Prison Act 1952, Section 7 of which states:

(1)   Every prison shall have a governor, a chaplain and a medical officer and such other officers as may be necessary …

(4)   … and the medical officer shall be duly registered under the Medical Acts …

(5)   Governors, chaplains and medical officers shall be appointed by the Secretary of State …

Secondary legislation has been amended many times. In relation to healthcare, the Prison (Amended) Rules include provision for medical attendance, special illnesses and conditions and notification of illness or death. Stated simply, the legal situation is that every prisoner has access to a doctor. That 24-hours-a-day access is subject to the similar constraints in immediate availability that apply to any member of the general public in their own home, who wants to see his or her general practitioner.

A brief history

Prior to 1993, prison healthcare was provided in what was known and signposted as the prison hospital in each establishment. At Headquarters, the policy leadership for health and considerable operational responsibility was vested in the prison medical service (PMS). Following the efficiency scrutiny of the PMS in 1990 (Home Office 1990) changes recommended in the scrutiny report were given visibility by renaming the PMS as the healthcare service for prisoners, managed by the Directorate of Healthcare and led by a dedicated director.

The efficiency scrutiny made 83 recommendations, predominantly on four themes: the role of the PMS should be widened to that of a service more closely aligned to the NHS; there should be a greater emphasis on health promotion and preventing illness; clinical practice and medical management should be more clearly distinguished; and the Prison Service should become a purchaser of healthcare, rather than a provider.

The first Director of Healthcare, Dr Rosemary Wool CB, wrote in the inaugural annual report of the Directorate (HM Prison Service 1993):

> It was, however, recognised that neither the NHS nor the PMS would be able to cope with so much change all at once. Moreover, the Scrutiny had been unable to deal with the number of crucial matters in the time available. These included: the capacity and willingness of the NHS to provide services to prisons; implications for industrial relations and for existing staff; and costs.

These comments foreshadowed three key issues for the 1998 joint NHS/Prison Service working group: funding, managerial responsibility and healthcare standards. Each of these issues is discussed below.

When the Prison Service issued a consultation paper 'Contracting for Prison Health Services' in August 1991, one particularly strong theme emerged in the responses received. In Rosemary Wool's words:

> The clearest message which came out of the consultation exercise was that a substantial injection of new funds would be needed to implement the Scrutiny recommendations. Indeed, if the funding of the PMS had kept pace over the years with that of the NHS, some of the criticisms appearing in the Scrutiny and elsewhere might not have arisen (HM Prison Service 1993, p. 2).

As Dr Wool implies, money is not a complete panacea, but it does help. There can be no doubt that the continuous efficiency savings required of the Prison Service can bite into healthcare provision, especially for hard-pressed governors at local level.

Change was reinforced by the impact of the Woolf Report into the prison riots of 1990 (Woolf and Tumim 1991) and the subsequent White Paper, *Custody, Care and Justice* (Home Office 1991). Lord Justice Woolf recommended increased delegation of managerial responsibility from Headquarters to local management. This has been implemented and includes healthcare management. However, a structure for providing expert healthcare advice at senior level in the operational line has been instituted to replace the principal medical officers, who were in place at

Figure 21.1: The functional model of healthcare management

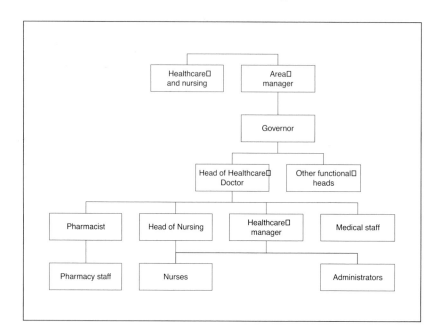

the time of the scrutiny. Line management accountability for prisoners' healthcare is illustrated in Figure 21.1.

Every prison has a healthcare service organised from a healthcare centre. There are four levels of service and the types and their distribution are illustrated in Table 21.1. In-patient facilities are generally found in all prisons where remand prisoners are held. This group have a very much higher prevalence of serious mental illness, drug and alcohol dependence and suicidal ideas. In-patient facilities are also found in high-security prisons, certain other prisons and YOIs. Patients are locked up every night in cells or dormitories within the prison healthcare centre. Due to night staffing levels and a general shortage of prison nurses, nursing supervision can be limited. In many prisons the in-patient facility does not provide a therapeutic regime. Also, these facilities are not suitable for seriously ill patients: there are no resident doctors in prisons. The term 'hospital' does not, therefore, accurately describe the in-patient facilities in prisons.

Lord Justice Woolf recommended that the Prison Service should set standards across the range of its responsibilities to prisoners and the public. In due course, that recommendation has led to the production and implementation of a

Table 21.1: Healthcare centres by type, 31 March 1998

Healthcare centre type	Level of service available	No. of centres	No. of staff
1	Day-time cover, generally by part-time staff	36	145
2	Day-time cover, generally by full-time staff	33	219
3	Healthcare centre has in-patient facilities with 24-hour nursing cover	61	1,490
4	As for type 3, but also serves as a national or regional assessment centre	4	172

programme of healthcare standards covering the structure, the process and, latterly – with the greater emphasis on audit, the outcomes required.

Healthcare staff

Primary care is provided on a similar basis to that available in the community via general practices, although historically these have had a very medical bias. 'Surgery' is often termed 'sick parade' in prisons – perhaps harping back to the old days where those wishing to see the doctor lined up. With the development of primary care teams in prisons and a closer alignment with the NHS, the term 'surgery' is preferred.

Prison doctors are employed on full-time, part-time, contractual or sessional bases to provide a wide range of medical services. Pharmacy services are centred in larger prisons (which serve other prisons), generally led by full-time pharmacists, but there are a number of systems. Psychiatrists, increasingly supported by mental health teams, provide psychiatric services, while a number of other specialists provide assessments of behavioural disorders, mental illness and of the suicidal; and a place of safety for detainable mentally disordered offenders, all within the Prison Service.

The NHS supplements primary care in prisons with a variety of specialist staff, including clinical psychologists, occupational and art therapists, radiographers and speech therapists. Some specialists visit prisons, particularly high-security prisons, when it would be difficult to escort the prisoner to an NHS hospital. In general, healthcare provided within prisons is the financial responsibility of the Prison Service, and that provided outside is the financial responsibility of the NHS.

The delivery of nursing services in men's prisons in England and Wales was traditionally undertaken by prison officers who had completed additional specialist training and who, until 1992, were called hospital officers. Prior to 1984, the training was three months in length, then it was increased to six months. Training was delivered by the Prison Service but included placements in NHS hospitals. This training ceased in late 1992 and hospital officers were renamed healthcare officers. Existing healthcare officers, without nursing registration, were encouraged to validate their skills by undertaking NVQs in care. Only first-level registered nurses who also satisfy the criteria for prison officer positions are now recruited as healthcare officers, undergoing prison officer training before commencing in post as healthcare officers.

Registered nurses have almost always provided nursing services in women's prisons. The situation was reinforced in the late 1980s by the Director of PMS undertaking, before a Home Affairs Select Committee, that women prisoners would be nursed only by registered nurses.

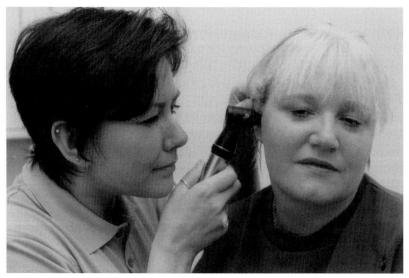

A registered nurse examines a female prisoner during a morning clinic.

Part Four – What happens in prison

The variety of entry routes for the healthcare workforce means that the skill mix is comprised, often quite randomly, of:

- healthcare officers with no nursing qualification who have completed prison officer training plus three- or six-month hospital officer training;
- healthcare officers with a nursing qualification who have completed prison officer training;
- nurses who have had training in security and control; and
- nurses who have had no training in security and control.

Since October 1992, Prison Service policy has expressed the aspiration that in future all nursing care would be under the supervision of a first-level registered nurse. Although the number of qualified nurses in the workforce has escalated, many healthcare managers are principal or senior healthcare officers or governor grades 4 or 5 without nursing qualifications. On 31 March 1998, only 15% of healthcare senior officers, 11% of healthcare principal officers and 20% of healthcare governors declared nursing registration in the annual statistics. The 1992 policy aimed to increase the overall number of healthcare staff from 1,300 in 1992 to approximately 1,750 by the end of the year 2000. Overall, these staff were to comprise 50% nurses and 50% healthcare officers. Additionally, the qualification split was to be 75% nurse-qualified, 25% non-nurse qualified. By 31 March 1998 the proportion of nurses in the workforce had risen to 54%. In addition, another 18% of the workforce were nurse-qualified healthcare officers, bringing the qualified work force to 72%.

Balancing care duties in custody

The delivery of every aspect of healthcare within prisons is dependent upon the custodial staff and systems. When coming into prison, offenders lose a substantial degree of control over their lives, including many determinants of health such as diet, access to exercise and occupation. Prisoners need to have access to healthcare services, and there must be safe systems for medication to ensure those that need prescribed medicine receive it at the right time. It is crucial that the trading of medication and bullying be minimised.

There are competing care and custody forces for all staff, who must provide a decent rehabilitative regime within a secure environment. Healthcare professionals train and often work in a primary care environment and the balance can be particularly difficult for them. The 1992 policy required that both nurses and healthcare officers have a 'dual clinical and custodial role' which has proved incredibly difficult to effect. Healthcare officers undertake Prison Officer Initial

Training (POINT) at the Prison Service College following a two-week orientation in their establishment. No officer begins work in his or her role unless he/she has successfully completed the POINT course. Furthermore, all officers have the 'powers of a constable', including powers to search, detain and arrest prisoners. They may be deployed on officer duties inside and outside the prison by the governor. It is easy to see the potential for conflict for healthcare officers, but good communications can and should ensure the right balance.

From 1992–97 it was mandatory for nurses joining the Service as nursing grades to attend, within six months, a centrally organised two-week security and control training course. In practice many nurses did not receive training until well after recruitment and some not at all. Since 1998, in order to ensure that many more nurses received at least the essential training necessary to function safely in a prison environment, a one-week course has been instituted. Run by the area training units, attendance is a local responsibility and no longer mandatory.

Terms and conditions

In addition to their differing preparation and powers, nurses and healthcare officers have different terms and conditions of service. Healthcare officers are prison employees and their terms and conditions are set by the Prison Service. Nurses are employed on the same terms and conditions as their counterparts in the NHS and thus their employment is analogous to the conditions set out in the Whitley Council Nurses and Midwives Regulations. The differences between the two types of employee include pay, hours, holiday entitlements and pension arrangements.

The healthcare officers' uniform is very like that of other prison officers, but with distinguishing insignia and access to protective clothing for clinical duties. Nurses' uniforms are distinctly different and defined in national guidance. The Chief Inspector of Prisons has criticised the disparity of the uniforms of healthcare staff, recommending a single recognisable uniform for all healthcare staff.

New healthcare staff now receive their training within the NHS or accepted over-seas health services. Doctors must be unconditionally fully registered with the General Medical Council and must therefore adhere to its Code of Practice; in the same way, pharmacists must adhere to the Royal Pharmaceutical Society's equivalent. Nurses must register and abide by the terms of the United Kingdom Central Council for Nursing, Midwifery and Health-visiting (UKCC). It is generally accepted that healthcare officers who have NVQ and not nursing qualifications should also abide by the professional nursing code, although this is not covered by legislation.

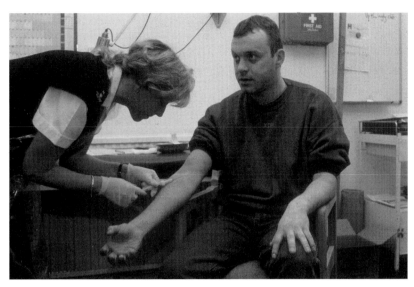

A nurse -qualified hospital officer provides treatment during an afternoon surgery.

Provision and practice in prisons

The joint NHS/Prison Service working group's investigations of current provision indicated that most prisons have a directly employed workforce, subdivided into those which comprise all nurses or all healthcare officers, or a mix of both in varying proportions. A small number also have contracted-in nursing staff, whether from an agency, a trust or a general practice. All but one of the contracted-out prisons has a contracted-in service, from either a trust or a private provider. The one exception has directly employed all the nursing workforce.

The common features of good practice in prison healthcare which emerged from the working group's review of 38 prisons were:

- a strongly committed governor;
- strong NHS links and positive relationships;
- a skilled and able healthcare manager;
- motivated and competent individuals;
- nursing and custody separated or clearly defined; and
- needs based healthcare.

In October 1997 a consultation paper on changes to the 1992 policy was published and disseminated widely within the Service and to selected outside bodies. The response produced no clear consensus and was polarised. Outside commentators supported radical change to a nursing-led workforce as soon as possible; individual healthcare officers and the Prison Officers' Association (POA) opposed almost all the proposed changes as unnecessary. A report on the consultation was submitted to the joint NHS/Prison Service working group, and any change in the way nursing is delivered in prisons will now be part of the group's overall deliberations and recommendations to ministers.

Prisoners' health

Assessment of health status on reception into prison is the key to the care which an offender will receive while in prison. When it is performed well by competent nursing staff, the assessment will result in an accurate plan of care for the individual. Unfortunately, at present, it is not uncommon for the initial assessment to be carried out under extreme time constraints by staff with limited knowledge. Ideally the assessment should be carried out by an experienced nurse, preferably with a psychiatric nursing qualification and knowledge of specialist areas such as substance misuse. The initial assessment is required to be followed by a full health appraisal by a doctor and nurse within 24–48 hours of reception. Best practice demands a high standard of record-keeping with shared care plans and, where relevant, integration with the prisoner's sentence plan and communication with his or her's previous health contact (GP, drug treatment manager or other), both of which improve continuity of care.

A picture of prisoners' health can be drawn from the annual reports of the Directorate of Healthcare. In the year ended 31 March 1997, 200,500 prisoners were newly received into prison custody and 202,056 health screenings were undertaken. The percentage of the average daily prison population who reported sick each day was 9.18%. There were 556,939 consultations with a prison doctor and 1,341,030 with another member of the healthcare team.

The annual reports for prison healthcare suggest that around 10% of male prisoners and 24% of female prisoners report sick each day, although this figure does seem to be falling. Undoubtedly, these figures reflect inappropriate medicalisation at times, for example it became normal practice for prisoners to have to report sick to obtain medical authorisation for wide-fitting shoes. Studies of individual prison surgery records also show high numbers reporting for minor injuries (which must be seen by healthcare staff, however trivial) and requests for diets needed for special conditions, such as a gluten-free diet for coeliac disease. With the advent of 'healthy diets' and many other positive 'healthy prison' developments, such requests are much less frequent these days. Nevertheless, those in prison do appear to perceive themselves as less healthy than the general population.

The Office of Population Censuses and Surveys (OPCS) study into the physical health of prisoners (1998) anticipated lifestyle prevalence (smoking, excessive alcohol, drug misuse). This study also confirmed doctors' impressions from reception medical examinations that prisoners are far more likely than the general population to report a long-standing illness or disability as Figure 21.2 demonstrates. Prisoners also report more frequently with acute illness than the general population, as Figure 21.3 shows. The level of prescribing of drugs by prison doctors, treatments provided by prison nursing staff, numbers of referrals to specialists and deaths of prisoners under 65 from cardio-vascular disease all suggest that prisoners may indeed be less healthy.

Figure 21.2: Self-reported, long-standing illness or disability

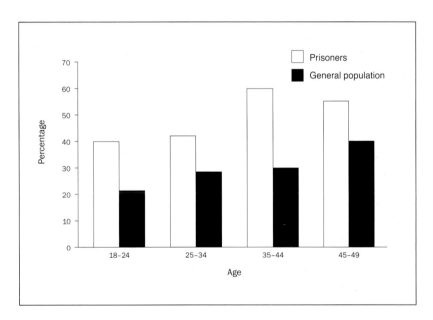

Much emphasis is given to the potential for the spread of communicable (infectious) diseases in prisons, and to the prevalence of diseases such as tuberculosis and hepatitis. In spite of the close proximity inherent in prison living, outbreaks of infectious diseases are uncommon. And yet the Prison Service has put in place many measures to counteract the risks inherent in institutional living, for example a hepatitis vaccination programme for prisoners. The figures on 31 March 1997

Figure 21.3: Acute illness within two weeks of admission to prison

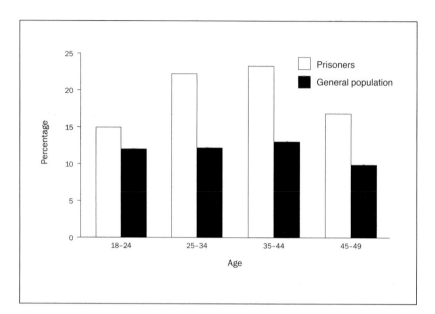

for known cases of infectious diseases were: active tuberculosis, two cases; acute hepatitis A and B, eight cases; chronic hepatitis B, 72 cases; and hepatitis C, 234 cases. Forty-three prisoners were known to be HIV-positive.

A prison environment presents special challenges where infectious illnesses are concerned. Intravenous equipment-sharing is the most important means of transmission of these infections. HIV is relatively uncommon in prison and the risk of transmission to staff is very low. Hepatitis B is far more infectious and staff are strongly advised to take advantage of effective immunisation and to keep up their level of immunity. Hepatitis C is not as infectious as hepatitis B, and there are fewer acute cases among the prison population than in the case of hepatitis B, although the number of prisoners with hepatitis C on admission to prison is roughly similar. Prisoner-patients are not routinely tested for hepatitis C and the results are not generally made available to staff unless they have a direct care role. Therefore, it is important to ensure good adherence to systems and procedures to minimise the risk of transmission.

Mental health is also an important aspect of prison healthcare. Large numbers of prisoners are mentally disordered so, ideally, will be transferred to NHS care. It is estimated that 14% of female prisoners, 10% of male remand prisoners and 7% of male sentenced prisoners have psychosis (a major psychiatric illness requiring

Part Four – What happens in prison

specialist care) compared with a community finding of 0.4% in the *General Household Survey 1997* (Office for National Statistics1997). Each year the Prison Service transfers about 700 prisoners to mental hospitals under the provisions of the Mental Health Act 1982. Many of these suffer from serious mental illnesses such as manic depression or schizophrenia, and these illnesses may have been the cause of their offending behaviour. Although most mentally ill patients are not dangerous, those coming to prison often are. They need expensive, scarce, medium-secure psychiatric beds. Unfortunately, a large proportion of offenders are considered to have the type of personality disorder that is not a treatable mental illness under the terms of the Mental Health Act, and they remain in prison.

Although there has been a massive expansion in medium-secure psychiatric places, patients often have to wait a long time for a bed. On 31 March 1997 the Prison Service had 1,733 healthcare beds, and the average daily occupancy was 1,138. Admissions can be broken down into categories: 26% were admitted for physical illness; 35% for mental illness; 13% for substance misuse and 14% for observation, because a risk of self-harming behaviour had been identified. Due to prison population pressures, the remaining occupancy was for non-medical reasons. The average in-patient stay was ten days (OPCS 1998).

Prisoners' health is the responsibility of the Prison Service but prisoners may need to be treated in NHS hospitals either as in-patients or out-patients. In the years 1996–98, there were 3,191 attendances at Accident and Emergency departments, 23,802 out-patient attendances and 2,374 in-patient admissions. Prison doctors and nurses also refer prisoners to specialists who visit prisons: psychiatrists, dentists, opticians, physiotherapists and radiologists, as well as other consultants in particular areas of medicine and surgery.

A high prevalence of physical illnesses is often associated with lifestyles in which drink and drug abuse, homelessness, unemployment, poor education and inadequate nutrition feature. For many offenders, being in prison may be a positive opportunity to address their health needs. Initial assessment and well-person healthcare screening can lead to effective intervention to treat, ameliorate or prevent illness.

Conclusion

The Prison Service standard for the provision of healthcare is 'to give prisoners access to the same quality and range of healthcare services as the general public receives from the National Health Service' (Home Office 1999). The Prison

Service is striving to achieve this aim, and closer partnerships with the NHS locally, regionally and nationally have already improved the arrangements and delivery of healthcare to prisoners immensely during the last decade. The Report of the joint NHS/Prison Service working group entitled *The Future Organisation of Prison Health Care*, was published by the Home Office in March 1999. It found that prison healthcare as a whole is characterised by considerable variation in organisation and delivery, quality, funding, effectiveness and links with the NHS. The working group recommendation that 'a substantial programme of change is needed' has been accepted and a formal partnership established between the Prison Service and NHS to take prison healthcare into the new millennium

References

HM Chief Inspector of Prisons (1996) *Patient or Prisoner?* Home Office

HM Prison Service (1993) *First Report of the Directorate of Healthcare*, HM Prison Service

Home Office (1990) *Report of an Efficiency Scrutiny of Prison Medical Services*, Home Office

— (1991) *Custody, Care and Justice: The Way Ahead for the Prison Service in England and Wales*, Cm 1647, HMSO

— (1999) *Future Organisation of Prison Health Care: Report of a Joint NHS/Prison Service Working Group 1999*, The Stationery Office

Office for National Statistics (1997) *General Household Survey 1997*, The Stationery Office

Office of Population Censuses and Surveys (1998) *Health in Prisons*, The Stationery Office

Smith, R. (1984) *Prison Health Care*, British Medical Association

Woolf, Lord Justice and Tumim, Judge S. (1991) *Prison Disturbances April 1990: Report of an Inquiry by the Rt Hon. Lord Justice Woolf and His Hon. Judge Stephen Tumim* (The Woolf Report), Cm 1456, HMSO

22

ACHIEVING SAFETY AND FAIRNESS IN PRISON

Stephen Pryor

In Chapter 1 Andrew Coyle refers to human rights in prison; Shane Bryans refers to staff cultures in Chapter 12; and WD2310 Jennings gives a prisoner's perspective in Chapter 24. This chapter, which is about coping with imprisonment, touches on all of these, aiming to help make sense of some of the most difficult dilemmas in society as they are reflected in prison. These issues can make the difference between a life worth living and hopelessness.

At the heart of the job of prison staff lies the fundamental conflict in the aim of imprisonment. The Prison Service looks after people who cannot be trusted to look after themselves. At the same time prison staff have to treat offenders with humanity while ensuring that their rights and freedoms are taken away. Very considerable discretion and authority is given by society, through Parliament, to do this. If the power which the role imparts is abused – whether by acts of commission or omission – life can be made a living hell for those meant to be looked after. When it is used wisely the prisoner can be helped to survive imprisonment and prison staff may well help to prevent there being future victims. The process prison staff are engaged in calls for a rare combination of strength and sensitivity; the detachment necessary to keep one's judgement clear, balanced against the involvement necessary to judge each person for him or herself.

By the time they arrive in custody prisoners will already have experienced a traumatic change in some of their closest relationships. When they are arrested they will experience a sudden sharpening of attention of those closest to them. They will need to explain how they came to be charged – to their immediate family, their children, their employer and their friends. Crime is mainly a young man's game, but even after many years a repeat offender will remember the first time this happened with stark clarity. The experience may become less unexpected each time, and the will to resist temptation correspondingly weakened, but the pain of strained relationships gets worse as one's credibility fails. The feeling of letting oneself and others down can become unbearable.

There are many views as to why people offend, and why some continue to re-offend. Whether they do so to keep up with others or because they do not care for themselves or others enough, offenders are often poor at forming or keeping relationships. The processes leading up to and beyond imprisonment weaken this further. Often by the time a court sees no alternative to imprisonment an offender will have accumulated several convictions, each weakening the resolve to go straight. It stands to reason that someone with several previous convictions is an unsuccessful criminal. Mercifully, most people stop offending before they reach middle age. Were it not so prisons would be full of pensioners. But the experience of making relationships in prison over a long period of time can lead to a distortion of what may already be a hazardous and threatening learning experience outside. It can take a long time to recover the necessary confidence to form balanced relationships based on mutual value.

Staff–prisoner relationships

Staff, especially those on prison landings have immense personal power and authority deriving from their role. They must use this carefully and consciously to provide safe systems and conditions for people in their care. This power and authority can usefully be seen as having three elements. First, staff know the rules and routines, and the limits of their authority in applying them. Secondly, they have knowledge of people – their strengths and weaknesses – which they can use to keep the incompatible apart and allow the compatible to remain together, to accentuate the positive and eliminate the negative. Thirdly, they are trained in person-management, however this training is often not as sophisticated as the job demands.

The use of incentives and earned privileges in determining the level of regime that each prisoner can enjoy depends on assessment by staff. But staff recognise that model prisoners are not the same as safe citizens after release. Some of those who adapt most successfully are the most institutionalised and may be the best able to convince themselves of their innocence.

Knowledge of people is both an art and a science. Above all it is necessarily a conscious process for prison staff. The good officer has to go out and get to know people: knowing **of** them is not enough. Dozens of staff will know of the most dangerous or odd prisoners, but few will actually know them. To get to know each other prisoners and staff both need some stability. High levels or unpredictable movement inevitably leads to short-term, superficial and uncommitted knowledge and relationships. Anyone who has worked on a remand wing will know the heightened anxiety caused by great uncertainty. It comes as a surprise to non-prison people to learn that almost all convicted prisoners were once remands, and that it follows therefore that the remand population has just the same proportion of dangerous and difficult offenders as the convicted. In fact they are more so, because the staff will not know them so well and remand prisoners themselves are in a heightened state of anxiety. It is not surprising, therefore, that remands have a higher self-harm and suicide rate than the rest of the population.

In some local prisons the convicted and the unconvicted are held in the same accommodation so that offenders do not have to move to another part of the prison on conviction. This allows knowledge and relationships to mature. But that by itself is not necessarily a guarantee of safety. Enmity and group cultures can also mature and fester where a population is static. At the opposite extreme of high levels of movement and uncertainty lie the long-term prisons where prisoners may spend many years and will have more knowledge of survival than most staff. Some long-termers like to be segregated with others like themselves so that they do not have to put up with younger, less mature people. Others like a mixture so that they can keep in touch with the world outside through talking with people serving shorter sentences. With both high and low movement, the understanding and skill of staff in the sensitive management of prisoners' lives is crucial.

At the level of basic safety, staff knowledge of individuals – of their normal and abnormal behaviour; of the tell-tale signs of stress or depression; normal contacts; family circumstances; of their illnesses, enthusiasms and dislikes – is vital. Landing staff usually have the authority to change cells within a wing. They can, by a careful Security Information Report, alert managers to danger. They can ensure like is kept with like. By omission they can fail to pass on vital information to other staff and departments, such as raising suicide management forms. Landing staff control the simplest vital procedures such as mail, food, exercise, communication, clean clothing, sanitation. How they do that will sometimes make the difference between a prisoner feeling like a human being or an animal. When people feel that they are being treated like animals they will naturally concentrate on their own survival beyond anything else. This is not the 'prisoner of war' or 'leper colony' morale that springs up against adversity; it is the cowed, fearful, sapped apathy that springs from lack of care, drawing on a deep anger and bitterness which destroys all decency between prisoners. Staff's ability to recognise this state of mind and deal with it is the lifeline on which prisoners depend.

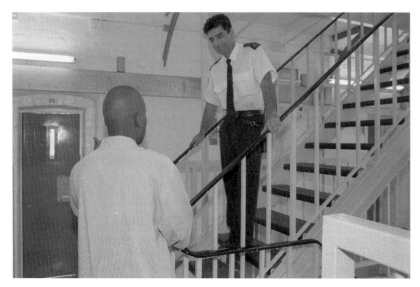

A prison officer takes time out of the busy wing routine to listen to a prisoner's problems. At the level of basic safety, staff knowledge of individuals is vital.

Many prisons, especially those holding young offenders and the long-termers, have personal officers who are assigned to deal with more sensitive issues. In some prisons the prisoner can choose their particular officer, in others the function is performed by a team of personal officers who provide constant access and have some special training. The job of personal officer can be a major part of an officer's work, requiring the completion of detailed and complex reports necessary for a range of decisions which will affect the whole future of a prisoner such as lifers or parole candidates. Prisoners can have some of their most 'positive' relationships with those who supervise their work or who teach them. This is because they do not represent authority as strongly as uniformed staff: first-name terms are not uncommon.

It is frequently said that one can tell whether a particular officer is on duty by the bearing of the prisoners on a wing. There are often very strong and friendly relationships between prisoners and uniformed staff, particularly where there is slower movement. However, it can be less easy to combine good relationships with the other roles that such staff have to carry out, such as reporting on prisoners, imposing an austere regime and removing prisoners by force, if necessary. And yet first-line relationships – between uniformed staff, work supervisors, teachers and the prisoner – are at their best the crowning glory of the Prison Service. Even those who do not believe that people can be trained for freedom in captivity recognise that the influence of a mature member of staff, combining

Prison staff are encouraged to form positive relationships with prisoners, while remaining conscious of security issues.

care with custody, is immensely important for a prisoner who has not had that role model. Experienced staff and prisoners will know very quickly that such an officer is on duty on a wing. He or she can change the atmosphere between prisoners: there is a general hum of voices, no tension, there is much incidental chit-chat, gates clang less stridently. The source of this may be invisible, but the presence and influence is undeniable.

Staff–staff relationships

As noted in Chapter 12, there are many staff groups, each with their own culture, history and rules. It is hard to imagine another occupation which calls for a wider range of skills, is less understood by those outside, has such an intensity of localised affiliation in each establishment and such a fragmented affiliation with other establishments and Headquarters.

Uniformed staff are often seen as the core staff comprising about half the total. They mainly work directly with prisoners, and are well aware of their authority over and personal power in managing them. Many will perceive other staff as belonging to layers outside this central core. The first layer includes the governor grades, chaplains and medical officers. Next come the administration grades, responsible for the handling of finance, personnel, IT, supplies, and administrative links with the courts. Beyond that come those often referred to as 'civilian' – mainly contracted or employed for their special skill or trade – such as teachers, trades instructors, maintenance staff and contracted staff. Still further beyond lies a diverse collection of people who have authority in their own right but whose authority within the prison environment is not so strong: visiting medical specialists and specialists from Headquarters. Finally there is a wide range of volunteers.

Members of Boards of Visitors are volunteers, but their direct and independent relationships with the Home Secretary can be a major influence on relationships within prisons. Staff at all levels, as well as prisoners, can find members of the Board to be a most valuable source of balanced judgment, reflecting both the views of local people and a cross-section of feelings within the establishment.

In common with a number of other organisations, more junior staff move around less than managerial grades. The effect of such frequent senior management movement can be a natural reluctance to commit oneself to big, long-term change in case the next manager changes it yet again. Again, there is a well-recognised paradox here in that each establishment is acutely sensitive to a change of governor. There are many examples of an entire establishment's culture and self-belief altering within days of the arrival of a new governor – for better or for worse. Given a governer's average length of stay of three years, this means that establishments tend to work through a three-year cycle. The first year is one of settling down, the middle year sees development and the third year is defined by growing anxiety. Set against a background of political planning framed by the lifetime of a government – with uncertainty rising as each election approaches, and changes in society's fickle view of crime and its causes – this often means that more junior staff will invest strongly in caution and stability. Add to that the fact that many people join the Prison Service as a second or third career looking for job security and the structure of a disciplined service, and it is not perhaps surprising that there are a number of tensions resisting change.

Prisoner–prisoner relationships

Relationships between prisoners are distorted under the pressure of imprisonment, much like the development of a plant in a greenhouse. They may be distorted by the lack of normal social contexts: with the opposite gender, with very young or the elderly; and by the unreal institutional goals and parameters imposed by security and control. While there are some strong cultural norms, there are higher proportions of people in their early 20s, a higher proportion of those with mental disorder, a compression of geographical areas and far greater difficulty in preserving privacy. Relationships can be very intense and very supportive. For those who are more accustomed to a solitary existence relationships in prison can be very threatening. Equally the sudden severance of an important friendship can be devastating.

Bullying

The physical or moral oppression of one individual or group by another – bullying – is not a simple manifestation. Bullying exists within and between staff and prisoner groups. Sexual harassment, denial of equal opportunities, nepotism, pecking orders, the exclusivity of one group versus another can all be forms of oppression. It is not peculiar to institutions where there is only a limited amount of power to be had by the inmate. However, it is particularly difficult to tackle where there is an inmate culture which derives its identity in part from opposition to the overall authority of the institution. Prisons can be frightening places. They become more frightening if the authority of staff is shown to be ineffective. Where staff and prisoners share a common ethos of respect for the individual, bullying will seldom take root. Where there is a great gulf fixed and there is a tacit understanding of 'no go' areas, that is a breeding ground for bullying.

Prisons institutionalise almost all behaviour to the point where they lose sight of its origins. Thus the worst offenders, who get the longest sentences, tend to develop the best skills for achieving a comfortable billet. At the other end, those who are on remand come off worse. The most institutionalised achieve the enhanced regimes most easily. High-security prisons have most staff attention – not always of the kind they want, but it is attention nevertheless – and they can present a formidable intimidation to staff. Bullying happens both ways across the span of relationships.

Arguably, the delineation and segregation of vulnerable prisoners – a group that scarcely existed ten years ago – is a form of institutionalised acceptance of a culture of hatred and bullying. These inmates are vulnerable to other prisoners. As soon as accommodation is designated for these there is no difficulty filling it. Here is a group of prisoners who are easy to handle because they are grateful for the protection. This phenomenon is often masked, however, by the tendency of sex offenders, chief among those who need protection from bullies, to behave in a way which shows that they are not, and should not be seen to be, criminals like others. These people 'in denial' are sheltered from bullying, but at the same time they are sheltered from legitimate expectations of self-criticism.

Oppression of one by another can be devastating and drive prisoners to suicide if there is no hope of an effective remedy, whether through the intervention of staff or other prisoners, or some other means of escape from the situation. The removal of one bully in a culture that does not otherwise change will only make room for another. There is no one who cannot be bullied, but using bullying to beat bullying only reinforces the lesson that it pays to bully. If bullying is endemic in most close-knit organisations, it is most destructive where people are already deprived of rights and freedoms. If a prisoner comes from a background where bullying is the norm, it may follow that we can expect it to be the norm inside. But prisoners differ, and some hate bullying as much as they need to feel safe. There is plenty of evidence to suggest that they will work hard to defeat it because they know better than anyone how terrifying it can be.

Bullying can be tackled, and tackled quickly, but it has to be done through determination. There are several ways of doing it, but all of them require the skilled and deliberate use of relationships. Little can be achieved by edict. Once tackled, bullying has to be kept down.

The determination and the lead to achieve fairness has to come from the top: it starts with senior management. Only if the most powerful show that they will not abuse their authority by exercising personal power can others feel confident in keeping to their role. That determination has to be transparent in every deed and word. Selection processes must be seen to be fair: access must be seen to be even-handed; bias and prejudice, privilege and favouritism must be condemned unreservedly. Drug-free wings or prisons; the confrontation of bullying as an institution-wide strategy; the appointment of strong, sound staff to lead an anti-bullying strategy; linking such a strategy with other strategies such as anti-suicide – all these will speak to prisoners about the determination from the top to outlaw oppression.

Suicide

Perhaps not surprisingly, the suicide rate in prisons is higher than outside them. In comparison with the rate of male suicide in the community, which was 17.4 per 100,000 in 1996, the rate in prisons is much higher at 117 per 100,000 average population (HM Inspectorate of Prisons 1999, pp. 12–13). A recent analysis by the Office for National Statistics found that there has been a clear trend in the community for suicide rates to fall: for men, by 9% and for women, by 43% between 1982 and 1996 (Office for National Statistics 1998). Suicides per 100,000 of the average annual prison population rose from 54 in 1982 to 128 in 1998, an increase of 237% (HM Inspectorate of Prisons 1999, p. 12). In 1999 there were 91 suicides in the prisons of England and Wales, the highest number ever (*Guardian*, 22 March 2000). And yet international comparisons indicate that the suicide rate in prisons in England and Wales is lower then in Austria, Belgium, France, Germany, the Netherlands and Ireland (HM Inspectorate of Prisons 1999, p. 14).

Though they are too rare to draw strong conclusions, prison suicides often occur near the beginning of an offender's time in custody and following important adverse decisions. Their causes are complex but research shows that staff can easily mistake what seem to them to be gestures for a genuine attempt to kill themselves. However, warning signs are often detectable, for example self-harm is a strong predictor of eventual suicide. Also staff should be aware that feelings of worthlessness can be aggravated by factors which staff themselves can do something about.

It is hard to imagine a more tragic event than a death in custody. For the families involved, burdened already by the events leading up to custody, this can be over-whelming. Since it often shows up missed opportunities, which are exposed in the public hearing of an inquest, these can be very stressful and prolonged traumas for all concerned. A self-inflicted death in custody often affects a whole establish-ment, reminding everyone of the harsh and bleak outlook for many inside, and of the need to keep a constant watch to see if future deaths can be prevented.

It also draws out the best in people. The Samaritans train prisoner-listeners to listen to their fellow inmates. (Sadly, staff often do not have the time to do that.) To be a listener gives a prisoner the opportunity to make a real contribution to another person's life. The staff support for such schemes can be one of the most rewarding pieces of work that staff do, as well as sometimes being deeply frus-trating and disappointing. Invisible though they are, the success stories should not be overlooked. Every day the work of staff, prisoners, volunteers and families is successful in preventing loss of life. There is no easy way of measuring this, and it largely goes unreported, but it is true none the less.

The current Prison Service strategy *Caring for the Suicidal in Custody* (HM Prison Service 1994) was introduced in 1994 and was recently subject to a review by the Chief Inspector of Prisons. His thematic report *Suicide is Everyone's Concern* (HM Inspectorate of Prisons 1999) was published in May 1999, and Prison Service policy is being reviewed in the light of these recommendations.

Justice

Justice can be considered in both individual and common terms. In prison, what is just depends on who you are and on what you have to do. The view of victims may also vary. Some may believe that the needs of justice can only be served by taking an eye for an eye. Others may hold that a just community is one which shares a common view of restorative justice, where families and friends of victims and offenders and the wider community work together to deal constructively with offenders. There is widespread acknowledgment that an offender's family may be the true victims, but that could be squared with the view that they may well have contributed to the offender's behaviour, too. The offender may see the adversarial court process as inherently unjust. Few prisoners admit to being wholly innocent, but many say that they are not as totally guilty as the verdict suggests. The judge's view as to what is just may be of less relevance than the decision he or she has to make when considering the jury's verdict and ordering an appropriate sentence within the limits of the law.

The White Paper *Custody, Care and Justice* (Home Office 1991, p. 4), which followed the Woolf Report into the 1990 disturbance at Strangeways (Woolf and Tumim 1991), said that prisoners should be required to exercise responsibility for what they do and they should be consulted and given explanations for decisions which affect them, adding that procedures for handling this must be effective and fair. That is a common view with which few would argue. A corollary of this might be that prison staff feel that justice has been served if the system they operate is open and accountable. However, they are still left with the dilemma of balancing what is right for a particular individual with what is deemed to be the tariff for all.

Another common view, seen clearly in the Articles of the European Convention on Human Rights, is that justice requires an effective remedy for a wrong. Few would argue with that either. A consequence of that for the Prison Service might be that prisoners can more easily and quickly take action if they believe they have been denied their rights. Yet staff are still faced with the dilemma that a contract or 'compact' with a prisoner leaves few real options for him or her if prison staff breach their side of the deal. Given the uncertainty inherent in imprisonment and the inability to predict accurately what is going to happen or be available, there will be plenty of loopholes to justify a departure from the desired best practice.

Many consider the hallmark of justice is mercy. The application of the law through the declaration of the sentence is not just unless there is a subsequent option to reduce its severity on evidence that the purposes of the sentence have been served. The underlying principle of parole is wholly distinct from that of an appeal, though both might be more just if they could take account of the feelings of remorse of the offender. Recognising this and committing oneself to it on paper when reporting on a lifer to the Parole Board is one of the hardest jobs that any member of the Prison Service has to do.

There are many common, basic views about fairness, integrity, honesty, straightness and justice. However, unless the conflicts and different perspectives are understood by each member of prison staff – whether contracted or directly employed, whether dealing directly or indirectly with the prisoner and their family – a prison cannot be held to be just. A filthy or dilapidated prison may only reflect a view of justice that prisoners get no more than they deserve. Such a view may be held by an individual prisoner in which leaving a filthy cell for a successor, residential staff acknowledge the substandard conditions in which to change clothing, or Headquarters considering the poor level of funding for refurbishment. Staff may quickly pick up on the same view of justice if they seldom see managers, or if their few encounters are driven by a need to apportion blame rather than understanding.

Staff will also be quick to sense an imbalance between prisoners' rights and their rights. In truth, these are rarely in conflict or mutually exclusive. In a prison where justice and humanity prevail, both staff and prisoners will recognise a mutual obligation. That will be reinforced by the governor through his or her senior management team, monitored by a keen and independent Board of Visitors.

Justice is about **how**, as much as about **what**. At its core lie the quiet arts: the skill and discipline of listening, observing, reflecting and sharing. The good prison staff member acts as a medium; a membrane; and a transformer of skills, understanding procedures into effective working relationships.

Summary

In this chapter I have looked at the key part which relationships play in running a safe, just and fair prison. To work effectively, staff need to understand some of the conflicts that lie at the heart of imprisonment, and the importance of their own judgement and personal standards as the foundations of their work. Without these insights staff become a menace to their colleagues. They reinforce the feelings of mistrust, unaccountability and worthlessness which helps people to give themselves permission to offend or otherwise destroy themselves. With these insights prison staff can operate more safely and effectively with everyone else who contributes to the work.

References

HM Inspectorate of Prisons (1999) *Suicide is Everyone's Concern: A Thematic Review of HM Chief Inspector of Prisons for England and Wales*, Home Office

HM Prison Service (1994) *Guide to Policy and Procedures: Caring for the Suicidal in Custody*, Instruction to Governors 1/94, Home Office

Home Office (1991) *Custody, Care and Justice: The Way Ahead for the Prison Service in England and Wales*, Cm 1647, HMSO

Office for National Statistics (1998) *Population Trends*, No. 92, The Stationery Office

Woolf, Lord Justice and Tumim, Judge S. (1991) *Prison Disturbances April 1990: Report of an Inquiry by the Rt Hon. Lord Justice Woolf and His Hon. Judge Stephen Tumim* (The Woolf Report), Cm 1456, HMSO

Newspaper article
Guardian (22 March 2000) 'Suicides in prison on the rise'

23

PREPARATION FOR RELEASE
Sue James

Introduction

With the exception of a very small proportion of the lifer population, upon reception into the prison estate, it is a certainty that at some future point the prisoner will be released back into the community. The second part of the Prison Service Statement of Purpose requires that prisoners are helped to 'lead law-abiding and useful lives in custody and after release' (see Annex A).

The Prison Service has to balance its responsibilities for containment and working with other criminal justice agencies, particularly probation services, to reduce offending behaviour. Both the Prison and probation services operate in a context of financial constraint, so whilst there may be a need to prepare all prisoners for release, priorities have to be established. These are underpinned by the Criminal Justice Act 1991, which establishes for adult prisoners sentenced to twelve months or more and all young prisoners (under 21 years) that a term of imprisonment should be served partly in custody and partly in the community, on licence to a probation officer. The following is an overview of the custodial and community aims of a prison sentence and highlights where probation services are involved:

For the Prison and probation services   Sentence management provides information to assist prison establishments and probation services to target resources more effectively, in order to ensure that prison regimes and probation service programmes more closely match the identified needs of offenders.

For the public   Sentence management cuts down the risk of re-offending by prisoners by identifying areas of risk and providing action plans aimed at reducing them during custody and while under supervision in the community.

For the prisoner   Sentence management:

- enables constructive use of their time in prison;
- provides strategies for avoiding further offending and consequently further periods of imprisonment;
- provides a more structured resettlement into the community; and
- minimises the destructive effects of imprisonment, within the context of lawful custody (HM Prison Service 1997b).

A number of interlinked processes can ensure, when effectively implemented, that appropriate plans and actions are followed to prepare prisoners for their return to the community. They are aimed at meeting the prisoners' needs for successful integration but, more importantly, to minimise their likelihood of further offending. At the heart of the sentence management or planning process are risk assessments. From these flow decisions about offending behaviour programmes, education, training and employment needs, community and family links, and parole.

Collaboration between the services: the shared task

Links between the Prison and probation services date back to the late 1950s when boys placed in detention centres were offered voluntary after-care by probation officers in the community after their release. Since then, the idea of a custodial sentence being partly served in a prison or YOI and completed in the community on licence has spread to all young prisoners and adults sentenced to twelve months or more. There have been tensions in the relationship between the two services and many reports advocating closer collaboration; which is seen as a means of smoothing the transition for prisoners from custody to the community and of improving their prospects for successful rehabilitation.

Politically, the pressure is on for the Prison and probation services to consummate their marriage and deliver a 'seamless [custodial] sentence' (HM Prison Service 1997b). This can be seen in *The Prisons–Probation Review* (Home Office 1998b) and the resultant consultation document from the Home Office (1998a), *Joining Forces to Protect the Public: Prisons–Probation*. Promoting this working partnership theme the *National Framework for the Throughcare of Offenders in Custody to the Completion of Supervision in the Community* (HM Prison Service 1993) was produced to guide staff in the two services. It stresses their shared responsibility to deliver throughcare, risk assessment and the confrontation of prisoners' offending behaviour. It states that: 'Planning for safe release should begin at the start of the offender's sentence' (para. 2.3), and that 'Sentence planning is the process by which throughcare work with prisoners is planned, co-ordinated and monitored between the two Services' (para. 5.1).

During the custodial phase of a sentence the two services are expected to identify the factors that contributed to a person's offending behaviour (risk factors). The Prison Service then has to provide opportunities for these issues to be addressed, along with opportunities to address other needs that might improve the prospects of the prisoner leading a law-abiding life on release. By the end of the custodial phase a plan should be agreed between the two services that will minimise and manage any continuing risk the person poses to the public, their families or themselves, which reinforces and complements the work prisoners have completed in custody.

The *Prisons–Probation Review* identified many barriers to the two Services' collaboration and therefore to the ideal of a 'seamless sentence', and yet there is a feeling that politicians are no longer interested in problems and excuses but want evidence of positive outcomes. The two services will need to demonstrate a reduction in offending and an increase in public protection from serious harm – challenge for both organisations, to overcome the barriers and implement the joint policies and procedures collaboratively.

Risk assessment and management

'The term "risk" has been widely explored in recent years in criminological literature' (Worrall 1997). It would be fair to say that risk assessment has been the business of the 1990s, even wider than the field of criminology. However, whilst the term is widely used, how many can define it? Of those who do define and explain its meaning, including academics, how many would offer the same ideas? More importantly for practitioners, how is it best carried out? These questions are echoed by Kemshall (1995; 1996), who concluded that there are no easy methods for risk assessment. For a start, it is necessary to define the kinds of risk being assessed. In terms of preparing prisoners for a safer release, risk assessment judges the risks that a prisoner's behaviour may present to the public.

> Risk assessment is about calculating whether harm will result from a particular behaviour or set of circumstances [and] is aimed at answering the questions: How bad? How soon? How often? How likely? And what triggers it? (HM Prison Service 1997b).

McGuire writing under the title *What Works* (1995), refers to two approaches. The first is **actuarial or statistical**, based on longitudinal studies of behaviour patterns. These give the statistical probability of a person with a particular set of characteristics being convicted of an offence within a certain period. Characteristics like age, age when first convicted, and aspects of sentencing histories and offending patterns are considered. The second approach is **qualitative**, based on information and professional judgement. While researchers would still argue for a structured, systematic procedure this approach relies on a worker's ability to collect, assimilate, and analyse information to reach informed judgements, based on experience and underpinning knowledge of criminal behaviour patterns. Bottoms and Stelman (1988) refer to 'predisposing hazards' (factors that research indicates predispose a person to offend) and 'situational hazards' (particular circumstances that can increase a person's susceptibility to offend).

Guidance to Prison and probation service staff suggests that a combination of approaches is most effective. The Prison Service uses a standard computer-based actuarial method, known as a risk predictor. For qualitative risk assessment, guidance is offered on how information should be gathered and documentation standardises its recording. It is suggested that assessment be based on observation of an individual over time, assessment, knowledge, experience and professional training:

> Risk assessment in itself cannot reduce risk but, through identifying the probability of harmful behaviour and who is at risk from it, strategies can be devised for addressing those factors which may reduce the risk of harm (HM Prison Service 1997b).

So, having answered the how questions relating to risk, one must decide on what will reduce the seriousness of risk. How can this be implemented. What dosage of treatment/level of restrictions will be necessary? How effective is the strategy likely to be in reducing risk? What indicators from the prisoner's behaviour can be used to measure the success or failure of a given strategy?

Sentence management and planning

The aims of sentence management are given in the *Manual for the Prison and Probation Services* (HM Prison Services 1997b) and were stated earlier in this chapter. Essentially, it aims to assess a prisoner's needs and the risks they pose, and establishes an action plan to address these during the custodial and community elements of the sentence. Sentence plans to provide prisoners with opportunities to prepare for release into the community and strategies to avoid further offending, and therefore to maximise public protection – one of the Home Office aims (1998a).

The purpose of sentence management is to have an integrated record to inform decisions concerning prisoners made by both services. These decisions include categorisation; allocation; attendance at specialist programmes; educational, training or employment placements; early and temporary release; and conditions in licences to safeguard the public. It is also to enable the deployment of resources efficiently and effectively when addressing offending risks and prisoner needs. The purposes in full are to:

- ensure that internal and external information within or received by an establishment is available for all relevant assessments and decisions;
- avoid duplication of information gathering;
- avoid duplication of effort or work in making assessments;
- ensure that assessments and decisions are not made separately or in isolation from each other;
- ensure continuity of decision-making:
  - when prisoners transfer between establishments
  - during prisoners' sentences within establishments
  - when prisoners are discharged from custody to licence; and
- ensure that decisions taken are the best possible ones, having regard to prisoners' needs, issues of risk, resources available and operational constraints (HM Prison Service 1997b).

Each prisoner has their own individual sentence plan, under the sentence management process. The priorities of these plans are 'To prepare for safer release [and] To make best use of the prisoner's time' (HM Prison Service 1997b). Objectives to meet these include:

- to identify factors relevant to the rehabilitation of the offender:
  - protection of the public from harm from the offender
  - prevention of further offending
  - successful completion of the licence
  - and to target resources to address these;
- to prepare the prisoner for release;
- to develop, improve or increase the offender's employment skills;
- to make constructive use of the prisoner's time in custody;
- to provide the focus for all work and interventions with the prisoner;
- to inform all assessments and decisions made in relation to the individual, such as release on temporary licence and parole;
- to provide the basis of the supervision plan for the licence period; and
- to provide the information base for regime development and service provision, and the consequent strategic management of resources (HM Prison Service 1997b).

Sentence management and planning are therefore the vehicles through which the Prison and probation services can collaborate to deliver the 'seamless sentence' that the Criminal Justice Act 1991 set in place. Information gathered and assessed is recorded in a standard format. Targets are formulated in areas of education, training and employment; offending behaviour; relationships and community ties; use of time; resettlement; residential behaviour; and any other area, associated with risk factors. These targets and assessments are regularly reviewed and fresh targets are set to further reduce risks and maximise the prisoner's chance for a successful rehabilitation. The areas of focus have been selected by the two services, based on evidence that they are important in reducing re-offending. The Prison Service should aim to release prisoners with sufficient skills 'to fit back into society, get a job and home and cope with life without re-offending' (HM Prison Service 1993).

Public value in the form of efficiency is demanded of all public sector organisations, and collaboration through sentence management and planning presents the Prison and probation services with an opportunity to deliver this: 'Public managers, then, are obliged to hold a vision of public value, good for today and into the future' (Moore 1995).

Release on temporary licence (ROTL)

Release on temporary licence: 'is designed to ensure that suitable prisoners are released only for precisely defined and specific activities, which cannot be provided in Prison Service establishments' (HM Prison Service 1995). Governors have had discretion to allow prisoners to leave the confines of prison on licence – to perform activities or re-establish links in the community, including family – for many years. However, the scheme became discredited when the media published details of activities regarded as purely social and where public protection was not adequately considered. In April 1995 tighter guidance was issued to ensure that prisoners released would not put the public at risk, that the activities had credible objectives and that those objectives could not be met in prison.

A facility licence is 'to enable suitable prisoners to participate in regime-related activities … and activities which have an element of reparation' (HM Prison Service 1995). Subject to a facility licence, a prisoner may be released to attend work or educational activities or carry out voluntary work of benefit to the community. Normally a prisoner carries out the activity during the day, returning to the prison at night. Their progress will be monitored and taken into account during subsequent sentence planning reviews. A resettlement licence is aimed at prisoners whose removal from the community has been for a substantial period of time. The purpose is: (a) to enable prisoners to maintain family ties and links with the community; and (b) to make suitable arrangements for accommodation, work and training on release (HM Prison Service 1995).

A prisoner's application for facility or resettlement licence should arise from assessments and targets in their sentence plan. Similarly, information in the sentence plan is the starting-point of a rigorous risk assessment, necessary before any prisoner is released. If the activity is assessed as making an important contribution to a prisoner's rehabilitation, the prisoner will only be approved for release if the governor can be satisfied 'that both public safety and public confidence in the system are maintained' (HM Prison Service 1995).

Community links and family ties

The importance of links with those outside prison walls has been acknowledged for some time:

> Extra visits to prisoners or privileges to send or receive communications from friends and relations would be beneficial to a prisoner and likely to assist in making him a better man (Gladstone 1895).

In more recent years, Blakeman (n.d.) has pointed out the very real benefits that can result from community and family ties:

> … it has been accepted that removing an offender from the community creates special problems when he [or she] is returned to it. In the vital months after release the community, and especially family ties, are seen as being essential in preventing re-offending.

The significance of positive community links and family ties to rehabilitation has helped to inform the Prison Service's commitment to regime and temporary release activity supporting these areas. For the Prison Service to fulfil the second part of its Statement of Purpose, maintaining (or building) community links and family ties must be an essential part of preparing a prisoner for release.

Community and family links, therefore, feature in assessments and plans made for prisoners during sentence planning, and are legitimate objectives for temporary release. Prison establishments strive to create a positive environment for prisoners' families to visit, within security constraints. Given those constraints, prisons also make arrangements for the community to enter the prison and, in certain circumstances and without placing unnecessary risk on the public for

Prisoners are encouraged to maintain close links with family and friends while they are in prison. Such links play an important part in reducing re-offending after release.

prisoners to attend activities in the community. Such carefully monitored activities help to prepare prisoners for a life outside the prison institution, where they will quickly need to rely on their own devices to secure housing employment and/or education.

Parole

Parole emerged from a blending of voluntary and statutory after-care. Voluntary after-care aimed to assist prisoners on their release and statutory after-care aimed to control those considered a high risk on their return to the community (NAPO 1976). Originally, prisoners were released, at the point in their sentence when they were assessed as most likely to be successfully rehabilitated. However, recently it has been suggested that some changes to the scheme have been driven by the need to manage the prison population (HM Prison Service 1997a).

> The aim of parole is to reinforce the training and rehabilitation of prisoners by giving an additional incentive to them to reform in prison and by providing support and supervision on release. Each parole decision is a pragmatic attempt to balance the benefit to the prisoner and his or her family against the risk to the public of re-offending. The public interest must always remain the most important consideration (HM Prison Service 1997a).

The parole scheme was reviewed and then updated by the Criminal Justice Act of 1991. The key points of today's scheme are:

- release is discretionary – there is no right to parole;
- it is an integral part of sentence management processes;
- prisoners serving four years or more are considered for parole at the half-way point of their sentence; and
- those released subject to parole have to comply with the supervision requirements of their local probation area.

The decision to release a prisoner on parole rests with the Home Secretary, who is advised by the Parole Board. To assist the Parole Board in making an assessment a dossier of reports is compiled at the prison where the prisoner is located. A full list of the documentation in the dossier includes:

Crown Court papers	sentence plan review
report of offences	prison probation officer's report
Court of Appeal papers	medical officer's report
previous convictions	psychiatric/psychological reports
pre-sentence reports	prison chaplain's report
pre-sentence psychiatric reports	parole assessment report (PAR)
prison offences	letters/other papers
previous review papers	disclosure form/representations
sentence plan initial profile	interview report
initial sentence plan	prisoner's comments

If granted parole, the licence runs to the two-thirds point of the sentence (when the prisoner would have been released had parole not been granted). During the licence period, parolees are expected to maintain regular contact with their supervising probation officer, keep them informed of their circumstances (employment and address details) and abide by any conditions imposed to reduce their risk of re-offending. Conditions can include exclusions from visiting certain places or people, specific requirements prohibiting alcohol or drug use, or requirements to attend offence-related programmes. The supervising officer supervises the parolee's compliance with the licence and monitors their attitude and behaviour. Any failures are reported to the Parole Board and immediate recall can be ordered if risks to the public are assessed as unreasonable.

Conclusion

While the Prison Service has a public duty of 'keeping in custody those committed by the courts' (HM Prison Service 1993, p. 4), the second half of the Statement of Purpose requires more than that. The Prison Service has a responsibility to provide prisoners with opportunities to learn how to stop offending and acquire the necessary skills to return to the community and play a useful part. This preparation for release has to start at the beginning of a person's period of imprisonment. If left until the end, community and family are harder to rekindle, skills will have been lost rather than developed, and anti-social attitudes and behaviour may have become entrenched.

The processes of risk assessment, sentence management and planning, release on temporary licence and parole all help prison and probation staff to manage prisoners back into the community. However, to be fully effective, prison establishments must have regimes that confront offending behaviour and provide education and training that enables prisoners to secure homes, gain employment and develop healthy relationships. The challenge is to implement processes and regimes in an integrated, coherent way so that decisions reinforce positive change in prisoners. It is important to recognise that preparing prisoners for release cannot happen in isolation behind prison walls. To be effective long-term, there has to be an exchange between prison establishments and the community and collaboration with other criminal justice agencies.

References

Blakeman, I. (undated) *Family Ties in the Prison Service*, Wakefield: HM Prison Service

Bottoms, A. and Stelman, A. (1988) *Social Inquiry Reports*, Aldershot: Wildwood House

Criminal Justice Act 1991, Royal Assent July 1991, entered into force October 1992

Gladstone, H. (1895) *Report from the Departmental Committee on Prisons* (The Gladstone Report), C 7702, HMSO

HM Prison Service (1993) *National Framework for the Throughcare of Offenders in Custody to the Completion of Supervision in the Community*, Home Office

— (1995) *Release on Temporary Licence*, Instructions to Governors 36/1995, Home Office

— (1997a) *Making the Parole Process Work*, Rugby: Training Services

— (1997b) *Sentence Management and Planning: An Operational Guide for the Prison and Probation Services*, Home Office

Home Office (1998a) *Joining Forces to Protect the Public: Prisons–Probation,* A consultative document, The Stationery Office

— (1998b) *The Prisons–Probation Review: Final Report*, The Stationery Office

Kemshall, H. (1995) 'Risk in probation practice', *Probation Journal*, Vol. 42, No. 2, pp. 2–7

— (1996) 'Risk assessment: fuzzy thinking or decisions in action?', *Probation Journal*, Vol. 43, No. 1, pp. 67–72

McGuire, J. (ed.) (1995) *What Works: Reducing Re-offending*, Chichester: John Wiley & Sons

Moore, M.H. (1995) *Creating Public Value: Strategic Management in Government*, Cambridge, MA: Harvard University Press

National Association of Probation Officers (1976) *The Work of Probation Officers in the Welfare Departments of Prisons: A Report by a Working Party of NAPO*, Thornton Heath: NAPO

Worrall, A. (1997) *Punishment in the Community: The Future of Criminal Justice*, Harlow: Addison Wesley

A PRISONER'S PERSPECTIVE
WD2310 Jennings

Before writing this I read some of the diary that I'd kept for sixteen months of the two years of my incarceration. It tells me quite a bit about myself at the time. Much of what I said then is alien to me now, some six years after my release. I have, therefore, elected to write this with little reference to that diary in the hope that it provides a more balanced viewpoint, rather than an angry one that might be gained from someone actually writing while still in prison, either physically or metaphorically.

In the beginning

My first contact with prison was in fact as a visitor, with a friend, to a YOI. While it was a daunting experience and I was glad to leave, there was little sense of doom emanating from the inmate we were visiting. This may have had some effect on my lack of anticipation or fear when being remanded, for the first time, after my own arrest. What I do recall is the sense of it not being real, like being in a play and disassociated from the outside world, causing me to lose any anxiety and just go with the flow.

My initial remand spell was spent in the hospital wing of one prison, where my first night was spent in a strip cell, due to a misunderstanding. That first week I spent reading books all day, rarely venturing out and then only to get a new book. After being bailed to my parents' house, which was worse at the time than being in prison – so much so that I attempted suicide – I broke my bail conditions and ended up in various prisons on remand, again reading a great deal, by way of removing myself from the horrors that I thought awaited me in an uncertain future. Oddly, the thought of suicide never arose while in prison.

The most shocking thing for me was being sentenced in court. It was then that it hit home – this was no play or dream: I had just been given a four-year sentence.

Later I realised how lenient the judge had been, but at the time it seemed like a life sentence to someone who had never been in that position before. I stood in the dock emotionless through shock, like many had probably done before me. It was not bravado or arrogance, which it is so often mistaken for.

Being inside

Once sentenced, life inside altered quite completely, from having to slop out and share a cell with three or four others to an establishment with my own cell containing a toilet and basin. Surprised and relieved, I found myself in a place that was so different from the scenes I'd just left, my spirits rose and there began to be light at the end of the tunnel. Though, as Mr Wilde wrote, 'Walls do not a prison make'.*

The regimes in remand prisons were too army-like for me, with their cell inspections, discipline-based routines and militaristic approach. Some of the staff were from army backgrounds and enjoyed enforcing the discipline a little too much. The officers' own opinion of 'nonces' (I was on Rule 43, segregated for my own protection) was little different from that of the general prison population: that prisoners' self-esteem is higher if they deem themselves better than another inmate. We are all in the same boat so there is therefore less of a threat from one another.

My own superiority complex ended up getting me transferred to another prison. The thought of it had sent a shiver down my spine, but the regime and staff attitude was much better and the cells were bigger, even with being back to slopping-out. It was in this other prison that I was part of a therapy group which had an annexed smaller wing off the main VPU, housing only about 50 inmates. This made for a far more humane environment, where you knew everybody and so felt part of a community.

The food was pretty dire in every prison, except at Christmas. There was always too much liver being served for my taste, which is why I chose to become a vegetarian and later went on the vegan diet – that at least got me a jar of peanut butter every week. Food becomes more than nutrition when it's how you mark the progress of the day. A breakfast including cornflakes would give you a lift so the day got off to a good start, whereas when you're served tomatoes on toast along with the standard ration of four slices of bread and butter you feel robbed and

---

* 'Stone walls do not a prison make' is from a poem by Richard Lovelace (1618–1658) and not by Oscar Wilde.

Prisoners collect their meals from the hotplate. The Prison Service provides a wide range of food for all dietary preferences.

thus are agitated from then on. Lunch, I recall, was the worst meal and I left it as many times as I ate it. The evening meal, which was served at 16.30, could be the highlight of a day, if chips were being served; or a cruel period between the end of the working day and association.

As I've never really been into anniversaries and the like, Christmas especially, the two birthdays spent in prison didn't upset me that much *per se*. The first birthday and Christmas did cause me to reminisce about the ones I'd had the previous year – having been taken out to dinner at an expensive restaurant and been generally spoiled. These thoughts made me both depressed and angry. By the time the second birthday came around I had begun the therapy and so was able to deal with my emotions better.

Christmas inside was, for me, less a time that brought mixed memories and more a time to fill my boots, as the food was much improved. It was the only time I regretted being on a special diet. There was often more joy about in prison at Christmas than I remember of family Christmases. With longer association and festive competitions, in which the staff participated, the atmosphere was often like being at school on the last day of term. There was always a pool and darts competition. As for New Year, it only ever meant extra football to me, so inside it meant more football on the radio. It was impossible not to notice that others were

A group of young prisoners enjoy a game of table football during their evening association period. Relieving the monotony and boredom of prison life is important for prisoners.

missing their wives and children, which might explain why everybody was nicer to one another, including the staff.

My radio was the greatest asset in prison. I'd go so far as to say life would have been unbearable without it. Having a cassette player was just a bonus. I got all my news from the radio and the majority of my entertainment, as most of the films shown during association tended to be Hollywood blockbusters or Chuck Norris-type fight movies. Thus Radio 4 was my daytime station mostly, though Radio 5's coverage of the football helped pass many an afternoon. I'd nearly always retune to Radio 1 in the evenings to hear the *John Peel Show*, but often found it clashing with a play on Radio 4. I went from being a casual radio listener to knowing the schedules.

The time spent 'banged up', once serving a sentence, is very different from being on remand, where your thoughts are of what you're missing and other things that only cause you misery. Once in a cell alone I was more productive (apart from the times I fell asleep in the middle of the day): reading, listening to plays (if it was Shakespeare, I'd read along) and writing numerous letters. I wrote to more people in prison than I ever did before or since. Mail is of huge importance to prisoners, as it not only keeps them in touch with family and friends but gives hope to thoughts that you'll see these people again soon. Furthermore, it makes you feel loved and wanted, a vital requirement for one to carry on.

The availability of educational courses allowed me to at least ensure my brain didn't cease to function. However, I soon discovered that most education departments catered, in the main, for basic, almost remedial maths and English, which, while I accepted was highly justified and necessary, was frustrating to me. Until one teacher I met, while still on remand, suggested I do an A-level English course. Unfortunately the education department of the prison I moved to after sentencing refused to fund such a course. This I found to be a big problem, especially with my length of sentence. If it had been longer, then there would have been less of a problem. Eventually I began a psychology distance-learning course after transferring to another prison, where there seemed to be a more open-minded policy. Ironic, considering the hostile appearance of the place. I was able to do this along with other things within the educational remit, such as art. This enabled me to increase my portfolio of work to show at the university interviews I attended while still an inmate.

Visits – inside and out

Leaving prison unescorted to attend university interviews was very strange. I had had such interviews some years previously as a naïve 18-year-old; this time I was going as a serving convict. The thought of absconding never seriously entered my mind. I was even anxious when the prison minibus wasn't waiting to collect me on my return – I had to phone to get it sent out. Travelling back on the train was the worst part, having enjoyed a spell of freedom and the company of friends. It was a similar story, only more gruelling, when returning from home leave.

Home visits can be quite stressful on all concerned. As part of my therapy I had an escorted visit with two of the officers involved. This was even more harrowing than having my mum visit me in prison, though it proved invaluable. I don't think I knew how much pressure my mother was under. She split from my father while I was in prison, though not because of it. During home leave it was the little things that really made an impact on me. Pulling on a freshly ironed T-shirt, a waft of air shooting up my nostrils, triggering a childhood memory of the safety and security you get from home. I lay down on the bed in a reverie, only to be pulled out of it sharply by my mum's call, back to the present and my current status with a shudder. Memories can be uplifting and depressing, often both at once, and I found it necessary to keep a tight rein on them as much as possible.

Home leave is a world away from prison visits, where family and friends see you dressed in the convict uniform of stripped shirt and blue jeans, you not knowing who wore them before you and hoping you can keep hold of the new pair of underpants you got this week. When my mother visited me on remand I was going through a period of defiance and had grown a full beard, causing me, with my long hair, to look either like a tramp or Jesus, depending upon your perception. Visiting me later in my sentence was no less harrowing for her for it was a 'real' prison and one we'd passed one family holiday, reading the 'No Stopping' signs with morbid curiosity. At least I was in a better frame of mind by then, but still I'd have preferred her not to visit, to see me there. Visits bring joy and hurt, it's inevitable. However, the visit of a friend can also bring the bonus of drugs.

Hash was the only drug I ever used inside; I was never 'up' for trying anything that might have been available. The only time I saw any other drugs was while on remand, when one of my cellmates bought some Temazepams from someone. Acid was the most sought-after drug in all the prisons I was in because of the escapism it gave. Drugs are bound to find their way into prisons, where they are an excellent way to escape the confines of one's cell and to relieve the boredom and monotony of prison life.

'Meaning' and therapy

Reading or listening to plays on the radio often helped me escape to another place or another world. Writing letters, poems, essays and the like, though, always seemed to give me greater enjoyment because they had meaning and were thus far more rewarding than pure escapism. To do something that will have an effect on others outside of your current domain means that 'they', the system, cannot lock you away entirely, and acknowledges the fact, to yourself, that your current residence is only temporary. I wrote bits and pieces for a number of football fanzines while in prison and received many letters from people who had bought them, commenting upon what I'd written.

There is definitely a fascination with prisoners out there which falls into two categories: first, those of a morbid nature wanting to know what terrible crime someone has committed, which I think is less common; and secondly, what I call the 'there but for the grace of God go I' syndrome, which is generally where people feel empathy towards your plight. I wrote to musicians, bands and record labels begging for cassettes, usually of stuff that I'd got already on CD at home. Without fail I'd get a reply and at least one cassette. The director of a small independent record company in London sent me six cassettes because I obviously impressed him with my love of what his label does, but I wouldn't have got anything had I written that letter from outside. Writing to radio stations to get records played has always been popular with inmates. I remember hearing many a request from someone in one of 'Her Majesty's Hotels' on the *Annie Nightingale Request Show*, on a Sunday night, which was a favourite of mine when doing my homework as a schoolboy. I particularly remember Annie announcing a request of mine because she'd never heard the track before and saying how much she had enjoyed it. Little things like that really make a difference to your evening. They do on the outside too, but being locked in a cell listening to someone warmly comment upon your choice of record is quite heart-warming. Tom Robinson, who at the time was presenting a Radio 4 show called *The Locker Room*, sent me a Christmas card and asked me to appear on the programme because I had written to the show about a subject-matter they were discussing which rang true with me. After consideration I decided against going on the programme, but, again, it shows that being in prison interests people. It makes interesting people of inmates and obviously gets others watching and listening. The reason I opted not to appear on *The Locker Room* was because, after quizzing myself over the reasons to do it against those not to, I realised my reasoning in favour had been malicious.

My anger did not subside really until I began the group therapy. It was easy to verbalise what I had done and to say how my own actions alone were to blame for my being in prison, but there was much internal resistance stopping me from actually feeling this and thus really taking the enormity of it on board. The twelve-week course was very tough and, as I mentioned earlier, involved an escorted visit to talk my crime through with my mother, which was no picnic. There were moments of great anguish and individual torment throughout the therapy for all those involved, including the officers directing the proceedings. They had to be, at times, both interrogators and a support mechanism for each inmate taking part. Without them I believe my actions would have taken me back inside within a year, quite possibly for life. There were, of course, other inmates within the framework of the therapy group who helped, and none more so than one particular individual, with whom I developed a very good relationship and had contact after my release, but not for some years now. I would like to wish him well, wherever he may currently be residing. The officers in these groups were bold enough to be different and wanted to try to make a difference, if not for the men in the group then for their next prospective victim. They ought to be congratulated, although they should be the norm not exceptions. The relationship built between those officers and the inmates in the group meant that outside of the therapy room there was a respect from the inmates that showed itself in other ways, like when someone was being awkward about banging up, often a swift rebuttal from a fellow con does the job better than an authority figure bellowing orders. I remember several times when I castigated one particular individual for his misplaced anger towards one officer, all because I had respect for that officer, as his attitude toward me had altered.

There were aspects of the therapy I found annoying and unproductive, person-ally. Namely, all offenders being adjudged to have behaved in a similar manner and thus our offending behaviour was deemed to fit into the predictable parameters set down by whichever psychologist established the therapy programme in the first place. There was a certain amount of brainwashing going on: disagree with anything that is put to you, and you're deemed to not have taken the lessons on board, you're said to be deflecting the truth. An example was me saying that I was middle-class because of the upbringing I'd had. The group contended that I was working-class because I worked for a living and so did my father. It was a point that could have been argued for weeks so I kept quiet and nodded my head when required and admitted I was wrong, otherwise I'd never have been paroled. The inflexibility of it needed working on and my misgivings were shared by the clinical psychologist I saw after my release.

Self-determination and adjudication

The thing that really used to wind me up in prison was the lack of self-determination. There was a procedure to make requests, but the adjudication system or kangaroo court (as it was known to inmates), which dealt with complaints, disciplinary matters and requests, was all but a waste of time. It was used, where necessary, to demonstrate that there was some internal system which looked into all prisoner matters impartially, or so it is said. So, where there had been an attack on an inmate by another it sat, assuming the victim was willing. Even then there was pressure upon the victim not to bother as (according to staff) it might only cause greater trouble. Justice has to be seen to be done, so the saying goes but in prison it's a case of not rocking the boat. I was amazed to hear that a prisoner who riots can be charged with mutiny. The whole adjudication system is weighted heavily against the prisoner because he is prejudged as being guilty, unruly or simply not to be trusted.

My first contact with an adjudication officer was while on remand. I complained about being moved from one wing to another and put in a request to be moved back. I was never given a good reason as to why the move was necessary, and when it was pointed out that there was someone in the other wing that wanted to move wings, my request was ignored. Eventually I went on hunger strike, as it seemed to be the only way to make myself heard. After about a week I was moved to the hospital wing, where I resumed eating and from where I was moved back to my original cell. I did get a 'result', once, after a complaint against an officer who gave me a verbal dressing-down while on exercise instead of taking me aside. He was the officer who had instigated my move and obviously felt he'd lost face and was trying to regain it. Another brush with the adjudication procedure came when I was first told of my move to another prison. My reaction was rather melodramatic, refusing to leave my cell, so I was taken to the segregation unit. There my appeal against the transfer was summarily dismissed. The reason given to me for my move was for security reasons. After my release I discovered the truth: someone had 'stitched me up'.

Being paroled, and after

By the time my parole came up I'd been moved to a Category D prison, though I was only there a matter of weeks. It was, however, very close to where I'd been living when I committed my offence, so I was a bit apprehensive about leaving. A friend agreed to collect me, so that apprehension soon disappeared and I couldn't wait to leave. As I hadn't had time to form any bonds, there was little for me to leave behind for anybody, which I'd already done when leaving the previous prison. That was quite an event because I'd been there for about fourteen months of my sentence.

There was nobody to really guide me. However, I was fortunate enough to have a friend within the Prison Service with whom I could chat. He was one of the governors at the prison where I did the group therapy and befriended me during my stay. We used to have the type of intelligent, circular conversations I have with my friends. He was the only governor I felt who actually cared about prisoners, because he listened. I'm still in contact with him from time to time, and he still never gives a straight answer. I know it took some courage for him to ask the prison authorities for permission to keep in contact with me after my release, but it didn't do his career any harm as he is now governing his own prison.

The difficulty upon release was fitting into an environment I'd not known since some time before my arrest. I was fortunate enough by then to have secured a university place and so I only had to wait to start at college. From one institution to another! In retrospect, I think this might have been a mistake. I dropped out part way through the second year due to a directional crisis, lack of interest and too many drugs. However, I'm back on the course now. Coming to university while still on parole meant I was required to see my parole officer every fortnight while being a regular student, which came all too easily. Thankfully I moved in with four other lads, who were all in their final year, and we quickly became good friends. Two of them I am in regular contact with, so prison hasn't damaged my ability to form friendships.

The most difficult part of being released was staying with my mother again. I love her dearly, but she soon got on my nerves and no doubt I got on hers just as much, if not more. I don't know if I was trying to make up for lost time, or trying to pretend the previous two years hadn't happened, but I was very restless. I had no point of reference to start each day from – no cell to clean, no job to do – and yet all the freedom to do anything. It was rather daunting. So maybe going to university **was** a good idea. It gave me routine and a purpose. Even now, looking back, it's difficult to know what was best or how I ought to have been reintegrated into society.

I had expected to be required to see someone other than a parole officer, while on parole. It took me a long time to get to see someone on a regular basis, just as a pressure valve. I was lucky and determined, others won't be. These sessions have long since stopped, but one of my fears when being paroled was not to have someone to talk through anything that was causing me problems, who could deal with the issues. My parole officer was pretty good actually, and easy to talk with, so again I was fortunate.

All things considered . . .

Everything considered, I have to concede that my time in prison was a positive experience. Though, given my life over, I wouldn't choose to repeat it. I've heard say that what doesn't kill you will make you stronger, and prison has certainly done that. It may have also made me more arrogant, in the belief that, already having hit rock bottom, my life can only improve. That is, so long as I remember what it was like to be stood in the dock having sentence passed against me, how it felt like the bottom had dropped out of my world. Then everything should be fine. The lessons learnt inside will always be with me and it's a chapter in my life that will not be forgotten easily, especially if I keep writing about it.

I would like to give thanks for being able to contribute to this book. I hope that my experiences can help, if not correct what is wrong within the prison system, then at least to give rise to more questions being asked of current policy and doctrine. I would also hope it encourages the development of directives such as the offender therapy groups, which should be extended to all offenders. It has to be the way forward with regard to what is expected from our prisons in the 21st century.

PART FIVE:
EXTERNAL MONITORING
AND ACCOUNTABILITY

THE INSPECTORATES, OMBUDSMAN AND BOARDS OF VISITORS

Nicola Padfield

Quis custodet ipsos custodes?

In 1997, the Prisons Ombudsman recorded in his *Annual Report:*

> Ms X complained that she had been held for 48 hours in an unfurnished cell in the female segregation unit and, apparently on the instructions of a particular named officer, had been refused all food and drink for at least 24 hours because she would not wear the canvas 'strip' dress she had been given … She claimed to have been given no opportunity to wash, or to use a toilet, throughout the 48 hours … I was distressed to find out that her account was borne out by the evidence … Nor were the accounts of members of staff borne out by the evidence … a member of the Board of Visitors had visited Ms X on the Sunday but had not brought an end to her detention in intolerable conditions, and had apparently been unaware that the cell in which she was held had no sanitation … no subsequent disciplinary action seems to have been taken against the named officer (Prisons Ombudsman 1998, p. 12).

This summary of an appalling case illustrates the need to ask the question, 'Who guards the guardians?' or *Quis custodet ipsos custodes?* It will be clear to any reader of this book that those who run prisons wield extraordinarily wide powers, and that the prisoner is vulnerable to the abuse of such powers. As has often been said, safeguarding the fair treatment of prisoners is a hallmark of a fair society.

A number of questions should be borne in mind: Do the bodies being considered in this chapter have adequate powers? Are they independent? of the government? of the Prison Service? Are they adequately accountable? To whom? to the government? to Parliament? to the public? And, perhaps most importantly, are the standards which they are there to uphold clearly articulated and understood?

The Inspectorate of Prisons

The role of the Chief Inspector of Prisons is governed by Section 5A of the Prison Act 1952:

1. Her Majesty may appoint a person to be Chief Inspector of Prisons.
2. It shall be the duty of the Chief Inspector to inspect or arrange for the inspection of prisons in England and Wales and to report to the Secretary of State on them.
3. The Chief Inspector shall in particular report to the Secretary of State on the treatment of prisoners and conditions in prisons.
4. The Secretary of State may refer specific matters connected with prisons in England and Wales and prisoners in them to the Chief Inspector and direct him to report on them.

A vision of the Inspectorate's role can be gained from its Statement of Purpose:

> To contribute to the reduction in crime, by inspecting the treatment and conditions of those in Prison Service custody, and Immigration Service detention, in a manner that informs Ministers, Parliament and others and influences advances in planning and operational delivery (HM Inspectorate of Prisons 1999, p. ii).

The Inspectorate carries out its work by way of announced and unannounced inspections. Reports include lists of good practice, as well as criticisms. A recent development has been the publication of thematic reviews, for example of Prison Service healthcare, women in prison, young offenders, and suicides in prison. Inspections are concerned particularly with the conditions in establishments, the treatment of prisoners and the facilities available to them, but the Home Secretary may direct the Inspector's attention to other matters. It is important to note that the Inspector only has power to recommend. Complaints from individual prisoners are not dealt with routinely although similar complaints from a number of sources might alert him or her to a problem. Nor does the Inspector enter into correspondence with MPs, organisations or the public.

The current Chief Inspector, Sir David Ramsbotham – a former army general, follows in a tradition of external appointments to the position, which suggests a certain independence (though it is the Home Secretary who appoints him). Judge Stephen Tumim, the previous Chief Inspector, developed a reputation for plain speaking and tough words. The same is true of his successor. Sir David's report *Women in Prison* concluded that 'there is an almost total absence of co-ordinated operational planning and day-to-day planning' (HM Chief Inspector of Prisons

1997). Perhaps this hard-hitting report was responsible for the creation of an Assistant Director of Regimes for Women the next year. The *Annual Report 1996–97* (1998) is again hard-hitting, complaining long and hard about over-crowding and the shortage of resources, and looking at prisons in the wider context (including that of United Nations and European Union human rights law). The style of the report is frank and honest:

> … in common with the rest of the estate, there is not enough money in dispersal prisons to conduct a full programme of work, training and offending behaviour courses … Unemployment in a training prison is a contradiction in terms, not least because … idleness breeds corruption, and is therefore contrary to the objective of preventing re-offending … I hope that thought will be given to tackling in a more determined way the problem of illegal drugs, and how they get into prison (pp. 10–18).

Comparisons to other Inspectorates

It is perhaps worth comparing here the role of the Chief Inspector of Prisons with that of the Probation Inspectorate, especially given the recommendations of *The Prison–Probation Review* (Home Office 1998). The Probation Inspectorate was established following the recommendations of the Departmental Committee on the Social Services in the Courts of Summary Jurisdiction 1936, and the first Inspector was appointed that year. The main purpose of that Inspectorate, as recommended by the Departmental Committee, was to exercise control over the payment of government grants, but with the wider objective of fulfilling the functions of advice, encouragement and stimulation. From the early days there was also an element in the work of the Probation Inspectorate directed towards efficiency and the maintenance of standards. These emphases came into greater prominence after the government issued a *Statement of National Objectives and Priorities for the Probation Service* in 1984. Efficiency and effectiveness became the main pillars of the inspection programme. Section 73 of the Criminal Justice Act 1991 put the Inspectorate of Probation on a statutory footing for the first time.

The Inspectorate is not there to deal with complaints, but to provide the government with a means of monitoring the 54 local and independent probation services. These probation services are not accountable to central government but to their local probation committees, which are composed largely of local magistrates. The Probation Inspectorate, therefore, is the government's eyes and ears, monitoring locally independent probation services. The latest *Annual Report* (1997), with pictures of Home Office ministers on the cover, states that the first 'key priority' of the Inspectorate is 'fulfilling Ministerial demands'. The Chief

Inspector, previously a chief probation officer, concludes his overview with a message which might well have been written by a chief probation officer rather than a chief inspector, as it is not very critical of the probation services:

> Overall, 1997 has been a year of achievement for the probation service. It seems poised and willing to change. Its understandable anxieties have not prevented it from being more efficient, and at its best it reduces offending. It knows its workload will continue to rise and that it must involve itself ever more closely both with prisons and the local community. My sense of overall performance during 1997 is that the service has achieved a great deal, maturely accepts the need for continuous improvement and is ready and able to contribute constructively to the challenging year ahead (HM Inspectorate of Probation 1998).

This 'watchdog' thus does not have the abuse of power central to its concern, but is more generally concerned with good management. The Probation Inspectorate's more hard-hitting, individual area inspection reports and their thematic reviews are perhaps a better guide to their success at improving probation practice than is the Probation Inspectorate's *Annual Report*. A quite separate question outside the scope of this chapter is whether there should be a separate Probation Ombudsman to deal with offenders' complaints.

Similarly, the police inspectorate – the Inspectorate of Constabularies – monitors the performance of 43 independent police constabularies. Originally, the Inspector was usually a high-ranking military figure who reported to Parliament on the good running of individual forces. Now the Inspector has a duty under Section 54 of the Police Act 1996 to inspect and report to the Secretary of State on the efficiency and effectiveness of every police force maintained for a police area, and to carry out such duties for the purpose of furthering police efficiency and effectiveness as the Secretary of State may from time to time direct. The HM CIC *Annual Report 1996–97* reports:

> HM Inspectors of Constabulary (HMIs) have no statutory powers and rely instead on persuasion and discussion in order to take forward their recommendations. The Inspectorate is not a part of the tripartite structure and is independent of the Police Service (p. 15).

Compared to these other Inspectorates, HM Chief Inspector of Prisons is more outspoken. The Prison Service is not a collection of independent services needing a central management monitor but an arm of government exercising huge powers over a vulnerable population out of the public eye. However, it is often the fabric of prisons or the general standards to be found within them which are subject to his criticisms, not the treatment. Until there are clear standards for prisoners' living conditions it is not difficult for some of the Chief Inspector's complaints to be ignored by the Prison Service. As Morgan concludes, the Chief Inspector's critiques have sometimes lacked policy bite because he is not always clear by what standards he concludes that provisions are 'impoverished', 'degrading', 'unacceptable' and so on (Morgan 1997, p. 1172).

The role of the Prisons Ombudsman

There has been a Parliamentary Commissioner for Administration (the Ombudsman) since 1967 to investigate complaints of maladministration generally. He has long been criticised for being ineffective in his influence on prison administration (see the Woolf Report (Woolf and Tumim 1991)). The government accepted the recommendation of Woolf that there should be an independent complaints adjudicator, but unlike Woolf, the government preferred the title Prisons Ombudsman. The first, Sir Peter Woodhead, was appointed in October 1994. No enabling legislation has been passed so he has no specific powers, for example to award compensation; and he cannot consider complaints made by prisoners' friends or families. The Parliamentary Commissioner for Administration continues to have jurisdiction. Only time will tell whether the Prisons Ombudsman proves to be more effective in dealing with brutal or oppressive treatment. As the Prisons Ombudsman's first *Six-month Review* (1995) points out: 'some initial problems in defining the interface with the Prison Service still need to be overcome'. Judging by the 1997 *Annual Report* matters did not change, within those two years.

In 1997 the Ombudsman received 1,960 letters from prisoners wishing to make complaints. Only 553 were eligible: the majority appear either not to have known of, or to have had no faith in, the Prison Service's internal request/complaints system. However, prisoners must use this procedure before the Prisons Ombudsman can get involved. In his 1997 *Annual Report* Sir Peter states:

> … it is apparent from the cases I have seen [in 1997] that the Prison Service's internal complaints system has been put under extreme pressure; it is still taking far too long to answer grievances, many of which are not satisfactorily considered. I am also concerned that the Prison Service does not appear to keep adequate records of the number of complaints it deals with and their outcomes; I consider this to be a serious flaw in the monitoring of the complaints system (p. 1).

He goes on to speak of the 'very poor record' (p. 8) of Prison Headquarters in replying to request/complaints in a timely manner. The main areas of complaints were adjudications, followed by complaints about property and cash, transfers and allocations, general conditions, security and categorisation, and regimes activities. More important, perhaps, than the subject matter of the complaint are the serious breaches of the legal framework which they reveal.

The Ombudsman himself raises three key issues about his terms of reference:

1. his inability to scrutinise official advice to ministers relating to a specific complaint
2. the fettering by the Prison Service of information relevant to the eligibility and investigation of complaints; and
3. the non-statutory framework of the Prisons Ombudsman.

These issues echo the recommendations of the House of Commons Select Committee on the Parliamentary Commissioner for Administration in 1996. Another problem arises from his inability to explore complaints raised by third parties, with the inevitable consequence, for example, that he cannot explore deaths in custody. There are practical limitations, too, on what he can achieve: with a total staff of sixteen the Ombudsman cannot be expected to be the panacea of all ills.

Boards of Visitors

Independent both of the Prisons Inspectorate and of the Prison Service should be the Board of Visitors. The duties of Boards are prescribed by the Prison Rules 1964 (as amended) and include:

- satisfying themselves as to the state of an establishment's premises, its administration and the treatment of its prisoners; rendering annual reports on these subjects to the Home Secretary;
- inquiring into and reporting on any matter at the Home Secretary's request;
- directing the governor's attention to any matter that calls for it;
- reporting to the Home Secretary any matter that they consider it expedient to report, informing him or her immediately of any abuse which comes to their knowledge;
- in any case of urgent necessity, suspending any officer until the Home Secretary's decision is known;
- hearing any complaint or request which a prisoner wishes to make (to the Board in full or to any member);
- inspecting the prisoners' food at frequent intervals;

- inquiring into any report made to them that a prisoner's health – mental or physical – is likely to be injuriously affected by any conditions of his or her imprisonment; and
- arranging a rota for visits to the establishment by at least one Board member between Board meetings (see Walker and Padfield 1996, p. 166).

Any member of the Board has the right to enter a prison establishment at any time and have free access to every part of it and to every prisoner (Section 6 Prison Act 1952, as amended). Each Board of Visitors is thus a sort of lay Inspectorate, but with responsibilities for dealing with individual prisoners' treatment and complaints, which the Prisons Inspectorate does not have. The principal issues of common concern raised by Boards of Visitors in 1996 included:

- healthcare for prisoners;
- delays in transfers of mentally disturbed prisoners for hospital treatment;
- availability of illicit drugs, and insufficient counselling and treatment;
- the accuracy and usefulness of mandatory drug-testing (there were wide variations);
- the increase in prison suicides;
- the effects on staffing of budgetary cuts;
- workshop closures;
- overcrowding; and
- the lack of mechanisms to monitor the use of 'basic level' incentives (NACBV 1997, pp. 6–7, 20–5).

Boards of Visitors are appointed by the Home Secretary, although these days the recruitment process may be more open. At least two members of each Board must be Justices of the Peace, and usually more are. Until 1992 Boards also discharged quasi-judicial duties in dealing with the more serious disciplinary charges. As a result, they were seen by many prisoners as part of the prison administration, rather than as the impartial providers of safeguards against maltreatment. Little research has been done to explore whether they are seen as any more independent of the Prison Service today. It seems unlikely: the Secretariat of the Board of Visitors is under the Directorate of Regimes. Maguire, writing in 1985, says that 'virtually all the evidence available about the work of Boards of Visitors suggests they have consistently failed to fulfil their potential (Maguire 1985, p. 143). More recently, Robinson-Grindley (1998) echoes this, questioning whether Boards are carrying out their duties appropriately.

There remains a lack of clarity about the role of the Board of Visitors. The Home Office proposed in 1995 that Boards of Visitors should be renamed Advisory Councils. But who are they to advise? Perhaps a fundamental concern should be that although a system of lay visitors' free to drop in on prisons at any time remains attractive, the reality is that the level of commitment expected of Board members is likely to deter the recruitment of conscientious new members. It should not be forgotten that the Ombudsman's case study with which this chapter started included the fact that a member of the Board of Visitors had visited the prisoner and failed to take any action. Is it appropriate to rely on unpaid volunteers to be the watchdog of prison malpractice?

The courts and the rule of law

Ultimately, a prisoner should be able to rely on the courts to uphold his or her legal rights. 'The rule of law' is a fundamental constitutional principle. According to Dicey (1965), the classic constitutional theorist of the 19th century:

> … the rule of law is contrasted with every system of government based on the exercise by persons in authority of wide, arbitrary, or discretionary powers of constraint.

> It means … the absolute supremacy or predominance of regular law as opposed to the influence of arbitrariness, of prerogative, or even of wide discretionary authority on the part of the government. Englishmen are ruled by the law, and by the law alone; a man may with us be punished for a breach of the law, but he can be punished for nothing else (pp. 188, 202).

To what extent does this concept of the rule of law apply in prisons? One difficulty is identifying the 'law'. Parliament has been inactive in this area: the most recent Prison Act was enacted as long ago as 1952. It is worth reading as an example of how not to make law. It has little internal consistency and is simply a consolidation of various earlier enactments relating to prisons. It grants 'all powers and jurisdiction in relation to prisons and prisoners …' to the Home Secretary (see Section 1). This includes, specifically, the power to alter, enlarge or rebuild any prison and to build new prisons, with the approval of the Treasury (Section 33). Another example is the power to 'make rules for the regulation and management of prisons … and for the classification, treatment, employment, discipline and control of persons to be detained' (Section 47(1)). The power to make prison rules is exercisable by statutory instrument (Section 52). Although the Act specifies that every prisoner shall have 'a governor, a chaplain and a medical officer and such other officers as may be necessary' (Section 7) the powers and duties of these officers are not spelled out. Section 8 provides that every prison officer shall have the powers, authority, protection and privilege of a constable, but this does little to clarify the legal role of the governor.

The law, therefore, has evolved largely through the decisions of the executive and those of the courts. The 'executive' in this context is both the Home Office and the Prison Service. Since April 1993 the Prison Service has operated as an executive 'Next Steps' agency of the Home Office. The basic principle underlying this was that the new body would be subject to the strategic control of the minister and the Home Office, but that once the policy objectives and budgets within that framework were set, the management of the agency would then have as much independence as possible in deciding how those objectives are met. As the review of the management of the Prison Service by the House of Commons Home Affairs Select Committee (1997) makes clear, there is still a great deal of uncertainty surrounding the autonomy and accountability of the Prison Service. Whilst the Select Committee would in general terms have supported measures to increase the Prison Service's autonomy, they were 'not sure that legislation is the correct route to achieving this' (para. 113). One factor influencing them was that they were 'very reluctant to open the door to possible legal actions by prisoners against the Prison Service for possible breaches of the legislation' (para. 113).

The supervisory jurisdiction of the High Court is based on the common law powers of courts to stop other legal bodies from acting outside their powers. Thus, a decision-maker's decision must not be biased; it must not be vitiated by illegality, irrationality or procedural impropriety. These essential points about judicial review were explored in the classic GCHQ case (*Council of Civil Service Unions* v. *Minister for the Civil Service* [1985] AC 374). Other recent judicial reviews of the rule of law in prison took place in *R.* v. *Secretary of State for the Home Department, ex parte Simms* and *R.* v. *Governor of Whitemoor Prison ex parte Main* [1998] 2 All ER 491. These two separate cases were heard together in the Court of Appeal since they both raised questions about the validity of decisions taken by prison authorities in relation to convicted prisoners and in accordance with orders reflecting policy at national level. In the first case, prisoners were visited by journalists who refused to sign notices that the material obtained during visits would not be used for professional purposes. In the second case, the governor introduced a new practice for searching cells (following the recommendations of the Woodcock Report 1994), which included examination of correspondence with legal advisors. The decision of the Court of Appeal reveals the limited powers of the Court in judicial review proceedings: decisions made by prison authorities can only be impugned if either the standing order or the governor's order in question is shown to have been made *ultra vires* (outside his or her powers) or if the decision itself was unreasonable, in the legal sense of being so unreasonable or irrational that no reasonable person could have taken that decision (see *Associated Provincial Picture Houses Ltd* v. *Wednesbury Corporation* [1948] 1 KB 223). The Court in the Simms case held that convicted prisoners have no right to communicate orally with the media, and that the governor's order that correspondence could be examined was no more than the minimal interference with the prisoner's rights which was necessary to ensure that security was maintained. It remains to be seen whether incorporation of the European Convention on Human Rights into domestic British law by the Human Rights Act 1998 will breathe new life into the concept of judicial review in this area.

Conclusion

It must be appropriate that the 'closed' world of the prison is monitored by a variety of checks and balances to safeguard prisoners against abuses of power. Perhaps the monitoring bodies described in this chapter would be less vital if more was done internally to deal with complaints and grievances. In the absence of that, any monitoring body has to have powers and resources to be truly effective. They also need to know where they stand, as Genevra Richardson argues:

> The Prison Act and the Prison Rules combine to place large areas of policy formulation in the hands of the administrative authorities, on whom they impose few procedural constraints ... The prison system, its aims and governing principles, belong to society at large, not just those who work and live within it (Richardson 1993, p. 108).

The existing legal structure is so loose as to provide little guidance or constraints upon the Prison Service: in spite of the major developments in prison policy over the last few decades, none of these has required any significant change to the legal structure. It is not surprising that many of those who examine the Prison Service have called for enforceable standards in prisons (see for example, Woolf and Tumim 1991; Loucks 1993) as a 'rudder by which overseers can steer' (Morgan 1997, p. 1171).

References

Criminal Justice Act 1991, Royal Assent July 1991, entered into force October 1992

Dicey, A.V. (1965) *An Introduction to the Study of the Law of the Constitution*, (10th edition), Macmillan

HM Chief Inspector of Constabulary (1998) *Annual Report 1996–97*, HC 246, The Stationery Office

HM Chief Inspector of Prisons (1997) *Women in Prison: A Thematic Review*, Home Office/The Stationery Office

— (1998) *Annual Report 1996–97*, HMSO

HM Chief Inspectorate of Probation (1998) *Annual Report 1997*, Home Office

HM Inspectorate of Prisons (1999) *Annual Report 1997–98*, The Stationery Office

Home Office (1998) *The Prisons–Probation Review: Final Report*, The Stationery Office

House of Commons (1997) *Home Affairs Select Committee, Second Report, Session 1996–97*, HC 57-I

Loucks, N. (1993) *Working Guide to the Prison Rules*, Prison Reform Trust

Maguire, M. (1985) 'Prisonsers' grievances: the role of the Board of Visitors', in M. Maguire, J. Vagg and R. Morgan (eds) *Accountability and Prisons: Opening Up a Closed World*, Tavistock

Morgan, R. (1997) 'Imprisonment: current concerns and a brief history since 1945', in M. Maguire, R. Morgan and R. Reiner (eds), *The Oxford Handbook of Criminology*, (2nd edition), Oxford: Clarendon Press

National Advisory Council for the Boards of Visitors of England and Wales (1997) *Annual Report 1996*, The Stationery Office

Prison Act 1952 (15 and 16 George VI, 1 Elizabeth II, c. 52)

Prisons Ombudsman (1998) *Annual Report 1997*, Cm 3984, HMSO

Richardson, G. (1993) *Law Custody and Process: Prisoners and Patients*, Oxford: Clarendon Press

Robinson-Grindley, S. (1998) *Board of Visitors: Whistle-blowers or Governors' Patsies?*, prison report No. 44, Prison Reform Trust

Walker, N. and Padfield, N. (1996) *Sentencing Theory, Law and Practice*, (2nd edition), Butterworths

Woodcock, Sir J. (1994) *The Escape from Whitemoor Prison on Friday 9th September 1994* (The Woodcock Inquiry), Cm 2741, HMSO

Woolf, Lord Justice and Tumim, Judge S. (1991) *Prison Disturbances April 1990: Report of an Inquiry by the Rt Hon. Lord Justice Woolf and His Hon. Judge Stephen Tumim* (The Woolf Report), Cm 1456, HMSO

This chapter was submitted in early 1999 and should be read in that context.

PRESSURE GROUPS AND THE PRISON SERVICE

Stephen Shaw

To left and right above the main gate into Wormwood Scrubs Prison in west London are two large white plaques. They feature the portraits of a man and a woman, the two most noted prison reformers in British history, perhaps in world history – John Howard (1726–1790) and Elizabeth Fry (1780–1845). There, in the very fabric of the prison wall, is a symbol of the close relationship that exists between the Prison Service and those who advocate reform within the penal system.

Both Howard and Fry derived much of their interest in prisoners from deep religious conviction. However, their views of what constituted prison 'reform' bear little resemblance to the agenda of organisations like the Prison Reform Trust today. For example, one noted historian has dubbed John Howard as much the

A female prison officer outside the gates of HMP Wormwood Scrubs.

father of solitary confinement as the father of penal reform. But the work of Howard and Fry demonstrates that there is nothing new in external monitoring of the Prison Service. Prison reform has a long and honourable tradition in the United Kingdom.

Yet some unfriendly critics from time to time unfavourably compare the number of organisations with an interest in the treatment of offenders with those who concern themselves with victims of crime. Even cursory examination of the facts shows that this alleged over-investment in prison reform versus victims is a myth. The Charity Commission lists over a hundred charities with the word 'victim' in their title. The largest, Victim Support, has a budget running into many millions – and quite right too. Still, some parts of the media tend to polarise victims' and prison reform organisations at either end of a spectrum, even though many people are sympathetic to both. In fact, important advances for victims like the criminal injuries compensation scheme actually grew out of the efforts of penal reformers.

The role of prison pressure groups

There are three principal prison pressure groups:

National Association for the Care and Resettlement of Offenders (NACRO)   the largest, with a wide range of interests including crime prevention, housing, training and education;

Howard League for Penal Reform   the oldest, which can trace its forebears to the 1820s, just 30 years after the death of John Howard himself; and

Prison Reform Trust (PRT)   the youngest and most clearly focused upon prison issues.

All three organisations monitor what happens in the Prison Service, carry out research, publish reports and, in the case of NACRO and the PRT, offer direct services to prisoners. These three groups are the most frequently cited in the media. However, there are many other bodies with an interest in prison matters, although not all would welcome the description 'pressure group'. These various other organisations have very different structures, histories and objectives, but most have come into being in response to the innate characteristics of imprisonment: its secrecy; its damage to family relationships and to work, education and housing; and its ever-present potential for abuse.

This is not to say that the Prison Service in England and Wales can been characterised in recent years by a lack of openness and a propensity for inhumane treatment. On the contrary, the Service's record on both scores compares very favourably with prison systems in the rest of Europe and North America, let alone the rest of the world. Published accounts of individual prisons or sensitive statistics on such matters as suicide or prison discipline are all much more readily available than they are in most countries, and serious staff malpractice is fortunately extremely rare. One reason for that outcome may well be the unusual degree of external scrutiny to which the Prison Service in England and Wales is subject. Although a lot of cant has been spoken about the ideal of 'community prisons' – jails serving and forming an integral part of the local community – there is no question that the whole Service has opened up enormously in the past twenty years. The number of community-based bodies coming into an average prison on an average day must run well into double figures. Examples include the Women's Royal Voluntary Service (WRVS) in the visits room, the Samaritans helping train listeners on the suicide prevention scheme, drugs agencies, community groups who use the gymnasium, arts organisations, volunteer helpers in the chaplaincy, and so on. The image of the Prison Service as a closed, inward-looking monolith is pervasive but it no longer reflects the reality, if indeed it ever did.

Not everyone welcomes openness, though. There is still a strain within the prison culture that relishes the isolation, is contemptuous of 'outsiders', and positively detests fresh ideas and new ways of working. This type of approach is much like that of the notorious Millwall Football Club supporters, with their self-mocking chorus 'No one likes us; we don't care.' Such views are far less common than was once the case but, sadly, they can still be heard on many prison landings. In other areas, there has been a lot of progress to challenge racism and misogyny, although the Service has a long way to go to rid itself entirely of racist and sexist behaviour. One woman governor I know was once asked outright by a member of staff if she was 'a bike or a dyke'. In most walks of life this would be considered a curious way of addressing your line manager.

Another reason for the number and range of external pressure groups is that the official watchdogs – Boards of Visitors especially – are often perceived by prisoners to be lacking in authority, energy and independence. Performance differs markedly from jail to jail, but all too often prisoners believe that Boards of Visitors are not sufficiently robust. As one prisoner once said to me: ' "I'll look into it." That's the kiss of death – you'll never hear anything again.'

As one prisoner said to me: rightly or wrongly, prisoners often have more confidence in something said or written by the Prisoners' Advice Service, PRT or NACRO than they do in something produced under the Prison Service's imprimatur. It is for this reason that the *Prisoners' Information Book* (PRT and HM Prison Service 1999), to which all prisoners should have access or their own copy, is produced jointly by the Prison Service and PRT. It is more trusted with the PRT logo attached to it.

It is a mistake, however, to regard the pressure groups as constituting a 'prisoners' lobby'. Sometimes, of course, the pressure groups do articulate the view of prisoners and their families. This can be a very important function so far as prison managers are concerned, especially those at the top of the Service whose day-to-day involvement with both staff and prisoners may be somewhat tenuous. However, all but the most radical pressure groups accept the legitimacy of imprisonment as a punishment and the need for effective security and control. Their focus is not just prisoners' rights but the activities of the Service as a whole. For example, PRT produced studies on the absence of sex offender treatment programmes in jails in the late 1980s. Another area where the pressure groups have been very active has been that of race – not just because it is a matter of justice and fair treatment for prisoners, but because equal opportunities and anti-discriminatory practices ought to be part of the very life-blood of the Service. Indeed, many members of the Prison Service in their private capacities are supporters of one or other of the pressure groups. The pressure groups would be much the weaker, and their arguments much less authoritative, were this not the case. In addition, the various reports and magazines that the pressure groups produce find a ready audience at all levels of the Service. I have, for instance, lost count of the number of prison officers who have told me that the *Prisoners' Information Book* has helped them to cram for their promotion boards. The PRT's magazine *Prison Report* and various offerings from the Howard League and NACRO are also widely circulated and read.

On occasions, the pressure groups act as 'the conscience of the Service', articulating deeply held values (like treating prisoners as individuals with particular wants and needs) which can sometimes get swamped under the pressure of events. At other times pressure group activity can be a useful (and public) adjunct to what the Service believes privately, for instance in expressing concern about the impact of overcrowding or calling for more resources for some aspect of prison regimes. The pressure groups also have an important formal consultative role when ideas for change are being floated. Thus, it is well worth the Service getting alongside the pressure groups, given the attention which their views and opinions receive from the media.

Prison staff often complain, and with good reason, that they and their work are misrepresented in the media. A serious interest in prisons is a minority taste, and newspapers in particular know that there is a vicarious public fascination in stories about life behind bars (whether accurate or otherwise). Certain tales – high jinks in open prisons, drug-taking, alleged over-indulgence in terms of prisoners' rights or prison regimes – are the staple diet of the tabloid press. It is also still standard practice for the term 'warder' to be used as a synonym for prison officer, even though the word has not been in official usage since the 1920s. In a small way, prison reformers can help to correct these distorted images. Much of the output of these organisations is designed to improve public awareness of what **really** happens in prison. This may include enhancing the public image of prison officers whose professionalism is rarely acknowledged in the media. Prison reformers do not see this as a disinterested activity, but believe that prison staff will perform better if they do not believe themselves to be oppressed and misunderstood. Higher public status means higher self-esteem, better morale and a commitment to more progressive work with prisoners.

Another, less healthy, reason why pressure groups have sometimes been given a welcome by the Service deserves a mention. Traditionally, the Prison Service has been wary of allowing a voice to prisoners, much less encouraging any organisation of prisoners. Although it has been more or less defunct as a prison-based organisation for many years, the very name of the national prisoners' movement, Preservation of the Rights of Prisoners (PROP), still exercises a certain terror over the longer-serving staff. The more orthodox pressure groups are seen by some as providing a filter through which prisoners' views can be mediated in more acceptable form. (This phenomenon has been termed 'buffering' by Marxist scholars. In this more radical version, the respectable pressure groups are not so much mediating grassroots prisoner opinion as doing the state's dirty work by extinguishing the revolutionary fires below.)

Of course, at times the relationship between the Prison Service and campaigning groups is less comfortable. One of the roles of the pressure groups, unelected and largely unaccountable though they may be, is to act as whistle-blowers. As campaigners, this must surely be at the very core of our work. For example, complaints about alleged ill-treatment of prisoners at one London prison were partly channelled to the authorities by PRT. The Howard League and PRT were also very active during the controversy surrounding the practice of shackling (using escort chains), in particular their use on pregnant and seriously ill prisoners in hospital. In one especially shaming incident a dying prisoner remained chained to his bed during his last hours alive in a hospice. The man's treatment was condemned as inhumane, a sentiment expressed by many of those within the Service who felt that an obsession with security had led ineluctably to a lack of human compassion. Following an inquiry, the Director General himself apologised to the deceased man's family.

Finally, as well as keeping a close eye and ear on what happens in prisons, another important role for the pressure groups is the development of public policy and the presentation of evidence to official inquiries. The high watermark for this activity was the 1990–91 Woolf Inquiry which followed the prison riots that began at Strangeways (Manchester) and spread, to a greater or lesser degree, to over twenty other establishments. For all the reasons stated above – the stimulus to thinking and action, the failings of the official watchdogs, being a conduit for prisoners, the public relations role – the pressure groups are usually afforded a place at the table when those at the top of the Service are considering change in policy or practice.

Improvements in prisons

Compared to a decade ago, physical conditions for prisoners have greatly improved. Prisons are cleaner, lighter and airier. No prisoner is held in police cells, and nor are prisoners held three to a cell designed for one. The disgusting ritual of slopping-out (the emptying of plastic pots used as toilets, once a key part of the 'regime' in many local prisons) has ended. Such was the overpowering smell that prisoners' letters used to be impregnated with a unique mix of tobacco, sweat and urine, which survived their passage through the post.

Regimes have also improved. Although activity hours were knocked back in the mid-1990s under the twin pressures of a rapidly rising prison population and cutbacks on spending, in general there is more time out of cells and more involvement in work, training and education. The Prison Service's accredited programmes are significantly in advance of anything elsewhere in Europe, and the newer focus on drug treatment and basic numeracy and literacy is also very welcome. Prisoners' rights have been extended too: better visiting entitlements; reform to the system of prison discipline; an independent element in complaints procedures – to take just three examples.

The Prison Service has also improved hugely its record on both security and control. For every ten prisoners who escaped five years ago, only one gets out now. However, most of the escapes used to be from Category C establishments and involved prisoners who were not dangerous and were soon recaptured. There is no benefit in treating a baby-faced burglar as if he represented the same risk to society as a terrorist – although, ironically, most terrorists have been set free anyway as part of the Northern Ireland peace process. Prisons must be secure, but there is such a thing as too much security.

Work, training and education opportunities are essential components of most prison regimes.

Future development

What now needs to be done? A good place to start would be the landmark Woolf Report (Woolf and Tumim 1991). Not everything Woolf said was sensible but, by common consent, his was the most important report on prisons to have appeared in a century. It is all the more regrettable that it was never the subject of proper debate in the House of Commons, and that while Michael Howard was Home Secretary (1993–97) the Report appeared to have been air-brushed from history like a disgraced Bolshevik in a photograph in Stalinist Russia. The Prison Service should report regularly (say, in its *Annual Report and Accounts*) on what has been achieved towards implementation of Woolf's recommendations.

So far as prisoners' rights are concerned, there should be a liberalisation of the rules governing release on temporary licence (ROTL), speedy installation of in-cell television and moves to allow prisoners to wear their own clothes. The grievance procedure needs to be speeded up, too: at present, it can be six months or more before a case reaches the Prisons Ombudsman. The incentives and earned privileges scheme is also crying out for reform to remove inconsistencies and ensure prisoners are treated fairly. Finally, why should convicted prisoners still be denied the vote if we are serious about tackling social exclusion?

The Human Rights Act (the measure that incorporated the European Convention on Human Rights into British domestic law) will also have serious implications for the Prison Service. Are adjudications sufficiently fair and judicial in their proceedings? When was a prisoner last granted legal representation? Can it really be justified for governors to have the power to order 42 extra days' of imprisonment (the equivalent of a three-month sentence) for breaches of prison discipline? And how come governors of Scottish prisons cope perfectly well when they can only order an extra fourteen days, not the 42 of their English and Welsh colleagues?

With the new money committed following the government's comprehensive spending review we must also see a major expansion in regimes and education. Despite all the public concern over paedophiles and other sex offenders, only one sex offender in three currently receives any treatment at all while in prison. (Wembley Stadium could be filled three times over with the number of convicted sex offenders in the population as a whole. There are over 250,000 men currently at liberty who have convictions for sex offences, including over 100,000 whose offences were against children.) As for education, nearly half of all prisoners have problems reading and writing (including very high levels of dyslexia). There is evidence from Canada which suggests that help with basic literacy and numeracy not only improves prisoners' skills but also is correlated with reduced rates of recidivism. Yet if prisoners can earn more in prison workshops than they can in education, there is no incentive to learn and improve. We should be encouraging activities that reduce re-offending, not those which merely pass the time.

Of course, it is not within the Prison Service's power to control the number of prisoners sent by the courts. No prison can erect a 'Full Up' sign (although systems of queuing for custody exist in a number of European administrations). The Prison Service itself cannot reverse the doubling in the number of women prisoners which has occurred over the last five years, nor determine for itself that it will no longer provide places for children under 18. Staff certainly face difficulties in finding space at times of acute overcrowding, but it cannot be right that so many prisoners end up serving their sentences far from their homes. Not only does it make visiting so much more arduous but, perhaps more importantly, holding prisoners away from the community to which they will return makes a mockery of the idea of throughcare and preparation for release. Among its Key Performance Indicators (KPIs) the Prison Service should develop measures to promote the allocation of prisoners close to their own homes.

The Prison Service cannot operate for much longer under a statute that has not been looked at for half a century. PRT has long held that reform of the prison system should be reinforced by a new statutory framework, replacing and updating the Prison Act 1952. This could lay down explicit standards and entitlements, as well as reflect the major changes in structures and procedures that have taken place over the past 50 years. Among the changes introduced could be Woolf's proposal that no prison should be overcrowded beyond its certified normal accommodation, except in certain specified circumstances.

Perhaps more important than the somewhat rarefied issue of legal structure is the spirit or ethos of the Prison Service. Ask any prisoner about the pains of imprisonment and he or she will not usually mention physical conditions, the lack of autonomy or the quality of prison regimes (although, as in all institutions, the standard of the food takes on an enormous significance). What prisoners talk about is separation from their families – even though they may not have been tremendously devoted to family responsibilities while on the outside – and the relationships they enjoy with prison staff. Are they treated as adults? Are their views afforded any respect? Are they told what is going on? Are their grievances and problems taken seriously? In other words, what is the calibre of the basic grade staff with whom they come into contact day by day? PRT, for example, is no enthusiast for privately managed prisons and the whole idea of running prisons for profit. However, the Service could learn a lot about 'customer care' from the private sector: calling prisoners by their names, wearing name badges and a less military-style uniform, openly acknowledging that prisoners have entitlements which must be met. That said, there are plenty of examples of good practice in the public Prison Service: the work of the staff at Grendon, which operates as a therapeutic community; those working in drug-free units; or in the small number of resettlement prisons (including Kirklevington Grange and Latchmere House), which cater for long-term prisoners coming towards their release, to name a few. Jails like Lancaster Farms YOI and the local prison at Woodhill are model institutions of which the Prison Service is rightly proud. Future developments in the Service should aim to ensure that these establishments are no longer the exception but the norm.

Changing images, improving performance

We live in an age in which 'image' seems all-important; the vogue occupations are advertising, marketing and public relations. Every profession seems to have its communications strategy, and politics these days is less about policy and more about spin-doctoring. Every idea, every product, even every film is first tested on focus groups to see whether it will pass muster. What impressions of the Prison Service would emerge from a focus group discussion? Familiar stereotypes, one suspects. At one extreme, it might be the law of the jungle, decay and decrepitude, brutality. We might term this the *Midnight Express* proposition: prisoners preying upon each other, or being preyed upon by staff. At the other extreme, it might be prison as holiday camp; calculating cons running rings round staff who are either naïve or lazy; no deterrence, no order, no control. We might call this the *Porridge* option: prison staff as 'wet behind the ears' incompetents. Popular images of prison often reflect the dark, dank, insanitary, inner-city pile that was Strangeways pre-riot rather than modern jails like Littlehey or Whitemoor. The more complex, mundane, inconsistent and contradictory reality of prison life probably would not feature much at all. Most people do not come into contact with the prison system, nor do they wish to do so. However, the reality is that seven in every hundred men will spend some time in prison at some point in their lives. Imprisonment is not that rare an experience.

Prisons and prison staff are often misrepresented and misunderstood. The pressure groups and the Service itself can make common cause to improve the way in which prisons are regarded by the taxpayers who fund them and on whose behalf they operate. I commend the efforts of the Prison Service to present a more balanced picture of itself. Great strides have been made in recent years, but the lesson of all advertising is that messages have to be repeated over and over again if they are to have any effect. However, image is only one part of the equation. The Prison Service needs to improve its performance too, and in this respect there is much that the pressure groups can do to monitor, criticise or support. A great deal has already been achieved: prisons today are unrecognisable from those that I first studied twenty years ago. Yet much more needs to be done. The key to success perhaps rests less with the big issues of prisoner numbers, resources or the leadership given by Headquarters (important though they are), and much more with the efforts and attitudes of staff on the landings. Prisoners judge prisons by the quality of the staff. So does HM Chief Inspector of Prisons. So should we all.

References

Prison Reform Trust and HM Prison Service (1999) *Prisoners' Information Book*, PRT/HM Prison Service

Woolf, Lord Justic and Tumim, Judge S. (1991) *Prison Disturbances April 1990: Report of an inquiry by the Rt Hon. Lord Justice Woolf and His Hon. Judge Stephen Tumim* (The Woolf Report), Cm 1456, HMSO

PART SIX:
THE FUTURE

THE PRISON SERVICE INTO THE 21ST CENTURY

Martin Narey

I am in the privileged position of being the Director General of the Prison Service in the 21st century. I am pleased to have this opportunity to set out my vision for the Service. I have taken over a Service which has worked hard, and shown good results, in recent years to regain the confidence of ministers and the public. The current government have made it plain that they want more from imprisonment than incarceration. Additionally, they want prison regimes which can reduce re-offending. In the context of that policy I want to state my personal beliefs about what prisons should be like. These have been formed by seeing prisons in action and by the real examples of the leadership an outstanding governor can bring.

Leadership in the Prison Service requires personal and moral courage. This is not a job that can or should be done in a detached or neutral way. I hope never to be unmoved by a prisoner's premature death, by the sight of a teenager arriving from court alone and afraid, or by the sight of staff putting their personal safety on the line for the benefit of their colleagues and the prisoners for whom they care. There is an inescapable moral dimension to the Service's work. Those of us who aspire to lead within it have to know what we believe to be right, and to trust that instinct both in moments of crisis and in charting a strategy for the future.

It is not enough, however, to depend on the moral instincts of those of us in the Service. Informed and objective scrutiny of those who understand and care about our prisons is vital. I very much welcome a strong, independent Inspectorate of Prisons. Sir David Ramsbotham, Her Majesty's Chief Inspector of Prisons, has shown the way in many areas, including the care of women, the care of the under-18s, and on reducing suicides. The relationship between the Prison Service and the Inspectorate is a healthy one and the two organisations are at one in wanting to improve the care of prisoners. It is for this reason that I welcome a Youth Justice Board that will demand high standards of us. I also want Boards of Visitors that get under the skin of an establishment, listening to prisoners, asking

Martin Narey, Director General of the Prison Service.

uncomfortable questions from a basis of close knowledge. I want all visitors to expect and receive high standards of courtesy and efficiency. I want a Service that welcomes the recruitment and secondment of people with a range of different experience. Above all, I want a Service which is safe and decent for all those in our care.

The challenge for the Prison Service is set out clearly in our aim: 'effective execution of the sentences of the courts so as to reduce re-offending and protect the public'. Starting with our duty to protect the public, it is the case 30 people escaped from prison custody in 1999–2000, compared to 232 in 1992–93. This is the bedrock of our credibility, and it is right that it should be so. I do not intend to lose the gains made in this key area. Everyone has a right to expect that the sentences passed by the courts will be enforced. The second part of our aim – reducing offending – is an extension of our duty to protect the public. For the overwhelming majority of prisoners, custody is an interruption in their lives rather than a final destination. Helping to protect the public from crimes committed following release has sometimes been portrayed as an optional extra. It must be a core element of our work.

What is new, however, is that we have an explicit objective to reduce re-offending. The rate at which prisoners re-offend following release has been remarkably constant for as long as researchers have measured it. It has fostered a 'nothing works' attitude that is both sterile and ill-founded. Prison has educated some to commit more crime, and removed the practical and social support that might have helped others go straight; but it has always helped some offenders to avoid a return to crime on release. The problem has been that we have failed to demonstrate that the investments in work and education, which are considerable, have made a real difference.

I am not so unrealistic as to believe that we can achieve a reduction in re-offending that is either quick or dramatically large. However, I am convinced we can and will make a measurable difference. The key is to make that difference while not losing our grip on security. There is no pendulum swinging between security and making prisons constructive places. Security, and the public and ministerial confidence it delivers, is the platform on which constructive regimes will be built. I would like to suggest three starting-points for a strategy which can, for the foreseeable future, deliver a balanced, purposeful penal policy.

First, we must bring the same discipline and skill to the task of reducing re-offending as we have to preventing escape and maintaining good order. That requires us to be much more scrupulous in learning from the evidence of what works and applying it more broadly. The Prison Service's current accreditation system for offending behaviour programmes has allowed us to intervene with a small minority of higher-risk offenders in a way that evaluation is now starting to show can be radically more successful in reducing re-offending than many of us ever dreamed. We are doubling the number of programme completions over the next three years.

Accredited programmes are important but only one element of what is needed. The Basic Skills Agency (formerly the Audit Literacy and Basic Skills Unit) is the national body responsible for literacy, numeracy and ESOL (English for Speakers of other Languages) in England and Wales. Since 1990 the Agency has been working with Training and Enterprise Councils and employers to develop work-place training. The Agency ran the Work Project from 1991–94 and in that time it was found that people with basic skills at level 1 or below have access to 1 in 25 jobs. By increasing our investment by 30% over a three-year period we can transform the employability of many thousands of prisoners. The discipline and skill to make this happen exists, and we have set ourselves a target to improve the literacy and numeracy of our least able prisoners by 15% by 2002. We are doing this imaginatively, complementing traditional teaching methods by using prisoners to teach others and – recognising the aversion to the classroom held by many prisoners – training PE staff and instructional staff in workshops as support tutors. We are beginning to get it right. At Huntercombe, young people there gained 336 NVQs in key skills in 1999.

Drug-related offending is another essential target. We have made strides in reducing drug misuse in prison (though there is much more to be done) and we now have a comprehensive, funded plan to help reduce drug-related crime. This includes a commitment to offer support to prisoners, where necessary, for eight weeks following release. It is often suggested that prisons encourage drug misuse. This might once have been so, but levels of misuse as measured by random testing have fallen sharply and are now down to about 15%, compared with 24.4% in 1996–97. At Parkhurst recorded levels of drug misuse have fallen to 0% and prisoners have told me that, as a result, it is now a safe place in which to live.

The second key element of a robust, long-term strategy is that we must enmesh our operations with the work of others. We need to become so interdependent with the work of probation services, for example, that it will become unthinkable to portray our objectives as in any way competitive or separate. We are already embarked on exercises to produce joint planning and joint training. I am very excited that we have been able to establish a joint accreditation panel for offending behaviour programmes. It is hugely significant that this panel has been personally appointed by the Home Secretary, that its membership includes some of the world's leading experts in 'what works', and that its chairman is to be someone of the calibre and experience of Sir Duncan Nichol. Area drugs co-ordinators will ensure our involvement in drug action teams. We are working closely with Young Offending Teams and, through Welfare to Work, we are forging a critical relationship with the employment service. Cementing our strategy means constantly looking out to the communities to which prisoners are returning.

My third point is perhaps a little less obvious, but in many ways the most important. To give staff and prisoners confidence about our seriousness about making prisons work we must scrutinise the way we deal with prisoners every day. That means demonstrating fairness. We must remember all the lessons from Woolf about disciplinary procedures and about due process in the minutiae of institutional life. Above all, it requires us to deliver a non-discriminatory service to ethnic minority prisoners, on which I know we still fall short. This aspect also requires us to show respect for prisoners as individuals. That means decent living conditions. It means avoiding the abuse of authority through unnecessary rules, or worse. Sadly, it still requires vigilance in weeding out a small minority – thankfully a very small minority – of staff who physically abuse prisoners. There is no place for such people in this service.

I want to conclude by offering a litmus test for whether we are serious about pursuing a genuinely constructive penal policy. There are many who deeply regret that it should ever be necessary to incarcerate a young person who has not even reached their 18th birthday. The reality, of course, is that many adolescents do continue to defeat the best attempts to divert them from custody. The Prison Service has the task of caring for the majority of these young people. We have to recognise that very often their behaviour has been out of control, chaotic and sometimes dangerous. We have to deal with their rejection by other organisations and agencies, and the history of suspicion and failure they bring with them.

The number of under-18s in our care, who number about 2,300 at present, has barely been recognised as a discrete group with particular needs. We now urgently need to demonstrate that we can make meaningful differences for these young people. The Prison Service can look after under-18s well. We have some way to go to convince everyone, but some very positive signs of what we can do are already being seen at Huntercombe and at Werrington, for example. At Huntercombe, casework has been transformed by employing a senior manager from Social Services to inform our practice with the best from community-based residential care. Werrington is in the lead in developing child protection arrangements which have been brokered nationally with the Association of Directors of Social Service, the Association of Chief Officers of Probation (ACOP), the Association of Chief Police Officers (ACPO) and the Local Government Association (LGA).

Steadily, a real improvement in all establishments that care for this age group will become apparent. But first we have to invest new resources. The local authority secure accommodation to which young offender institutions (YOIs) are so often

Martin Narey, Director General of the Prison Service, has an informal conversation with young prisoners during one of his frequent visits to prison establishments.

unfavourably compared cost an average of six times as much as the typical YOI. The achievements at Werrington and Huntercombe are, in part, due to extra funding which we managed to find last year. So it has been immensely encouraging that the government has given the Service an additional £51 million over three years to replicate this achievement elsewhere. These funds will help develop two broad initiatives:

- the creation of a distinct estate in which almost all under-18s will be held separately from other young people and adults; and
- the development of high-quality regimes.

Unless we accommodate under-18s separately we cannot easily or effectively identify and meet their needs, abilities and aptitudes, which really are different from those of other young offenders. The significant investment we are making in the fourteen establishments of the under-18 estate will facilitate the really important changes.

As I have mentioned already, the under-18s for whom we care have largely failed or been failed by schools, families and the interventions of other agencies. At Moorland more than 50% of young offenders there have spent time in care. At Wetherby 19% of young offenders have children of their own; 50% have fathers who have been in prison. Most of the under-18s at Wetherby had been excluded from school from about the age of 13.

Whatever has happened beforehand, when they arrive in our receptions these young people are usually leaving lifestyles that are chaotic and sometimes dangerous. We are determined to ensure that their time with us provides some stability, a chance to reorder their lives, to catch up on what they have missed. So the new regimes will quite rightly place great emphasis upon education, both remedial and vocational. These young people will earn responsibility in personal relationships and self-respect based upon recognised achievement. Critically, our approach will not simply be about doing things to and for them: we will seek to nurture their initiative so that, to borrow Sir Alexander Paterson's words 'they will regulate their conduct aright'.

These changes are crucially dependent upon the role of staff, so we will recruit and train staff specifically for this work. It will be entirely routine for prison officers who care for these young people to have more specialist training, and to conduct their work out of uniform. We know that adult role models matter to young people which is why we are placing great emphasis upon staff performing the role of the 'significant adult', modelling attitudes and behaviours in the development of good relationships with young people. We know that young people can change and that we can influence that change for good.

In 1999 we published standards for the delivery of regimes for the under-18s. We consulted widely on the drafting of these and we believe they are ground-breaking. They will require us to deliver on the statutory task of preventing future offending by putting the young person's welfare at the centre of the regime. I believe that we are well placed to meet the needs of the Youth Justice Board following the introduction of the new Detention and Training Order on 1 April 2000. And I positively welcome the pressure that the existence of alternative providers will create for us to meet and maintain high standards.

Transforming the treatment of under-18s is a real test for the Service. First, because we must demonstrate to the Youth Justice Board that we can be trusted to deliver to a high standard and the Board will judge our success. Secondly, because the fundamental values we need to care properly for this population are those that must also inform our care of adults. A Service that cares properly for teenagers will know how to care for all prisoners. Experience shows me that many of the Service's most influential leaders and staff have had their commitment moulded by their role in looking after the youngest and most vulnerable of those sent to us by the courts.

In this short concluding chapter I have presented both the traditional values of the Prison Service and the ambitions I have for the future. I genuinely believe that there is now an unparalleled opportunity to make a balanced, moral and purposeful penal policy part of the permanent landscape in England and Wales. I very much look forward to the challenge of helping to make that happen.

PART SEVEN: ANNEXES

ANNEX A: THE PRISON SERVICE'S VISION, STATEMENT OF PURPOSE, AIM, OBJECTIVES AND PRINCIPLES

Statement of Purpose

Her Majesty's Prison Service serves the public by keeping in custody those committed by the courts. Our duty is to look after them with humanity and help them lead law-abiding and useful lives in custody and after release.

Aim

Effective execution of the sentences of the courts so as to reduce re-offending and protect the public.

Objectives

- Protect the public by holding those committed by the courts in a safe, decent and healthy environment; and
- Reduce crime by providing constructive regimes which address offending behaviour, improve educational and work skills, and promote law-abiding behaviour in custody and after release.

Principles

1. Deal fairly, openly and humanely with prisoners and all others who come into contact with us;
2. Encourage prisoners to address offending behaviour and respect others;
3. Value and support each others' contribution;
4. Promote equality of opportunity for all and combat discrimination wherever it occurs;
5. Work constructively with criminal justice agencies and other organisations; and
6. Obtain best value from the resources available.

ANNEX B: PERFORMANCE TARGETS FOR 1999–2000 (KEY PERFORMANCE INDICATORS)

KPI 1a: To ensure that there are no Category A escapes from prison.

KPI 1b: To ensure that the number of escapes from prisons and escorts undertaken by Prison Service staff, expressed as a proportion of the prison population, is lower than 0.05%.

KPI 1c: To ensure that the number of escapes from contracted-out escorts is no more than 1 per 20,000 prisoners handled.

KPI 2: To ensure that the number of positive adjudications of assault on staff, prisoners and others, expressed as a proportion of the average population, is lower than 9%.

KPI 3: To ensure that the rate of positive testing for drugs (the number of random drug tests that prove positive expressed as a percentage of the total number of random tests carried out) is lower than 18%.

KPI 4: To ensure that the number of prisoners held two to a cell designed for one, expressed as a percentage of the prison population, does not exceed 18%.

KPI 5: To ensure that prisoners spend on average at least 24 hours per week engaged in purposeful activity.

KPI 6: To ensure that at least 60% of prisoners are held in establishments which normally unlock all prisoners on the standard or enhanced regime for at least 10 hours per weekday.

KPI 7: To ensure that there are at least 3,000 completions by prisoners of offending behaviour programmes, accredited as being effective in reducing re-offending, of which 700 should be completions of the sex offender treatment programmes.

KPI 8: To ensure that the average cost per uncrowded prison place does not exceed £26,208.

KPI 9: To ensure that, on average, staff spend at least 6.5 days in training.

KPI 10: To ensure that staff sickness does not exceed 12.5 working days per person.

KPI 11: To ensure that 95% of correspondence receives a reply within 20 days by October 1999.

FURTHER READING

Some recent publications on prisons and imprisonment

Bosworth, M. (1999) *Engendering Resistance: Agency and Power in Women's Prisons*, Dartmouth: Ashgate

Bryans, S. and Wilson, D. (2000) *The Prison Governor: Theory and Practice,* (2nd edition), HMP Leyhill: Prison Service Journal Publcations

Caddle, D. (1998) *Research Findings No. 80: Age Limits for Babies in Prison – Some Lessons from Abroad*, Home Office

Cameron, J. (1983) *Prisons and Punishments in Scotland*, Edinburgh: Canongate

Cohen, S. and Taylor, L. (1972) *Psychological Survival: The Experience of Long-term Imprisonment*, Harmondsworth: Penguin

Department of Health (1996) *The Patient's Charter and You*, DoH

Flynn, N. (1998) *Introduction to Prisons and Imprisonment*, Winchester: Waterside Press

Gendreau, P. (1996) 'The principles of effective intervention with offenders', in A. Harland (ed.), *Choosing Correctional Options that Work*, Sage

— and Goggin, C. (1997) 'Correctional treatment: accomplishments and realities', in P. Vouris, M. Braswell and D. Lester (eds), *Correctional Counselling and Rehabilitation*, Cincinnati, OH: Anderson

Goodman, A. and Mensah B. (1999) *The Prison Guide*, Blackstone Press

Gravett, S. (1999) *Coping with Prison: A Guide to Practitioners on the Realities of Imprisonment*, Cassell

Gunn, J. and Robertson, G. (1987) 'A ten-year follow-up of men discharged from Grendon prison', *British Journal of Psychiatry*, Vol. 151, pp. 674–78

Harland, A. (ed.) (1996) *Choosing Correctional Options that Work*, Sage

Hedderman, C. and Sugg, D. (1996) 'Does treating sex offenders reduce offending?', in *Research Findings No. 45*, Home Office

—, — and Vennard, J. (1997) *Changing Offender's Attitudes and Behaviour: What Works?*, Home Office

HM Prison Service (1998) *Annual Report of the Directorate of Healthcare 1996/1997*, HM Prison Service

— (1999) *Briefing*, (May)

— (1999) *Vision Document*, HMSO

Hollin, C.R. (ed.) (1996) *Working with Offenders: Psychological Practice in Offender Rehabilitation*, HMSO

Home Office (1990) *Crime, Justice and Protecting the Public*, HMSO

— (1999) *Quinquennial Review of the Prison Service: Evaluation of Performance*, The Stationery Office

Lappi-Seppälä, T. (1998) *Regulating the Prison Population: Experiences from a Long-term Policy in Finland*, Helsinki: National Research Institute of Legal Policy

Leech, M. and Chenery, D. (1999) *The Prisons Handbook 2000*, (4th edition), Winchester: Waterside Press

Livingstone, S. and Owen, T. (1999) *Prison Law*, (2nd edition), Oxford: Oxford University Press

Matthews, R. (1999) *Doing Time: An Introduction to the Sociology of Imprisonment*, Macmillan

May, T. (1995) *Probation: Politics, Policy and Practice*, Milton Keynes: Open University Press

Moczydlowski, P. (1992) *The Hidden Life of Polish Prisons*, Indianapolis, IN: Indiana University Press

Newton, M. and Thornton, D. (1994) Grendon Reconviction Study Update, unpublished correspondence cited in E. Cullen, 'Grendon: the therapeutic community that works', *Therapeutic Communities*, Vol. 15, No. 4

Prison Commissioners (1879) *Prison Statistics Report*, HM Government

Prison Reform Trust (1997) *Race Equality in Prisons: The Role of RRLO*, PRT

Research and Advisory Group on the Long-term Prison System (1987) *Special Units for Long-term Prisoners: Regimes, Management and Research*, HMSO

Shaw, A.G.L. (1966) *Convicts and the Colonies*, Faber & Faber

Simon, F. (1999) *Prisoners' Work and Vocational Training*, Routledge

Statham, R. and Whitehead, P. (1992) *Managing the Probation Service*, Aldershot: Ashgate

Van Zyl Smit, D. (1998) 'Life imprisonment as the ultimate penalty in international law', unpublished article

Warren, F. (1994) 'What do we mean by a "therapeutic community" for offenders?', *Therapeutic Communities*, Vol. 15, No. 4

Weiss, P. and South, N. (1998) *Comparing Prison Systems: Towards a Comparative and International Penology*, Amsterdam: Gordon and Breach

Whitfield, D. (1998) *Introduction to the Probation Service*, (2nd edition), Winchester: Waterside Press

Wilson, D. and Ashton, J. (1998) *Crime and Punishment: What Everyone Should Know*, Blackstone Press

INDEX

Page numbers in *italics* refer to figures and tables.

Index compiled by Anna Wynne of **INDEXING SPECIALISTS**
202 Church Road, Hove, East Sussex BN3 2DJ
Tel: 01273 738299 Fax: 01273 323309

Printed in the United Kingdom by The Stationery Office
TJ2129 C20 1/01 19585